A Song in YOUR HONOR

KAY EVANS

Christian Light Publications, Inc.
Harrisonburg, Virginia 22802

A SONG FOR YOUR HONOR

Christian Light Publications, Inc.,
Harrisonburg, Virginia 22802

Third Printing, 2007

Cover design: Elizabeth Mong
Cover photo: Matthew Weaver

Softcover Edition ISBN: 978-0-87813-627-8
Hardcover Edition ISBN: 978-0-87813-644-5

Dedication

We dedicate this book to our heavenly Father. Through our experiences He has proved Himself to us as the Father of the fatherless and the Defender of widows. He has become our rock-solid Foundation as well as the Head of our home. We owe all that we are and have to Him. He is the one who has truly set us free.

A father of the fatherless, and a judge of the widows, is God in his holy habitation (Psalm 68:5).

Preface

Many people have become dear to our hearts through our experiences. It would be impossible to recount all of the kind ways people served us. We are very grateful to each one.

There are others, some of whom we may not meet until eternity, who labored in prayer for our family or who blessed us in ways unknown to us. We were deeply touched by all of the people who sought the Lord on our behalf.

May God Himself give each person the reward he deserves for the love shown to us, which helped carry us through.

Contents

Introduction

The making of this book has been a family project. It was written by me, the mother in the story, and my two oldest daughters. My son and younger daughters helped with editing, and I depended heavily on their computer skills. If it had not been for the faithful assistance and cooperative spirit of my children, I don't know how this story could have made it into book form.

You may have noticed on the cover the absence of an author's name. There is an explanation for this. After prayerfully considering the sensitive family issues in this story, it seemed best to change our family names and a few others, as well as the name of my hometown, in an effort to guard the identity of those preferring anonymity.

And as I pondered the Lord's mighty hand, it seemed fitting that only one name should be truly honored anyway. I pray that the events recorded in the following pages will cause you to exalt with us that precious and enduring name that is above every name . . . the Lord Jesus Christ.

As you read this book, you will discover that I, the mother in this story, made mistakes as I faced various decisions. While it is humbling to expose them to you, may it give you a greater appreciation for our glorious God Almighty who is willing and able to help His children, even when they fail.

A special thanks to Harvey Yoder for being an adviser and coach to us while we wrote our story.

We are also very grateful to Christian Light Publications and specifically Leon Yoder, for working with us so respectfully and helping us polish our story.

It has been our desire and commitment to tell this story as accurately as possible. Please give us grace where our memory failed us, and we took writers' liberties to recount various conversations or minor details.

CHAPTER 1

The Call of Death

– March 29, 1996 –

I turned over in bed, sleepily wondering, *What is that noise?*
Once again the phone rang, and this time I recognized the sound.
I sat up quickly and reached clumsily for the receiver. Squinting
my eyes, I stared at the blurry numbers of my digital clock. They
stood out in stark contrast to the dark room. I tried to make sense
of the woman's voice on the other end of the line.

"Hello? Is this Kay Evans?" she asked.

"Yes, it is."

"Mrs. Evans, if you want to see your husband alive, you had
better come in to the hospital right now. He is going downhill very
quickly."

I was standing now, barefooted, on the cool, hardwood floor.
My heart thumped as I answered, "Yes, I'll be right in."

Slamming down the receiver, I grabbed my glasses from their
place next to the phone. The clock read 1:38 a.m.

In the living room, my brother David and his wife Sue Beth
were sleeping on an air mattress. They had been staying with the
children and me during the past few weeks while Ron was so ill.
I shook David awake.

"David, the nurse just called and said that Ron is dying. Could
you get ready and go with me to the hospital?"

"Yeah, sure," he mumbled, rubbing his eyes.

Back in my room, I closed the door behind me and switched on
the light. "I can't waste any time," I told myself as I dashed over

to the closet. "Let's see, my blue printed dress will be fine," I decided, jerking it off the hanger. *Can this be real? Is it true that Ron is actually dying?* My thoughts spun around and around as I hurriedly dressed.

Minutes later, David and I were on our way. The street lamps cast shadows on the vacant thoroughfares as we sped toward the Houston Medical Center. Lighted billboards flashed by: "Coca Cola . . . the real thing." Another read, "Got Milk?" and showed a young girl, smiling and displaying a milky mustache. The gaiety of these advertisements seemed to mock the gravity of the moment.

Glancing at the speedometer, I slowed down a bit. My brother and I stared blankly ahead, lost in our own thoughts. Could it really be true that the man I loved so deeply, my husband of twenty years, was actually dying? A verse kept flashing through my mind. *God is our refuge and strength, a very present help in trouble. Therefore will not we fear, though the earth be removed, and though the mountains be carried into the midst of the sea; though the waters thereof roar and be troubled, though the mountains shake with the swelling thereof. Selah.*[1]

As we hurried into the hospital, everything was quiet except for the staccato of our footsteps down the empty hall. We turned into the familiar surgical intensive care unit where Ron had been lying motionless for weeks. There was no time to greet the nurses as we rushed into his room. Where he lay all was dark; the only light was streaming through the open door behind us. Ron's mother, Jan, sat in the corner, as still and blank as a statue. No monitors beeped. No oxygen hissed. No IVs dripped. All was eerily still and quiet. I glanced at the monitor, which for days had traced Ron's every heartbeat.

Glancing over at Jan, I broke the deafening silence, "Why isn't the monitor on?"

"He is deceased, Kay," she responded hoarsely.

In my heart, I screamed, *NO! It can't be!* And yet, one look at my husband's ashen face told me it was true. I leaned over the metal railing of the bed and kissed the cold lips of this man so dear to me. As the horrible reality began sinking into my very

---

1. Psalm 46:1-3

being, I started to pray silently.

A nurse tiptoed in and led Jan out, leaving David and me alone in the room with the still form half-covered by a white sheet. Minutes later, two nurses slipped in and came over to me. They had become close friends of ours in the past few months, volunteering to help our family with Ron's many needs and often staying up with him through the night.

Debbie wrapped her arms tenderly around me. "I'm so sorry," she said. "Are you going to be okay?"

I nodded. Debbie was always reassuring and understanding; her kind words were such a comfort. Seeing I was okay, the two women left together quietly.

I had known this horrible moment might come. While Ron had been alive, I had been determined he would be healed. My in-laws had focused on the doctors and every decision they made. When things had gone well, they praised the doctors. But I had determined to approach it differently.

The children and I had prayed for Ron's healing every day. I had carefully selected Scriptures that focused on healing, and we had faithfully read them aloud every day to encourage ourselves and Ron. But now that he was dead, I switched to Plan B.

"Surely this means God is going to raise him from the dead," I told myself, mustering up my courage. My brother and I had even talked about it, and he felt the same way.

With mounting excitement I picked up the phone in the hospital room and dialed our home number.

Hannah answered. "Hello, Evans' residence. This is Hannah speaking."

"Hannah, this is Mommy."

"Yes, Mommy, what is going on?"

"Well, Hannah, it happened. Your daddy has died."

"Oh, Mommy, I can hardly believe it. Sue Beth, Lissa, and I have been praying ever since y'all left. I just know this means God intends to raise Daddy from the dead. Isn't it exciting to think that He would do such a thing in our day and time?"

"Yes, honey, it is. I'm proud of your faith. It bolsters my courage just to hear you."

As I left the room, I noticed Jan standing alone in the hallway.

She looked so empty and crushed. The dreams she had for her eldest child now lay broken and unfulfilled. She had loved him, too, and watched him grow from an active little boy into a promising trauma surgeon. And now he was gone.

I walked up and hugged her. "How are you doing, Jan?"

After a moment of silence, she replied coldly, "I'm grieving, Kay," and pulled away from my embrace.

CHAPTER 2

Years of Training and Trial

Ron and I had met in high school and married while he was in college working toward a medical degree. Becoming a doctor had been his childhood dream, but he still had many years of hard training before it would be realized. During his four years of medical school in San Antonio, Texas, the Lord richly blessed us, and we joyfully received a precious baby girl, whom we named Hannah. About three years later He sent Lissa, another darling daughter.

After completing medical school, Ron was accepted into a general surgery residency in Phoenix, Arizona. I needed to support our growing family, but I hated leaving my children in the care of someone else. I found I could baby-sit for other working mommies and still stay at home with our daughters, which was where I wanted to be.

Cooper pounded his spoon on the high chair, and screamed, "Food!"

The microwave chimed and I popped open the door. "Cooper, be patient. I'm getting your food right now." Stirring the warm spaghetti in the bright yellow bowl, I set it in front of the hyper little boy.

"Okay, Daniel, Amanda, Geri, put away the Legos and go wash your hands. Mandy, Kimberly, and Hannah, did you already wash your hands? Good, then come to the table. It's time to eat!"

Lissa was already asleep in the high chair, her lunch smeared across her face and throughout her wispy blonde hair. Kimberly climbed up into her chair and grabbed her fork, flying it through the air like an airplane. Hannah sat next to her, rubbing her eyes sleepily, her brown curls swaying back and forth. I spooned warm spaghetti onto all the bright, plastic plates and then onto my own Corelle dinner plate.

"Let's pray, children," I announced, and all the little heads bowed except for Cooper, who was busy squishing noodles between his fingers. "Lord, thank You for this food, and for the many blessings You have given us. We love You. In Jesus' name. Amen."

An explosion of noise followed my prayer as forks hit the plates with a vengeance. I slid into my chair with a sigh. The morning had been long, and I was tired. The radio on the counter played soft, classical music, calming my nerves.

"Lissa," I said, pulling her high chair close to me, "wake up, sweetie. Don't you want any more to eat?"

Her eyes fluttered open, and she lifted her head from the spaghetti-smeared tray, only to doze off, her head sinking down again.

"I guess she's done," I said. "Hannah, please go get me a washcloth, and I'll wipe her up and take her to bed." I pulled off the tray and unsnapped the sleepy little girl. "It will be nap time, y'all, as soon as you're through with your food."

Lila knocked lightly and then opened the glass door smudged with tiny handprints.

"Come on in!" I called from the living room where I was changing Lissa's diaper on the dark-brown carpet. "Daniel and Cooper, your mommy is here!"

They ran to her happily, and she hugged the boys tightly. "Were you good today?"

They both nodded emphatically.

"Pretty good," I added. "Cooper bit only one of the children twice today, so that's an improvement!"

She screwed up her face and looked disapprovingly at her little son. Grabbing the blue diaper bag from the bench by the door, she called, "We'll see you in the morning!"

I snapped up Lissa's pink sleeper and nodded. "All right, we'll see you!" I said.

The door slammed shut, and day care was over for the day. The other moms had already picked up their children. I closed my eyes and enjoyed the silence. Hannah stood on the couch and peeked through the blinds.

"Daddy is here!" she cried.

I hopped up from the floor and slid open the glass door, catching the sound of bicycle wheels clicking to a stop at our back gate. "Welcome home, honey," I called as he guided his bike into our patio yard and snapped his helmet onto the seat. He smiled lovingly down at Hannah and Lissa and gave me a long, tender embrace before scooping each of them up in his arms. I could tell by the tired expression on his face that this had been a wearying day for him too.

I set the heavy box down on the kitchen counter and looked around. Jan hurried into the kitchen with another box labeled "silverware."

I turned to her, "Jan, did you clean in here this morning? Everything looks spotless. There are even new towel sets in the bathroom!"

She smiled, and nodded, opening the box and proceeding to carefully unpack the contents.

"Thank you, Jan," I said. "I really appreciate it."

My brother Don rushed in through the back door. "Kay, where are you going to want the couch? Ron and Nick are pulling it off the truck now."

I stepped into the den. "What do you think about putting it right here?" I asked, pointing to a spot along an empty wall.

He nodded and opened the door wide as Ron backed into the room, carrying one end of the heavy couch.

We were discovering that meeting all the training requirements for the medical profession often means moving. So we had once again packed up our things and loaded them onto a truck. This time we moved to Dallas, Texas, where Ron would complete a two-year trauma medicine training program. Our family totaled five now, since our lively baby Isaiah had joined us.

Ron's parents and several of his brothers, as well as my brother, had all come to help us move in. It had eased my load tremendously.

"Mommy, look! I found the box of schoolbooks!" Hannah's excited voice clamored over my shoulder as I placed a stack of dinner plates into the cupboard.

"Sure enough!" I exclaimed after glancing down at her, proudly holding the box. "Why don't you just put it on the table in the living room," I instructed. "That way it will be easily accessible when we start back to school next week."

I had homeschooled our girls from the very beginning, and Ron and I had become increasingly excited about this style of education, especially since it made us both feel so involved with our children's learning.

But homeschooling was a new idea for both sets of our parents, and they naturally had questions. Ron's parents were both professors who trained college students majoring in education to become public schoolteachers. It was difficult for them to accept that their own grandchildren would be home educated, particularly by a mother who didn't even have a college degree. In their way of thinking, one was not qualified to even teach her own children at home unless she had first been certified to teach or had completed a college education. We began to sense strong opposition from Ron's parents about our choice to home educate.

One evening Ron burst into the room. "Kay, do you have plans for supper?"

I brushed some hair from my face and shook my head. "No, not really."

He smiled. "Good, because I just ordered pizza!" he said, jabbing my side playfully.

"Ron!" I yelped.

He grabbed my hand and pulled me toward him, a mischievous glint in his eyes. I scolded him, smiling, and he darted out of the kitchen, tweaking Lissa's ear on his way. I watched him go, delighted to see him enjoying life.

My heart swelled with gratitude to God for the work He was doing in Ron. My husband had begun to view life differently than he used to. He was discovering purpose through Jesus Christ instead of satisfaction based on his profession. He had become a committed husband, so that our marriage could grow more fully. We were beginning to do more and more things differently from the way in which we, especially Ron, had been brought up. But these changes brought friction between us and his parents.

————————————

"But Ron, they are *our* grandchildren. Don't we have a right to spend time with them without you and Kay being right there?" my mother-in-law asked pointedly as we glided past miles of lush green woods.

Beads of sweat formed on Ron's forehead, and he pursed his lips. Grasping the steering wheel tightly, he turned to his dad in the front seat of the van and then glanced back at his mom seated beside me in the first bench seat.

"Mom and Dad, you want to know why we haven't been allowing the children to spend time alone with you lately? Okay, that's a fair question." Looking intently at the road in front of us he continued, "Well, to be totally honest with you, Kay and I do not appreciate how our authority is undermined when the children are alone with you."

I prayed silently for Ron, knowing this was hard for him. I greatly admired his courage to stand for truth even when it put him at odds with his parents. I knew Ron had a way of being lovingly frank, and this instance was no exception. He addressed the sticky issue boldly but graciously.

Isaiah waved at us from the rear window of the van we were following. This meeting with Ron's parents had been carefully prearranged so that we could discuss the matter privately with them. Though we had visited back and forth regularly in each other's homes, tension had continued to build. Clearly they disapproved of the way we had chosen to raise our children.

Comments they had made to our children in our absence worried us. Our relationship with them had come to a place where something had to be done at once. Only recently Jan had asked Ron, "Why is it that we never get to have the children to ourselves anymore?"

Ron thought a short trip together would provide an opportunity for the four of us to discuss the matter while our children rode in his sister's van up ahead.

"On occasions when the children have been alone with you, they have come home with reports that have been very unsettling to us. It has put our children in an awkward position. And that's why we've begun limiting your visits with them to include Kay and me. Dad, we don't want our children to be involved in some sort of tug-of-war between us and y'all. That doesn't help anyone."

"Son, what do you mean? When have we put the children into an awkward spot?"

"Well, Dad, there have been quite a few instances. Let me see . . . Okay, for example, our choice to homeschool. I know that has been something you and Mom have not approved of from the very beginning. Do you remember the time we left the children with you and Mom, and then ya'll took them on a tour of a public school without asking our permission? How were we supposed to feel toward you when our children told us about it? Or like the times you played a video our children felt uncomfortable with? Hannah said she told you she did not feel right about watching some of those movies. Dad, were those movies important enough to force the children to sit through them?"

Jan leaned forward and clutched the seat in front of her. "But Ron," she interrupted defensively.

Walter turned around sharply and stopped her with an authoritative look. "Jan, let him finish."

She sat back dejectedly.

Ron went on. "Look, Mom and Dad, I don't want to go through a whole big list of offenses today. I don't see how that will help. But I think what is happening is that Kay and I are raising our children differently than you raised me. Hey, I want to thank you for the way you raised me. I know you did what you thought was best, and I commend you for that. But, you see, now it is our turn to give this thing called parenting our best shot. It is true that our children are your grandchildren. No one is denying that. But Kay and I are the ones who will someday stand before God and answer for the way these children were raised. You have to be willing to let us do things with our own children the way we see fit. I know you have your doubts about our children's home education. Maybe you think they will grow up inadequately educated or socially maladjusted. I don't know what all your concerns are. But I would like for you to honor our decisions since we are the parents and realize that, by God's design, we have the greater authority over our children. I know this is going to sound harsh, but I have decided I must protect my children from any environment that I perceive could be spiritually or emotionally harmful, even if that environment happens to be the home of their own grandparents."

There seemed to be nothing more to say. An awkward silence ensued as I glanced at my watch and realized we still had another thirty minutes before reaching our destination. It must have been a terrible insult for Walter and Jan to realize we felt we needed to shield our children, even from them.

"And by the way, Hannah and Lissa, I posted an article on the tackboard that I found in the *Houston Chronicle*. I want each of you to write a report about it today in school," Ron carefully instructed as he finished up the morning devotional. Turning to me, he ran his fingers through his dark hair. "Kay, I'm sorry, but I won't be home in time for supper tonight. Just go on without me, all right?"

After more than fifteen years of training to become a trauma surgeon, Ron had been accepted for a position on staff, working with the University of Texas Health Science Center and Hermann Hospital in Houston, Texas. Trauma surgeons lead a demanding life, running back and forth from their homes to the hospital and wearing beepers that go off frequently. Their body rhythms are constantly thrown off by irregular sleep patterns, since they spend so many nights in the operating room. It is a tricky profession for a family man.

Nonetheless, Ron had a heart for his children and loved being personally involved with each of them. Whenever he was home, no job was too lowly for him. He was happy to change our baby's diapers when I was busy or even help put a meal on the table when our small children were hanging on my skirt.

By now we had more children. We had been blessed with three more daughters since the birth of our son, giving us a total of five daughters and one son. How rich we felt with God's blessings. Ron liked to lead devotionals for our family at 6:00 a.m., whenever he was home. Sometimes, to wake us all up before a devotional, he would lead us outside on a short walk along the bayou trail. Together we would marvel at the stars still hanging in the black sky. If his work required him to fly to a medical meeting somewhere, he faithfully sent a postcard to each of the children just so they would know he was thinking of them.

Although Ron's job required much time and energy, he found the work thrilling. The work was multifaceted. His inquisitive mind was challenged by the medical research and experiments he was involved in. A gifted teacher, he delighted in helping educate other aspiring physicians. Not being satisfied with the norm, he found it gratifying to search out ways to improve the system in hopes of providing better quality health care.

He also found it fulfilling to operate on patients at Hermann Hospital, especially when they pulled through and recovered. Judging from the letters of thanks from patients or their families, I concluded that my husband was a competent, compassionate, personable, and gentle doctor. He gave his utmost on the job and was the kind of physician I would hope for if I were involved in a serious accident.

Observing how busy he was, I remembered what I had said after the first few weeks into his new job. "Ron, I think they got a bargain when they hired you. It seems you are working enough to fill the place of several men."

He merely smiled and shrugged. Ron was a very energetic and enthusiastic man, totally committed to his work, but I could see that even he was being stretched to the limit.

"Kay, I'll be back late tonight," Ron said, as he kissed me. "I love you, honey," he whispered.

"I love you too, Ron." Guiding his bike from the garage, he wheeled it out onto the driveway, latching the metal gate behind him. The children and I gathered on the front porch, waving as he hopped on his black bike and quickly pedaled down the driveway onto the street.

"I'm glad we live close enough to the medical center so he can bike sometimes," Hannah mused as he disappeared from view.

I could picture him as he sped along the canal bike trail, bypassing traffic altogether and making it to work in only 15 minutes. "Me too," I agreed, opening the front door as we all filed inside.

"Okay, it's bedtime. Is anyone ready to hear more of 'The Man Story'?"

"Me!"

"Me, too!"

"I am!"

"Oh, yes, Daddy!"

Ron liked to think up stories and tell them to the children. Actually, the children seemed to prefer this approach, since he created such interesting ones.

"Isaiah, let's put your horses away so that I can tuck you into bed."

"Yes, sir," Isaiah said. He climbed up on his bunk and began hurriedly gathering plastic horses into his arms.

"Beverly, crawl onto your bunk too. Good girl! Shhh, Emily. Let's not sing right now. Daddy wants to tell you a story, so lie down in your crib and be very quiet."

Ron eased into a chair and propped his feet up on the bed while the children settled quickly onto their bunks. Even though Hannah and Lissa slept in the next room, they never wanted to miss an episode, so they crowded into their siblings' bedroom too.

"Let's see . . ." Ron began. "Do you remember last night in the story there had been a huge storm at Thomas and Joseph's house, and the rain was beating down so hard when the big tree crashed to the ground just outside their fence?"

"Yeah, and all duh vegables were bwown ovah by duh wind."

"That's right, Grace. Okay, listen carefully so that we can find out what will happen tonight."

The children lay frozen in their beds, not wanting to miss a single word, as Ron dramatically told the next portion of the story, complete with sound effects.

Tonight, as usual, he abruptly ended at just the most critical point, leaving the main character, Thomas, in extreme danger. Everyone would have to wait and find out what would happen to him tomorrow night or whenever Ron got a chance to continue. By the grin on his face, I could tell he delighted in making everyone terribly curious and impatient to hear what would happen next.

Kissing each child good night, Ron headed toward the door, his hand resting on the light switch ready to flick the light out. Every pair of eyes stared in disbelief. Surely he couldn't possibly stop the story at such a critical place! But he had.

"Oh, Daddy," Lissa pleaded as she hopped up from the bed and ran to him, wrapping her arms tightly around his waist, "what's going to happen next? Can't you just give us a little, tiny hint?" she asked looking up into his face pitifully.

He smiled down at her lovingly. Smoothing her hair, he looked into her blue eyes. "Lissa, I won't know myself until I'm telling it the next time," he confessed with a mischievous grin.

It was a fresh, beautiful morning in Houston. The city was only beginning to stir, and the roar of the nearby freeway was not yet audible. I really enjoyed early morning walks along the bayou just one street behind our house. It had a good walking trail, and more than a few people could be seen jogging or walking their dogs. I came out to pray.

As a busy mother of six, time alone was precious. We had enjoyed our years in Houston, and Ron was well-respected and in great demand everywhere he went. He was a surgeon, and a good one, from every report that came my way. But he was also my husband, and the father of our six precious children. We loved every minute he was home, even if it was brief. My mind went back to an event last night. It was so typical.

We had just prayed and were enjoying the first bites of Ron's favorite meal, taco salad. Beep, beep, beep! Ron grabbed his pager and held it up to his ear. We all paused and strained our ears to catch what the call was about. Sometimes we heard that Life Flight had gone to pick up an unconscious male, wounded in a gun fight, or a young child who had been hit by a car.

But last night it had been a call from the hospital. One of Ron's patients had taken a turn for the worse. Ron got up from the table and stepped to the phone in the kitchen. We could hear snatches of the conversation. "Hey, John, what's up? It's Mrs. Crompton, right? Uh-huh. Gotcha. Okay, no problem. I'll be right in."

And with that, he had hung up the phone and kissed me as he dashed out the door, saying, "Just save me a plate, Kay, and I'll eat later."

I couldn't hide the disappointment on my face. We hated it when he had to leave, especially when we were having family time. More than once, the children teasingly threatened to flush the dreaded pager down the toilet. It tugged at my heart to raise our children so much in his absence. More and more of the home responsibilities were falling to me. How I wanted to see more of Ron; we all did.

On my walk this morning I was especially weary and burdened. Our future seemed spiritually bleak to me. "Oh, Lord," I prayed, "how will it be possible for the children to grow up totally committed to You if their daddy is away or preoccupied with his work so much of the time? Lord, what kind of 'fruit' will result from this fast-paced life of ours?" I questioned. "Truly You have brought us through to a better season, and I am certainly grateful for this, especially compared to the grueling years of Ron's training. Yet, Father, I am increasingly concerned about the direction of our family."

I confided in God about my desires and aspirations for the children. I told Him how intensely I wanted our children to grow up with an intimate relationship with their eternal Father. "Oh God," I prayed, "would You give our family an assignment that would help our children to grow up to be mighty in faith? I am willing to go through *anything* if You will use it to train our children to become fully committed to You." I had no idea what I was asking for.

Still wearing his green scrubs at the end of the day, Ron tossed a big pillow onto the living room floor next to the couch. "Okay, children, who wants to hear the next chapter of *Swiss Family Robinson?*" Wedging the pillow behind himself, Ron opened the book where the marker held its place.

"Oh, yes, Daddy!" The children giggled and squirmed into a spot on the floor, pressing up next to their daddy as tightly as possible. Ron smiled affectionately at each of them as he began. The children listened attentively to the lively story, their eyes glued to the dramatic expressions on their daddy's face. But after a couple of pages, Ron began to grow sleepy and his speech became slurred. His eyelids drooped and as his muscles relaxed, the book gradually slipped from his fingers. His mouth formed the words of the story in slow motion as his head nodded toward the book.

"So the Swiss Family Robinson built a trauma center underneath the bridge." He woke up with a jerk as giggles erupted from his children, delighting in this sudden, new twist to an old classic.

Ron yawned and said, "Okay, children, time to go to bed."

He jumped up and scooped Grace and Emily into his arms, heading for the bedroom. As the children scrambled into their beds, Ron bent over his little son. "Good night, Isaiah," he said, kissing the restless little boy. "Don't you want to take your boots off before you go to sleep?"

"I guess so." Isaiah sighed as he pulled off each one and tossed it over the edge of the bed.

"Good night, girlie," Ron called affectionately to Beverly, stooping over to kiss her. A quiet giggle sounded from the bottom bunk, and I smiled.

"Oh, look, dear," Ron said turning to me with a wink. "Grace must already be asleep. Look how tightly her eyes are closed. But she is smiling. Do you think I should tickle her to see if she might possibly be a little bit awake?"

Squeals of shrill laughter followed while I looked on. Emily, who was standing up in her crib and clutching the railing, began bouncing happily. She hoped her Daddy would tease her next.

I leaned on the door frame contentedly. *Ron is such a sweet daddy,* I thought.

I stepped into our room and got dressed for bed. Ron wearily shut the bedroom door and went into the bathroom. I heard the water turn on, and then his toothbrush scrubbing. I slipped between the cool sheets and pulled them up to my chin. My eyes drooped. "I'm tired, honey, do you have to be at the hospital early again in the morning?"

"Uh-huh," I heard him mumble. Several minutes later I opened my eyes and looked toward the bathroom. The light was still on, and the water was still running.

"Ron?" I called. No response. *What's taking him so long?* I wondered. Shoving back the covers, I hurried to the bathroom doorway.

Ron was frowning at himself in the mirror, his toothbrush lying forgotten in the sink. With an alarmed expression, he stuck out his tongue and then shook his head.

"What's wrong, dear?" I asked, concerned.

He slowly rinsed his hands under the running water and dully turned off the faucet. Turning, he looked into my eyes, and then shook his head. "Something is wrong with me, Kay. I don't have complete control of my tongue."

Drawing on all his medical training, he mentally flipped through the possibilities. What he found was not promising.

I leaned against the doorway and asked, "What do you mean?"

In August of 1995 Ron had begun having severe headaches. But when his tongue no longer responded normally, he knew something was really wrong. He was suddenly experiencing extreme pain most of the time. Although the original CAT-scan revealed that he might have only an infection of some type in the base of his skull, we eventually learned he had a fast-growing type of bone cancer called Ewings sarcoma.

Cancer. The word sent shivers down my spine. My own mother had died of cancer fourteen years before. With horror I had observed her losing weight, strength, and hair because of chemotherapy. My beloved mother had fallen victim to this terrible disease, and now my husband was dying from it too.

Ron's diagnosis was a devastating blow to us all. The

oncologist at M.D. Anderson Cancer Center in Houston gave us
little hope of Ron living very long. After hearing the grim prognosis, Ron and I made our way to the oppressive medical library and
leafed through forbidding volumes, gathering information on
Ewing's sarcoma. We discovered that what the doctor had said
was true: the prognosis looked bleak indeed.

We began researching natural approaches to cancer treatment. No one needed to encourage us to seek the Lord through
prayer for divine guidance; we were on our knees, begging for wisdom. I know that reflecting upon my mother's death biased me
against chemotherapy and radiation, so I wanted my husband to
be cautious. It was such a huge decision! Family and friends of
opposing opinions called us to discuss the matter. Some began
bringing books and videos to our door for us to evaluate. Ron even
put out a fleece, asking God to give him a clear and specific sign
regarding whether he should pursue chemotherapy or take a natural approach. He chose the natural approach, a choice some considered a serious mistake.

After my mother died, my dad married a lady who had lost her
first husband through illness. They were both deeply concerned.
Ron's parents worried day and night.

Our approach to Ron's medical treatment accelerated the conflict in our relationship with his parents. Understandably, they
were anxious about their son's health and wanted so much for
him to choose the right treatment. But what was the right treatment? How could anyone know? It must have been a frustrating
time for Ron's parents as they stood helplessly looking on. It was
a terrifying and agonizing time for us too.

The room was quiet, and Ron lay restlessly on the bed. A tube
from the oxygen tank in the corner snaked its way to the bed and
up to Ron's nose, where it hissed softly. His breathing was slow,
but steady. I glanced at the gauge to make sure the reading was
where it should be. We had recently come across a new problem:
Ron was requiring more and more oxygen. If he needed more than
what he was getting now, he would have to be admitted to the
hospital again.

At home we had been able to provide him with vegetable juices all through the day. But that halted when the tumor at the base of Ron's skull pinched off his ability to swallow effectively. Now he was fed intravenously with a milky white substance. At first, a nurse had to come to our house each time he needed a new bag, but eventually she taught Hannah and Lissa how to do basic nursing. Daily they flushed his line and periodically changed his Total Parenteral Nutrition (TPN) bag. Ironically, Ron had always been the medical person in our family; now he was the patient, and our oldest girls were the nurses.

I looked at the form of my dear husband, stretched out on the bed with his face toward the wall. His bones jutted up sharply against the sheet; he was so terribly thin. His cheeks had sunk in, his eyes had a hollow look, and his arms were simply bone with some loose flesh clinging to them. Clearly, neither the juices nor the conventional medicine was working. Every day Ron grew weaker. He was literally wasting away.

My eyes returned to the Bible beside me on the couch. I just knew God was eager to show His mighty power on our behalf, to reach down and heal my husband. It sounded radical, but this situation had become desperate. We had so badly wanted Ron to be healed and had found many verses on healing. Surely that was God's will too.

My eyes looked past the page, and I was soon lost in thought. God was already teaching us valuable lessons through this trial. Our friends eagerly did anything they could to help us. People from church sometimes took the children home when Ron needed to go to the hospital. Other friends mowed our yard, for which we were so grateful. The lawn was the last thing on our minds.

A couple of months before, we had all come down with a terrible virus and had to go to bed. A family from church took care of us all that day, not only providing Ron with fresh carrot juice but also making enough for us as well. Debbie, a nurse who had worked with Ron when he was healthy, was now offering her nursing skills and much spare time to help us out. Sometimes she came just to visit. She was more than a nurse; she became a dear friend. And many others had done just as much for us. Yes, we were learning to accept help from others, which was humbling at times, but a good lesson for me.

I thought back to when Hannah and Lissa had been home alone with Ron and heard coughing sounds from his room. When they rushed in to check on him, they were startled at what they found. Ron was sitting on the edge of the bed with his legs dangling, bracing himself with his arms. With his head bent low, he was weeping loudly.

When the girls asked him what was wrong, he shook his head. "How I have grieved God with my life!" he said between sobs. The girls knelt beside him.

"Mommy, it felt like we were kneeling on holy ground," they confided to me later.

The Lord had done a breaking work in Ron's life through this sickness, and although painful, it was a beautiful thing to behold. Though his body was deteriorating, his heart was increasingly soft in the Lord's hands. He never asked God "why" nor grew bitter, but rather accepted this as a lesson from God. He was just as convinced as we that God was going to heal his body.

The doorbell rang and Hannah opened the door wide for the paramedics who had come to take Ron back to the hospital. I led them to his room where they deftly unfolded the stretcher and gently transferred my husband onto it. For the ninth time Ron was being rushed to the hospital for critical care. One of the paramedics handed me a form to sign, permitting them to transport Ron to Hermann Hospital. I scribbled my name and handed back the clipboard, following them out into the living room and to the door with a heavy sigh. Fear hung in our household like a gloomy cloud.

Ron was alert as he was rolled through the living room. Weakly, he tried to sit up and smile at the children as he passed by, but he didn't have the strength to manage it. Determined to communicate, he whispered, "Good-bye, children. I love you."

Lissa choked back tears and told him that she loved him too. The children watched, wide-eyed, as their daddy rolled past them through the door, and out to the waiting ambulance.

Minutes later, I kissed the children good-bye and pulled the car door shut behind me. "I don't know how long we can all go on like this, God." I prayed desperately as I drove myself to Hermann Hospital. Our life revolved around Ron and his failing health, so for now, I would be at the hospital as much as possible. Sometimes Hannah or even Jan took turns sitting with him through the night so I could go home and get a little rest.

It was during this very stressful time that my brother David and his wife Sue Beth came to live with us. They kept life as normal as possible for the children, whether it was putting meals on the table or just being there to tuck the little ones into bed. They were such a blessing to us, not only for all the work they did but also for the moral support. They even provided a needed laugh now and then when a day got too intense.

Ron had appointed me to be his power of attorney if the time should come when he could no longer make decisions about his medical care. So, when he lost consciousness in the hospital and those final decisions regarding his medical treatment, indeed, fell to me, my relationship with his parents became almost unbearably tense. But I still believed that God was somehow going to heal my husband. He just had to! I was stubbornly determined about it and wouldn't let myself think any thoughts to the contrary.

In the now familiar hospital room, I caught myself worrying anyway as I stared at my husband's motionless form lying on the bed. A trache had been placed in his throat a few days earlier. The bag hanging above his bed dripped fluid steadily into an IV line, giving him nutrients he could not give himself. I opened the Bible in my lap and read out loud the Scriptures I had marked, which reminded me that God certainly had the power to heal.

"Lord," I prayed, "I'm not feeling very full of faith today, but I offer to You this little bit of faith I do have. Please forgive me and help my unbelief."

A doctor entered the room briskly with a clipboard in hand. Her crisp white lab coat rustled as she shook my hand. "Hello, Mrs. Evans," she addressed me professionally. "Well, things are not looking very hopeful for your husband. I'm sure you realize that by now. I'm really sorry. I do need to find out what your wishes are at the point of his death. Do you think he would want to donate his organs?"

"Um, no ma'am, I don't think so."

She jotted it down on her clipboard and glanced quickly at Ron before patting me on the shoulder. "Hang in there, Mrs. Evans," she said sympathetically as she turned and vanished into the hallway.

A lump formed in my throat, and I felt very alone.

Moments later, my mother-in-law and sister-in-law, Elaine, entered the room and stood across the bed from me. Tension arose within me as my mother-in-law glanced around the room, observing the monitor's bleak readings. She studied her son gravely.

"Kay, surely you can see by all of this that Ron is dying," she said.

Something in me wanted to cry out against her hopeless outlook. *Lord, somehow give me Your love for my mother-in-law,* I prayed silently. Gripping the cold bed rail, I looked directly into her face. "But Jan, I've been praying for him to be healed. I believe God still has the power to heal him, even though it looks grim right now. And even if God should let him die, I believe He would raise Ron from the dead."

My mother-in-law glanced smugly at her daughter, my words confirming her suspicions. As the door clicked shut behind them, I slumped into the chair and gazed out the window. *What have I just said? Ron's body is obviously deteriorating more and more every day. But then again . . . I do believe God wants to use such a miracle to show Ron's parents that His power alone can revive their son.*

Late that night I gazed at the lights of the city from the hospital window. Vehicle lights headed down the street as medical personnel made their way home after another busy day in the medical center.

How I miss normal life, I thought.

Ron lay exactly as he had for the past who-knew-how-many days. He was alive, although I had not heard his voice in over a month, nor seen him move in several weeks. He had been unconscious ever since the trache was placed in his throat. I glanced at his monitor, which showed a slight improvement. I was encouraged.

In the eight grueling months since Ron had gotten sick, his health had grown steadily worse. It had been especially strange during these past few weeks with only the monitor showing signs of life. Yet I always looked for anything hopeful. Was I hoping against hope, or was it worth noticing the progress on his monitor this evening?

CHAPTER 3

Life Without Ron

Apprehensively I stepped toward the chaplain seated just outside Ron's private room. Although this man had become a frequent visitor of Ron's, I was still nervous about how he would respond to my question. I cleared my throat, and he glanced up, adjusting the glasses on his nose.

"Can I help you, Mrs. Evans?"

"Yes," I responded hesitantly. "I was wondering . . . would it be possible to have my husband's body taken to our home this morning rather than to the mortuary?"

He stared at me in disbelief, but I was too far into my plea to quit now. "Is that possible?" I inquired.

He sputtered, and then looked back at me. "Um . . . I think . . . well, I guess you could ask the funeral home director. He could tell you what you are legally allowed to do."

I thanked him and turned back into the room, but I could feel his questioning eyes staring into my back.

Looking through the phone book, I found the funeral home section. "Landis, Elmwood . . . Earthman, there it is." I put my finger at the phone number and held the receiver to my ear. After dialing the number, I glanced at the empty bed beside me. *Funeral arrangements . . . I can't believe I really need to speak to a funeral home. Ron is actually gone . . .*

A monotone voice answered, breaking into my thoughts. "Earthman Funeral Home. How may I help you?"

I started and then said, "Ummm, yes, I have a question for you . . ."

On the way home from the hospital, David and I talked about why Ron had not been healed. We both knew God could have touched Ron's body and healed him in a flash. Why hadn't He? Or why hadn't He allowed the organic juices to work? I thought we had asked in faith, believing He would answer. I knew some would argue that Ron was cured, since now he had a perfect body beyond this life. But death was not the answer I had in mind when I asked the Lord to heal Ron.

Could it be that God had an even mightier miracle in mind? Couldn't God just raise Ron from the dead, and bring even more glory to His name? I thought of the time Jesus lovingly raised Jairus' dead daughter. Wouldn't the Lord do the same thing for me now? His Word said if we ask, we shall receive.

Arriving at home I acknowledged to my children that their daddy was dead. There was no way we could deny that. But I decided we were still going to pray and ask the Lord for one more miracle, even now.

It felt very strange, looking at Ron's lifeless form, draped in a white sheet, lying on a gurney in our living room. I had never asked God for anything like this in my whole life. "What am I doing?" I asked myself with a heavy sigh. I stooped over and picked up Grace, who was standing on her tiptoes, trying to get a better view.

"Do you see your daddy's body, Grace?" I asked.

She nodded slowly, and her little brown curls bounced. I looked at my other children gathering around me, quietly observing the reality of death. Isaiah, although a lively seven-year-old boy, understood this was a sober time. As always, he was wearing his cowboy boots and a hat that was much too big for him. Right now he was subdued, and his eyes looked troubled as he gazed at his daddy's pale, motionless form. It was a strange sight for us all, especially since it was the body of someone we all loved so much.

David and Sue Beth stayed to support me in this unusual petition we were bringing to the Lord today. A friend of theirs was also there, who was reportedly full of faith. I hoped to lean on their faith, because I was not feeling very strong. It was so reassuring to have them around during this stressful time.

We all sat down for a time of singing and praying. I explained to the children that although we had asked God to heal their daddy, He had chosen not to.

"I don't know why . . . Beverly, please sit still, honey! I don't know why God did not heal your daddy, but I know He has enough power to even raise him from the dead if He wants to," I said.

We became excited at the prospect of such an incredible miracle.

"Let's pray," said David, bowing his head.

But just then the doorbell rang, interrupting us. Sue Beth quietly got up from the couch to answer it. In a moment she was back.

"Kay!" she said urgently.

The tone of Sue Beth's voice startled me, and I looked up. She was obviously concerned.

"Kay, someone from Child Protective Services is at the door. They need to talk to you."

Dread filled my heart, and I followed her to the door, wondering what they wanted with us. In the doorway I managed a weak smile at the man standing there.

"Um, excuse me, Mrs. Evans. I work with the CPS. A report has been filed concerning your family, and we have some things we must check out. We would like to talk with you. Would it be all right if we come inside to interview you and the children now?"

After an awkward pause, I said, "Sir, my husband died just this morning." My voice cracked, and I whispered, "Do you think you could come back another day?"

The man looked down at his shoes and mumbled, "Yes, I'm sorry. I am very sorry to hear about your husband." He handed me his business card and said briefly, "Call me back later when it is more convenient."

By the tone of his voice and the look on his face, it was obvious the CPS interview was not optional. One day soon, I would have to allow them to interview me and the children. Sue Beth had been a CPS social worker in the past and gave us important information about such an interview.

"And don't let them in the door," she said. "Once they step inside your house, they legally have more jurisdiction over you. When the social worker interviews you and the children, don't permit them to interview the children alone. Maybe David or I could be there with them, and it would be ideal if we could have the interview taped . . ."

We had heard horror stories about the CPS ripping families apart. That they were now wanting to investigate our family was a nightmare.

It was almost lunchtime, and the children were getting hungry. But food was the last thing I wanted. It was getting later, and the morticians were growing frustrated that the body had been kept in our home all morning. I had no idea that bringing it to our house would be such an explosive issue. Unknown to me, it had caused quite a stir among our extended family.

"Elaine," I had told Ron's sister, "I just want to have a day of prayer. I really would prefer not having visitors today. I know it's strange, but please just try to understand!"

As Elaine passed the word around, family members did not understand. Furthermore, when they heard I was asking God to raise Ron from the dead, some of them were outraged. How dare I ask the Lord to perform such a miracle in these modern times! Most of our extended family members were disgusted. Others concluded I was not accepting the reality of Ron's death very well. Normally, I would have agreed, but somehow I believed from the bottom of my heart that God wanted to raise Ron.

I had no idea that in the months and years to come God would lovingly show me His higher plan. Although He well could have raised Ron, it was more important that I learn to accept God's sovereign and perfect will for my life rather than insisting on my will over His. I did not realize how much Jesus, my risen Lord, wanted to become my All in All.

Little Emily tugged at my skirt, reminding me I still had hungry children. The phone rang, and Hannah ran to see who was calling. A moment later, she returned.

"It's Earthman Funeral Home again," she whispered with her hand over the mouthpiece. "Do you want to talk to them?"

I sighed and accepted the phone. I knew these men had a job to do. "Yes, you may come get the body. In ten minutes? Sounds fine. Thanks."

I hung up the phone, feeling a great weariness.

The smell of Church's Fried Chicken filled the living room, as Sue Beth and Hannah served hot chicken onto paper plates. Lissa poured water into the cups and set them by each plate around the table. Isaiah always loved having Caleb, Timmy, and Drew, his three cousins, at our home. He had managed well enough being the only boy, but when he had masculine companionship, he relished it!

Today their game was the usual: a cowboy and Indian chase scene. My three youngest daughters followed behind, delighted to be included in the game; the boys had captured "Indian squaws." Sounds of whooping and hollering floated in as David opened the back door and called the troops in for lunch. Soon high-pitched excited voices and thumping boots could be heard in the kitchen.

Hannah directed them to the sink. "Over here, boys, you need to wash your hands first. No, you can't just rinse them, you have to use soap! Yeah, that's good. Okay, get to the table!"

After the blessing, I sat on the couch and watched as Beverly picked up a chicken leg and chomped on it. All the children enjoyed fried chicken, and I was glad David had gone out and bought lunch. This day had already been so draining, and making lunch was just one more thing to do.

I glanced at the vacant spot on the floor where the gurney had stood all morning. Now that the morticians had removed my husband's corpse from our house, I somehow felt strangely relieved. A car door slammed, and I looked toward the window, wondering who could be here.

"We are just starting to eat. I wish the meal didn't have to be disrupted," I said groaning.

Lissa turned from the window with a frightened expression. "Mom, it's police cars . . . lots of them!"

I stared at her in disbelief. "What could possibly be going on!"

A firm knock resounded on the front door. David and Sue Beth exchanged strained glances. Sue Beth made her way resolutely to the door and opened it. There stood a short, stocky officer; his demeanor commanded respect. Sue Beth eyed his Houston Police Department badge warily.

"May I speak with Kay Evans, please?" he demanded.

"Yes, she is right here."

I got up from the couch and hurried to the doorway. We stepped out onto the porch, and Sue Beth shut the door behind us.

Once outside, I could see five, six, no, it was *seven* bright blue police cars parked along the street! My mind reeled. For what reason would they send so many officers to my home? Several of them were on their walkie-talkies.

"Mrs. Evans, I have some questions for you." Once again the policeman was speaking, and I tried to concentrate as he talked on and on. A report had been filed . . . The police had heard that Ron's body had been here this morning, and that concerned them. I tried to answer each question and was so glad Sue Beth was beside me.

After the officer had asked many questions and filled out a paper, he said, "All right, Mrs. Evans, I just have one last thing. I would like to take a quick look around inside your home, just to make sure the children are all okay. Is that all right?"

"Of course," I said, and Sue Beth and I followed him into the house, leaving the other policemen outside, some leaning against the closest police car.

The children stared with interest as the uniformed man stepped through the front doorway. After a quick tour of our home, the officer returned to the living room where we all waited.

"Everything looks fine," he said. Noticing Isaiah's eyes riveted on the shiny pistol at his hip, he paused and smiled. He slipped his gun from its holster, and crouched down, explaining to the boys how a pistol works. They were fascinated. When he was finished, he winked at them and straightened up to face me.

"I guess that will be all, Mrs. Evans. I'm sorry to have disrupted your meal."

"Oh, it's no problem." I shrugged as he stepped out the door.

After they left, we sighed in relief. But we were concerned that someone had filed a report against me. Why? And why today of all days? How I related to David of old, who said, *They prevented me in the day of my calamity: but the LORD was my stay.*[1]

How thankful I was that even in this, one of the hardest days of my life, the Lord was giving me strength.

The chapel was filled to capacity, and people were standing in the lobby. It was April 1, only three days after Ron had died. I slowly looked around at the sea of faces. Ron's mother and father sat near the front, just across the aisle from me. Jan dabbed her eyes with a tissue, and Walter's gaze rested, as if unseeing, on the casket in front of us. He looked up, his eyes meeting mine, and then he glanced away.

Just before the service, they had cornered Lissa, and tried to convince her that what I had done was wrong. Lissa had made it clear she did not agree with them. Although she was only twelve, she had a very strong opinion of her own. After the confrontation, she had rushed to my side and quietly recounted the whole scenario for me.

I knew my in-laws were extremely upset. An uneasy feeling grew in my heart that something more painful than the death of a loved one was taking place. What a horrible day to be at odds with extended family members, yet it was a reality. Years later, when I looked back on this day, I would have deep regrets about the way I avoided people during this extremely difficult time. How I would wish I could go back and undo the damage caused by my not receiving their sympathy in the way I should have. I pray they can forgive my insensitivity.

Behind Jan and Walter, I saw Debbie and several other nurses who had worked with Ron at Hermann Hospital. Farther back, families from church crowded into the benches. Behind them I could see others standing, peering in through the open door. Ron's life had touched many people.

Ron's brother, Leo, got up and read passages of Scripture and shared favorite memories of Ron. I felt so distracted, I could hardly concentrate on what was being said. I stared at the open silver-colored casket only a few feet in front of me, embellished

---

1. Psalm 18:18

with red roses. From where I sat, I could barely see Ron's pallid face against the satin pillow. His dark hair was combed straight back in such an odd way. He had never combed it like that.

With the funeral behind us, cars lined the street in front of our house, and people milled in and out, including Jan and Walter. Flowers and plants from the funeral gave the house a new, jungle-like appearance. The living room now smelled just like the funeral home. Our guests had kindly provided lunch, and ladies in the kitchen busily dished out steaming plates and passed them around.

My younger children ran, screaming and playing in the backyard with a number of other children, running off some of their abundant energy. I was so grateful for all these people and the concern they showed for my family. Nonetheless, I was simply exhausted.

One couple sat down across from me, wanting to help me outline the direction our family would be going from here. "What are you going to do, Kay? How will you make out financially?" they queried with worried expressions.

Their words spun evasively in my tired brain. "I just don't know," I said apologetically.

My house was swarming with precious people wishing to comfort me. I tried to smile at each one of them and answer every question they asked, but what I really wanted was a nap.

"But Mommy, what if I say something wrong?" Hannah's troubled eyes looked into mine. The day had arrived for the CPS interviews, and 15-year-old Hannah was especially concerned. My most sensitive child, she felt responsible to help this interview go well.

"Honey, don't worry about it. I am sure God will show you what to say, so just ask Him to give you the right words," I said.

I also dreaded this event, but I knew God would guide us. How could it be otherwise? God's Word spoke so clearly to me saying, *When thou passest through the waters, I will be with thee; and*

through the rivers, they shall not overflow thee: when thou walk-
est through the fire, thou shalt not be burned; neither shall the
flame kindle upon thee. For I am the LORD thy God.[1]

That morning we had called the CPS and arranged for the
social worker to come in the afternoon. We were all in the front
yard when the white Dodge Caravan drove up. A short woman
climbed out of the van and walked toward us, smiling.

I stepped forward and shook her hand, saying, "I'm Kay
Evans."

Her smile grew wider. "Yes, and I'm Judy," she bubbled. "It's so
nice to meet you. Why, you have such a beautiful family! I am terribly sorry to hear about your husband. I know this must be so
hard. Are you Italian?"

I shook my head, and wondered why she was asking such an
odd question.

"Oh, well, my family is from Italy, and it is common practice to
have the bodies of our loved ones at home for a day or two before
we bury them. When I heard you had your husband's body
brought to your home for a few hours, I just couldn't help wondering!"

I had not expected the social worker to be so personable. Was
this friendliness just a front? In spite of our suspicions, she
quickly put us at ease.

"Now I need to interview Hannah, Lissa, Isaiah, Beverly, and
you. I think Grace and Emily are probably too young for an interview."

I readily agreed.

The paper on her clipboard fluttered in the spring breeze. I sat
on the cool, stone planter watching her mouth as she read off the
report that listed abuse and neglect. I was simply appalled, and
could not believe what was being said of us.

"Why would anyone make up such blatant lies about me?" I
exclaimed.

Judy was clearly relieved to see the horror in my face and realized the accusations must be false.

"Judy," I asked, "would you like to speak with a nurse that has
been very involved with our family during the past few months?

1. Isaiah 43:2, 3

She might be able to give you an objective viewpoint of this whole situation."

She nodded gratefully, and I hurried inside to see if Debbie could come over.

Meanwhile, Judy continued with the interviews in the front yard. Sue Beth sat next to Isaiah, holding a tape recorder. It was reassuring for the children to have their aunt there with them. It was also a comfort to me, knowing Sue Beth was listening in on the conversations.

As the social worker spoke with Isaiah, she said, "Do you know what the CPS is, Isaiah?"

He looked up at her from beneath the wide brim of his cowboy hat and said, "No ma'am."

"Well," she said, "we help children who are in abusive or neglectful situations, okay? Now, I want to ask you a few questions. Do you ever get spanked?"

He looked down, quite embarrassed. "Sometimes," he admitted.

"When you do get spanked, where does your mommy spank you?"

He looked up. "Ummm . . . in her room," he admitted slowly.

She laughed. "No, I mean, where on your *body* does she spank you?"

He squirmed and said very quietly, "On my bottom."

Once all the interviews were finally over, Judy said to me, "Kay, it would look much better on the records if you would let me into your home. I understand why you didn't want me to go in, but I really think it would be better for you if you just let me walk through your house."

I decided she was right, and so I gave her a tour of our home and then led her back outside where Debbie was waiting to talk to her. After I introduced them to each other, the rest of us went inside so that they could talk alone.

Occasionally, I glanced out the window. *What is taking them so long?* I wondered.

Years later we learned of the incredible miracle that happened on that day. Judy had come to our house with strict orders from her boss to remove all my children and place them in foster homes that very day. The Lord worked in the heart of our social worker and prevented this from happening. She felt our home was not abusive and no action was necessary.

Meanwhile, Judy's boss, Kimberly, went to an evening church service. The speaker's topic was on the death of Christ, and as the preacher spoke, he began to weep. When he regained his composure, he apologized to the audience.

"This is an especially difficult message for me to share just now. A good friend of mine, Ron Evans, just died. He was a dear man, and has a fine family . . ."

Kimberly stared at him in horror. "What have I just done?" she asked herself.

A friend seated next to her whispered, "Yeah, I knew him too, and he was a really nice guy!"

Immediately after the service, Kimberly grabbed her cell phone and dialed Judy's number.

Judy had just finished up at our house and was driving home. Picking up her phone, Judy saw it was Kimberly calling. What would Kimberly say when she learned Judy had not carried out her instructions? "Hello?" Judy said tensely.

"Yes, Judy, I need to talk to you."

Judy didn't know what to do. Stalling for more time, she shouted back into the phone, "Hey, Kimberly, this is a terrible connection. We'll have to talk tomorrow at work, okay?" And with that, she hung up the phone, feeling miserable.

The next morning, the two ladies met in the hall, and Judy grabbed her boss, saying, "I have got to talk to you!"

Kimberly looked confused. "But Judy, I have to talk to you!"

As the two women told their stories, they were awed to discover what had transpired.

We were relieved when they informed us that CPS had decided to dismiss our case. Only an awesome God could work behind the scenes like that!

———————

I dug my toes into the sand and watched Grace and Emily squealing happily at the receding waves and picking up shells just washed ashore. Beverly waved at me from where she and

Hannah and Lissa were jumping into the waves. I could just see the top of Isaiah's head as he tried out a cheap snorkeling set we had bought yesterday. Every once in a while a big wave would sweep over him, and he would come back up spluttering.

I smiled; I was very grateful for this vacation. The past few months in Houston had been so stressful that I had decided we needed some time away, just as a family. I wanted to get away from the ever-ringing telephone, and even from all the people so eager to "help" my family grieve. All we wanted was to enjoy normal family life again, away from all the pressure.

My thoughts drifted back to the events of the past few weeks. Ron's burial in Amarillo had been on an unseasonably cold and snowy day in April. His grave was right next to where my mother had been buried years before. Inside the funeral home's dark green tent, we viewed Ron's body one last time. As I bent over Ron's face, snowflakes blew in through a crack in the tent and gathered on his eyelashes. I brushed them off. Ron's cheek felt as cold to my touch as the snow. He looked so plastic and made up, not at all like himself. After each of the children peered briefly at their daddy's face in the casket, we left the little tent and headed, shivering, toward the van, the snow crunching under our feet.

Yes, it was a good time to take some short trips within Texas and just relax. But before we left home, I sat down and wrote a lengthy form letter to our friends and relatives, thanking them for all their kindness to us over the recent months. I felt it important to explain that we needed some extended time away in seclusion. I also dropped a brief note to my in-laws, informing them of our plans.

Then we had packed up the van and headed to South Padre Island. It was wonderful. Only a few people were around, and we were able to be on the beach almost all the time. The gulls above us screeched, and little sand crabs crawled by sideways. We laughed and played in the water and buried each other's bodies in the sand by turn. The children had taught me how to build dribble castles just as their dad had shown them. They imitated his skill perfectly.

I had found a nice, furnished apartment near the shore, so we were able to enjoy family devotions on the cool sand. We loved watching the orange sun come up over the horizon, like a ball of fire, illuminating each wave as it rolled in. The children and I enjoyed the peace. The never-ending song of the waves calmed my heart, so troubled after Ron's recent illness and death.

Another time we went to the hill country, which for years had been one of our favorite family getaways. We took walks through the woods and waded in creeks. We lay out under the brightly shining stars, far away from the city lights of Houston. Then we headed for the door of a rustic, rented cabin and crawled into bed.

On this visit, three-year-old Grace began to coax me, "Friend, let's go down to the lake." "Friend, let's go take a walk." "Friend, may I sleep with you tonight?"

All day long she addressed me as "Friend." I was delighted that her toddler ways did not appear to be hindered by all the stress I was experiencing. It was hard to resist entering into her child's play when she addressed me so affectionately. I knew that maybe even tomorrow she would forget and call me Mommy again, but for now I decided to play along. After all, I wanted to be her friend as well as her mommy.

These times of relaxation provided an opportunity to let God restore us, allowing the stress of the recent months to drain away.

I clasped the stiff, red-white-and-blue envelope in my hand while the Federal Express truck backed out of our driveway. When I noticed the return address, I shuddered. We had just returned from one of our little vacation trips, and this envelope struck fear in my heart. Opening it, I found a letter from my father-in-law.

It was brief, getting right to the point. "Kay, the fact that you are not permitting Jan and me to spend time with the children is un-Christian, unloving, and illegal."

It was a scary letter. I pondered its implications. Another time he contacted me by telephone, saying I had wrongly handled my differences with them. He said I had not followed the proper steps given in Matthew 18:15, 16. *Moreover if thy brother shall trespass against thee, go and tell him his fault between thee and him alone: if he shall hear thee, thou hast gained thy brother. But if he will not hear thee, then take with thee one or two more, that in the mouth of two or three witnesses every word may be established.*

My heart sank. *He's probably right,* I thought. I hadn't handled our differences according to that passage. In fact, I hadn't even thought of that passage. And so I called and asked his forgiveness.

After that, I began to reevaluate what I was doing. Was it right for me to deny them access to their grandchildren? On the other hand, I feared their apparent desire for power and control over my family. When Ron was alive, we had made a strong stand together. We had decided to protect our children from potentially damaging influences, even if those influences were from their grandparents.

Yet how could I stand up to his parents all alone? I found myself wavering, uncertain what to do. Taking small trips helped me avoid my in-laws, but it didn't solve the problem. I poured out my concerns and questions to God, begging Him for guidance. *Lord, what should I do?* I would pray. Often, while praying, I envisioned a court scene. I wondered what that meant.

———————————

The familiar landmarks flew past us once again. By this time we knew almost every mile between Houston and Amarillo by heart. We had traveled these same roads only a month before, when we had buried Ron. But now we were heading back for my grandfather's funeral. I had a hunch this was going to be another awkward and stressful time with my in-laws.

Sure enough, a few days later the phone rang at my dad and stepmom's home where we were staying. I answered. My father-in-law was on the line.

Walter cleared his throat and plunged in. "Kay, just what are the Scriptural reasons behind your not allowing Jan and me to spend time alone with the children?"

Shakily I asked, "Do you think I could call you back a little later?" He agreed, but made it clear he expected an answer right away.

I knew I needed to pray about it before saying anything. And to prayer I went. Wearily I climbed the stairs to find a spot where I could be all alone. "Okay, God, what should I say to him? Oh, this is so touchy . . . Do I dare give him the growing list of Scriptures I believe You have shown me on this subject lately?"

This was not something I would have voluntarily shared with my father-in-law. Yet, he was demanding I give him a Scriptural basis for my decisions. Nervously I dialed the number, dreading to hear him answer.

"Hello?"

"Yes, Walter, this is Kay."

"Go ahead, Kay."

What an unpleasant phone conversation this was going to be. What I had to say would be a bomb, exploding upon him and likely intensifying his animosity toward me. I dreaded the outcome. With trembling hands I unfolded the piece of well-worn notebook paper on which I had jotted a list of Scriptures. Nervously I told him that according to the Scriptures, I felt I had to guard my children. When he insisted on knowing *which* Scriptures, I looked down at the notebook paper in my hand.

"Well," I said, "I can read you a few . . . Let's see here . . . , *'If any man teach otherwise, and consent not to wholesome words, even the words of our Lord Jesus Christ, and to the doctrine which is according to godliness; he is proud, knowing nothing, but doting about questions and strifes of words, whereof cometh envy, strife, railings, evil surmisings, perverse disputings of men of corrupt minds, and destitute of the truth, supposing that gain is godliness: from such withdraw thyself.'"*[1]

I knew he felt I was taking these verses out of context. But I didn't think so. Glancing over my list, I wondered which others I should read. There was Psalm 1:1; Romans 16:17; Exodus 23:32, 33, . . . *Lord,* I prayed silently, *shall I read any more?*

Walter sounded more than hurt; he was angry. My words were like an explosion in his ears.

I also informed him that I felt we still needed some time apart from them. I could not specify how long, because I did not know. It was hard for me to explain why I was denying them the time with their grandchildren they wanted.

---

1. 1 Timothy 6:3-5

But he must have known. Surely he remembered the meeting Ron and I had had with them in the van before Ron's illness, when Ron had voiced our concerns about their times alone with our children.

Our approach to these grandparental conflicts had been possible while Ron was able to "call the shots" as the leader of our family. But taking a stand on my own was a completely different matter. And I was not managing very well.

I didn't know how to cope with the pressures I was now facing with my husband's parents. In the past, I would have gone to Ron and cried on his shoulder, and he would have understood. But now, I felt helpless. I had yet to learn just how powerfully God would step in to be my Defender.

CHAPTER 4

"By My God, I Can Leap Over a Wall!"

We were almost home from a weekend getaway. The road sign read, "Houston, 40 miles." I glanced at my watch, and calculated what time we would get home. David and Sue Beth, their boys, my children, and I had spent a wonderful few days together near Austin; but now I was eager to return home.

We had stayed at Sue Beth's parents' house, which had a lovely view over a lush green golf course. David had taken Lissa, Isaiah, Beverly, Grace, and his three boys hiking in the woods that lined the course. There, they had collected dozens of golf balls and had a great time just trekking with David. I was glad he could provide some masculine influence for my children. My mind went back to the serious conversation with David and Sue Beth just this morning. It was about going to court.

"I don't know why, David," I had said to him, "but oftentimes when I am praying or spending time with the Lord, I find myself envisioning a court scene."

Concerned, he leaned forward in his chair. "Kay, you do *not* want to go to court. Court battles are awful . . . and bloody. Accusations would be thrown at you, and the only way you'd win is to throw accusations back! Believe me, that is not what you want!"

"Hey, you don't have to convince me. I have no desire under any circumstances to take anyone to court. In fact, I feel strongly it would be wrong to get involved in a court battle, unless I am forced into it. It seems totally un-Christian."

I looked at Sue Beth, Hannah, and Lissa, who were sitting

with us in the little den area of the well-furnished basement. Suddenly Beverly, Grace, and Emily came bounding excitedly down the stairs.

"Mommy!" Beverly spoke eagerly, "we were looking out over the golf course from Mrs. Edwards' back porch when a deer and twin fawns came almost up to us. I was standing as still as a statue!"

"Really? That's very exciting."

"We're going back to see if they're still there," she exclaimed as they turned and scampered off merrily.

I looked back at David. "I know what you're saying, David. Taking someone to court wouldn't portray the Spirit of Christ either."

He nodded in agreement, his face sober.

Sue Beth leaned forward, placing her hands on her knees. "But Kay, do you realize it's possible for them to summon you to court against your will?"

"Yes, that's what scares me."

Sue Beth's experience with Child Protective Services proved extremely helpful. "You see," she continued, "all they have to do is hand you a subpoena, which is a legal invitation to court, and then you are automatically pulled into the system. A government agent must place it into your hands; a third party cannot deliver it. So, if a stranger comes to your house, and you suspect he is there to give you a subpoena, don't answer the door. Do whatever you need to do to avoid him!"

I was still mulling over this conversation when we pulled into our driveway late that night. After tucking my sleepy younger children into their beds, Hannah checked the message machine. Several friends had called and left loving messages. One man, without identifying himself, had even called to sing an encouraging hymn for us. Hannah, Lissa, and I crowded around the phone and laughed. Only one man at church sang like that.

Several callers hung up without leaving messages. The caller ID showed an American Investigation Association had called us four times while we were gone. Frowning, I jotted down the name and telephone number, wondering what that could be about.

Though it was late, I went to the pay phone at a nearby

grocery store and called the AIA number. I had decided to play it safe and remain anonymous. The phone rang repeatedly, and then the message machine began playing, "You have reached the American Investigation Association offi . . ." Click. I quickly hung up the phone and returned home, still wondering what they wanted with me.

The next morning I drove back to the grocery store and tried again. This time a man with a deep voice answered.

"Hello," I said quickly. "Do you mind if I ask you what kind of work your company does?"

"Well, who is calling, and why do you want to know?" the man responded.

"Ummm, I noticed on my caller ID that your company called my home recently, and I was curious to know what type of work you are involved in," I said.

"Well, in order to tell you, we'll need to know your name," he replied curtly.

Once again I remained elusive, and the conversation ended abruptly, leaving us both to draw our own conclusions.

Back home, I called David to tell him what had happened. Hannah was making lunch, and Lissa was helping the little girls put away their things from our trip, when someone knocked on the door. Flinging the door wide, Isaiah burst into my room.

"Mom, someone's at the door!"

My first thought was, *Don't answer it!* But, of course, he already had.

Hannah dashed into the room after Isaiah. "Mommy, the neighbor is here, and she has some important news," she said. "Can you please come talk to her?"

I nodded and quickly told David I'd call him back later. As I neared the front door, I recognized our neighbor standing there, holding her baby. I invited her in.

"No, thank you, I have only a minute," she said hurriedly. "I'm terribly sorry to bother you. I know you just got back last night, but something strange has been going on. Somehow your mother-in-law got my phone number and has called me almost every day. She has told me some personal stuff I really don't need to know, and she wants to find out where you are. She asked me to call her as soon as I saw y'all return, but of course I didn't. I thought you should know she's looking for you. She sounds desperate. They have hired private investigators, and have filed charges against you for not allowing them to see your kids. I think you even missed a court date or something!"

I reeled under the weight of her words.

"Please be careful!" she pleaded.

My mind was spinning; I could hardly believe what I now knew to be true.

"So, Walter and Jan are, indeed, pursuing me through the court system . . ." My voice quavered as I told David the latest news.

I knew he was worried. So was I. "Kay," he said gravely, "we will pray for the next two hours, and then you give me another call, all right?"

"Okay, talk to you later," I said as I hung up.

Hannah and Lissa's faces were concerned as I recounted his words to them. "I think we should take another trip, just to get out of the house and out of the reach of Grandmom and Granddad until I decide what to do."

Hannah sprang into action, pulling out the suitcases that had been emptied just this morning. She and Lissa began repacking them hastily. We did not know what we would need, because we had no idea how long we'd be away. A week? A month?

What if we never return? I wondered. It seemed only remotely possible, but the thought did go through my mind. This situation was getting more and more desperate all the time.

I threw the last towel into the dryer and slammed the door shut. Pulling out the lint screen, I peeled off a thick layer of lint and tossed it into the trash can.

"I sure hope this load dries quickly before we have to leave," I said. Picking up the empty laundry basket, I looked down at Lissa. "When I started this load, I had no idea our plans would change so suddenly."

"Mommy, this is so strange, isn't it? I mean, going on another trip so unexpectedly."

I reached over and adjusted the dial on the dryer. "Yes, it is, honey," I said, wrapping my arm around her. "Lissa, I know things have been pretty tough the past couple of months since your daddy died. I want you to know, though, that I'm proud of you and the way you're handling all the pressure."

"Mommy, I miss Daddy so much," she confided as a tear slipped down her cheek. With that, she pressed her face hard against my chest and sobbed.

"I know you do, honey; I do too. Somehow God will help us get through this if we trust Him," I assured her, smoothing her silky, brown hair. "But right now, I'm going to need you to help Isaiah, Beverly, Grace, and Emily get their things packed up quickly again."

"Yes, ma'am," she responded, wiping a moist eye with the back of her hand.

"So, let's hurry inside and get organized as fast as we can," I said as we headed toward the house from our detached garage.

"Mommy, look!" Lissa hissed, pointing.

A gasp escaped my lips as I caught sight of a red sports car parked behind our van in the driveway. Together we dashed into the house, the back door slamming behind us.

"Mom, do you think they saw us?" Lissa asked breathlessly.

"No, I think our van hid us from their view."

Hannah rushed toward us from the living room. "Mommy, I just peeked through the blinds," she said urgently in a low voice. "There is a red car in the driveway. I didn't recognize it or the two women inside of it."

"I know. We just saw it too," I told her. I glanced around the living room where Emily, Grace, and Beverly were playing church and rocking their babies on the "pews." Isaiah sat on the hardwood floor surrounded by Legos, carefully putting together a small airplane.

I peered through a crack in the blinds at the red car. *Could those women be private investigators?* I wondered. *Are they coming to deliver a subpoena?* My heart sank. Turning from the window, I noticed my younger children all looking up with wide eyes, not understanding our alarm.

Suddenly the doorbell rang, and I jumped, even though I had

been expecting it. I had no idea what to do, but mustering courage, I said in a low voice, "Children, I want you to go to my room very quietly."

Obediently, they filed out in a silent procession. Fingering the front door lock, I tiptoed to the back door and double-checked that one too. Then I walked softly after my children to the back of the house.

Even from my room we could hear the doorbell ringing again and again. When that proved unsuccessful, the women began yelling.

I turned to Hannah. "Sneak into the living room and listen to what they are saying," I said.

She nodded and disappeared down the hall. Moments later she returned, her face pale. "Mom, they're saying, 'Kay Evans, please come out here! This is Harris County!' I think they want to deliver a subpoena to you. Mommy, it was really scary because one of the ladies was peering in the windows and rapping loudly on the glass. I had to duck under the piano so she wouldn't see me!"

My children and I stared at one another, wondering what to do. Time crawled, yet what was I supposed to do? I couldn't imagine. A little later, I sent Lissa into the living room to see if the women were still there.

Lissa came running back. "They're gone!" she blurted. "I didn't see them or the little red car anywhere!"

"All right, children, let's load up the van very quickly!" I called as I snatched up my purse, trying to think what we might need for such a spur-of-the-moment trip. The children began throwing things into the van in no certain order, and soon it was almost totally loaded. Everyone helped. Five-year-old Beverly took out all the shoes we might need. We could put them on later. Isaiah put some of his favorite airplane books in his spot in the van. While he was still there, the car returned.

I froze when I heard it. "Quickly!" I said urgently to Hannah. "Go to the van and get Isaiah! If the women ask for me, tell them I'm not available."

Hannah:

"Isaiah, Mommy wants you to hurry inside!" I said sharply.

Isaiah's eyes widened. He nodded and darted quickly toward the front door. I turned to follow, but the women had gotten out of their car and were making their way toward me. I felt weak and shaky.

"Hello," I squeaked.

The women glared at me.

"Are you Kay Evans?" asked the one in charge.

I shook my head. "No, ma'am," I said, "I am her daughter."

"Well, I need to talk to Kay Evans," the woman demanded.

"I'm sorry, ma'am," I said slowly, "but she is not available."

Without taking her eyes off me, the woman grabbed her wallet from her pocket and opened it, flashing a shiny badge in my face. "We have the Houston Police Department standing by on your street," she said coldly, and waved her arm in the direction of the street. "If you don't let me speak to your mother, then we are going to have to barge our way in! Do you understand?"

I gulped. "Excuse me just a second," I said. Backing away from her, I turned and ran up the steps and into the house. Mommy shut the door behind me and locked it. Panting, I repeated the conversation to her.

Kay:

Back in my room, I once again dialed David's number. After ringing five times, David's voice came on the line. "Thank you for calling . . . Please leave your name, message, and number . . ."

What a terrible time for them to be gone. Where could they possibly be? After the irritating beep, I said, "David, this is Kay and we have an emergency. Give me a call right away!"

Moments later I jumped when the phone rang. The number on the caller ID was not David's, so I didn't answer. After our family's message ended, a female voice said, "Kay, we know you are in there! This is Harris County and we need to talk to you!"

I grimaced and looked over at the children, who were trying to keep quiet. I could tell they were starting to panic. I tried calling David several more times, but hung up each time when his answering-machine recording started again. I wished desperately they were at home.

I grabbed my well-worn Bible. To calm our nerves, I read aloud some verses. "He only is my rock and my salvation; he is my defence; I shall not be greatly moved."[1]

Again, the phone rang shrilly, and we all glanced toward it, fearing it would be the private investigators. But this time it was David. I breathed a grateful prayer and snatched it up.

"Hello, David? You won't believe what is happening here."

David and I discussed options and then I hung up to think about them and pray. I felt a huge weight pressing on my shoulders. I slipped out of my room and went to be alone. We had closed all the blinds, so the living room was dark. I stretched out on the hardwood floor, facedown, and cried out to God.

"Oh, Lord, You see what is going on here. You see the trouble I am in. You see the strange women stalking my house right now, demanding that I come out. They are just waiting for us to give up like a cat waiting for a mouse to come out of its hole. God, I'm scared. My children are scared. We cannot hide in here indefinitely. We have to do something. But what? Lord, when I spoke to David on the phone just now, he suggested I call some neighbor to come and pick us up on another street. What do You think? Is that what You want me to do? Should we escape from our home in this way? It sounds so extreme! God, please protect us. I am willing to do whatever You want me to do, but please guide me."

I lay there praying and thinking about the dilemma we were in. Finally a peace washed over me. Somehow I felt a confidence that fleeing with my children was what I should do, and I believed the Lord would see us through and give us a clean escape. I felt a fresh courage and strength from the Lord. Getting up from the floor, I took a deep breath and walked back to my bedroom with a plan forming in my mind . . .

Lissa:

I sat quietly on Mommy's bed, and looked around at everyone's frightened expressions.

Mommy pushed open the door. "Well, children, I've been praying about this situation," she said. "I've decided we are going to do

---

1. Psalm 62:2

something that might sound really strange." She pointed to the window. "I think we are going to climb out that window and escape from here."

I stared at her blankly. She had said we were going to escape. Run. She actually wanted us to climb out of her bedroom window and just flee on foot. I glanced at the window in disbelief. As her words slowly registered in my mind, a feeling of panic enveloped me.

"Mom, surely we will get caught!" I pleaded. "How can we simply walk away from here without those ladies in the driveway seeing us? This sounds crazy! We will surely be seen."

But Mommy was sure God had directed her. She picked up the telephone and called our trusted friend, Laura, a few streets over. After giving a quick version of what had happened in the past few months with my grandparents, she explained that, even at this moment, we were trapped inside our own home.

Then she asked the question burning on her heart, "Laura, it looks like we are going to have to flee our home. I was just wondering. Is there any way you could come and pick us up on South Braeswood?" Mommy paused, awaiting her answer. Looking relieved, she took a deep breath and said, "Oh, Laura, I can never thank you enough!"

Kay:

I called my family together for a quick prayer that God would protect and guide us through this scary adventure we were about to embark upon. We grabbed up a few things we would need to take with us.

"Let's see, here's my Bible and my purse." I checked the diaper bag to make sure I had everything on hand for Emily, who was not yet two. I glanced down at my bare feet and stepped over to open up the closet door, intending to slip on my shoes. "Ahhh," I said, tapping the heel of my hand against my forehead, "that's right. I had y'all pack all of our shoes into the van when we were still planning to drive away."

It was normal for our family to be barefooted inside the house, so we hadn't figured on needing shoes until we had driven away. But now, none of us had any way to get our shoes without going outside to the van. "Well," I sighed, turning away from the closet, "we'll just have to leave without shoes then. Okay, does anyone need to run to the bathroom or to grab anything else important before we leave?"

I glanced around the room one last time and then studied the window before Lissa opened it. "Isn't it funny that the two people who offered lately to do odd jobs for us hadn't gotten around to putting a screen in this window like I'd asked. Well, it is proving to be a blessing now since we all need to climb through it."

As soon as the window was raised high enough, agile Isaiah jumped out, and then watched me slowly climb through. Soon we were all standing outside, except Hannah who held Emily.

"Mommy, can you take her?" Hannah asked as she handed her out through the window. Emily's head accidentally bumped the window frame, but she didn't even whimper.

"Thank the Lord," I thought as I stretched out my arms for her.

Hannah carefully crawled out, and I whispered, "Now shut the window."

I peered briefly through the fence toward the street, hoping the two women had not noticed our bold escape attempt. The afternoon light was beginning to fade into dusk, but I knew we could have been visible from the street. Thankfully, we did not see anyone.

Our next-door neighbors on this side of the house were still new to us. They had put up a tall wooden fence when they moved in. Once when my in-laws visited us, they had gone next door and befriended them. Now I knew that this fence, erected for privacy, was serving as a protection for us.

As my family trekked silently across our backyard, we approached the chain-link fence separating our yard from the neighbors directly behind us. This was the only segment of fence low enough for us to climb over easily. I had wondered before why this fence was so low in one spot. Now I understood. God had set everything up to make this moment flow as easily as possible.

Since our neighborhood had no alleys, we needed to go through the neighbors' backyard to get to the street on the other side of their house. New neighbors had just recently moved into this house too. The people before them had a big dog, but the new neighbors did not. Trespassing through their backyard, I was grateful no animals were in sight. Once we were safely on the other side and closing their gate behind us, we huddled together near their garbage cans by the carport. There was nothing to do but watch for our getaway car.

I could see through the windows into this home and was grateful the neighbors were engrossed in a television program. Colorful images changed rapidly on the screen, which we were facing. If the TV had been on the wall closest to us, we would have been easily noticed.

Lissa:

"Hey, Mommy," I whispered, "I have an idea! Remember when Yeller got out one time? I had to come down here looking for him. What if y'all stay hiding back here, and I walk to the curb, acting like I'm whistling for a dog. That way I can watch for the Magees' mini-van to come pick us up."

"Okay," Mommy agreed, motioning for me to go ahead.

I casually strode down the driveway to the curb, occasionally whistling and calling out, "Here, puppy . . . Here, puppy."

All the while I kept a sharp eye out for our ride. Our whole family of seven would have been more conspicuous at the curb, waiting together. It wasn't very long before Laura's husband, Kevin, spotted me on the sidewalk and slowed to a stop. Mommy and the children all hurried over and quickly piled in, and the little blue minivan took off. God had given us a clean escape!

CHAPTER 5

"What Should I Do, God?"

K_{ay}:

Kevin pressed the accelerator, and the van slipped rapidly away from the curb. We rode nearly a block in absolute silence before I spoke.

"Thank you so much for picking us up," I said. "We appreciate it more than you know."

"Hey, no problem," he replied. "I'm glad to help!"

It must have been an awkward moment for Kevin Magee, my friend's husband. Not every day does someone have the opportunity to drive the getaway car for a family of seven. It was awkward for us, too, to suddenly be so dependent on someone we had rarely even spoken to before. I had gotten to know Laura, his wife, over the past year through a neighborhood Bible study, but her husband was a stranger to us.

He turned to me. "Where would you like me to take you and the children?" he asked cheerfully.

I smiled, thinking, *This is what I would expect a cab driver to say.*

I collected my thoughts. "Well, what if you just drop us off at some hotel? Then I can get in touch with my brother, and he and his wife can come get us later."

Kevin shook his head, dissatisfied. "I would rather take y'all where you really need to go, so please just tell me." He didn't seem willing to negotiate.

After hesitating, I said, "Well, when I spoke to my brother on the phone, he told me he was planning to load his family and head to his in-laws' house near Austin tonight."

"Then what if I just take you there?" Kevin asserted eagerly.

"But that would be nearly four hours out of your way!" I said, trying to discourage him. "I wouldn't feel right about having you do that."

"Well, I would feel better just knowing you and the children end up tonight where you really need to be," he stated calmly. "But, if you don't mind, I'd like to stop and make a call to Laura, so that she won't worry."

"Oh, of course!" I replied, overwhelmed that he was willing to do this for us.

So we stopped, and he called his wife, and I called David. Thus the plans for our evening were set.

Traffic thinned on the outskirts of the Houston metropolis, and we stopped at a grocery store. We were all hungry, and I needed a few things that I had not thought to grab on our way out the window. Taking Beverly and Grace by the hand, we walked, barefooted, across the lighted parking lot. The other children stayed in the car with Kevin.

It must have been strange for him to be away from Laura and their children like this. Only moments before, he had glanced at me and confessed, "You know, when you called and talked to Laura earlier, I was taking a nap. We had been planning to go out on a date tonight. But now that the night is turning out this way, I am beginning to see why God allowed me to have that nice nap." He chuckled, putting me at ease about missing a wonderful date with his dear wife.

Approaching the store, I scanned the automatic door for the common sign, "No shirt, No shoes, No service!" Seeing no such sign, I breathed a sigh of relief, but I still felt nervous. Was it because we were running away or because we were entering a grocery store without shoes? It was hard to know the source of my uneasiness. But here I was, shopping in a very undignified way.

After bagging up a few bananas and quickly grabbing crackers, juice, and an assortment of other things, we joined the line at the checkout. It was a relief to notice that a woman in the line ahead of me had her toddler dressed in pajamas. Relaxing a little,

I hoped the management would not frown upon our bare feet.

It was almost midnight by the time we pulled into the wide driveway of an upscale neighborhood. The porch light was still on, and as Kevin slowly approached, the garage door opened mechanically.

Inside, a dark-haired lady wrapped in a housecoat was peering out at us. She looked tired, but was smiling nonetheless. She was Sue Beth's mom, whom I had met only a few times.

Climbing out of the vehicle, I greeted her. "Hi! Thank you so much for opening your home to us, Mrs. Edwards."

"Yes, dear, and I know you all must be very tired. Come on in and make yourselves at home. I have the beds ready for you in the basement."

I gave her a grateful hug and then followed her down the stairs to a well-furnished apartment. In fact, it looked like a complete home down there.

"Here is a room for the gentleman that drove you here. I'm sorry; I didn't catch your name, sir." She glanced toward Kevin. "Okay, Kevin, that room has its own bathroom, and the towels will be easy enough to find." Kevin thanked her and disappeared into the room.

We skirted a kitchen area and rounded a corner where Mrs. Edwards pointed out another big bedroom with its own bathroom. "I think you'll find everything you need in here. Sue Beth and David won't be in for another couple of hours, and they know where to sleep once they're here. I think I will head on up to bed if you don't mind. Sleep well!"

We thanked her as we closed the door and soon fell into bed, exhausted. There was no need to change into pajamas. The only clothes we had with us were those we had on.

———————

The next morning we were all sitting in the breakfast room discussing our perplexing situation, and how to go on from here. Many details had to be carefully sorted through.

"David, I really don't think it's safe for us to go back to our house, even to collect our things. Someone must surely be watching the house. To go back would mean getting caught!"

"Yeah, I agree," he replied. "And you need to understand that living in hiding is more than just not going home. You can't use your credit cards; you cannot write checks. You must even change the way you get your money from the bank, like your social security money. Kay, you must make yourself untraceable!"

I sighed deeply, thinking how different this new lifestyle would be. I was not accustomed to using cash for purchases. It was clear I would have to change the way I did many things.

Isaiah burst through the back door, followed by his cousin, Caleb. They were obviously soldiers at the moment, being chased by the enemy. Seconds later David and Sue Beth's twin boys threw open the screen door and stalked into the room, wooden guns in hand. Stealthily, they crept around the room, checking each corner for their enemies. Isaiah had tied a brown bathroom rug around his waist—a genuine "buffalo hide," he claimed.

Sue Beth tried to keep a straight face, but once the boys crept past us, she broke into a low giggle.

"Anyway, Kay, as we were saying . . .," Sue Beth continued in her thick southern accent, "living in hiding will be a very delicate and risky matter. You must be extremely cautious. Even our communication with each other will need to be guarded. When you contact us, it would be best if you call from a pay phone and don't even tell us where you are. Who knows, our phone lines may even get tapped!"

"Hey, about the stuff left in your house, I can go back into your house and get things you need," Kevin volunteered bravely. "I doubt I would be stopped, and even if I were, they couldn't really get me in trouble."

I didn't want Kevin and Laura to get into legal problems because of me, but how could I turn down his offer? I worried about them doing this, for I could imagine our house swarming with detectives by now. Could word already have gotten out that we had fled?

I shuddered to think of the fun the news media could have with this one. "Deceased doctor's widow flees out the back window of home with six children."

After Kevin returned to Houston, he and Laura did go into our house, in broad daylight, and packed up the most critical things on our list and loaded them into their car. They reported they felt an incredible peace, and no one bothered them at all. They also removed phone lists from the wall and gathered a few important documents we didn't want to fall into the wrong hands. Later they carefully boxed up our things and mailed them to us.

I arranged for a mover to put our other possessions into storage until we could figure out what to do with them. I also notified our landlord and the utility companies that we were no longer there. It was the easiest move we had ever made, in one way, since we simply left. In the past, it was always a struggle getting our deposit money back. This new approach, though terrible for one's credit record, was certainly less hassle!

We talked and prayed and planned about our unsettled future. While we discussed each detail of hiding, knowing we were being hunted gave me a tremendous sense of urgency. I learned of a way to obtain what were supposed to be official passports, but under assumed names. It sounded as if such identification could become necessary in order to purchase a vehicle, to obtain a motel room, or to relocate to a foreign country. It would be a drastic measure, but so was going into hiding.

I wondered if showing my Texas driver's license could allow me to be traced. I knew my in-laws were serious about finding us. Child Protective Services, the Houston Police Department, and private investigators had already been enlisted. I figured if they were so serious about finding me, I should be equally serious about staying well hidden. Extra precautions seemed in order, so I hastily chose to obtain these passports.

But once I had secured them, I found myself doubting the wisdom of my actions. "God, please forgive me," I prayed. "I didn't pray over that decision the way I should have. Maybe I was trying to help You like Sarah did when she offered Hagar to Abraham. I should have waited on You so that I could have peace about whatever I am supposed to do. In waiting, I would either have been given Your confirmation or I would have been given faith to just sit still."

I did not yet know about His amazing desire and commitment to protect the fatherless and the widows as Psalm 68:5 describes.

A father of the fatherless, and a judge of the widows, is God in his holy habitation. I had a lot to learn.

I double-checked the number scribbled on the paper and read the address on the door.

"Here we are," I said. "Okay, Lissa, are you ready for this?"

Lissa shrugged her small shoulders. She dreaded visiting the attorney as much as I did. We walked to the door, grateful for the shoes Mrs. Edwards had given us this morning from her own closet. After we rang the doorbell, the lawyer's wife greeted us warmly and ushered us into a cozy living room. Pictures of their grandchildren hung artistically on the walls.

The lawyer was a big man with silver hair. Motioning for me to take a seat across from him, he eased into a recliner.

Timidly, I explained how I was being pursued in court and did not want a court battle. After giving him a brief history of our situation, I sat back and waited for his advice.

His expression was anything but encouraging. His mouth screwed up into a tight frown, while he tapped his fingers impatiently on the armrest of his leather chair. When he spoke, his words crashed down on me in a wave of despair.

"Well, you should never have fled," he said brusquely. "You have got to face court cases head-on. Running only makes everything worse. My only suggestion to you is to write your in-laws a gracious letter and promise to let them spend time with the children on a regular basis."

In my heart I knew, in order to guard my children as God commanded, that I couldn't allow them to have the children alone. Blinking back the tears that stung my eyes, I stood and thanked him for his time. "What do I owe you?" I asked weakly.

With a hint of compassion in his eyes, he shook his head. "You don't owe me anything," he said. "Just take my advice."

Sue Beth poured David a cup of steaming coffee, and he reached for a plastic spoon, nodding for me to continue.

"About a year ago, Ron and I read a book together about the

covering mentioned in 1 Corinthians 11. I don't know why, but that passage has fascinated me for years. I have long since wondered if Jesus would like for me to wear a covering on my hair."

Sitting cross-legged on the double bed of the motel room, I faced the other bed where David sat sipping his coffee. Sue Beth walked over to the mirror near the bathroom and began brushing out her thick brown hair. Hannah and Lissa had brought up trays from the breakfast bar piled high with packaged cereals and sweet rolls for the children in the next room so that we adults could have an uninterrupted talk.

"Ron and I both read the book and tried to research the idea of women covering their heads as a sign of submission to God's order in these modern times. He never came to any definite conclusion about it, so I dropped the issue. It seemed to me that if Ron wasn't sure, or did not have convictions about it himself, then I should just leave the matter in the hands of the Lord."

"But, Kay," David broke in, setting his paper cup down on the phone stand, "don't you think the covering was just for the women in that culture and in that era?"

I shook my head and sighed. "That is what some people say, but I'm not convinced. I just can't see why it would be written to us as instruction in the New Testament if we really don't need to obey it. But now that I am a widow and on my own, I feel this strong yearning again to follow this Scripture literally. God is, after all, my only husband now. And I really want to please Him, even if it means I do something other people don't understand or agree with.

"Anyway, when we fled from our house in Houston, I had felt prompted to read 1 Corinthians 11 again. It seemed so clear to me. As I read it that morning, I was impressed to find something that might serve as a covering, like that verse mentions. The only thing I found in the house was a doily. I tucked it into my purse and then forgot about it. I just remembered it this morning as I was praying."

David and Sue Beth sat quietly listening as I shared my heart. In our background, women were not encouraged to wear head coverings of any type for religious reasons, especially in public.

Yet, as I shared with them that I believed this was something the Lord wanted me to do, they were very supportive.

David leaned forward and spoke. "Kay, if you think that is what the Lord is leading you to do, then just do it. Don't worry what we might think, or anyone else, for that matter. Just obey the Lord." I appreciated the way he encouraged me to follow God no matter what.

The next morning I carefully pinned the little white doily onto my hair. "Hmmm. There must be some trick to this. Hannah, does this look right to you?"

I stepped back from the mirror in the motel room, looking at my head from as many angles as possible.

"Well, Mommy," Hannah said, "it makes you look very different. I don't know exactly how something like that is supposed to look."

I chuckled quietly. "Well . . . this is definitely going to take some getting used to!"

I was still smiling when I knocked on the door of the next room. Sue Beth answered and invited me in.

"Hey, I see you put it on," she said, eyeing me curiously.

David was sitting on the bed, bent over his Bible. He peered up at me over his glasses. A grin spread across his face, and he slapped his knee. "Well, now aren't you cute?" he teased.

My face flushed. I pretended to be offended and pouted, crossing my arms over my chest. He certainly wasn't going to miss an opportunity to tease me, as only a brother could.

But he quickly turned serious. "Kay," he began, "I've been thinking about something . . ." He laid his Bible on the bed and turned to face me. "We need to talk about your finances. You need to get in touch with someone who can help you secure your money. You may want to invest it somehow so that you will not be paying taxes on it each year."

"Oh," I responded, "I hadn't even thought of that. I've never dealt with these kinds of decisions before and wouldn't have a clue how to invest money."

"I know," he assured me, "but you need to give it some serious thought. That life insurance check and the social security funds will be your and the children's means of support now. You have got to be careful how you handle them. Hey, Sue Beth, do you remember the name of that guy we talked to once who helps people invest their money?"

"Um, let me think," Sue Beth paused from clipping her nails and looked up at David. "I'm pretty sure it's in that little address book in my purse."

"Thank you, sir," I said, taking up my pen to sign the form in front of me. "I am relieved to know it is this simple to get the money invested safely."

The man smiled from across the conference table, shuffling the stack of papers he had just gone over with me. "I'm just glad I could help you."

Kevin's fingers flowed over the keys effortlessly, "Like a river glorious is God's perfect peace, Over all victorious in its bright increase . . ."

We were standing around the piano of Kevin's parents' home in Mississippi. I closed my eyes as the music swelled from my very heart, and I felt soothed. The past few weeks had been tremendously stressful with all the decisions I needed to make. But for the moment, I just relaxed and praised the Lord.

The younger children were all in bed, but Hannah and Lissa and I had stayed up. Kevin and Laura had loaded up their children and had come up from Houston to be with us. This made getting to know Kevin's parents and two brothers easier. It was so sweet to sing God's praises together.

"The battle belongs to the Lord. We sing glory, honor, power, and strength to the Lord." Laura's high soprano blended harmoniously with her husband's voice, and the rest of us joined in.

I had bought a used van, and Mississippi was our first stop. We were thankful that Kevin's parents had opened their home to us. Kevin had told them we were in a desperate situation and needed a place to stay while I made some decisions.

"Kay, I'm sorry for the trouble you are facing so soon after your husband's death," Kevin's mother had said. "Why don't you stay with us until you figure out what to do next?"

For nearly three weeks, we stayed in this nurturing environment. Sensing what a critical time this was for my family, they held an all-night prayer vigil, asking God for wisdom and guidance in the decisions I was facing. After Kevin talked with his parents about my situation, his dad urged me to seek legal advice again.

"Kay, it doesn't make sense to us for you to be on the run and not even know the charges against you," he said. "What if this is something that could be easily resolved in court? It seems to us that you should at least get some more information before you give up entirely on going to court. Don't you think so?"

Their questions made sense, and I prayed earnestly for direction. I contacted several lawyers, gingerly inquiring about what to do under these unusual circumstances. But as I considered retaining a lawyer, my uneasiness grew. Several attorneys spoke harshly when I tried to explain my situation over the phone.

"Look lady, this doesn't add up. You fled your home just because you don't want your kids to be alone with their grandparents? That's nonsense! I don't have time to be bothered with this kind of a petty case!"

Not usually prone to tears, I was unable to hold them back. Talking to legal professionals and thinking of entering a courtroom were very disturbing to me.

After we had fled our home in Houston forever, a "doorhanger" was evidently placed on our front porch. This was a "summons to court" for me, initiated by my in-laws. I did not personally find it there; it was given to me later by someone who picked up our mail. A lawyer later told me it could not hold much power in court unless an authorized person had handed it directly to me.

Finally, I met with a lawyer who had been in our homeschool support group back in Houston. I told him my concerns up front. "I don't want a messy court battle, and I know this could easily turn into one. Is it possible for me to retain you for the sole purpose of having you delve into the files? I may just want you to find out what the charges are."

"Yes, that is possible," he assured me. "I would need to show up in court initially to say I am representing you. But I could represent you in one hearing, and then show up at the next one and say I am declining the case, if you want."

After looking into our files, he commented, "Well, this sure looks like a Goliath of a case, but I'll get my five smooth stones and come running."

Calling back a few days later, he sighed wearily. "Your in-laws have gathered quite an amazing list of offenses against you," he said. "And they are pushing to get six weeks a year alone with your children."

"Six weeks? I could never in good conscience allow that!"

"Now, just listen," he continued. "Based on my research, you could possibly negotiate with them and whittle it down to four weeks out of the year, but that is probably the best you can hope for, unless you can make your in-laws look really awful before the eyes of the judge."

"I refuse to play that game," I said firmly.

"I know, Kay."

I shook my head, trying to take it all in. But he wasn't finished.

"You know, the grandparent laws in Texas right now favor the grandparents in cases such as yours, giving them a great deal of liberty."

"But I would be violating my conscience if I agreed to let my children have unsupervised time with my in-laws. My husband and I agreed on this."

"Well, Kay, I'm not here to tell you what to do, but you do have a serious decision to make. I know that taking your family and running is not going to be an easy path. But on the other hand, there is no way of knowing just how things will turn out once you are in that courtroom either. To put it simply, there are big risks either way."

"Well, I need to spend some time in prayer and ask the Lord whether or not I should retain you beyond this," I said.

Hanging up the phone, I began to pray. "Lord, how can I know for sure what You want me to do? I have always desired to be a law-abiding citizen. But Lord, even more importantly, I don't want to dishonor You or Your laws. Please help me discern what Your will is on this."

Reading Acts 4, I found Peter and John's response very interesting when they were arrested for preaching Jesus to the people and were commanded not to do it again. "Whether it be right in the sight of God to hearken unto you more than unto God, judge ye. For we cannot but speak the things which we have seen and heard."[1]

With a shaky voice, I continued my heartfelt prayer. "Lord, like Peter and John, help me to be courageous when the laws of our land conflict with Your laws. When I am forced to choose between You and my earthly authorities, please help me to be loyal to You since You are my very highest authority."

Almost immediately, Kevin's parents urged me to spend time in the Word and in prayer. "Kay, we'll take care of your children. Take your Bible and go spend some time alone with the Lord. We will be praying that He will show you just what to do."

I gathered up my Bible and kissed each of my children, giving them simple instructions. "I want you to obey Mr. and Mrs. Magee while I study my Bible. Okay?"

I walked out to the porch and turned the rocker to face the woods before sitting down. I stared into the forest and wondered, "Where do I begin to search for the answers I need today? Hmmm. Maybe I'll start off with the Psalms."

No matter where I turned, whether Old Testament or New Testament, I kept noticing Scriptures pertaining to hiding, and how God protects His children. I had never realized how many of God's people throughout history found it necessary to go into hiding. Why had I never noticed that in the Bible before? These passages took on a whole new meaning for me. God began to assure me that He would protect us, no matter what lay ahead. It would take more courage, I thought, to be stepping further into the unknown. Yet I began to feel strangely confident that the Lord was directing us to continue hiding.

As I rocked back and forth on the quaint porch with my Bible open on my lap and listening to the rhythmic creaking of the rocker, raindrops began to fall. I breathed deeply, taking in the lovely fragrance of the fresh air. The rain became heavier, drowning out all other sounds.

----

1. Acts 4:19, 20

Hannah came out on the porch to ask me something. Our conversation was suddenly interrupted by a deafening clap of thunder. A fiery bolt of lightning shot across the sky scorching a tree only a few yards in front of us. We screamed and jumped; then laughed at ourselves as we stared wonderingly at the injured tree.

"Hannah," I cried excitedly, laying my hand on her arm. "Look what I just read in Psalm 81:7. 'Thou calledst in trouble, and I delivered thee; I answered thee in the secret place of thunder.' "

It was true; God had delivered us from trouble, when my in-laws were hotly pursuing us. During a thunderstorm, while we were tucked away in a secret place, He answered my questions. To me, this was a landmark confirmation. Now, I knew for sure He wanted us to continue hiding.

I contacted the lawyer waiting on my answer. I thanked him for his help, but asked him to withdraw himself from my case.

I felt a sense of urgency to get out of the country to ensure better safety. I learned Argentina's extradition laws were more favorable than some countries. That meant my in-laws could have a more difficult time forcing us back to the States if we were in Argentina.

While acquiring second-identity passports, I was told many people use these passports to travel internationally. It was explained to me that we should have no problem getting into other countries with them. The only country in question seemed to be the U.S.

It sounded as though we could potentially travel only one way with these passports. That was a bit scary. To think, we might be moving to some foreign destination without the possibility of ever returning. That would mean we might never again see our old friends and family members. I didn't want to dwell on that.

"Hannah, could I please lean on you?" I gasped. "I don't know what happened to my left hip and leg, but I can't seem to put any weight on them today."

Hannah supported me as I clutched her arm tightly and hobbled toward the entrance of the bank. I felt like Jacob who had
struggled with God and suddenly limped severely.

"It's so strange," I muttered, "I didn't even injure myself, so
why is this happening?"

It seemed like terrible timing. I had already bought airline
tickets for us to fly from Miami to Argentina, and we were scheduled to leave tomorrow. But some of the children had come down
with a virus, and now my leg was nonfunctional.

"How will I manage, arriving in a new country with a sick family, a crippled leg, and not even knowing the language? What a
way to start a trip!" I shook my head.

Hannah pulled open the heavy door and helped me inside.
"Are you going to be okay?" she asked with growing concern.

"Just help me to a seat," I panted. "This is just so odd."

"Here, Mommy, you can sit here."

I gripped the armrest and sank into the leather couch.

"Do you want me to go ahead and get in line, or shall I stay
here with you?" Hannah asked sympathetically.

I looked up and saw a courtesy phone on the coffee table in
front of me. "I don't know . . . Maybe I'll call Kevin and Laura and
ask their advice about this trip."

Hannah looked at me quickly. "About what? Isn't it a little late
to get advice about going to Argentina? You've already bought our
tickets!"

I sighed and waved her aside. "I just want some reassurance
. . ." Pulling my purse into my lap, I dug out my wallet and opened
it, sliding my prepaid phone card from its slot. Trembling, I dialed
their number.

"Hello, this is Kevin."

"Hi, Kevin, this is Kay . . ." I told him about our plans to fly to
Argentina the very next day.

"Really?" he said. I could tell by his voice he was disturbed.
When I had finished speaking, there was silence on the other end.

"Are you sure this is what the Lord wants you to do?" he asked.
"It's a pretty major step, isn't it?"

"Yes," I confessed. Suddenly my chest felt tight.

Kevin, usually a man of few words, continued. "You know,

some people will question your sanity for such a rash move as this. I do hope you are absolutely sure this is the right thing, because I'll have to tell you, I'm certainly NOT convinced it is!"

I was speechless. Proverbs 27:6 says *Faithful are the wounds of a friend,* and I was indeed cut to the heart as I listened to the stinging words on the other end of the line. Yet I believed God had used Kevin to speak truth to me. I had not felt at peace about flying out either. Maybe I just needed to hear another human voice confirm my inner fears, that there was too much risk in this plan.

It had been one thing to step out in faith to go into hiding. God had opened every door and made the way clear for us to do that. I had an unexplainable peace about that decision. But the decision to move to Argentina was fraught with complications. I began to wonder if God was closing the door for us to go.

Hannah:

Mommy groaned as I helped her up into the van seat. I gingerly shut the door and ran over to my side. After I got in I looked over at Mommy. She sat still, fidgeting with the keys in her hand, but she didn't start the van. Her expression was downcast, and she leaned forward, resting her head on the wheel with her eyes closed.

"Hannah, am I going the wrong way? I feel like I am teaching my children to lie! Is it right for us to go to another country, hoping to become missionaries, when we are lying about something so basic as our names? I feel terrible about this, as if I have violated my conscience."

She had successfully used her second identity passport in order to get money for our trip. My heart grew heavy at her words.

"But what should we do?" I asked quickly.

She slowly turned the key in the ignition and said, "I don't know, Hannah. I really don't know . . ."

In the motel room, Mommy called a meeting. We sat facing her on the bed, watching her grave expression.

"Children, what would y'all think if we wouldn't fly to Argentina tomorrow after all?" Mommy asked, looking from one surprised face to the other. "I mean, I'm beginning to wonder if it is really the right thing to do," she continued.

We all stared at her, wide-eyed, not wanting to believe our ears. We had all grown excited about moving to Argentina, learning Spanish, and becoming missionaries.

"Mom, surely you aren't backing out now. We've been planning this for weeks!" Lissa pleaded.

"I know, but suddenly I just feel very uncertain about flying out tomorrow, children. I'm really not sure what God's plan is for us, and I don't want to lead you wrong. Let's pray."

Kay:

I rolled over in bed, blinking in the darkness. A heavy, unsettled feeling pressed down on me. "What is wrong? Ohhh," I moaned, "I remember now. We are scheduled to leave for Argentina today."

The troubled feeling washed over me anew. I sat up, and pushed the covers back. It was two o'clock in the morning. Silently, I slipped into the bathroom to pray.

"Lord, I don't know what to do. Please make it clear if You want us to fly out today or not. What am I doing? Am I leading my family in a wrong direction? Show me what to do, God!"

I poured out my confusion before the Lord. After struggling and agonizing, I had to admit the Lord was shutting the door to Argentina. I groaned inwardly, realizing this would not be welcome news to my children. This also meant I would need to cancel our flights, even though our tickets were nonrefundable. I hated to think about wasting so much money. Nonetheless, knowing that God was watching over us and that He had strong feelings about our future made me feel secure.

Hannah:

I clicked the gate shut behind us and followed Mommy to a little table with two plastic chairs beside the pool. She scooted one out and sat down on it.

"This is actually a nice place to talk," she said.

I nodded and slipped into another chair by the table. I watched as the lights under the water shimmered and glittered, reflecting on our faces. Hotel rooms are not the best place for private talks, but tonight Mommy had told me she wanted to talk to me. So after the other children were tucked into bed, Mommy and I had headed outside. It was a cool evening, and no one ventured into the pool. I was glad, because that meant Mommy and I could be alone.

"Hannah, I know this has been a hard day for you. Can you tell me about it?"

I nodded and looked down, tracing the edge of the glass table with my hand. "It's just . . ." I sighed. "I was so excited about going to Argentina, and then suddenly the whole trip is off. Being in hiding gets so old, and I guess I felt like I hit complete bottom this morning after you told us that we weren't going after all. I was really discouraged and kept asking myself, 'Does God even care?'"

Mommy smiled at me tenderly. "Do you think He does?"

I shrugged and said, "Well, I know He does. And today when I locked myself in the bathroom and cried for a while, God reminded me that the best time to have faith is when I am too weak to hold myself together. Then I know that it is all Jesus' strength that is holding me up, and none of my own . . . But Mommy, sometimes I wonder how much longer we are going to be living in motel rooms. It gets so tiring, and even thinking about it is overwhelming. I get frustrated when we have nothing to do but watch the Summer Olympic Games on TV!"

Mommy leaned back in her chair and looked up at the distant moon glowing softly in the night sky. "Well, surely there is something profitable we can be doing while we are traveling. Can you think of anything that would be a worthwhile project?"

"Hmmm," I mused. "Well, I had wondered about piecing together a quilt. All of us children could get involved and put our own stitches into it. It could be sort of a journey quilt."

"Oh, I like that idea! Hannah, I cannot tell you how much longer we will be traveling and staying in motel rooms. Only God knows that."

Staring out over the glistening water, she added, "Let's trust God to lead us where we should go, and patiently learn the lessons He has for us here and now."

CHAPTER 6

Step By Step You Lead Me

Kay:

"Welcome! Thank you for choosing America United Bank . . ." The message scrolled leisurely across the teller machine screen. The little plastic card flashed in the light as I stuck it into the slot, and then rapidly punched in my PIN number. I hummed a tune, feeling quite upbeat. Traveling can get tiring, and being in hiding itself was certainly stressful; but together they became overwhelming at times. Nonetheless, at this moment, we were all excited about the prospect of a good meal.

After leaving Mississippi, we had traveled constantly, stopping to enjoy beautiful sites and making a grand homeschooling tour of it all. We had visited many historical places, keeping record of each one and enjoying this new approach to education. Also for fun, we kept a notepad in the front of the van with our eyes alert for license plates, especially those from states farthest away. We also found that singing together was a sweet way to pass the time. Many of the hymns had more meaning now that we had fallen upon hard times.

Although a bank account was set up for our use, we occasionally ran very low on cash. And since we used cash for every purchase, this could be a problem. Times like these stretched our faith as we observed how the Lord provided for us.

Once when we had a money shortage, I decided to handle things differently. "I think I'll let you children help me do the grocery shopping for our food today. We will split up into groups and scatter throughout the store to see who can figure out the cheapest way to eat. Then we'll meet over there by the checkout, and see who has come up with the best plan."

The children smiled, eager for the challenge. We ate a lot of string cheese, bread, and yogurt in times like that. To this day, some of my children won't touch string cheese unless they are required to!

During another financial pinch, I tried having money wired to us, but for some reason there was a delay. I called the bank that was helping us and pleaded with them to do something.

"Don't worry, ma'am," the bank manager had said, "we are sending you a 24-hour teller card; it will arrive promptly."

I swallowed, thinking of the few remaining bills in my wallet. Just today the children had eaten the last of the graham crackers, and we were completely out of food. But this afternoon the card had finally arrived, much to our relief.

Now I stood at the ATM machine, tapping my foot and watching the screen. "One moment, please . . ." it read. The ATM beeped and read, "Please enter your information again." Slowly I punched in my PIN number and hit "Enter."

Maybe the machine is having a hard time accepting the new card, I thought with concern.

The children's happy voices floated to my ears from the van. They must have sensed my tension over the past few days while our last few dollars dwindled away. They were curious to see if Mommy's disposition improved just by inserting a plastic card into a machine, a strange modern phenomenon.

Suddenly, there was an unfamiliar sound, and my attention focused fully on the machine in front of me. I could not believe my eyes. My little plastic card was slowly, but surely, being "eaten" by the machine.

"Oh, no," I groaned in horror. There was nothing I could do but stare in disbelief. Finally, I turned and pulled open the van door. The children's excited voices fell silent, eager to hear that we had at last gotten the money.

With a weak voice, I said, "Could y'all pray? The teller machine ate the card."

I shared the sad story of the plastic card that had brought so much excitement earlier. I knew this was a good lesson from God *not* to put my trust in money. I swallowed hard, trying to surrender to the lesson God had in this. *Wilt thou set thine eyes upon that which is not? for riches certainly make themselves wings; they fly away as an eagle toward heaven.*[1]

"Okay, children, now we truly need to walk by faith. Let's pray that God will provide for us." After our prayer, and not knowing what else to do, I drove to a motel. Pulling open the lobby door, I walked toward the desk. *This man looks friendly enough,* I thought.

Hearing the door close, he looked up with a cheerful smile. "Hello! Can I help you?"

I nodded. "I sure hope so!" I said. In a few words, I explained my predicament to him.

He laughed. "Oh, the same thing just happened to me recently! Isn't that frustrating?" he said sympathetically.

I nodded, not quite seeing the humor in it that he did. "Yes, sir, it sure is. But I am hoping to receive money from my bank tomorrow, and then I should be able to pay you for a room. How much is a room here anyway?"

He smiled reassuringly. "Well, how about if I lower the cost of the room a little bit?" he asked, and then quoted me a price much lower than normal.

My eyes grew wide at his offer. "That would be a big help. Thank you."

Fingering our last bills, I realized I just might be able to afford both the room and a small supper for my family. I knew God was causing this man to have compassion on us in our desperate situation, and I was very grateful.

"Yes, I'll take the room. Thank you so much for lowering the price!"

Handing me the key, he said, "No problem. Everyone gets in a pinch at some time or another. I'm just glad to help."

I hopped back into the van and joyfully announced, "God provided us with a room, and we still have a few dollars to buy supper!"

---

1. Proverbs 23:5

I sat at the Burger King table with Lissa, Isaiah, and Emily. In the window a big sign promoted their 99-cent Whopper sale. I watched other patrons carrying plastic trays of hamburgers tucked inside their boxes. Turning to Isaiah and Lissa I said, "Wasn't it sweet of God to let Burger King have their Whoppers on a special sale today of all days, when we were nearly out of money?"

Isaiah rubbed his stomach. "Yeah, 'cause I was getting pretty hungry."

Hannah arrived at our table, grinning, as she set the tray of food down in front of me.

"Mommy, the lady at the counter gave me two free drinks when she saw me counting out each dime and nickel! Isn't God good to us?"

I smiled in agreement as I handed hamburgers to each of my children. Beverly passed out drinks to each of us, while Grace handed around paper crowns.

"Hannah, would you offer thanks for this wonderful meal the Lord has blessed us with this afternoon?" I asked as everyone sat down, crowding around the two tiny tables.

"Yes, Mommy. Dear God, Thank You for providing everything just when we needed it most. Thank You that You always take such good care of Your children. In Jesus' name. Amen."

I felt especially in awe of the Lord right then, while the children and I sat, eating our "manna" from heaven. Between bites I exclaimed, "This is the best hamburger I have ever eaten!"

They heartily agreed.

Traveling had been fun back when we had a home to return to. But after being on the road for so long, and with no end in sight, it had lost its appeal. I never knew where we would be from one week to the next, as God led us in a new, unknown way. We stayed in motels, cabins, beach houses, and sometimes rented trailers. Other times we simply drove through the night until I got too tired to drive any farther, and then we simply pulled off somewhere and slept in the van. Eating out, sleeping in unfamiliar beds, seeing famous places, mapping out where to go next, looking for coin-operated laundries, trying to school along the way—all of it had gone stale.

In addition there was the stress of having to tell motel clerks that I needed a room for myself, plus my children. Once in a while, a clerk forgot to ask how many children I had. Actually, we got into a routine of praying that motel clerks would forget to ask.

If they did discover I had six children, they inevitably urged me to get two rooms. If we weren't permitted to stay in one room together at one motel, we drove on to another. We began feeling an intense longing to live in something more substantial than a van.

Occasionally, I called David for any news. I longed to hear how our family members were. And I always wondered if there might be any updates on what my in-laws were up to. We always left town right after such a phone call, moving on to another city, just in case Jan and Walter had some way of tracing those calls. We did not know if David's phone lines might be tapped or not, so I had long since decided to play it safe. We knew God was protecting us, but we were cautious anyway.

Because we were in hiding, we were unusually attentive to happenings around us. "Why is that car driving so slowly past?" Lissa would say. "Is that man standing in the corner wearing dark glasses spying on us? Look, he is talking on his cell phone!"

It was almost comical how many people looked like my in-laws! More than once we were sure that we spotted one of them, only to discover, to our great relief, when they turned around that it was not them after all. Ahhh . . . Praise God!

Because I was now wearing a veiling, I wanted to go where we could see and be with other women who believed in covering their heads too. We had heard that Amish ladies wore some sort of covering, so we went to Lancaster, Pennsylvania, and saw Amish folks for the first time. We soon realized we would never be Amish, for we didn't share their convictions about no electricity or not owning automobiles. Nonetheless, I felt we could learn a great deal from them, and we observed them with keen interest. We researched the Anabaptists and appreciated the stories about their forefathers.

As we traveled, we began checking the papers for rental housing. But every place we considered required a credit check on me and character references.

Oh, no! I thought. I had not figured on this. I couldn't give out any information about our past at all. We were trying to avoid giving any information that could be traced and get us caught. So, we continued our nomadic traveling. I related to the passage in Psalm 107:4, 5, *They wandered in the wilderness in a solitary way; they found no city to dwell in. Hungry and thirsty, their soul fainted in them.* That was exactly how we felt.

But that passage gets more encouraging in verses 6 and 7, *Then they cried unto the* Lord *in their trouble, and he delivered them out of their distresses. And he led them forth by the right way, that they might go to a city of habitation.* I remember crying to the Lord about this very thing, asking Him what I should do.

Surely, we should be settled down before winter, I thought. Being a southerner, I had limited experience driving on icy roads. And besides that, it was getting too difficult to accomplish schooling when we were always traveling.

The clerk behind the desk handed me the receipt and our room key. "Here you are, ma'am. Is there anything else I can do for you?"

I nodded, tucking the key into my purse. "Yes, may we please have some extra towels and blankets?"

The young clerk smiled, bobbing her head. "Of course. I'll bring them to your room in about fifteen minutes."

"Thank you," I called, as I pushed open the door and hurried into the parking lot. The thin metal bell tied to the door handle clanked sullenly against the glass door.

Snow was falling steadily on this cold November day of 1996; the little flakes were illuminated by the Super 8 motel sign. A fat snowman stood cheerily in the yard, his crooked arms outstretched and a scarf wrapped around his thick neck.

I shivered and hurried toward the van. Snow was a rare and special thing where we came from, but to think of winter moving in made me nervous. I was frustrated that I had not managed to get my family settled anywhere yet. In spite of my best efforts, we still had not found any place to call home. And after five months on the road, we had spent too much money on overnight lodging and eating out.

Arriving in Elkhart, Indiana, that late, snowy afternoon, I sighed. "Hopefully we will find something here," I said.

In the restaurant we sipped our scalding soup, warming our hands on the bowls. Peering out the window, we watched the beautiful, large snowflakes drifting thickly to the ground. Despite my discouragement, I couldn't help admiring God for designing such a beautiful way to send moisture to the earth.

Anxious thoughts still loomed in my mind, but I tried to fight them off. *God has encouraged us along our way just when we needed it most. Surely He will meet the needs of this moment too, when the time is right,* I assured myself, dishing more salad onto my plate.

———————

Hannah cleared the wadded napkins from the table beside the indoor McDonald's playground and piled them onto a tray. "That breakfast was good," she said. "Thank you so much, Mommy."

"Oh, thank the Lord," I returned, pulling out the morning newspaper. "I wonder if we will find any rental options today?"

"I hope so!" Hannah said, as she dumped the last of the trash through the swinging door of the tall garbage can.

Digging a pen from my purse, I slowly perused the housing options. "Hmmm, here is a two-bedroom house. Oh, but it says, 'No children.' I guess that one is pretty clear."

Hannah peered over my shoulder, studying the fine print in front of me. A shriek echoed through the playground, and I looked up just in time to see Isaiah jump from the steps into the ball pit. The girls showered him with a volley of balls. I shook my head and smiled.

"What about this one, Mommy?"

I looked down at the ad Hannah pointed to. "Let's see, a three-bedroom house, one bathroom. It doesn't say much, but it's worth a try. And look, the ad below it might work too." I circled them both and turned the page to inspect the next column.

Later in the hotel room, I flipped on the wall lamp and perched on the edge of the bed. Spreading the paper out in front of me, I carefully reexamined the ads before taking a deep breath and picking up the phone. Slipping a prepaid phone card from my wallet, I dialed the number and held my breath, as I listened to the phone ring. This little calling routine was so familiar to me by now.

Lord, we are trusting You to provide us with a house, I prayed quietly.

"Hello?" a man's voice said on the other end.

"Um, hi. I noticed your ad in the paper about a rental home. Do you run a credit check or require character references on someone interested in your rental property?"

"Well, no," the man answered cheerily. "I don't like to run credit checks on people or require character references. I've been burned many times, that's for sure, but I still like to give everyone a chance."

My heart leaped with joy. *Hallelujah! Here is our man!* I thought. "Sir, is there any way we could see the place today?" I spoke more calmly than I felt.

"Why, certainly!" he assured me. "How 'bout you come by my place at one this afternoon. Let me give you directions . . ."

My heart was overwhelmed with gratitude to God as I gingerly ran back across the street to McDonald's to tell my children the wonderful news.

The snow crunched under our feet as we walked carefully up the sidewalk. "The house will have to be pretty bad for us to turn it down, you know?" I said to the children.

Lissa agreed, "Yes, since he doesn't even want to run any checks on us, this could be our only option."

Stepping up to the door, Hannah pressed her gloved finger against the doorbell.

A kind, elderly face appeared in the window, and the screen door swung open. "Come on in," he called, holding the door wide for us. Pointing to a long bench, he added, "Have a seat."

Glancing curiously over my family, he turned to Isaiah. "Well, young man, how do you manage to get along with all these girls?"

Isaiah looked up seriously into the kind man's weathered face. "God helps me."

The man laughed heartily, patting Isaiah on the head. Turning my way, he handed me the keys. "The house is a small white one on Okema Street. It is about fifteen minutes from here. To get there you will take a left at the end of this street, and then take a right at the blinking red light."

Pulling up into the driveway, we all quietly scrutinized the place we had been directed to. It was a basic white house on a quiet street. Nothing really special grabbed our attention except for the gorgeous fir tree that rose proudly from the front flower bed, dwarfing the house beneath it.

"Hey, this doesn't look bad at all," I said encouragingly to the children. "Let's go inside and take a closer look."

Entering the kitchen, I pulled off my gloves and placed them on the dusty counter. *Yes, this could definitely work,* I thought.

We walked from one end of the house to the other, thinking and dreaming about living in a home again. The place was far from beautiful, but it could certainly meet our needs. There were three small bedrooms, one bathroom, a fenced backyard, and a detached garage.

My little girls ran from room to room with mounting excitement. "Just think, this could be our bedroom, and Mommy could sleep in the one at the end of the hall!"

The mere thought of actually living in a house again was thrilling to us all. I wondered how I could be sure what the Lord wanted us to do.

"Hannah and Lissa," I called down the hall.

They answered from one of the bedrooms. "Yes, Mommy?"

"Girls, I think I am going to take a short walk and pray about this. I'll be back in just a little bit, okay?"

Tugging my warm gloves back on, I made my way out onto the front porch and peered up into the beautiful fir tree. "Lord, I don't want to be hasty in my decision," I prayed out loud, "so please show me Your will. Is this the house You want us to rent?"

As I walked down the street, the Lord filled me with a peace about renting this house. "Thank You, Lord!"

I quickly turned around and quickened my pace to go tell the children that I believed God had shown me what to do. I knew it would be welcome news.

CHAPTER 7

"Any Spot on the Globe?"

Kay:

"Okay, Mommy, everything is out of the van now," Isaiah announced proudly as he set another heavy load onto the living room floor.

"Already? Good work!" I praised my children. They had just finished distributing the contents of the van throughout the house. "Y'all pulled together and got that done very fast! Thanks!"

With my hands on my hips, I observed how empty the living and dining rooms looked without furniture. "Well, I'm sure there must be a Goodwill here somewhere. Isaiah, see if you can figure out how to take the bench seats out of the van so that we can go and do a little furniture shopping."

"Yes, ma'am," he answered as he darted out the back door.

"Hannah, I think there's a phone book in the drawer by the refrigerator. Could you look up Goodwill Industries?"

"Oh, yes, ma'am."

One trip to Goodwill took care of all the basic needs. A dining table and chairs, a couch and corner chair that matched, and a corner lamp improved our house tremendously. It was definitely on its way to becoming a functional home.

I decided we would buy egg-carton foam mattresses at Wal-Mart and just sleep on the floor, campout style, in the living room. We had grown accustomed to sleeping in the same room over the past months and liked the coziness of it. Instead of making official beds each morning, everyone was responsible for rolling up his own bedding and carrying it to one of the bedrooms where we stacked it all in a closet. It was a cheap solution to bedding, plus I wanted my family to get accustomed to sleeping on the floor.

"We might find ourselves sleeping on dirt floors someday on the mission field," I reminded my children with a smile. "This will be a step in that direction."

"Hey, that's right," Hannah and Lissa agreed enthusiastically as they showed their little sisters how to roll up a mat tightly.

It was fun living in a place where snow could fall so heavily. We enjoyed digging a trail through the snow so that the mail carrier could get to our mailbox on the porch. Our yard averaged more snowmen than others on our street. The beautiful fir tree that hid much of the front of our house from sight provided a squirrel playground. Cardinals loved it too, as they hopped cheerily from one low-hanging branch to another. We hung a bird feeder in the center of their playroom to sustain them through the cold months. It all provided delightful entertainment for us from our window.

Living in this part of the country also increased our fascination for the lifestyle of the Amish and Mennonite people who lived in the area. *Why did these people dress and live in such a peculiar way?* we wondered as we drove slowly past each Amish buggy. We collected books about their origin and the convictions that had initially prompted their strange customs. We were sobered to learn that some of their early ancestors had bravely faced hardships and even death without wavering because of their allegiance to the Lord Jesus Christ.

Each morning, after family Bible reading and prayer time, we were inspired as we read aloud thrilling accounts of these daring individuals from long ago who had not wavered in the face of persecution.

"Children, hard times are coming," I would say, closing the book. "The Bible tells us so. Will we be ready to face whatever tests the Lord sends our way?"

Every face looked earnestly into mine.

The Amish auctioneer leaned into the microphone. "Now here is a right nice mare, only three years old. A little spirited but that won't take but some training. C'mon, who's gonna get this perty one? Do whatcha gotta do, Joe!"

The horse pranced excitedly around the small corral several times until an old man lifted his weathered hand and signaled he would take her. Another hand shot up, and the price climbed higher, until the auctioneer hollered, "Sold, to the man with the green shirt."

Seated high in the bleachers, my children and I watched, fascinated. I had grown up just a mile or so from the local cattle auction, and we regularly heard the echo of cattle lowing through the creek hollow. But this auction was very different from the Texas auctions I'd seen. This crowd was made up mostly of Amish men, leaving me and my girls feeling rather conspicuous. I had never seen so many pairs of suspenders and so many beards in one room in my entire life!

"But really," I told myself, "this field trip is too fascinating to be concerned about so trivial a matter as looking out of place. After all, the announcement in the newspaper had stated that anyone was welcome."

As a homeschooling mom, I always kept my eyes open for educational experiences that would broaden my children's understanding of other cultures. After seeing the notice about an Amish horse auction, I had decided we would go. So this morning we had driven forty-five minutes from our home in Elkhart to Topeka, Indiana. Now we found ourselves surrounded by a culture starkly different from our own.

"Now here is a stable, calm one with a nice white blaze down her face, and just as nice of a gait. Come on, who'll claim her?"

Isaiah watched in amazement as the auctioneer's gibberish flowed, with never a moment of silence. The words seemed to pour from behind his mustache-less beard.

Finally the gate clanged shut behind the last horse, and the auction was over for the day. I leaned forward and stretched, looking into the faces of my children. "Y'all liked that, didn't you?"

Lissa grinned and teased, "It's too bad we didn't buy a horse."

I feigned horror. "And just where would we keep it?"

"In the garage!" Lissa replied quickly.

Hannah laughed. "I don't think so! Mommy, look, everyone is leaving."

I stood and slid my black purse onto my shoulder. "Yes, we should go too."

We made our way down the wooden stairs to the dirty concrete floor, our shoes echoing in the drafty building. Isaiah held the door open, and we stepped out into the cold wind. The sky was dark and overcast.

"Looks like we might get some more snow," Grace predicted as she knotted her scarf tightly under her chin.

A low barn stood the length of the parking lot, and one by one, black-coated men disappeared into its yawning door to hitch up their horses. Our gray and white van, alone in the parking lot, looked quite out of place.

Quietly we climbed into the van and buckled our seat belts. Methodically, I pulled the key from my purse and inserted it into the ignition.

Suddenly, Emily's small voice broke the silence. "Mommy, an Amish man is coming to our van. Look!" she said excitedly from her car seat behind me.

I turned and looked out my window. An old, bent Amish man, hobbled slowly toward us, motioning for me to roll down my window. As my window slid downward, I found myself face to face with the wrinkled, little man. Heart thumping, I wondered what this ancient patriarch wanted.

The cold wind whistled around him as he shouted, "Pardon me, ma'am, but do you ever haul Amish folks?"

I studied his kind face, wondering just what he could be talking about.

Noticing my puzzled expression, he repeated his question louder, "Do you ever haul Amish?"

Slowly I shook my head uncomprehendingly. Where I came from people haul hay, pigs, cows, and all kinds of equipment in the back of a truck, but I was not familiar with the term of "hauling Amish folks." Then it slowly dawned on me what he must have meant.

"Oh, no, sir," I responded, "but if you need a ride, we can take you somewhere."

Scratching his chin underneath a wispy, gray beard, he continued, "Well, I was jist wonderin' 'cause one of our kinfolk is laid up in the hospital, and a group of us wanted to go see her tonight. Our usual driver can't haul us over there this time, so I was jist wonderin' if you might be able to."

How could we resist helping this dear old man? I thought.

"And o' course we'll pay you, for gas and yer time and all," he added quickly.

"Don't worry about the pay," I returned, "but what time and where shall we pick you up tonight?"

"Well, the name is Crist Nissly, and it's real simple to find my place."

That was how our friendship with the Amish began. God seemed to have an interesting twist to this little field trip, as we arranged to "haul" Crist's group of friends to the hospital that evening.

"Yer gonna want to pull in that next drive there, the one with the phone booth out front. Jonas and Libby live here. Yep, here they come!"

Crist Nissly, the old man we had met this morning, peered through the window at the Amish couple approaching our van. "This here is the last stop we need to make. Know how to get to the hospital from here?" he inquired.

"I'm sorry," I told him, "I don't know this area very well. Can you tell me how to get there?"

His black hat bobbed. "Sure nuf, I kin tell you how. It's simple, really."

I watched the couple hurry toward the van, the woman's dark shawl fluttering in the wind. Old Crist pushed the door open and called out something in Dutch. A guttural response came from behind the man's big bushy beard.

This is by far the most interesting group of people that have ever entered this van! I thought as I carefully passed a buggy on the narrow country road. Our van was bulging with beards, bonnets, straight pins, and the Dutch language. Behind me words flew back and forth in Dutch; I wondered how anyone could understand it. But they were also surprisingly comfortable in English.

My six children were crammed tightly onto the back bench, silent and wide-eyed. I could have left them at home, but who would want to miss an opportunity like this? We were never this close to Amish people before and couldn't help but be fascinated.

After a brief visit at the hospital, the bunch loaded back into the van, and I retraced our way over the winding roads back to each passenger's home. Soon our van held just one Amish lady, and she chattered away in the passenger seat next to me.

"I'm Saraetta Kauffman," she had introduced herself. Her relaxed manner put me instantly at ease. I hadn't known what to say, but she carried on a lively conversation, telling me about herself and her family and asking me about mine. As we pulled into her gravel lane, the van headlights shone on a modest double-wide home.

"Yes, this is our house," she said, pointing to the dimly lit home.

I pulled the van to a stop in front of the porch, and with her hand on the door, Saraetta turned to me.

"I do wish you would stop by for a visit sometime," she said.

"Really?" I nearly gasped. I had assumed Amish people wouldn't cultivate friendships with ordinary folks like us.

"Oh, yes," she insisted as she tied her black bonnet strings under her chin. "Please do come back someday when you have a little time to stay." Her eyes sparkled as she smiled at me.

I decided then and there that I would definitely take her up on that invitation. "Oh, thank you. I hope we can come by sometime."

Since Amish don't have phones, I'll just have to drop by unannounced, I resolved. And sure enough, one afternoon not too many weeks later, we did drop in on Saraetta and her family. She greeted us at the door with a welcoming smile and graciously invited us into her kitchen. Stamping the snow from our shoes, we entered timidly.

She chatted with us as she quickly poured us each a cup of steaming balsam tea, frozen from last year's garden. As we warmed up, sipping the hot drink, she announced, "Oh, you must stay and have supper with us. It would be such a good way to get acquainted! Do you have the time?"

"Well, yes, if you're absolutely sure."

She was so hospitable that she made us feel like we were doing her a big favor by staying.

Oh! I thought. *I have so much to learn from this woman's hospitality.*

We had just picked up ice skates at a garage sale. Once Saraetta's children found out, they encouraged mine to go skating with them on the frozen pond out back. We had a lovely evening getting to know her family of seven and experiencing things the Amish way.

David's voice sounded very close. I could tell he was under a lot of pressure. "Kay, I want you to stand strong in what God has led you to do, but make sure this is, indeed, His plan for you."

The wind was cold, and I turned toward the telephone booth, trying to escape the chill. I was glad I had worn my big coat.

David went on, "The district attorney's office has been contacting me constantly, and they assure me that everything can be worked out smoothly, even now. I just don't know, but pray about it, okay?"

"All right, David, I will. And I am very sorry this situation has disrupted your lives so much. I'll call you again next month. Love ya."

I hung up the phone and ran quickly to the van, where Lissa sat nice and warm, enjoying the heat. As I slammed the door behind me, Lissa asked, "What did he say?"

"Well," I said, still shivering, "it sounds like they're under a lot of stress. He's beginning to have doubts about us being in hiding. I'm nervous. Where's my Bible? Let's spend some time reading. I need some comfort."

Lissa looked at me worriedly before reaching for my Bible.

When I called David, I always took extra precautions to ensure that we wouldn't be traced. While we lived in Elkhart, I drove to Chicago and called from pay phones using prepaid phone cards.

It was a blessing to hear his familiar voice again and to learn the latest on our case. But sometimes what I heard struck fear in my heart.

Not long after talking with David, I called the lawyer who had originally gone into the files to find what the charges were against me. Many months had passed since I had last talked to him. By now I was well established in this life of hiding, yet here I was, calling him again. I leaned against the wall in the motel lobby as the phone began to ring at the other end. I hated to bother this busy attorney, but I couldn't get the nagging question out of my mind.

Should I keep on hiding or not? Surely, he will have an opinion about this. Oh, God, please give this man the very words You want him to say to me, I prayed silently.

The lawyer answered the phone after only a few rings. I passed on to the lawyer what David had been hearing from the district attorney and then waited breathlessly for his advice. The lawyer paused only for a second before he spoke.

"Kay, the time of decision has passed. You cannot go back," he said, his voice strong and unwavering.

It felt so good to hear strong words of direction from a masculine voice. I took his counsel as from the Lord.

Another time those working for my in-laws asked David to pass along to me an urgent message that I should "give up and turn myself in" at once. Such news always struck me with a paralyzing fear and caused me to burn a great deal of "midnight oil" to see what the Lord would have me to do, if anything, in response.

As I feverishly turned the pages of my Bible, the Lord brought Galatians 5:1 to my attention. *Stand fast therefore in the liberty wherewith Christ hath made us free, and be not entangled again with the yoke of bondage,* I read and sighed with relief. "Giving in to my in-laws' threats would surely be accepting a yoke of bondage," I whispered to myself as I closed my Bible and jotted down the verse.

Another time I was supposed to send word back through my brother saying whether I was willing to "give up" or not, when the Lord led me to Luke 17:32. *Remember Lot's wife,* I read. "Oh, yes, Lord. I know I should not look back when You clearly directed me this way. Please help me not to doubt Your direction anymore." In fearful moments of doubt, I took great comfort in these Scriptures that the Lord put in front of me.

Goshen, Indiana, seems to be the headquarters for every size, shape, stripe, and brand of Amish and Mennonite group, sometimes referred to as plain people. With keen interest, we quietly observed the variety of clothing worn by Mennonite and Amish women. My girls examined these styles because we, too, had become increasingly convicted that God wanted us to dress modestly. We noticed many of these ladies wore what we later learned was called a "cape dress." We had looked through the McCalls, Butterick, and Simplicity pattern books to see if we might find a pattern for such a dress, but found no such thing.

Hannah finally took courage and asked a few women about their dresses. "I like your dress pattern. Was it hard to make?"

One especially helpful woman told her, "Oh, no, it is extremely easy. All you have to do is cut an extra piece to cover the bodice. Just fold the front bodice piece here and here," she said, pointing to her shoulder and waist, "and there you have your cape pattern!"

Hannah smiled, trying to visualize what the woman had just said. "Thank you!" she said.

Back at home Hannah folded the bodice pattern as instructed. "Oh, I get it!" she cried exultantly. And then, very carefully, Hannah began to make our very own cape dresses.

I had long since wanted a larger, more adequate covering than the small, lacy doily now balanced on top of my head. Hannah and Lissa, who were by now also covering their hair, wanted something more modest too. We had quickly learned that you could tell what kind of Mennonite a woman was by the shape or the number of pleats in her covering. Lissa wondered how to duplicate what we saw. Time and time again she sat down at our sewing machine to experiment. But despite her diligent efforts, she grew frustrated with the project.

"Oh, Mommy," she said to me one day, "these things are turning out to look like something that belongs on a box of Rice Krispies! You know, one of those little guys, 'Snap,' 'Crackle,' or 'Pop'!"

We all laughed with her, but I could see the growing frustration in her eyes.

The card tables set up in the dimly lit garage were lined with odds and ends. Saraetta Kauffman's daughter browsed through the small, homemade Amish dresses, while Lissa and Hannah looked at the books. We had started taking our Amish friends to garage sales, since it was so much easier in a van than a buggy. I slowly strolled past the loaded tables, my eyes examining each item as I passed. Dishes, aprons, socks, a stack of white Amish coverings, a few sweaters. I paused, my eyes returning to the stack of crisp, white coverings. Reaching out, I pulled the top one off the stack, my fingers running over the stiff material. "I wonder . . ."

Saraetta picked up a gray sweater from the table. "This is a nice one," she said to herself. "I wonder if it would fit Kenny?"

"Saraetta," I said, breaking into her thoughts.

"Yes?"

"Tell me . . . How would your people feel if they saw what they call an 'English' woman wearing one of their type of coverings?" I held up the covering for her to see.

"Well," she said, looking down apologetically, "the Amish would see that you drive a vehicle. A lot of them would be offended, seeing you wear the Amish covering but don't live the Amish lifestyle."

"Ohhh," I said, nodding. I gently returned the covering to the top of the stack. "I'm so glad I asked you. Thank you so much for being honest with me."

I certainly did not want to offend any of these dear people. Buying these had seemed like a perfect solution to our problem, but it obviously wouldn't work. It was quite a letdown for us, but we continued to pray that God would help us find a way to get better coverings.

I stared at the grocery list, and crossed out the detergent. "Okay, I think all we lack are some socks for Grace. Let's go down this aisle and head toward the girls' department."

Lissa pushed the Wal-Mart cart after me, one wheel clicking monotonously. Behind me trailed my family, bundled in coats, thick socks, and warm boots. The girls also had black scarves on their heads. Emily sat in the seat of the cart, playing with her doll. We didn't get away from the house very much, so when we did, it was a family event.

I slipped the list into my coat pocket and smiled as we neared a friendly-looking Mennonite lady in the aisle. It was easy to tell who the conservative Mennonite ladies were. They always pulled their hair up, pinning the bulk of it underneath a white net covering, and they wore modest dresses. Just as we passed her, I suddenly decided to gather my courage and speak with her.

"Excuse me, ma'am. Do you mind if I ask you a question about the covering on your hair?"

She stopped and looked at me quizzically. "Oh, no, that would be just fine."

"Well," I continued, "is the type of covering you wear just for the women of your church, or would it be acceptable to you if an outsider wore one like it?"

I was suddenly very self-conscious. My solid pink, cape dress hung a little below my knees, and my hair was pulled up on top of my head with the doily pinned over it.

The woman smiled. "Oh, well, you know, my husband and I believe that if a woman outside of our church feels directed to wear a covering in obedience to the Lord, we just want to help her in any way we can. So, you don't have to be a member of our church in order to wear one of our coverings," she said. She leaned closer, her eyes twinkling. "I actually make them for the ladies in our fellowship. So, if you could come over to my house, I would be most happy to get you fitted for one too."

"Oh!" I said slowly, hardly daring to believe my ears. "Yes, I would love to get your address. Maybe sometime we could come and get fitted."

She nodded, and graciously wrote down her address and phone number. "I hope to hear from you," she said.

I thanked her, and we continued our way down the aisle. I could hardly believe that God had directed me to ask this particular woman, who actually knew how to make the coverings. I was excited and nervous at the same time. *How am I going to handle this since we are in hiding?* I wondered. *If she asks me, I'll just have to give her my assumed name, Christin, as we have done with our Amish friends. Hopefully, she won't ask too many questions.*

Life is so strange when you are in hiding!

———————

A few days later I double-checked the address on the mailbox and then turned into the long driveway leading to the Weavers' home.

"That big barn on the left looks like a dairy barn," Isaiah decided. As we hopped out of the van, the smell confirmed his guess.

"Apparently the Weavers are dairy farmers," I whispered.

The screen door creaked open as Sheryl greeted us with the same warm smile I remembered seeing in the store. "Welcome! Welcome, all of you. Come right on in."

She led us through her orderly house to a sewing room. "This is where my daughters and I do our sewing."

I nodded silently, noticing a whole wall of plastic ice-cream buckets with a label on each, indicating a size. *Now, that is interesting,* I thought.

Sheryl seemed to read my mind and began to explain, "Since every woman has a different size head," she said, pointing to the wall of buckets, "each requires a different size covering, as well."

"Oh, yes, of course," I responded, studying the rows of buckets stacked nearly to the ceiling.

"Now, if you will just sit here," she said as she pulled out a chair, "my daughter Lillian can measure you."

Lillian smiled shyly and very gently measured me, Hannah,

and Lissa. Laurel, another daughter, showed us how to pin our hair underneath such a covering. "You want to make the bun oval-shaped so that it will fit into the cap, see?"

She pointed to the covering, and I nodded.

"We have your measurements now," Sheryl said when Lillian was finished. "You can come back in a week for the coverings." She looked at us curiously but didn't ask any questions.

"I thought you might want a statement of faith," she said as she handed me a small booklet explaining the doctrines of their church. "We would love for you to come some Sunday."

I bit my lip and wondered what to say. "Um, thank you," I stammered. In our fugitive status, I couldn't imagine facing a whole church full of new faces. It would doubtless bring unwanted questions.

"Mrs. Evans, I really think you should not have retained that first lawyer to research your case, because doing that tied you into the court system whether you wanted it or not. If you had just left things alone, there would have been no proof that you knew anything about the charges being filed against you."

I listened nervously. After I first went into hiding, my investor had employed this lawyer to set up a foreign bank account for me because of our unusual circumstances.

"Yes, sir," I said, squirming. "I am sure you are right. But the fact is, I did know there was a case against me, and I did retain that first lawyer. It seems pointless for us to go back and reevaluate what I should have done back then, when I cannot change it anyway."

He agreed and quickly moved on to his next point. "I have spoken with the gentleman in charge of your account, and we both agree you should remove yourself and your children from the United States as soon as possible. Simply pick a spot on the globe and go there! I cannot express how urgent this is. It is simply too risky for you to remain here while your in-laws are pursuing you with every dime they have. There are some small details you will need to take care of first, like getting U.S. passports. Oh, and you will need to decide where you are going, of course."

Simply pick a spot on the globe and go there! My lawyer's words rang urgently in my ears, and so we began the search. That was a very overwhelming thought . . . *anywhere in the world!*

I was stunned. I had spoken with both my lawyer and investor that morning, and they had each urged me to leave the country. I had always thought mission work would be a wonderful experience for my family, but I had never pictured our leaving the United States in this way.

Standing on my tiptoes, I craned my neck to read the titles on the top shelf. "Hannah, can you see what those books are called?" I asked.

Hannah was thumbing through a colorful book with dark Colombian children smiling back at her. She looked up and slowly scanned the shelves. "Ecuador . . . El Salvador . . . No, I don't see any books on Chile up there."

We had begun making regular visits to the library, walking up and down between shelves of books, always browsing earnestly through the country section. I had never realized how many countries there are in this world! In our family times we were praying daily that God would somehow make His will known to us.

Last week I had discovered a shelf full of books about Chile. I remembered the colorful pictures of mountains and black, sandy beaches. I wondered if we should move there. Since then, I had decided we would examine every book on Chile we could find.

"But, Lissa, where could all the books on Chile be? Weren't they right up there just last week?"

Lissa looked up from the book she was holding. "Yes, I'm sure they were because those books up there on Ecuador were right next to them."

"It is so odd that the books about Chile have all suddenly vanished," I said with a sigh. "God has unique ways of closing doors, and I am at a loss as to where God might want us to go. Sometimes it is confusing trying to figure it out. I have an idea it might be a Spanish-speaking country, since He laid it on my heart so clearly that you and I were to start taking those Spanish classes."

Glancing at my watch I frowned. "Oh, that reminds me. We have only a little over an hour until the class starts. We need to hurry home to drop Hannah and the children off if we are going to be on time for class."

For months the question remained unresolved. "Where am I supposed to take my family?" I prayed over and over. My investor and lawyer had both made it clear that I should get things in order right away and leave the country at once. Yet, I had no earthly idea where we should go.

"Help, Lord!" I cried desperately.

The words of Ezra spoke to my need. *Then I proclaimed a fast there, at the river of Ahava, that we might afflict ourselves before our God, to seek of him a right way for us, and for our little ones, and for all our substance. So we fasted and besought our God for this: and he was intreated of us.*[1]

I studied the airline tickets in front of me. *I wonder if I can redeem these?* I thought.

Earlier that morning I had dug through my file to find these Argentina airline tickets we had never used. I found the phone number of the travel agency that had helped me and stuck the paper into my purse.

"Children, I'm going to drive to a pay phone," I said. "I want you all to obey Hannah, do you understand?"

"Yes, ma'am," they answered dutifully.

As I backed out of our driveway, I prayed, "Lord, make Your will known to me. I really have no idea what You want me to do, or where You want our family to go."

Minutes later, I pulled into the parking lot of a restaurant that I knew had a pay phone inside. After turning the van off, I sat still and decided to pray some more before proceeding.

"Maybe I'll read just a bit," I mumbled to myself as I reached over and grabbed my Bible from the passenger seat. "Lord, please give me some sort of direction as I read Your Word. I feel

---

1. Ezra 8:21, 23

desperate to know Your will."

Picking up my Bible, it fell open to Isaiah 52:12. *For ye shall not go out with haste, nor go by flight: for the* LORD *will go before you; and the God of Israel will be your rereward.*

I read it again, and thought, *What a specific and clear word from the Lord!*

I grew excited to think that God had communicated with me. "All right, Lord, I will rest in Your decision. We will not fly. What is money anyway?" Hadn't God provided everything we had needed? Losing the money from those tickets had taught me a very important lesson, if nothing else.

As I drove back home, I pondered how the verse I had just read would impact our future. Well, it would certainly narrow the options and clue us in a little better on which country God had in mind for us. I took this direction literally and assumed we would be driving, rather than flying, to our destination.

"Children, pray that we will make it in time!" I urged. "The passport office closes in just one hour." Worried, I glanced at my watch and then at the dense Chicago traffic closing in on me. "Lord, please let us get there before they close the doors."

Soon tall skyscrapers surrounded us, and we passed the building housing the U.S. Passport Office.

"Okay, now to find a parking spot. Hannah, do you see any place where I can park the van?"

"What about that parking garage on the left?" she offered.

Seeing no other options, I quickly turned in and rolled down my window, motioning the attendant to come. "Will my van fit in your garage, or is it too tall?"

"Um, I think you might make it." He sized up the height of our van and shrugged. "Just drive in slowly, and if you hear a scraping noise, stop!" he said, grinning.

I groaned inwardly, but I knew I did not have time to hunt for a more promising space. We inched into the garage. When no scraping was heard, we all sighed with relief. We took the first parking space we found and piled out. Hannah grabbed up Emily, and we raced up the street toward the passport office.

I laid my purse and the bag of our important papers down on the conveyor belt and watched them disappear into the scanning machine. Then straightening my new head covering and pushing the thin ribbons behind me, I walked with my children through the metal detector. We picked up our bags again in front of the stern-looking guards, and then all but ran toward the elevator, not wanting to waste any time.

On the fourth floor, we went through the doors marked, "Passport Office" and breathed a prayer of thanks to God that we had made it before they closed. Several lines of people were waiting for clerks, standing like banktellers behind a long counter. I scanned the room, and my uneasiness grew. I had been nervous about dealing with the officials here, especially since we were going to use our real names now. After living in hiding for more than a year, it felt strange to suddenly use our actual names again.

Could these people have some way of detecting that we are in hiding? I shook my head, chiding myself, *I must not let my thoughts run wild like this.*

Trying to ignore my nervousness, I glanced up at a poster on the wall to my left. It showed a picture of hands, securely handcuffed. In black bold lettering were the words, "Fake Identification? We'll find out!"

I glanced away. I couldn't let the children know how anxious I felt. The atmosphere in here was more than intimidating—the whole room provoked terror. I felt like turning around and leaving. But if I wanted my family to have U.S. passports so that we could leave the country legally, this was the procedure I knew we had to walk through. So I swallowed hard and tried to stay calm.

An unfriendly official stepped up and asked to see my paperwork. After looking suspiciously at each of our documents, he finally nodded and directed us to wait in another line for the next available agent.

"Next," droned a woman, slightly younger than I, with brown hair hanging limply around her face. Without a trace of a smile, she looked at me disdainfully and motioned for us to step forward.

I presented our valuable papers to her, and she immediately set to work, pushing her glasses up on her nose, studying each document critically.

As she thoroughly scrutinized both the paperwork and me, we got the impression that she was disgusted at our very appearance. Or maybe it was irritation, realizing that she would need to process the paperwork for a family of seven this close to the end of her workday.

We should have gotten here sooner, I thought grimly.

The woman spoke harshly, barking out one question after another, as if she suspected I was a criminal trying to slip through the cracks of the system.

"Ma'am, just exactly where are you wanting to go?"

Her cold eyes sent chills down my spine. I paused. "Well, I'm not exactly sure right now."

The woman frowned. Obviously, that was the wrong answer. "Well, we cannot just leave it blank on the form, now can we? We have to put down *something*. So, where are you going? Or, don't you even know?" She waited impatiently.

"Well, um," I responded hesitantly, "we are thinking of going to Mexico and then possibly Central America."

The woman glared at me, obviously perturbed, then looked down again at the form in front of her and began writing.

She paused at one photo and then looked up, disturbed. Studying the row of us, she quickly matched Lissa with the photo in question and motioned for her to step forward.

"Why are you wearing that thing on your head?"

Surprised, Lissa cleared her throat, straightened herself, and tried to explain. "It is a religious conviction of mine, to wear one of these on my hair because of what I have read in my Bible in the New Testament."

The woman stared back at her, unimpressed. "Well," she muttered, "since yours shows up in the picture, you will have to write out an explanation on a separate sheet of paper explaining your reasons. It doesn't show up in the photos of your mom and sister, so they don't need to. Here, take this sheet of paper and pen and write it all out quickly."

She shoved the paper toward Lissa. Meanwhile, the lady stared at the rest of us disapprovingly. Awkwardly, we tried to smile back at her.

Finally, Lissa nervously handed back the piece of paper containing the written explanation.

After everything seemed to be in order, the lady spoke to me. "Raise your right hand and swear that all of the information you have provided is correct."

I appealed to her, "May I affirm that it is all correct?"

With a sneer the lady turned to one of her co-workers, openly mocking my choice to affirm.

I couldn't help wondering why this woman was being so rude. Was she just having a bad day, or perhaps she was tired and anxious to go home? Or was she "breaking in" a new pair of shoes that hurt her feet, causing her to feel grouchy? Whatever the case, we stood there very uneasily, hoping it would all be over soon.

Finally we passed what had begun to feel like an interrogation process. And, amazingly, we were granted approval to receive passports. It seemed unbelievable. We went home rejoicing and thanking God for His faithfulness to us in spite of the frightening application process at the passport office.

A few weeks later a large, manila envelope arrived at our mailbox. After ripping it open, I found seven beautiful dark-blue American passports. I smiled and held them to my chest.

"Thank You, Lord, for blessing our way and providing us with these needed documents. You are a wonderful Guide!"

CHAPTER 8

Ready, Get Set, Go!

Lissa:

Customers surged through the store. Snow was in the forecast, and it seemed that everyone wanted to stock up before the storm hit. In line at the deli counter, we watched as overwhelmed workers sliced meats and cheeses as fast as they could.

"Mommy, what are you going to get?"

"I really don't know. Let's see . . ."

We were looking at the labels on the glass case when a woman next to us spoke, "Excuse me, ma'am, I have a coupon you may have. See, it is for turkey breast."

"Why, thank you! I really appreciate that," Mommy said, smiling at the woman.

She is clearly a Mennonite, I decided. *A solid cape dress, white covering, black stockings and shoes . . . I wonder what kind of Mennonite.*

The lady was very friendly. "I am Rhoda Bontrager," she introduced herself. "Do you live around here?"

Mommy nodded and the lady went on, "So where do you go to church?"

I could tell Mommy was a little uneasy, and understandably so. We were in hiding and tried not to give out more information than absolutely necessary.

Mommy smiled shyly. "Actually we don't attend church anywhere, but we are Christians."

"Oh, I see. You have a nice family. My husband and I have three children ourselves. Oh, I have a picture of them right here in my purse somewhere . . . Let me see, here it is!"

She handed the photo to Mommy, who looked at the picture of three smiling faces.

"They look very sweet!" Mommy commented, and handed the photo back to Rhoda.

"Oh, you may keep the picture, but let me write our phone number and address on the back. That way we can stay in contact."

She quickly wrote the information on the picture and handed it back to Mommy.

"Well, I should go, but it was very nice getting to meet you!" she said.

We smiled at her as she turned and disappeared into the crowd.

"That was a close call," Mommy breathed. "She gave me her name and number and even a photo of her children, but she forgot to ask my name!"

"It is too bad that we're in hiding," I whispered, "because she seemed like a very nice lady. I wish we could get to know her."

Mommy nodded, and then the worker at the deli counter called, "Next!"

Seeing we were at the head of the line, we quickly stepped up to the glass display full of meats.

With cars roaring past me, I looked to see how Isaiah was doing. "Stay on the sidewalk!" I shouted above the din.

He nodded and kept on pulling our red wagon with several empty water jugs bouncing around in the back. We often bought purified water at a nearby grocery store. Another vehicle passed, stirring up a gust of wind and whipping my skirt against my legs. People stared as they drove by, openly gawking.

I looked down and grinned. *Is it possible people actually mistake us for Mennonites?* I wondered. Dressing this way was not intended as a disguise, but we often bought Amish dresses or shirts at the plain garage sales we shopped at with the Kauffmans. The dress I was wearing now was fastened in the front with straight pins.

Oh well, let them think what they want! I thought.

Another vehicle passed, but then slowed and honked. Isaiah and I quickly looked up, and saw a Mennonite lady pointing at us as she said something to the driver. The minivan pulled into a parking lot on the far side of the street. The driver, wearing a small, black hat, jumped out and dashed across the street toward us. He stepped briskly onto the sidewalk and stuck out his hand.

"Hello, I'm Thomas Bontrager," he said. "My wife said she met you last week at the store. Do you live around here?"

I nodded.

"We would like to get to know your family. Where do you live?" he asked.

Despite our family's unspoken policy not to give out information about ourselves, I found myself feeling at ease about giving this man directions to our home. After our brief conversation, he ran back across the busy street, and Isaiah and I continued on our way to the store, musing over the unexpected encounter.

Kay:

As I turned the page of the book we were reading, Beverly glanced out the window and gasped.

"Mommy!" she exclaimed. "A minivan with Mennonite people just drove into our driveway!"

Being in hiding quickly taught my children to be extremely observant to anything unusual. Unanticipated visitors certainly fit that description.

Dashing into the bathroom, I glanced at the mirror to see if I looked presentable. Quickly, I guided some stray hair behind my ears and muttered to myself, "Well, it's not great, but it will have to do. Oh, there's the doorbell!"

I smoothed my dress as I approached the door and opened it to find a man and woman. The woman was the very lady I had met in the grocery store.

How could this be possible? I wondered. I had been so careful not to give out any information about myself, yet here she was at the front door of my home. I had to trust that God was up to something.

"Oh, hello! This is a pleasant surprise. Um, won't you come in?"

They smiled back at me. "Thank you. I am Thomas Bontrager, and I think you met my wife Rhoda at the grocery store a few days ago. Yes, we would love to come inside for a few minutes," he said as they walked into our living room.

Glancing around the room he explained, "We live over in Goshen, but occasionally we come over here to see a chiropractor. That is why we were in your neighborhood when my wife recognized your children pulling a wagon down the street a few minutes ago."

Rhoda smiled. "I was telling my husband about meeting you the other day. He couldn't believe I had given you my name and number but forgot to ask how I might reach you."

I smiled back, not wanting to admit that I had been praying throughout that conversation that she wouldn't ask me anything.

"Then when I spotted your children just walking down the street, well, we just couldn't let the opportunity slip by," she said, chuckling.

I nervously invited them to sit down.

"Just call me Christin," I said. When you're in hiding, it is hard to make conversation with someone who wants to get acquainted with you. Sitting on the couch, I tried to be friendly, hoping desperately that they would not ask any awkward questions.

Beverly slowly approached the couch and stared at Rhoda. Gathering her courage, she quietly asked, "Do you want to see our kitties?"

"Of course," Rhoda answered, following Beverly to the back door.

Emily stood soberly near Thomas, timidly answering a few questions as she looked up at the man fingering his black hat.

Joining Rhoda and Beverly at the back door, I heard Beverly say, "Yes, that fluffy gray one is Spitfire. That calico by the steps is named Presumption. My mommy named her Presumption because she presumed she could live here with us, and so she did. And those three white ones are Eeny, Meeny, and Miny, and that orange one is Mo; he's my favorite."

"Yes, I like your kitties. They are very pretty," said Rhoda.

A wonderful idea popped into my head. "Rhoda, would your children like to have a kitten or two? You see, our landlord wasn't happy when these two mother cats adopted us as their owners, but he liked it even less when the cats made our garage their maternity ward. Now with fifteen little kittens running around here, he has had about enough of this cat business. He told me just the other day that I must get rid of them, or else he will. So if you want, you can have some!"

We had grown attached to our little furry friends, and I knew the children did not want to see them go to the pound. But just maybe a few could go home with the Bontragers.

"Thomas, did you hear that?" Rhoda called into the living room.

"No, honey, I didn't," Thomas said as he walked into the kitchen.

"Christin just said they need to get rid of their cats. Look at all of them." Rhoda pointed out the window.

He peered over her shoulder and smiled at the lively kittens. "Christin, we have a big dairy farm, and we can always use cats around the place. It just so happens that we are running low on cats right now, so we can take them all, if you really want to get rid of them. If you can bring them out to our place, I'm sure they would be more than welcome," he assured me.

I was stunned. "You mean you could take *all* of them?"

"Yes!" Rhoda chimed in. "We have lots of land and plenty of mice for all of these cats."

My children and I looked up at them with relief flooding our faces. "Wonderful!" I cried. "When do you want them?"

"Well," Thomas said, scratching his head, "how about next week?"

"Rhoda, even the name I gave you at first was an assumed name. And my lawyer says it is increasingly important that I take my family out of the country. Living in the United States is too risky, since my in-laws are evidently putting forth their best efforts to track me down."

Sitting beside her on the couch, I could hardly believe I was actually telling her all of this. I had grown accustomed to being vague about my situation, but this morning I had felt the Lord nudging me to confide in my newfound friend about my fugitive status.

Through the window I saw Beverly, Grace, and Emily playing with Rhoda's daughter, Jennifer. Occasionally, a shriek of laughter echoed from the barn where Isaiah and the other children were making tunnels in the hay and helping all our cats settle into their new environment.

"So, anyway, I just felt I should tell you all that." I looked into Rhoda's face to see what she thought of me now.

Unflustered, she thoughtfully tucked a strand of dark hair back under her covering. "Christin, I mean Kay, our church supports an outreach in Belize, Central America. I really think you and your children would fit in with that group quite well. And that would get you safely out of the country. Let me get Joe Weirich's phone number. He's quite involved with the work in Belize and would be a good contact person."

She got up from the couch and disappeared through the doorway. While she was gone, my mind reeled under this new information. *Lord, are You opening the door for us to go to Belize? Are You handing me a new piece to the puzzle?*

Minutes later Rhoda pressed a paper into my hand. "Here is his number. I put a few other names and numbers on there, too, in case you can't get in touch with Brother Joe right away."

"Hannah, that looks like a Christian bookstore over there next to Belk's. Why don't you take the children and go browse a few minutes until I'm off the phone?"

"Yes, ma'am," she answered instantly.

I could tell the children were distracted by the brightly-lit shops clamoring for customers, but they trailed off with their big sister as I had requested. I slipped the prepaid phone card from my wallet and rummaged in my purse until I located the folded-up piece of paper with the list of names Rhoda had given me.

"Let's see, the first name is Joe Weirich," I said to myself as I punched numbers on the keypad to call his home.

Glancing around the gaudy mall, I hoped Mr. Weirich would

not be able to hear the abrasive music. My appreciation for malls had steadily declined over the years, but on chilly days I looked for pay phones inside.

After another ring, someone picked up. "Hello."

I cleared my throat and introduced myself and explained how I had heard about him. Then I told him what was on my mind.

"Rhoda Bontrager told me about the mission in Belize, and I was wondering if you could give me some more information. You see, my children and I may be going to Central America in a few months, and I would like to know more about the work there."

After a brief conversation, Joe Weirich said, "Yes, let's see, you say you live in Elkhart? That's interesting. My wife Effie and I will be going to Indiana from Missouri and plan on visiting the Bontragers' church this very weekend. Do you think we could talk some more then?"

"Oh, that sounds wonderful," I assured him. "Rhoda invited us to visit her church this Sunday, so we will just plan on meeting you then. Thank you so much, Mr. Weirich."

"What did he say then?" Lissa asked.

"Well, he said he and his wife will be at Thomas and Rhoda's church this Sunday, so we can meet them then. When I called Rhoda, she said we should just plan to eat Sunday dinner at her house because she's going to invite the Weirichs too. Hopefully we'll hear more about Belize then. Isn't all this incredible, children? For weeks we have wondered where God wanted us to go, and now, in one day, it seems He has plopped the answer right in my lap! Aren't God's ways awesome?"

The rest of the way home, Grace bounced in her seat chanting over and over the exciting new word, "Belize, Belize, Belize . . ."

———————————

"No, Kay," Rhoda assured me, "don't you bother helping with the dishes. Your girls and I can take care of them. You and Brother Joe and Sister Effie can go to the sitting room and visit."

"Are you sure?" I asked.

Rhoda nodded, giving me a gentle push toward the sitting room.

Timidly I sat down in a chair across from Sister Effie and

Brother Joe. I had met them only today. Brother Joe had preached this morning, and we had all shared lunch, but still it was awkward to know where to begin with such a woeful tale as ours.

Sister Effie sensed my nervousness. "Now tell us about your family," she suggested.

"Yes," agreed her husband.

"Well, it's kind of a long story," I said, "but you're welcome to hear it. You must wonder why we are a runaway family. It started years ago, really." Even as I spoke, it seemed like a strange, unbelievable story, even to me.

Sister Effie listened with interest, and shook her head as I told about Ron's illness and death.

"Oh, that must have been so hard," she said compassionately.

Telling the story became easier because they both seemed sympathetic to my cause. Brother Joe was quiet and thoughtful, asking an occasional question.

"So, you see why my lawyer is encouraging us to leave the States? I guess that is God's direction," I said.

Sister Effie nodded, and then quickly turned to her husband. "Joe, don't you think we should give her Tim's phone number in Belize?" Turning back to me she explained, "He is one of our missionaries in the northern part of the country."

Reaching inside her purse, she pulled out a simple white veil. "This is what the ladies wear at the Mennonite churches in Belize," she said. "It covers the hair in a similar fashion as a handkerchief."

Hannah and Lissa had migrated into the room by now and were listening with interest. Effie continued, "I'll slip into the rest room and put it on so you can see how they wear them." Moments later she returned, having traded her usual covering for what some people call a flowing veil.

She turned around slowly to demonstrate. "See! It's just that easy!"

I was immediately impressed with the simplicity of it, and said, "Oh, I like it! A wash-and-wear covering! It looks so practical."

Sister Effie smiled. "Oh, I think you would love it in Belize," she assured us.

Suddenly, I was very aware of this godly couple's blessing on our going to Belize. It was such an incredible feeling to sense the Lord's direction on where we should go. The burden lifted and my shoulders felt light!

———————————

With our destination settled, I plunged into high gear. I bought a big, yellow book full of medical information about international travel, which listed immunizations recommended for various countries. Feeling like pincushions, my children groaned through all the vaccinations and physicals we needed.

"And, yes, I want us all to have eye examinations, dental appointments, and to basically take care of everything possible, just in case the medical standards in Central America are deficient."

I set a date for our move and notified our landlord. As we asked questions and prepared to move to the tiny country tucked underneath Mexico, it appeared God was throwing open wide every door.

"Mommy, we have now given away everything we own except what will fit in the van," Lissa observed, carrying out another big load.

"Even the red wagon?" I asked, taking a heavy box from her arms.

"Oh, no, I completely forgot about that," she said, frowning.

From inside the van, Hannah overheard our conversation. "Hey, Mommy," she said, "what if we give our wagon to Mrs. Maples? Now that we are moving, we won't be able to take her grocery shopping anymore. Maybe she can pull the wagon to the store and then haul her groceries home."

"Hannah, that is a great idea!" I exclaimed.

So it was decided that the little, red wagon would be our going away present for the old woman without a family whom we had befriended in Elkhart.

———————————

I turned the key, and immediately the engine started. Before we started off, we bowed our heads for a prayer of protection.

"And, Lord, I pray You will go ahead of us every mile of the way. I know You are leading us, and I ask that You place Your hand of protection over us. Thank You, Lord. In Jesus' name I pray. Amen."

For the last time, our big gray and white van pulled slowly out of the driveway. We all looked back at the place that had been our home for the past ten months.

It has been a quiet, peaceful season, I thought to myself. But it was over, and now God was leading us toward Central America.

Our van bulged with our belongings, from the bedding crammed into the storage container perched atop the roof, to the pots and pans wedged under the seats. The back of the van was stacked full all the way to the roof, thanks to faithful Hannah's organizational skills. We had all pitied her as she carefully worked each item into the ever-diminishing space. But now all that was over, and we were on the road.

Whoever would have thought that I would drive with my family to Belize? I pondered, shaking my head incredulously. *I guess God has bigger plans than I could ever have.*

"I can't believe this!" I exclaimed to Lissa as we approached the Mexican border. She only nodded, too busy peering out her window to look at me. In the rearview mirror, I could see my other children also staring out their windows at the scenes around us.

The many days until now had been busy, but today had been especially full of last minute preparations. I had phoned a few of our friends who knew about our journey and then made one final call to my brother David and Sue Beth. Calling them from a foreign location wouldn't be safe.

We had also dropped a few notes in the mail, changed our money into pesos, and visited the auto insurance company on the U.S. side. I was delighted when the insurance company had asked for my destination and highlighted the route on a complimentary map. Handing me a very detailed guidebook, they had described the exact route. It was incredible. Our last stop had been Burger King, where we enjoyed one last American hamburger.

Although we were still on the U.S. side of the border, it surely felt like Mexico. It had not occurred to me that there would be a traffic jam just getting into Mexico. I glanced at my watch. It was 4:30 p.m., Friday, October 10, 1997.

Heavy traffic and determined drivers crowded the designated three lanes into about six, bumper to bumper, door to door. We were so close to the cars on either side of us, that I could have adjusted my neighbor's side mirror for him if my windows had been down. In fact, I noticed people rolling down their windows and pulling their side mirrors inward, so they would not get knocked off by vehicles on either side. As we inched forward, I held my breath and prayed.

"I'd sure hate to begin our trip with a fender-bender before even officially getting onto foreign soil," I said, turning to the children.

Proceeding through the border booths cattle-drive style, I chose the lane stating, "Duty to Declare."

The officer smiled and motioned for me to pull into a parking spot on his right. Opening the side doors, he stuck his head into the van. His smile broadened as he saw my six children peering back out at him.

"¿Hablan español?"

We shook our heads apologetically.

"Oh, I see," he said in broken English. "What you have in de van?"

I handed him the two and a half page list of all our earthly belongings, and he motioned to an English-speaking officer to come translate it. Someone had suggested that we carefully prepare a complete itemized list of everything we were bringing into the country. I was very grateful to have the list ready. Stroking his mustache, the officer studied the papers in his hand.

In my lap lay my husband's death certificate. *Just in case he needs to see it,* I thought. Yet no one questioned why a lone woman was carting six children through a foreign country.

After studying my list, the officer confessed sheepishly, "I not read English very good." Then he explained that because of something called *franquicia,* I would be exempt from paying any customs duties on our belongings. After the officer took a quick peek into our tightly packed van, he waved us to the next point, immigration.

We smiled at each other, rejoicing at God's goodness in getting us through customs so easily. I read the sign over the gate, *Inmigración*. The place was surrounded by high walls, topped with barbed wire. Soldiers holding machine guns waited beside the gate.

"Seems like an unfriendly way of welcoming us into their country, doesn't it?" I said as we drove through a deep puddle of water.

The soldiers gestured us to a parking spot, and I hastily obeyed. As we stepped out of the van, the guards directed us to walk toward a nearby building.

"Who would argue with men standing ready with guns?" I whispered to the children. They all watched the armed guards out of the corners of their eyes as we walked obediently onward.

Quickly, we took our place at the back of a long line. The line led to several worn-out, carnival-looking trailers that had become makeshift offices. Several dogs wandered around the compound, and the noise of buses barreling down the streets floated over the block wall. Empty chip bags blew across the hard-packed dirt. Everything seemed filthy.

Fingering the papers in my hand, I checked to make sure I had everything we needed to obtain van insurance. "Let's see, I have to show our passports, the title, and proof of U.S. insurance. Entering Mexico with a vehicle involves a lot of red tape."

The man ahead of us was watching me carefully. Finally he turned and said, "Ma'am, do you speak Spanish?"

I shook my head. "No, sir, I do not. I am hoping some of the officials will speak English."

He frowned. "I really doubt they will," he said. "I have been through here before, and they haven't spoken English, but I'll try to help you. I can translate if you need me to."

The man next to him nodded. "Yeah, I can too. Let us help you out, okay?"

I gratefully accepted their kind offer. God was taking such good care of us! *Lord, thank You so much for going ahead of us and providing even an interpreter!* I prayed.

The line inched forward. Concerned, I watched the light fade from the sky, leaving us in darkness.

Now is not a good time to think about all those stories I've heard of the dangers at night in Mexico, I thought. *There is absolutely nothing I can do but pray.*

No one in charge seemed in any kind of hurry. My children tried to be patient, standing on one foot, then the other, as the hours crept slowly by.

Finally we stepped up into a dejected-looking trailer to fill out the necessary paperwork. I smiled, remembering that a smile is understood internationally, and handed my stack of papers to a young man seated behind a small desk. Over to one side sat an ancient television, and perched in a window was an equally primitive air conditioner, covered with lint and missing its front cover. It was obviously broken.

My family and I stood awkwardly in the little office, crowded shoulder to shoulder. We tried making room for another secretary who made her way through the door and over to the desk. She set down a stack of papers and spoke rapidly to the typist. He glanced up at her blankly, nodded, and went back to his typing.

"Doesn't that ancient typewriter look like it belongs in a museum?" I asked quietly. Evidently, this was *the* typewriter, so workers appeared and reappeared to process various papers and forms for each tourist.

Isaiah leaned against the back door, only to discover it had not been securely closed. The door promptly swung open, and Isaiah, Lissa, and I almost fell out into the mud a few feet below.

"Whew!" I gasped, as we moved quickly away from the door. The worker never looked up from his typing, and my children and I exchanged glances of relief and amusement.

"I'm glad we didn't fall out!" Isaiah said, chuckling.

The primitive conditions astonished us. The metal floor under our feet was rusted out in several places. The trailer's front door had been kept open to ventilate this metal box of an office. Flies buzzed in and out freely. Crossing the border had brought us into another world.

Eventually the worker reached for my forms and began typing away methodically. After waiting at immigration for almost four hours, we were finally handed our papers.

"Muchas gracias," we said thankfully as we filed out and down rickety steps. We felt excited and grateful for the Lord's provision for us on this day. With a new spring in our steps, we strode one last time past the guards holding their machine guns and climbed back into our van. The shiny, new sticker on our windshield indicated that we were granted permission to drive through Mexico.

"What a blessing to be out of there!" I commented as we drove down the street. "Oh, look at the time. It is already 9:30. We should find a place to stay for the night. Children, keep your eyes open for anything that looks like a hotel."

We had been warned, in no uncertain terms, not to drive at night in Mexico, and I was more than happy to follow that advice. We drove down a main street in the border town of Reynosa, trying to read each sign as we passed.

"Did that place back there look like a hotel to y'all?"

"Not really, Mommy."

Even though we were just a few miles from Texas, things were very different here. Suddenly I realized I was thirsty. We knew we couldn't drink the water, and without knowing what was available, we had planned ahead and brought water and snacks.

The streets and the town looked dirty, even at night.

This is kind of a scary place to be driving with your family when it is past bedtime, I thought as I slowed to a stop at a red light.

A young boy ran out in front of the cars and began blowing fire from his mouth. We stared wide-eyed as he performed.

"Mommy, why is he doing that?" Grace asked.

"Honey, I don't know. Oh, look, he is going up to the stopped cars and asking for money. Grace, I guess that's how he makes money. How sad! How terrible that someone would need to take such drastic measures in order to survive."

"Mommy, that is awful! He shouldn't put fire in his mouth, should he?"

"No, Grace, you're right."

CHAPTER 9

Beyond the Border

Kay:

Behind the desk sat a young Mexican lady wearing a tight-fitting dress. She was clearly preoccupied with a male co-worker who was having difficulty keeping his hands off of her.

"Please, we need a room," I attempted in Spanish.

The clerk looked bewildered, so I repeated my request, still without success.

Hannah and I used every motion and action we could think of to help her understand us, but she only shook her head and said something rapidly in Spanish.

I felt helpless. The words I had looked up in the dictionary and tried to say didn't seem to register as Spanish to her. And our gestures seemed to be equally unintelligible. It was like a game of charades where no one could figure out what we were trying to describe.

I had already left another hotel in frustration and was not giving up a second time. I sighed, and tried again.

"A room, please. I need a room!" I said desperately.

"I don't have any rooms available," she seemed to say, glancing at the young fellow beside her.

"Okay, if you don't have a room for us, where can I find one? Where is another hotel?"

She glared at me, rolling her heavily outlined eyes.

"Where?" I insisted.

Clearly exasperated, she hastily fiddled with the room keys

110

and begrudgingly slammed one on the counter for me.

"Ah, success!" I exclaimed, looking triumphantly at Hannah.

We walked out the door, much relieved. "I guess she decided the fastest way to rid herself of us was just to give us a room after all."

"Yeah, I guess so," Hannah agreed, with a weary smile.

We climbed back into our van with the wonderful news that we had a room for the night. Moments later I laid a suitcase on the king-sized bed and looked around. The walls were an overwhelming yellow, and the bedspread a deep, blood red. The furniture was a dark, Spanish style. A small table in the corner was graced by a tall, clear pitcher with two wine glasses tastefully placed beside it. I quickly moved the glassware to a high shelf in the closet before my little ones could accidentally break them.

"This must be a pretty nice motel," I said, picking up what looked like a room-service menu from the table and studying, uncomprehendingly, the jumble of words and prices. I shook my head in confusion.

Hearing a squeal of laughter, I turned to see my three little girls tumbling on the bed. It was about the only way my younger children could exercise and release their energy after being confined all day in the van.

Someday, I thought, *I'll have to retrain them not to do this, but for now, I really don't care. After the day we've just endured, I almost feel like jumping on the bed myself!*

But Grace was disappointed. "Mommy, this bed is hard!" she complained as she climbed down.

It was true. The bed had absolutely no bounce, and the children's usual game was spoiled.

A quick peek into the bathroom revealed the same offensive yellow as the bedroom.

"Let's see, there is no bathtub in here, just a shower. The place does look remarkably clean though."

Glancing at the sink, I remembered the advice of more experienced travelers and asked myself, "What can I do to remind us not to even brush our teeth with the notoriously polluted water?"

Remembering a small box of Ziploc bags packed into the suitcase, I went to dig it out. Back in the bathroom, I covered the faucet with a bag and stood back to admire my solution. "There, that should do it."

Some of our own blankets were spread across the floor since one king-sized bed would accommodate only a few of us. We slept soundly in the strange room, grateful that God had provided a safe place.

————————————

Refreshed from our night of sleep, we piled back into the van to get an early start on the day's driving.

"Don't they have any traffic lights around here?" I cried in dismay.

With no traffic lights, the center of the intersection was chaotic, and my nerves were on edge. Cars streamed back and forth, horns blaring and arms flailing out of open windows. I found myself following the surge of vehicles as they headed bravely into the intersection. After a few near-accidents, we were safely across the busy thoroughfare.

I sighed with relief and wiped my sweaty forehead with the back of my hand. "Whew, I am not used to this style of driving. But praise the Lord, He has protected us so far. Children, you keep praying, and I'll keep driving." But, of course, I was praying too.

Surrounded by new sights and strange smells, my children's faces were glued to the windows. But my eyes looked for one thing only—road signs. I just wanted to get out of this city and onto the less crowded roads again.

"Mommy, look over there! See all those people jammed into the back of that pickup?"

"Oh my, look! The ladies in the back of the truck are all dressed up, and their hair is styled. I'm sure it will be all messed up by the time they get to work or wherever they are going."

We carefully passed men walking along the side of the road, wearing big sombreros, their machetes tucked into their belts.

"Look up ahead!" I called.

The children craned their necks to get a good glimpse.

"It looks like a walking haystack! All I can see underneath are two rubber boots."

I swerved around him, and the children looked back with

interest. "Poor man! That must be heavy! But it looks like he has done it before."

"Mommy," Isaiah's voice piped up from the second seat, "what do they need all those sticks for? I have seen lots of people carrying loads of sticks, but what do they do with them?"

"I'm not sure, Isaiah. Maybe they use them for their fires or their roofs. Your guess is as good as mine."

"Hey, look out, Mom!"

Honk! Hooonk!

"That one barely made it! It seems most of the chickens around here have a tendency to dart across the road right in front of us. I almost creamed that one for sure!"

As the busy city traffic finally thinned, I began to relax, and we found the road winding south.

Now I can enjoy the view, I thought. *Just look how green everything is out here!*

Our eyes feasted on the beauty surrounding us. Adobe houses with thatched roofs were tucked behind banana trees and thick vegetation. It seemed as if we were going back in time, to some era I was unacquainted with.

An elderly lady stood in the doorway of her small, mud home, looking out at our van as we drove by. We waved at her, and she lifted her hand in response. The children watched till her form grew too small to see anymore.

As we ventured farther south, we occasionally caught tantalizing glimpses of the blue Gulf of Mexico beyond the palm trees to our left.

Oh, I thought, *I would love to park and take a walk along the beach. Wouldn't it be wonderful to bury our toes in the grainy sand and feel the refreshing spray in our faces? But who knows, maybe it wouldn't be a safe thing for an American woman and her six children to do alone.*

So, we just enjoyed the view and kept going.

———————————

Plates clinked and soft voices rose and fell. I looked around the table and smiled at my six children. We were all happy to be out of the van stretching our legs a little. And, of course, we enjoyed stopping for a meal.

Apparently we were not the only ones hungry this afternoon. The waitresses bobbed from table to table, taking orders and delivering trays loaded with steaming food to the crowd of hungry patrons.

"This is clearly the upper class," I said quietly. "I don't think the poor people we've passed along the road would have enough pocket change for even a sandwich in a place like this. Just think of how hard life is for those poor people. I wonder how many of them know who Jesus is and what He has done for them? Will they have a chance to know that Someone has died to give them hope to live?"

I looked deeply into Beverly's eyes and then at Isaiah seated beside her. I had always wanted my children to get a taste of another culture, hoping it would spark an interest in missions. I wanted their interest to be transformed into the compassion of Jesus, who hung on the cross for every soul. Would they grow up caring enough to bear His Word to distant lands? I prayed so.

———————

Double-checking the road sign, I turned off in the direction of Manuel.

"Hmmm. I don't know about this," I mumbled to myself. "This little dirt road has not taken well to all the rain. I hope we don't get stuck in the mud."

Eyeing the deep ruts in the ditch to my left, I grimaced. Someone apparently had gotten stuck there not too long ago.

"Lord, You safely guided Your people through the Red Sea, and now I beg You to lead our big van safely through this sea of mud."

We slid our way down the road, slowly turning as the road twisted and wound its way through fields of sorghum. I recalled Rhoda Bontrager's words to me before we left Indiana.

"Kay, there are three families in Manuel, Mexico, who are ministering to a large settlement of Russian Mennonites. Two of the couples came from that background but are now reaching out to their own people with the Gospel of Jesus. I think you might enjoy a break from your trip, and they might enjoy getting to know you. It would be a chance to relax a bit before heading on."

I had to laugh as I remembered her words, because I never dreamed it would mean attempting a road like this. "Oh well, Lord, You wanted us to have an adventure!"

I turned off the van and dropped the keys into my purse. "Okay, y'all pile out. We are here." Shyly, we made our way to the door of the humble house. It was our first time staying in a Mennonite home, and I quickly saw that gracious hospitality was a way of life for John and Eva Harder. My heart was touched.

Ten children lived at home, and the five daughters gave up their room for my family. The house was not large, and I wondered where these dear girls slept. But they assured us they were glad to have us there.

The food in Manuel was scrumptious. For the first time ever, we saw chicken feet floating with the vegetables in a big pot of delicious soup. To get a chicken foot when the steaming soup was ladled into someone's bowl seemed a special award. We watched with amusement but were happy to let them enjoy the "treat."

Just a few days before, Hurricane Pauline had battered the Pacific coast of Mexico with heavy rains and high winds. Eva shook her head with a worried frown.

"At least 230 people have been killed and hundreds of others injured by floods and landslides," she said. "Why don't you and your children stay on a day or two more until the roads dry up a little bit? We would love to have more time with you!"

I wasn't ready to face those roads again until they were dry, so I nodded gratefully, accepting her invitation.

After my children were in bed that evening, John and Eva said they wanted to talk.

"I'll be there too," said Nettie, their older daughter, "in case my parents need me to translate anything. You see, even though Mom and Dad speak English, they are really more comfortable in German. They want me there in case they don't understand something you say."

Leading the way to a spacious porch where her parents sat waiting, we seated ourselves in chairs across from them. They were eager to know our story but hesitated to ask. Why were we here? Why would a woman, especially a widow, leave the United States with her six children? There had to be a reason.

The cool desert breeze swept up off the prairie surrounding us, and I buttoned up my sweater. Coyotes howled in the distance as John asked, "Would you mind explaining to us what you have been through and what brings you here?"

It was a sensible question. They were sharing what they had with us. They had every right to know why we were on the run. I began to recount my story for them.

". . . and my in-laws wanted six weeks out of the year alone with my children," I said. "But I did not believe God wanted me to expose my children to their worldly philosophies. I could not compromise and allow my children to be alone with them for even four weeks."

John Harder leaned forward. "No, sister, you cannot let them be alone with your children even for one week!" he exclaimed, holding up his index finger as he spoke. The expression on his face showed he knew what it meant to face persecution.

It was so good to hear someone agree so emphatically with the decision I had made. The Lord used his words to encourage me greatly.

While in this home, God taught me a beautiful lesson on servanthood. As we were packing up the van to leave, Eva sat outside near their running-water supply. She had taken a break from her usual bustling schedule in order to clean off each of my children's muddy shoes before we set off for Belize.

At the sight, I stopped in disbelief. This dear woman was a busy mother. She did not even have an automatic washer or dryer. She had to work so much harder than American women do to keep things running smoothly for her large family. Yet, here she was, taking time out of her schedule to serve me in this way. God was showing me how to be a humble servant.

Oh, Father, I prayed. *I am so humbled by the way these people have blessed my family. Help me learn to serve people in the spirit of Christ as I have seen here!*

We had spent three days in Manuel, days of incredible refreshment to me. In a very short time, we felt a kinship with these people that encouraged us very much. It is so beautiful to experience the bond Christians have together, even when they haven't been acquainted before and when they are from such different backgrounds. Yet sharing the same desire to love and serve Jesus Christ gives us a common bond.

Before we knew it, it was time again to slip and slide our way across their country roads back to the main road and continue on our way toward Belize.

Hannah looked over the map. "Um, Mommy, there is that sign again," she said quietly.

Sure enough, there it was, *Aeropuerto*. We had been in Tampico for the past hour, and I was trying to find our way out.

"Hannah, I just can't understand this. We are going in circles, and just when I think we should surely be out of it, we drive past that same sign to the airport again!"

Driving in Mexico was quite toilsome for me, and getting lost didn't help. "I guess I'll just try again, but, Lord, please help us find the right road this time!" I pleaded.

Finally I saw a small, obscure sign that directed us south and away from Tampico. We were all happy to move on to new territory.

Hannah sighed. "I'm sure glad we got out of there. I couldn't figure out what we kept doing wrong!"

I looked over at her and thought about all the responsibility that had fallen on her shoulders. Hannah and Lissa had become my navigators, and they tried to follow the directions explicitly.

"Tampico Alto," I read aloud. "I guess that is a subdivision of Tampico?"

Hannah bent over the map and nodded. "Yes, it looks like it to me too. So we must be headed in the right direction."

The driver of a big blue truck in front of us slammed on his brakes and took a sharp turn to the left. I slowed down in confusion at a fork in the road. "Hannah, quick, can you tell me which way I should go here?"

Cars behind me honked, and I quickly took the road that turned slightly to the right. The pavement changed as I veered onto this road and moments later I voiced my concern.

"I don't think this is the right way. This is clearly a residential section. Let's see . . . where can I turn around?"

"Look, Mommy," one of the children called, "up there at the end of the street goes that big blue truck that you were following! The main road must be just straight ahead."

Of course I didn't know who drove that truck, but I concluded he knew more about these roads than I. The road he had chosen back at the fork evidently ran perpendicular to this one. I accelerated with confidence, eager to get back on course. But in my eagerness to catch up, I failed to notice a low-hanging wire over the street.

Suddenly I heard a strange sound—a high-pitched screeching and then a thud. Quickly I glanced in my rearview mirror and saw, to my horror, our nice Sears storage container sitting awkwardly in the middle of the street a short distance behind us.

"Oh, no!" I groaned as everyone's head turned to behold the sight. *I can't believe this!* I thought to myself. *I've really done it now!*

I could just envision this interesting scene: I would jump out of our 15-passenger Ford van, clutching my Spanish dictionary. My children and I would all walk over and stare at the big plastic box in the middle of the road. We would say to the crowd gathering, "Yes, that's our box. Oh, is that your power line now lying on the road? Strange, isn't it?" We would all laugh nervously and I would say, "I am really sorry."

But in reality, we couldn't say those things because we did not know how to. Yes, a nice crowd of curious people did gather to see what the excitement was about. I'm sure it was not every day that a U.F.O. landed on their street.

I stood by the storage box and scratched my head. One of the straps that held it on the van was snapped.

"Hannah, I don't think we'll be taking this with us. Someone around here will get a nice new sandbox!"

She nodded and giggled with embarrassment for me. A short man with a mustache smiled and jabbered away, pointing to the box.

I smiled nervously. "Sir, I don't understand Spanish," I said, "but I am terribly sorry about knocking that wire down."

His blank stare assured me he had not understood a word I had said. I looked into the faces surrounding me, all curious and interested.

"Well, who wants some bedding?" I said, holding up a piece of egg carton foam.

A lady near me said something and reached out for it. I handed it to her, nodding. The others now understood what I had in mind. Bed mats were soon carried away in every direction. Minutes later, its proud new owner was toting the storage box itself down the street.

I was actually glad to see it go, for I had been constantly concerned about scraping something with the extra height on top of the van. I wouldn't have to worry about that anymore. What I did have to worry about was the police officer standing among the diminishing crowd.

Quietly I prayed that I would not be fined for knocking down the wire, which lay on the street at his feet. Learning that we spoke almost no Spanish, the officer smiled graciously and waved us on, as if to say, "Well, what if you foreigners just move along and try a little harder to stay out of trouble?"

I smiled at him gratefully, having been pardoned from my offense, and we drove off thanking the Lord.

"Okay, children, it looks as though we're coming to some sort of checkpoint again. Pray hard!"

A uniformed officer stepped out onto the road and raised his hand, motioning me to stop. My heart always beat faster at checkpoints. I had heard horror stories about them, but we always prayed through them.

I rolled down my window and attempted a smile as the officer walked over to us. *Lord, please help us to get through this without problems!* I prayed.

Though he looked threatening with his rifle, he seemed delighted to see Americans. When he opened his mouth, a stream of Spanish syllables poured forth.

Shaking my head, I reached for my dictionary kept conveniently on the dashboard. I scanned the pages for any clue to what he might have said but found nothing.

After a long silence, he rolled his eyes and waved me on. He didn't have time to be bothered by someone so inexperienced in his language.

We all sighed with relief, thankful that God had yet again proved faithful on our behalf. This happened at several checkpoints, and although it was humbling to be so handicapped and unable to communicate any better, God was certainly giving us an easy passage. We had heard many stories of fluent Spanish speakers being stalled at such checkpoints. Often they needed to bargain, either with money or their goods, in order to be on their way again. But God had delivered us from such delays. Regaining speed on the road, I thanked the Lord for His guidance.

Rain beat heavily on the windows, and I squinted to see through the rivulets streaming down the windshield.

"This heavy rainfall is a result of Hurricane Pauline," Hannah commented.

Red taillights crept along the road directly in front of us. In the pitch black, I occasionally caught a blurry view of a long line of car lights ahead.

What a time for a traffic jam! I thought.

We inched forward, hoping the rain would let up. More alarming was our left windshield wiper. Its screeching grew louder until suddenly the wiper flopped uselessly.

Quickly I pulled over, and we sat trying to think of what to do. The rain pounded deafeningly on the roof as a long line of cars slowly passed us on the left.

"Children," I spoke up, "I'm sorry. The wiper needs help again."

The children had already been discussing what to try if the wiper flopped apart. "Let's try a ponytail holder this time!" Hannah suggested.

"Sure! It's worth a try."

Seconds later, Hannah, Lissa, and Isaiah were on the hood in the downpour, fiddling with the lame wiper. Dripping wet and shivering, they hastily climbed back into the van.

As we started out again, I marveled at my children's ingenuity and at how much better things were going.

"Lord, please let the windshield wiper stay in place until tomorrow when we can replace it. And please let us find a hotel to stay in tonight. Children, let's praise God. He has been very faithful to us on this trip so far. Can anyone think of a song?"

Though the driving was stressful, God blessed my family with a sweet praise time together that kept our courage up. By the time we reached Villa Hermosa, it was pushing 10:00 p.m. I pulled up to a hotel that had some unusual activity going on, but we were too tired to care. The lady who took our money did not even ask our name.

This is an odd setup, I thought, as we drove into a carport and entered our room. We fell into bed and soon were dozing. But off and on throughout the night I heard honking in the carport next door.

What could be going on? I wondered as I turned over in bed. *This neighborhood seems suspicious, but I know God is carefully guarding us.*

As I lay in my bed, I meditated on one of our favorite passages. *I will both lay me down in peace, and sleep: for thou, LORD, only makest me dwell in safety.*[1]

The next morning dawned sunny and dry, and we drove through the attractive city of Villa Hermosa. The main street was accented by a median strip of beautiful palm trees. Everyone was hungry for breakfast until we spied a big white horse lying dead on the grass strip.

"Ooh, yuck!" the children exclaimed, wrinkling their noses.

"I guess we were not the only ones who had a rough night, huh?" I mused as we drove past.

Our first priority was to gas up the van and have our wiper repaired. I pulled into a gas station with a service and repairs shop. After filling the van, the attendant gave me my total. Instantly, I knew he was giving me an exorbitant and dishonest price. We had driven long enough in Mexico that I had some idea of what a tank of gasoline should cost.

I looked him in the eyes and shook my head. On a piece of paper I scribbled what I thought the price should be. Then I wrote down the price he had given, and dramatically crossed it out while frowning and shaking my head.

---

1. Psalm 4:8

He watched me with wide eyes, and then understood. When I pointed again to my price, he shrugged his shoulders and agreed.

How about that! I thought. A *"name your own price" gas station! Whoever heard of such a thing?*

Pointing to the broken windshield wiper, I asked him what to do about it. He motioned for me to drive over to the little mechanic shop only yards away. Two young workers stood idly by the garage. One of them eagerly came over to investigate my problem. When I demonstrated my wiper's handicap, he smiled and darted across the street. In a flash he was back with the very piece needed to make it work.

Quickly and skillfully he put it on for me. When I asked him what to pay, he just smiled and indicated I didn't have to pay anything. When I held out money, he refused. I pulled out a small stash of Spanish New Testaments we had brought along and handed one to him. He was thrilled. Delighted, he ran and showed his buddy his new treasure.

Suddenly I had an idea. *Surely God would want me to give one to the man who meant to cheat me on gasoline.*

I walked back to the gas pumps and held one out for him. He wouldn't make eye contact, but he did accept the New Testament. It gave me a secret thrill to plant this seed in his heart. It was the first opportunity I had been given to return good for evil on our journey.

As the road wound its way south, we relished the tropical scenery. I had been cautioned that this last leg of the journey to the Belize border was considered the most dangerous. It was reported that along this route bandits occasionally lie in wait for unsuspecting travelers. I pushed such thoughts as far from my mind as I could.

The roads look pretty typical, I thought. *I can rest in the confidence that we have an Invisible Escort who is personally seeing us through safely.* My mind went to the verses in Psalm 91. *There shall no evil befall thee, neither shall any plague come nigh thy dwelling. For he shall give his angels charge over thee, to keep thee in all thy ways.*[1]

And truly He was guarding over us in all our ways; whether it

---

1. Psalm 91:10, 11

was a dumped storage container or a windshield-wiper problem, He had aided us. *Thank You, Father!* I prayed.

CHAPTER 10

Joining the Missionaries

– October 18, 1997 –

Lissa:

"We are finally at the Belize border!" Mommy said with relief. "What a blessing to make it all the way through Mexico with no flat tires and no problems at the checkpoints. The Lord has been so faithful to us."

We turned into the parking lot at the border office, and Mommy parked the van near the small building. Slowly we unbuckled and looked around.

"It's hot here, but at least there's a breeze," Hannah said, as she rolled down her window to get a better view of our surroundings.

"I guess we can get out and stretch a bit," Mommy said. "When I talked to Rhoda Miller this morning, she said they would meet us here, so keep your eyes peeled for a Mennonite couple."

"Why don't we try to tidy up our stuff in here. The officers will probably look through everything, you know," Mommy announced before turning off the ignition and slipping out of her seat.

I shoved my green backpack under the bench seat. "Oh," I said, "I hope they aren't too particular today. The stories we've heard about people having to unpack everything at the borders sound horrid. Wouldn't it be a headache to have to unload? We have everything wedged so tightly in here, I'm not sure we could get it all back in!"

Hannah groaned wearily from the front seat. "I don't even want to think about it," she said.

I crawled out of the van and stretched my stiff legs. A sea of tall grass grew on both sides of the road. I watched as it rippled in the wind like waves on the ocean. Flapping high above us, a Belizean flag proudly displayed its bright colors.

"Mommy, I see a lady walking this way, and she is wearing a white veil!" Beverly said, pointing excitedly.

I turned around, and sure enough, a Mennonite woman was making her way toward us. As she neared, the lady smiled broadly and said, "You must be the Evans family. I am Rhoda Miller. Welcome to Belize!"

Her warm, friendly manner instantly put us at ease. Minutes later her husband and daughter joined us.

"Kay, this is my husband Tim and our little girl, Abigail."

With a friendly smile, Tim reached out and shook Mommy's hand. "It's nice to meet you," he said.

Abigail smiled shyly and looked curiously at Beverly and Grace.

"Isaiah," Rhoda said, after being introduced to each of the children, "I think you will feel at home around our son Richard. He has a face full of freckles, just like you."

Isaiah smiled bashfully and looked down, kicking the dust.

Tim and Rhoda led us into the office, where they walked us through the procedure of entering the country of Belize. We filled out papers and handed them back to the dark-skinned officer, who stamped them with his big, official stamp.

A uniformed black woman approached Tim and said she needed to see what was in the van. We all filed back outside and opened the van doors where luggage and boxes were stacked all the way up to the ceiling.

I hope she doesn't have to go digging! I thought to myself.

After a few minutes of poking around, she said, "You are fine," and waved us on.

"Kay," Tim said, "you can follow us to the mission house. We live in Carmelita, which is near the town of Orange Walk. The small Nissan truck over there is ours," he said, pointing it out.

Mommy nodded. "Okay, that sounds great. I'll just follow you, then."

We soon found ourselves behind the Millers, driving past miles of green sugarcane nodding in the wind. Water buffalo grazed in pastures of knee-high grass. Occasionally we saw workers wearing wide straw hats and swinging machetes in the fields.

"So far, we've seen mostly African people here," Mommy said, "but I've heard there are also Spanish people."

"This must be the town of Orange Walk," Hannah said as we drove by a town square. "It may not be very big, but it surely is busy!"

Small shops lined the streets, selling anything from brightly colored shoes to plastic tubs and washboards. One vendor stood beside a trailer piled high with beautiful oranges. As we approached a gas station, a slender Latino boy waved at Tim, motioning for him to stop. Tim quickly pulled into the station and rolled down his window.

He said something and laughed, and the boy jumped in the back end. The gray truck pulled back onto the road, and the boy balanced himself on the edge of the bed, his shirt flapping.

"Do you suppose a lot of people travel that way here?" Hannah wondered.

Soon Tim's truck pulled off the main road onto a smaller dirt road and slowed to a stop. The fellow in the back jumped off, smiled, and waved good-bye as he turned and headed down a trail.

"I guess those with vehicles are considered the local taxi service!" Mommy exclaimed.

We followed the gray pickup as it lurched and shuddered through each pothole in the primitive thoroughfare, throwing up clouds of dust. Tim pointed out his window to a two-story house surrounded by a cheery picket fence, then drove into the gravel lane and parked in front. Several coconut trees, heavily laden with fruit, stood like guards in the yard. A clothesline strung from a second-story balcony to a coconut tree on the far side of the yard was draped with fresh laundry. Light-colored dresses and shirts flapped cheerily in the warm breeze like flags welcoming us to this beautiful tropical land.

The second-story door of the mission house flew open, and a boy and two girls ran onto the porch and peered at their new visitors through the railing. Little by little, as the word spread that we had arrived, a group gathered around us. They all smilingly introduced themselves and quickly set out to make us feel at home.

———————————

Kay:

"This will be your room, Kay," said Rhoda, leading the way into a modest guest room. "And I thought your little girls could sleep in here with you."

"This is very nice," I said, looking around. "Are we putting anyone out of their beds? I mean, we can easily sleep on the floor."

"Oh, don't worry," Rhoda assured me, as she opened the closet and made room for our dresses. "No, this is our guest room. And your two older girls can sleep in the room just around the corner," she said, motioning over her shoulder. "It's the room of one of our teachers, but she will be staying with one of the other girls. By the way, around here we often refer to the voluntary service workers as VS'rs. And I thought maybe Isaiah could sleep with our little boy, Richard, up in his room."

I set our blue suitcase on the concrete floor and put my purse on the nightstand. "Yes, I'm sure that will be just fine. Thank you so much for all you have done for us!"

She shrugged her shoulders and smiled. "Oh, we're glad to. Is there anything else in the van I can bring in?"

I quickly counted our bags. "Here's the suitcase, two backpacks, and my purse. No, Rhoda, I think that's it."

She stepped to the doorway and rested her hand on the frame. "Good," she said. "Now if you want to come with me, I'll show you the shower room and where we keep the towels."

As we stepped into the starry night, we were greeted by a loud chorus of crickets.

I leaned closer to the mirror and adjusted the new veil on my head. "These feel so much more comfortable than the other coverings we had," I confided to Hannah.

"Yes," Hannah agreed. "I have a feeling they are much more practical for missionary life."

I smiled at her and tucked a strand of hair beneath the white fabric. "Yes, this seems much more natural to me."

I stepped back from the mirror to survey my work. Last night I had asked Rhoda where to find the kind of veil she and the ladies here wore. She had promptly gone to her room and gathered up a few for us to try.

Hannah and I looked up as Lissa burst through the open door.

"Church starts in just a few minutes," she exclaimed. "Tim and Rhoda are walking out the lane now. Are you ready?" She grabbed up her Bible and handed me mine.

"All right, Hannah, let's go," I said as we hurried out the door.

The little church house was a literal stone's throw down the road. As we turned in the gate, I thought to myself, *I have never seen such a quaint little church house.*

It had pimiento wood for walls, a thatched roof, and open-air windows. The most modern thing about it was the concrete floor.

Stepping inside the door, the girls and I slid onto a bench on the ladies' side, while Isaiah walked up farther and sat with his new friend, Richard. I looked around at the many faces. Everyone seemed delighted to be here to worship God. The atmosphere was relaxed and cheery.

After a few songs, Tim Miller made his way up to the pulpit. Opening his Bible, he looked out over the group seated before him. "This morning I want to speak about the importance of waiting on God, and on God's faithfulness to His own . . ." he said, beginning his message.

What a blessing to be in a foreign country and yet hear an English sermon, I thought.

A rooster crowed above Tim's voice. The natives didn't even notice the distraction, but it was new to my American ears, and I had to restrain a smile.

A slight breeze flowed in and ruffled the thatch above me. A butterfly fluttered in through the door, and later a big, hairy tarantula crept slowly along the top of the wall.

What a wonderful way to worship God, I thought, *where you are constantly reminded of His creation.*

But beauty and nature can distract from a worship service. Beverly, an avid nature lover, had been sitting quietly beside me. Suddenly she patted my arm and cupped her hand to my ear.

"Mommy," she whispered, "may I dig through your purse for the binoculars? I think I saw something through the window out on the banana tree."

I shook my head in amusement. "Not now, Beverly."

Just then something stung my leg, and I quickly reached down and slapped. "Oh, too late," I whispered, holding up my hand and seeing a smear of blood.

Rhoda had warned me before church to put on mosquito repellent before coming to the service because the windows have no glass or screens. I had sprayed each of my children but had forgotten about myself.

A testimony time followed the sermon. I appreciated the open and honest way the brethren shared what was on their hearts. Meeting together were blacks, Latinos, and Indians, as well as the American missionaries whom we had already met. It was refreshing to see such a mix of backgrounds happily worshiping God together.

This seems just right, I thought. *It feels like a little taste of heaven, where all cultures will be one before God's throne.*

I rested my arm out the open pickup window, and my white veil flapped against my sweaty neck. Tim, Rhoda, and I, all squished into their small truck, were going to look at a prospective rental house. We passed small block homes surrounded by thick tropical vegetation. I looked curiously at the round, black water tanks perched atop so many of the flat roofs and asked Tim about them.

"Rainwater is too precious to waste here," he informed me, "so everyone who can afford a tank collects rainwater like that."

Tim slowed the truck and pulled into a small driveway. "The landlady lives here, and the rental house is behind her house."

A large, dark woman emerged from the front door and greeted us. "Are you Tim Miller?" she asked.

He stuck out his hand and said, "I am. And this is the lady who is looking for a house. Her name is Kay Evans."

She eyed me carefully. "Well, you can follow me out behind da house," she said. "It's a nice lil house. You might want to put some linoleum on de floor, but udder dan dat is bout ready to go."

We followed her single file through her backyard and into a big clearing. Nestled in the far corner was a newly-constructed, square house with a flat roof.

"This place has two bedrooms and one bathroom," the landlady said as we stepped through the door.

The house was small and had absolutely no frills like closets, cupboards, pantry, or warm water. In fact, the water supply line to the house had yet to be laid. But I decided, with a little determination, the place would be satisfactory.

Our new home was just off the main road heading into Orange Walk town and only a ten-minute drive from the Carmelita mission where Tim and Rhoda lived.

After nine days of living with the Millers, our moving day, Monday, October 27, arrived bright and clear. All the missionaries from the three nearby missions came and helped us unload and settle in. Our yard bustled with activity as women carried boxes from our van and piled them high just inside the door. When the fans were brought in, I quickly turned them on to get some air moving. The ladies put things away, generously adding canned goods, bedding, and many other things from their own homes. More and more donated things were carried through the door. A table, chairs, and even a stove were brought in. I was awed as the house was transformed into a home. I felt so unworthy.

Outside, the men were busy too. A determined young man grabbed the push mower we had brought from Amish country and set out to conquer the thick, green grass. Someone else raked up the lemons that had fallen from the big lemon tree. And others began digging the trench for the water supply line.

It felt good to be settling in somewhere again.

———————

The stars above us glittered in the pitch black sky.

"I don't think I have ever seen the stars so clearly before," I whispered as I gazed upward.

Emily yawned and rested her head on Hannah's shoulder. "Mommy, shall I go inside and put Emily to bed?" Hannah asked. "She is going to sleep."

I reached over and brushed a strand of hair out of Emily's face. "Let's just all go in," I said. "It's past bedtime, and besides, we'll get eaten alive by mosquitoes if we don't retreat soon."

I stepped onto the porch and opened the door. At the sink I filled a big pot with water and then struck a match and lit the burner. "Lissa, get the big metal tub ready in the bathroom. I want the children bathed before they go to bed. The water shouldn't take too long to heat up."

Hannah and Isaiah laid out the mats on the bedroom floor and spread sheets on them.

A minute later, I heard a squeal from the bathroom. "Yuck! Look, there's a frog!" exclaimed Lissa.

I rounded the corner and saw a slimy-looking tree frog stuck to the wall next to our pink toilet. Lissa and I exchanged disgusted looks and laughed.

"I guess I need to ask the landlady for a screen to put in that window. That should keep such unwanted visitors out of the house!" I said.

While Beverly sloshed in the washtub in the bathroom, Hannah, Lissa, and I sat around the table, discussing the evening. We had gone with the Carmelita church to San Román, a Spanish village back in the bush. At least it had seemed way back in the bush to me. We had traveled through miles of thick jungle and crossed a floating bridge before finally arriving at the village.

"I hardly understood any of the message," Hannah said with a sigh. "I wish we could help out more with the Spanish outreaches, but it's difficult when we speak so little Spanish."

I nodded. "I know what you mean. I asked Connie Bear about that, and she said they had attended a Spanish school over in Guatemala."

Lissa rubbed a painful bite on her arm. "Yeah, I think Dave and Kris Martin and Chad Miller went over there too," she said. "It seems a lot of the missionaries go over there to school."

We heard a loud clink as a beetle flew into the window glass. The bugs were attracted to the light and did all they could to get in.

"Anyway," I went on, "I think it would be a very good experience for us to go to Spanish school. I would feel much more useful here. Until then, we can't be much help in the Spanish villages. But I know after several weeks of school, we'll be eager to get back to our friends in Belize."

So I made plans for us to spend eight weeks at Spanish school in Antigua, Guatemala. Rhoda encouraged me to leave the van in Belize and bus to Guatemala.

"That way, you won't have to deal with all the paperwork and confusion of taking a vehicle into their country. Plus, their buses go nearly everywhere. Tim can arrange for missionaries there to pick you up from the bus station and take you to the language school."

———————————

On November 21, 1997, we were ready to cross the Guatemalan border. The closer we got, the more apprehensive I became. I leaned forward. "Chad, have you ever had problems at this border?"

Reaching over to turn up the air conditioner, he shook his head. "Not that I remember."

"Good," I said. "My children and I always dread border cross-ings. And the Spanish language here will be an additional stress. I am so glad you can translate for us. Thank you so much for doing us this big favor."

He glanced back. "Well, Sister Kay, I am glad for some little way to help you and your family. I know some Spanish, and so I thought I could just lend you a hand. This is the same border I went through when I went to school, so I remember a little of how things work at this crossing."

As he parked the van and pointed to the building, my stomach felt tied in knots. *Maybe he can't see how nervous I am. I hope not!* I thought to myself and turned to watch the children get out of the van.

Chad spoke up again. "Maybe it would be a good idea to have a bathroom stop before you all actually cross the border. You never know when you can find one, but I see one over there." He pointed to a small building and then motioned for us to follow him.

Grabbing our backpacks, we fell into line behind our leader. Between the men's and women's rest rooms was a little brown boy behind a small card table. On the table was a sign posting the price to enter the rest room, and beside it were little stacks of neatly folded toilet paper. My eyes grew wide, and I fought to keep from laughing out loud.

"Children," I said in a low voice, digging through my change purse, "let's just hope I can find enough change for each of you to enjoy this little privilege!"

The official behind the desk accepted our passports from Chad and examined them closely. I stood with my children in the dark office and let Chad do the talking. "I think border crossings are one of my least favorite things," I whispered to the children, "but at least Chad is taking care of all the paperwork for us!"

They nodded, and we watched intently as the official spread some papers out before him. Chad explained to the man in Spanish that we were headed to Antigua to attend Spanish school.

The brown-skinned man looked up approvingly. "*¡Sí, es muy bueno!*" (Yes, it's very good.)

Glancing around the dim room, I noticed several brightly colored posters on the wall. One featured a massive Mayan temple. "TIKAL," it read in bold lettering. Another poster had a colorful bird with a long tail, and neatly printed at the top was *Quetzal.*

"Children, look at the poster over there with the green bird on it. I think that it might be the bird the Guatemalan money is named after."

"Ohhh," exclaimed Beverly, "it's so pretty!"

After a few minutes, the official stamped our passports, filled out the necessary papers, and waved us out the door.

I sighed with relief. "Praise the Lord, we had no problems there!"

As we left the dark office, three money exchangers rushed forward and surrounded me crying, "*¡Quetzales! ¡Quetzales! ¡Quetzales!*"

I held my purse close and wailed, "Chad, what do I do?"

He laughed. "Well, if you want your money exchanged from Belizean dollars into Guatemalan *quetzales,* you can do business with them. Here, how much do you want to exchange now? I can do it for you."

Seeing my perplexed look, he spoke up quickly, "Don't do too much right now. You can always exchange more later at a bank."

I handed Chad several Belizean bills, and he showed them to the closest exchanger, who eagerly whipped out his calculator and punched in the amount I wanted to exchange. Then the little man grabbed a pencil from behind his ear and scrawled the number on a dirty piece of paper in his hand and showed the total to Chad. When Chad nodded, the exchanger quickly reached deep into his pocket and pulled out a well-worn billfold. Flipping it open, he counted out the colorful bills and then fished some change from his other pocket.

Chad accepted the money, counted it again, and said, "Yep, this is right."

I took the wad of bills and held up a bright piece of paper for the children to see.

"That looks like play money!" Lissa exclaimed.

"You should see the coins," laughed Chad, pouring them into my hand.

The children crowded around as I held my hand toward them.

"Mommy, look at that little bitty one!" Isaiah yelped.

I lifted it up. "It's so light too. Why, it hardly weighs anything at all!"

Chad cleared his throat and said, "The bus stop is not far from here. I'll walk you there before I leave."

Lissa:

We waved good-bye to Chad, who had graciously walked us through the whole border crossing process, and then we turned and walked toward the bus bound for Guatemala City.

I looked at the bus skeptically. "It's not a very impressive vehicle!" I muttered. The bus was an ancient-looking box, which had once been painted blue and white but had long since lost its true color. We hiked up the high steps and walked down the aisle, nodding at the other passengers seated in the benches. Finding seats, we settled down to wait.

"I wonder where the driver is?" I asked, but none of us knew.

Twenty minutes later Mommy glanced at her watch and looked up, puzzled. "I guess they are rather relaxed with their schedule around here," she said.

This was our first taste of the Guatemalan way of life in which you "hurry up and wait."

Seated by a window, I peered out at the people meandering by. "Emily, can you see that lady over there?" I asked.

Emily sat on Mommy's lap and leaned forward to look. "Oh!" she exclaimed in amazement. The woman had a big bucket full of clothes balanced on her head, and in each hand she carried a basket.

During the long wait, more and more people got onto the bus, and soon the vehicle was jammed. Finally the driver and helper hopped on, and with a tremendous roar we were off, leaving everyone behind us in a cloud of black smoke. The engine was right next to the driver, with little to muffle the noise. The driver bounced in his seat, occasionally grasping the gearshift and wrestling it into another gear, grinding the whole way.

The scenery was incredible—a solid wall of lush greenery and dense jungle. The windows were down, and the air rushed in and cooled our sweaty faces.

The driver apparently had a love for speed and was constantly accelerating, only to be slowed by an occasional pothole in the road. Three of us were now crammed onto our bench, sitting on what was originally meant for two. We flew around turns, trapped inside this bus, bouncing this way and that. I clung to the back of the seat in front of me, frantically trying to stay in my seat.

I laughed. "Yes, we are in Guatemala!" I shouted above the roaring motor.

With my nose pressed against the window, I tried to catch a glimpse of what this place looked like, but it was just too dark. I turned and shook Grace awake, who had drifted off to sleep near the end of our incredible ride.

How could she have slept through that? I thought to myself.

People pushed their way toward the door of the bus, but we waited until the aisle was empty. Then standing to our feet, we gathered our bags and stepped wearily off the bus. I jumped off the high step and onto the dirty street. Directly in front of us loomed the gloomy bus station, swarming with travelers. We followed the other passengers into the dirty little building and looked around at the huge mob of tired people. It seemed as though everyone was trying to do the same thing—purchase tickets for the next bus.

"I think this would be a good time to find a bathroom," Mommy said, exhausted. "Do you see one?"

I stood on my tiptoes and scanned the room for any sign of a bathroom, but saw nothing.

Mommy bent down and spoke to a German girl seated on top of her suitcase, surrounded with backpacks. "Excuse me, do you know where a bathroom is?"

The young girl took a wad of blue gum from her mouth and shook her head. "Sorry, no speak English."

Mommy yawned and sighed. "Hannah, why don't you and the others find somewhere to set our bags, and I'll stay in line and get the tickets for the rest of the trip."

Hannah looked warily at the filthy floor and then led the way to an empty spot along the wall. I set my heavy backpack next to the wall and sat on it.

"This room is gross!" said Emily.

Emily was so exhausted that she was nearly in tears, and Hannah pulled her onto her lap. We all watched as the line toward the ticket counter inched its way forward.

A man stumbled toward Mommy and stood only inches from her. "I need money," he said loudly in broken English. "Brother sick. I need money to help brother. You Christian . . . help me. Give money. God is love. God is love . . ."

Catching a whiff of alcohol on his breath, Mommy tried not to look disgusted. After several minutes of his rigorous begging, Mommy handed him a little money in a desperate attempt to get him away.

"God bless you!" He thanked her profusely.

On sudden impulse, she asked him a question. "Sir, do you know where the bathroom is?"

He nodded and assured her, "You go with me, I know where is bathroom." He took a few steps and eagerly pointed to a dark doorway. "There is bathroom." Then he staggered out the front door and into the night.

Mommy peered into the cave-like room, and saw a toilet in the far corner, standing alone like a white monument. She grimaced, noting there were no walls for privacy. And who knew what else was crawling around in that dark room. Looking back at the line of people, Mommy's eyes met the gaze of a woman about her own age. The woman had watched the whole scenario and shook her head as if to warn us to not even dare enter that forbidding room.

After Mommy got our tickets, she hurried over to us. "They say our next bus will have a bathroom. But until then, there is apparently no real bathroom around here," she said. "This could be a long night."

My eyes slid closed, and my head slowly fell forward until I jerked it back up, trying in vain to keep my heavy eyes open. We all sat waiting for our bus until it seemed it would never arrive.

This is so strange, I thought. *To think, our family is sitting in this filthy bus stop in the wee hours of the morning, surrounded by a language and culture that we do not know. When will that bus ever get here?* My tired thoughts drifted on and on until a sound jolted me to attention.

Loud screeching just outside the door announced that our desired bus had finally arrived. We quickly got up and slung our bags over our shoulders, joining the mob heading for the door. As we got closer, I could see this bus was big and shiny.

"This is a first-class bus! What a welcome sight!" we exclaimed.

When we stepped up into the dimly-lit bus, a wave of cool air washed over us. It felt wonderful after sitting in the stifling-hot bus stop for hours. I followed Mommy to the back of the bus where we found our seats. Suddenly I had a wonderful appreciation for individual seats. That other bus had been so crammed! We wedged our backpacks up into the rack above our heads and then collapsed into our seats.

"Ohhhh, Mommy," Hannah sighed contentedly, "these seats are cushioned and they feel so good! Now we can really go to sleep."

With a lurch the bus started, and we all relaxed, eager to rest. Our bus would arrive in Guatemala City early the next morning, so we had plenty of time to sleep. That announcement was music to my ears. I was so drained, and my eyelids grew heavier every moment.

But sleep did not come as easily as I had hoped.

The road was horrible; we were constantly hitting potholes. I couldn't see the road, but it felt as if the driver was trying to hit every bump! Slowly I drifted off to sleep, only to awaken minutes later by being thrown out of my seat until I was almost standing up. But the floor under me suddenly jolted the other way, and I toppled back, nearly landing in the next seat over! I felt the back of my head just to make sure my veil was still in place. To my dismay I found it holding on by only one pin.

As I securely pinned it on again, the whole situation suddenly struck me as funny. I peered through the dark and saw Mommy and Hannah both busily re-pinning their veils too. Even though we were exhausted, it was hilarious.

Leaning back in my seat, I closed my eyes and wondered, *Will the morning ever come?*

CHAPTER 11

Fleas, Homework, and Tortillas

Lissa:

The sun was just peeking over the horizon when the bus began descending the twisting road down into the valley. Through the smudged window, I could faintly make out the city far below.

I glanced around at our fellow travelers. Apparently, most of them had fallen asleep sometime during the night. One by one they began to awake and stare blankly out their windows.

Entering the city, the bus wove in and out of traffic, eventually rolling to a stop. Our family and the other passengers staggered out the door, exhausted and groggy. I yawned as the cool, morning air washed over my face.

A mob of short men shouted, "¡Taxi! ¡Taxi!"

When Mommy realized they were speaking to her, she stammered, "Oh, uh . . . *no gracias.*"

Lugging our suitcases into the dirty bus station, we found ourselves surrounded by sleeping people, slumped over in the black, vinyl chairs lining the wall. Men snoozed with hats tipped over their faces and with their feet outstretched. Others chatted loudly with their neighbors.

Mommy sank into a nearby seat, pulling Emily onto her lap. "Well, it is too early to call the family who is picking us up, so we might as well sit down too," she said.

A young man wearing a baseball cap meandered in, lugging a case of shiny watches. *"¡Relojes! ¡relojes! ¡Bonitos y nuevos!"* He offered his wares to anyone who looked up. He soon completed his rounds and wandered out the door to find other potential customers.

By the door sat an old beggar lady, shivering in the cold. Propped next to her against the wall was a dirty wooden cane. A filthy bandage on her foot told of a life of pain. Staring gloomily at the tile floor, she slowly pushed a greasy braid over her shoulder with her bony hand.

Hannah watched the woman in the shadows for a few minutes. "Mommy," she said quietly, "may I give her my jacket? She looks so cold."

Mommy studied Hannah's face for a minute and voiced concern. "You already gave your other jacket away while we were in Mexico, and I don't know how easy they are to be found here in Guatemala." After hesitating a moment, Mommy nodded her consent. "All right, I guess you may."

A few minutes later, Hannah returned to her seat, contented. "The woman seemed so grateful!" she said.

The light coming through the door slowly grew brighter. Glancing at her watch, Mommy said, "Children, I know you all are hungry. Let's venture down the sidewalk to see if we can find a restaurant open this early."

Isaiah jumped up from his seat, anxious to stretch his legs. After the long night's ride, we were all very hungry. So we gathered our baggage and stepped boldly out onto the city street.

The morning sun had crept over the mountains and was illuminating the downtown buildings. The language, the sights, and the smells were all so strange and foreign to us. Buses roared by loudly, leaving behind them great clouds of smelly exhaust.

We walked along the sidewalks, peering into store windows.

"Do you think this could be a restaurant?" Mommy wondered, staring at the bright letters painted on the wall.

I looked uncomprehendingly at the words, and shrugged.

After walking several blocks, we found a little restaurant. The proprietor was just shining the windows as we passed. She cheerfully welcomed us in and led us to a large rectangular table in the middle of the room.

Ordering breakfast in Spanish may be challenging, I thought.

But Mommy soon figured out a way. "We'd like to have this," Mommy said, pointing to a picture on the menu. The patient waitress nodded, and disappeared through the doors leading into the kitchen.

Minutes later, she produced a steaming and delicious breakfast unlike any we had ever eaten. We were served scrambled eggs, black refried beans, thick slices of white Guatemalan cheese, corn tortillas, and fried plantains with a dollop of sour cream artfully placed on top. Cups of hot Guatemalan coffee were carefully set before us.

Mommy thanked the waitress, and then we passed around the plates.

"Mommy," I said softly, "did we order beans and plantains?"

Scooting a plate toward me she smiled. "I think the waitress saw our feeble attempts at ordering, and then just decided to serve us what she thought best. It smells delicious anyway, doesn't it?"

I couldn't argue. After tasting it, we all decided we loved Guatemalan food, even though we had never eaten sour cream at breakfast. After scraping our plates clean and paying the waitress with the strange Guatemalan money, we lugged our bags back to the station.

The streets of Antigua were lined with small houses and tiny shops. The van chugged along over the town's rustic cobblestones and then slowed as Rogelio turned into an alley.

"The language school is right here," he announced enthusiastically, pointing to a brightly painted building. Parking the van right outside the door, he turned to Mommy. "The director of the school told me she will be here this morning to meet you."

Rogelio pushed open the van door and hopped out onto the dirty street. He was a cheery little man with a ready laugh who loved to tease my brother and sisters and me. He loved children and made us feel relaxed and welcome. We had spent the past two days with Rogelio and Janet Pichiya and their large family in the bustling town of Chimaltenango.

Knock, knock, knock . . . Rogelio pounded firmly on the black, metal door.

I craned my neck to read the small sign above the doorway, *La Enseñanza* (the teaching). Antigua boasts of many Spanish schools.

A woman opened the door and greeted us warmly with a big

friendly smile.

"This is Aura, the director of the school," Rogelio said.

We all smiled and shook her hand.

She held the door wide for us to come in, and proudly showed us a wall full of pictures featuring other students seated at small tables with their teachers.

After we signed up for classes starting the next day, Rogelio spoke up. "Let me take you to a hotel very close to here. You won't have far to walk to your classes from there."

Kay:

The door closed behind Rogelio, leaving us alone in the hotel room. He was going to ask the hotel owner about borrowing another cot.

Standing in the middle of the room, I looked around in disappointment. The place was dark and musty. Shoved up against the wall were two single beds with sagging mattresses. There was only one high window, but the wooden shutters were closed forbiddingly.

"It's a roof over our heads, children. We can be thankful for that," I said, trying to sound more positive than I felt.

Hannah nodded and smiled faintly. "The room is big, even if it is poorly furnished," she said.

I slid my purse from my shoulder and set it on the bed. "Well, children, let's get settled in."

I marched to the window and unlatched the shutters, determined to cheer the place up. After tugging for a minute or two, the shutters creaked and swung open. Shoving the tinted window glass upward, I peered out onto the street. Strong iron bars secured all around the window made me feel like a prisoner looking out of my cell. Nonetheless, looking upward, I could see the deep blue sky.

"Let there be light!" I exclaimed, but I quickly withdrew my head as a brightly colored bus rumbled past, belching fumes of thick black smoke. "Ewww . . . " I coughed and quickly pulled the window back down with a deep sigh. "Oh well, at least some light still manages to come through the glass."

A light knock sounded at the door. Hannah opened it a crack and saw Rogelio smiling back at her. She held the door open and he stepped inside.

"The owner will be bringing a cot later on. But for now, is there anything else you need? Do you need to go somewhere? I would be glad to take you."

I adjusted a pin on my veil and said, "Well, I do need to fax my lawyer in the States. Could you take us to a place that has a fax machine?"

He smiled widely and motioned toward the street. "Yes, I would be glad to take you. Hop in the van, everyone!"

Spread out on the bed around me were several papers and a fax sheet. I added up the figures while twirling a pencil between my fingers. Shaking my head, I sighed. "Hmmm, I did not realize how low on money we were."

At the bottom of the fax to my lawyer, I had scribbled, ". . . and please wire the money FAST!"

Rogelio didn't know what I had faxed, but as he returned my children and me to the hotel, he had handed me some money with a twinkle in his eye. "This is for you and your children," he said.

It was humbling, but I accepted it gratefully. So now that he had left, I seated myself on the bed, adding the bills he had given me to those I had remaining in my wallet. "Well, let's see. It will be at least a week till the money wire will come through. That leaves us with about thirty *quetzales* a day for the next seven days."

I was not accustomed to thinking in *quetzales,* so I slowly figured up what it would be in dollars. I stared at the figure on the scrap of paper in front of me, just a little over $4.00 U.S. per day to feed my family of seven.

Whew! Lord, this will be a faith project, won't it?

Although our room felt oppressive, only steps from our door was a beautiful courtyard. A fountain that had once shot sprays of water now stood motionless. But the pool below it reflected the fluffy white clouds in the sky above. As I climbed the stairway that curved up to the terrace, a beautiful view of the town of Antigua spread out before me. My children were downstairs unpacking, but they had told me about this spot, so I had come exploring. A slight breeze rustled the tall fuchsia shrubs next to the terrace wall, and I suddenly wished for my sweater.

Stepping to the railing, I gazed out over the town as the sun dipped behind the mountains surrounding this valley. In the street below, the last buses of the day headed out, leaving the town in a quiet hush. I could see above the rooftops, several tall cathedrals, standing proudly as if to remind me that this was, indeed, a land under strong Roman Catholic influence. And beyond, towering over the town, was the beautiful volcano Agua.

"Lord," I whispered, "this view is so awesome! And this place will be a perfect location to come and pray . . . or study," I added, noticing the round table and chairs. "This beautiful spot makes up for the dingy room below."

Taking one last look at the setting sun, I scurried downstairs.

The air was chilly as Beverly and I strode briskly down the vacant sidewalk. It was early morning, and the vendors of the *tiendas* were just opening their tiny shops. The buses hadn't started their routes, and everything was quiet, except for a dog barking as we passed.

A short woman stood in front of her small business, sweeping up the trash from yesterday's traffic. She paused as we passed and cheerfully greeted us, *"¡Buenos días!"*

I smiled and returned the greeting, *"¡Buenos días."*

Hurrying back to our hotel, Beverly held the small package of fresh tortillas to her chest. "These are so nice and warm!" she said happily. "I don't feel cold anymore!"

I nodded. "I am just so glad that we found that *tortillería* the other day. And they are so inexpensive—over a dozen tortillas for two *quetzales!*"

"I'm glad too," returned Beverly. "I like watching the ladies pat them out before they lay them on the hot griddle."

We had discovered some inexpensive food options, like beans, and rice, and the local rolls called *panes*.

"Beverly," I said quietly, "up ahead is that bar. I think I see a drunk man lying out front. Let's go by as quickly as we can."

Beverly's blue eyes grew wide. As we approached, I could see the man on the sidewalk was asleep, his head resting on the doorstep of the bar. As we passed, we stepped carefully over his leg, sprawled out across the sidewalk. Saliva dribbled from his lips and an empty bottle lay at his fingertips. A red curtain in the doorway fluttered as eerie music wailed from within the creepy establishment.

"What a terrible thing drink is!" I muttered.

I pushed open our door and inhaled the wonderful aroma of black beans boiling on the small stove.

"We are back," Beverly exclaimed happily, "and the tortillas are still warm!"

Hannah looked up and nodded, dishing out rice onto seven plates. "Great! Breakfast is just now ready." She glanced at her watch. "Spanish classes start in an hour."

"Yes," I agreed, "and after you and Lissa get back from your classes, I think I'll take Isaiah with me down to the Internet cafe. I want to use the phone there to call and make sure the lawyer received my fax. It would be nice to know exactly when we can expect the money to arrive. Okay, children, let's sit down and eat."

Grace laid her doll aside and joined the rest of us as we sat in a circle on the floor. Since our room was lacking a table or chairs, we simply "made do" by sitting on the brown tile. On each of our plates was a heap of rice and beans, a few tortillas, and a shiny orange tangerine.

"Let's pray," I said, and we all bowed our heads. "Lord, we thank You so much for this food You have provided . . ."

———————————

"Yes, Kay, we did receive the fax, and we are presently working on processing everything. In about seven to ten days the money should be in your hands. Oh, there is something else I need to tell you. Missing persons posters with your photos are beginning to appear in public places like Wal-Mart. I just saw one the other day. Flyers with the same pictures are being sent to thousands of people across America. And I guess you knew a warrant was issued for your arrest two months after you left the U.S.?"

The secretary's words continued to ring in my ears after I hung up the phone. Numbly, I sat down at a nearby table, and rested my head in my hands. My mind spun wearily. *A warrant? Issued only two months after we crossed the border?* I looked up. "What a blessing that we left when we did," I said. "It was perfect timing. God's timing is always perfect."

The money wire did arrive just when we needed it. I had only forty *quetzales,* the equivalent of $7.00, left in my purse when it came. God had never failed us even once. And here again He allowed the money to arrive just before our supply was depleted. What a wonderful Provider!

I stared at the page of homework and fought back a wave of frustration. The lines of Spanish verbs needing to be conjugated swam before me on the paper. While growing up, school had never been my favorite thing, and I was discovering it did not thrill me now either. Hannah, Lissa, Isaiah, Beverly, and I were all being tutored four-on-one, five days a week, at the Spanish school. It was a very demanding, rigorous schedule: shopping, cooking, cleaning, parenting, schooling, e-mailing, making sure we all made it to class on time, as well as always having Hannah, Lissa, or me at the apartment to be with Grace and Emily.

Each day we were given lengthy assignments to tackle before the next day, like the page I was staring at now. It was very challenging. Isaiah and Beverly's classes were mostly fun and games with no homework, so there was little stress for them. How glad I was. If they had been given difficult assignments, how would I have been able to help them?

Lissa tended to dread her classes and homework just like her mother. But she hated missing out on a conversation, so she was picking up the language quickly by all of our dealings with the natives.

Hannah, too, loved learning from conversations. But she was

the only one of us who delighted in the academic classroom setting. She was a born student and loved the mental challenge of learning a foreign language. The more homework she was given, the happier she was.

I have enough to occupy myself with, I reasoned, *running a household and training my children without having to study a list of words.* I tried though. Besides, I was learning lots of market words, mostly through trial and error. If I failed miserably, I remembered the next time.

Gripping the pencil, I stared again at the page in front of me. *"Yo hablo, Tú hablas . . ."*

Hannah:

We all paused at the corner and waited for the cars and buses to pass. As soon as we could, we dashed across the street and into the square. Antigua's town square was beautiful; a big fountain in the center sprayed streams of glittering water. Tall shade trees hung leisurely over the meandering sidewalks. The square was dotted with benches, and the sidewalks were often full of white-skinned people, or *gringos* as the natives called us. But the natives also swarmed here; they knew this was an ideal place to sell their handmade crafts.

A young mother approached me, balancing on her head a large basket, heavily laden with brightly colored, woven cloths, balls, wallets, and headbands. Her chocolate-eyed baby with thick black hair was tied onto her back. I smiled admiringly at the little one as she peered shyly around her mother at me.

The woman held out a beautifully woven placemat and asked if I wanted to buy it.

I smiled but shook my head. *"No, gracias,"* I said.

She reached up to the basket on her head and pulled down a small doll. "You want? Your sister want? I sell cheap."

Again I shook my head. *"No, gracias,"* I said.

She pouted and turned away as if insulted, looking around for another potential customer.

"These ladies are the best saleswomen I have ever seen," I muttered to Mommy. "They make you feel so guilty if you don't buy."

She laughed. I was glad to see her relaxed. Studying got stressful sometimes, and often after a day of classes and study we would go as a family to the open market, the town square, or just exploring. It was a wonderful change of pace.

Market was our favorite place to go. We filled our backpacks with the fruit and vegetables we bought there. The market displayed a beautiful array of colors and sights, sounds, and smells. Vendors shouted out the prices of their wares, dogs barked at each other, and pigs squealed as they were carried away by their new owners. We enjoyed watching the natives buying and selling because it was then that we observed the art of bartering at its best. We soon learned to love buying things this way.

Mommy headed down a row where women sat on the ground surrounded by piles and baskets of produce. I spotted a young lady nursing her baby while selling pineapples.

Mommy nudged me and said, "Hannah, let's get a pineapple. They look very fresh."

I stopped in front of the woman, pointing to the pile of fruit. "How much do you want for your pineapples?"

She looked up quickly. "Seven *quetzales* each."

I feigned a shocked expression. "Really! That's rather high," I exclaimed.

Setting her baby on her lap, she adjusted her embroidered blouse. "Yes, but they are high right now." Reaching for a large pineapple, she nodded. "Here, smell it. These are very good ones."

I held the fruit to my nose and sniffed. She was right; it smelled very sweet. "Will you take five for it?"

She frowned and exclaimed, "Five! Oh, no, it just won't work!"

I tried again. "All right, what about six *quetzales?*"

She paused and then nodded. "Well, which one do you want?"

"Oh, I'll take this one. Thanks." I handed her the money, and she reached into her blouse, pulled out a very tattered wallet, and slipped the money inside.

Isaiah pulled his backpack from his shoulder, unzipped it, and tucked our purchase inside. Shopping in the market had proved to be our family's favorite way to learn Spanish.

We wound our way into the inner market where many of the *tiendas* were. I blinked in the darkness until my eyes adjusted to the dim lighting. A radio blared from the butcher shop on our right. Flies buzzed from the pig heads piled high on the counter to the slabs of meat and intestines hung up in the shop window.

"It's enough to make a vegetarian out of anyone!" Mommy groaned.

The smell was nearly overwhelming, and we hurried past, looking for a shoe shop. Since I was nearly a head taller than most of the ladies in Guatemala, it was difficult to find shoes my size. I looked down at my battered shoes and sighed. The local cobbler had already mended them twice, and I doubted that I could extend their life much longer.

"Here is a little shoe shop," Mommy said, peering through the dirty glass at a dusty display of shoes. "Hannah, we should step inside and see if they have anything your size."

I entered the shop and smiled at the clerk who hurried toward us.

"How can I help you?" she asked.

Mommy looked at me and raised her eyebrows, letting me know that I was to do the talking.

Peering at the wall lined to the ceiling with shoe boxes, I tried out my Spanish. "Well, I am looking for a pair of shoes my size. Do you have any like those?" I asked, pointing to a basic black shoe.

Her eyes slid from my face down to my feet. "Well, let's see," she said doubtfully. "I am sure we must have something that would work. Just a minute."

She grasped a long stick with a metal hook at one end and squinted at the rows and rows of shoe boxes stacked on top of each other.

How do they ever find what they are looking for? I wondered incredulously, shaking my head. Suddenly the saleswoman spotted the box she wanted perched near the ceiling and expertly hooked the edge of the box, pulling it down and catching it skillfully. She opened the box and eagerly showed me the pair.

I shook my head sadly. "No, I'm sorry; these are much too small. Do you have any that are larger?"

She looked back at the wall of boxes and chewed on her fingernail. Her face lit up, and once again she pulled down a box and held out a pair for me to see.

I almost gasped, for she held out a pair that was indeed big enough for me, but they were men's!

"Oh, no, I don't think those will work either," I said, heading toward the door. Just before stepping onto the sidewalk, I turned. "But thank you for looking anyway!" I called to the clerk.

Kay:

A loud hissing and screeching of brakes accompanied the approaching bus as it slowed to a stop. The helper instantly jumped to the trash-littered curb and shouted, "Hurry!"

We clambered up the steps. The driver nodded in time with the loud radio music, and just as Emily and I were inside, he hit the gas pedal, sending us scrambling for something to hold onto.

Falling into a seat, I sighed in relief as the bus lurched forward. "We made it!" I exclaimed. "What would we do if we had missed the bus for Chimaltenango?"

Lissa stood up to slide the window open. "Well, we would just have gotten to Chimaltenango late and missed the Pichiyas heading to church. I guess we would have sat on the doorstep until they returned home!"

She sat back down next to me and continued, "But I'm glad we caught the early bus. Where did Hannah and Isaiah have to sit?" she asked, craning her neck to look behind her.

It wasn't hard to pick them out among the many faces staring back at her. We were often the only ones on the bus with fair skin, freckles, and light-colored hair. Nearly all the Guatemalans had brown eyes, beautiful brown skin, and thick black hair.

As the bus wound its way up toward our destination, my thoughts drifted to Rogelio and Janet Pichiya and their children. Besides owning a hardware store, Rogelio was pastor of the Mennonite church we attended in Zaragoza. Sundays were a welcome break from our grueling school routine. After we attended morning services with the Pichiyas, they always fed us a delicious lunch. And after we enjoyed their fellowship all afternoon, they insisted that we eat supper with them, and then they would take us back to Antigua themselves.

They invested a lot of time in us, even checking on us sometimes during the week to make sure we were okay and often leaving groceries for us.

Once again the bus screeched to a stop, and the helper waved for us to get off.

"Oh, we are here! Lissa, quickly motion for the others to come, and I'll grab the backpack," I said, holding Emily's hand.

One by one we stepped off the bus and onto the sidewalk. With a quick honk of the horn, the bus was off, leaving us behind in a cloud of dust.

I covered my nose and choked out, "Okay, we have to hurry!"

We had several miles yet to walk before we reached the Pichiyas' home. As we trotted briskly down the sidewalk, buses and trucks roared past. Our family of seven made quite a parade, all dressed in our best clothes. But we soon felt plastered with dust and diesel exhaust.

I was jolted awake; something was shaking my bed. At first I thought I was dreaming, but when I sat up, the swaying continued.

Lissa clutched the edge of the bed and whispered, "Mommy, this is a big tremor!"

Although we knew tremors were common in Guatemala, this was the first time we experienced a big one. Pots and pans in the kitchen rattled and hangers clanked in the closet.

"What time is it?" I croaked, trying to find my glasses.

Lissa held up her watch and punched the glow button. "It's 2:30 in the morning," she said.

After a few seconds the rocking stopped. The other children had slept through it all! Lissa and I could hardly wait to tell them what they had missed. Soon we drifted back to sleep.

Returning home from school the next afternoon, I said to Hannah, "When I told my teacher about the exciting tremor in the night, he was very serious. His face was grave as he told me about the big earthquake in 1976 in which some of his own family members were killed. That put a whole different light on the subject. My excitement turned to shame when I saw his deep concern."

Hannah and I paused as a truck loaded with pigskins turned in front of us to enter the big black gate of a tannery. After it had rumbled into the tannery courtyard, we continued homeward.

"The walk to our house is definitely longer now that we moved, but I don't mind a bit. Even if we do have to walk past that smelly tannery," Hannah said as we rounded the corner.

I agreed. "It was really nice of Rogelio to find this place for us. I could tell he did not like the other place, and I am glad. I can hardly believe this nice little rental house is cheaper than the hotel room!"

"I don't know why either," Hannah responded. "But since this rental house is so much cleaner, maybe we won't struggle with sickness or lice and fleas like we did at the other place."

"I sure hope you're right," I agreed.

Our new little place was a wonderful blessing. It had three rooms—a living room, a bedroom, and a kitchen. All three opened into an outdoor courtyard that led to the bathroom and shower. We were delighted to have a real kitchen, complete with a table and chairs. The whole house was painted a very bright aqua color, except for the front, which was a bubblegum pink.

Hannah and I paused in front of the door and knocked. I heard the sound of pattering feet, and Isaiah's little voice queried, "Who is it?"

I smiled and called, "It's your mother!"

The metal door creaked open. "You missed the parade!" Isaiah said excitedly. "A big procession went down the street awhile ago. Lissa said it was Catholic, because they were carrying a big figure of Mary."

"Oh," I said as we hurried down the hall, "I think it may have been the same one that passed the school during my class. The teachers and students all went to the window to see what was going on. Where is Lissa?"

Lissa poked her head through the living room doorway and smiled. "Welcome back," she said. "How did your class go?"

"Fine, but are you ready to run with me to the Internet cafe? I got a fax from the lawyer, and I need to call him. Let's go as soon as you are ready."

When Beverly saw me, she shrieked in pleasure. "Mommy," she exclaimed, "come look at the little people village we made around the tree."

Grace giggled. "It's funny; our little doll house is in the tree!"

I crouched to see their little houses made from twigs. "Oh," I exclaimed, "you even have a car!"

Emily nodded seriously. "Isaiah made it from a Jell-O box. Look, it even has a license plate."

Lissa tapped me on the shoulder. "I'm ready when you are," she said.

"Good," I said, standing to my feet. "Let's go, then. Hannah, we will be back as soon as possible. Do you think you could have supper ready by the time we get home?"

"I can hardly believe this is our last week of school. These streets are so familiar by now. Aren't you excited about going back to Belize?" Lissa asked, panting as we trotted down the cobblestone street.

I was silent and lost in thought, wondering what the lawyer's fax could mean. All it had said was, "Call me right away." My stomach felt uneasy, but I tried to ignore it.

"Mommy," Lissa said, touching my arm.

I turned quickly toward her. "Were you talking to me?" I asked.

"Yes," she said, trying to hide a grin. "I was wondering if you are eager to go back to Belize."

I dialed the number and held the phone to my ear, staring at the calendar, which read Tuesday, January 13, 1998. The phone rang once, then twice. I tried to brace myself for any important news he might have.

"I need to remember to ask him to send more money to the bank in Belize since we will be there next week," I said to myself.

Someone answered the phone. "Hello?"

"Yes, this is Kay Evans. I got your fax yesterday, and I'm calling in response to that."

"Kay, your in-laws have contacted me," my lawyer said tensely. "They told me they are aware of the money wire I sent to you when you first arrived in Belize. They also told me to let you know that they are on your trail. They said you should turn yourself in. I am required by law to relay this message to you from them. Kay, you need to stop all contact with me. I cannot help you anymore. If I continue to help you, it will make problems for me.

Forget the social security money. Use the other account now. Don't go back to Belize. I'm sure they are looking for you there. You need to relocate. That's all that I can say. Good-bye."

His words were brief and to the point. I heard his phone click. Slowly I hung up, stunned.

I went numbly through the motions of paying the bill for the call and walked slowly out the door. Lissa looked up from the bench where she was waiting, and, in a stupor, I sat down next to her.

"Well?" she asked quietly.

It was clear by my expression that something was really wrong. I stood up and said, "Let's go. He said we can't go back to Belize."

Lissa looked at me intently, uncomprehending.

"Lissa, I'm sorry, but he said we must not go back to Belize," I repeated. "Grandmom and Granddad traced the money wire to us after we first arrived in Belize, and so they know we were there. If we return, we could get caught."

Her eyes filled with tears. We had quickly grown to love the little church fellowship in Belize. To hear we could not return was shocking news. It would take awhile to let all this sink in. I replayed my lawyer's words over and over in my mind to be sure of every detail, wondering how this news would affect us.

"He was so tight-lipped that I wondered if his phone was tapped," I said. "I had some questions, but our conversation was over before I had a chance to ask them. Grandmom and Granddad obviously tracked us to Belize through the social security money. You know, Lissa, I have felt uneasy for a long time that the social security money could be a link to us. Back when we lived in Indiana, I even told the Lord that if He wanted to stop those funds, it would be fine with me. So, here it is actually happening."

The sky was growing darker as we hurried home. We pondered what we should do next. I knew God would provide for our needs, but it was unnerving to think how close on our trail my in-laws really were. *Lord God,* I prayed silently, *what will we do since we can't go back to Belize?*

My in-laws' previous threats had often frightened me. I would remember 1 Peter 3:14, *And be not afraid of their terror, neither be troubled.* After each threat, once the fear subsided, I became more solidly anchored in my hope in Jesus Christ.

The threats also taught me to cling to Galatians 5:1, *Stand fast therefore in the liberty wherewith Christ hath made us free, and be not entangled again with the yoke of bondage.* I knew I would rather continue living like a hunted animal in order to have the liberty to teach my children about the true freedom that comes from knowing Christ. I believed this to be far better than compromising and allowing my in-laws to "normalize" my children, bringing them into the bondage of this world's false freedom.

I reflected on our time of hiding in the U.S., how David and Sue Beth had frequently faced people at their front door—people with questions about me and about where we were. What a relief that we had never told them. I recalled how David had once called me with a message from my in-laws urging me to turn myself in. "Things might ease up for you if you would just come back and turn yourself in," they had said.

Another time David had relayed the district attorney's message to me, "If Kay would just turn herself in right away, the charges might be dropped and everything could go much easier for her." My response then was that I would pray about it and ask the Lord if I should change course.

Recalling this conversation from months ago, I remembered how God had given me the same familiar verse of Galatians 5:1. And the following day, Luke 17:31, 32 had jumped off the page at me, *And he that is in the field, let him likewise not return back. Remember Lot's wife.*

I felt God was making it very clear that I was not to turn back! He did not want me to give in to these endless threats. A tremendous peace comes when I know God is giving me direction from His Word. So with my mind made up, it was time to move on in faith.

By now we were nearly home.

"Lissa, this is almost funny!" I burst out. "Before we came to Antigua, I prayed about when to come and about how long we should be enrolled in school. Remember, I had decided on eight weeks? Now, here we are in our eighth week, and we just got this major news flash. While we are here in Guatemala, Grandmom and Granddad may already be in Belize looking for us. They could have gone to the bank or to the electric company and easily found our address, and then gone and quizzed our landlords. God moved us out of their way just in time."

Lissa whistled. "That sounds too close! Do you really think they might be in Belize hunting for us?"

I nodded.

Going into hiding is difficult because it involves leaving behind friends and loved ones. But God was exceedingly gracious to me because, next to Jesus Christ, my six children are my favorite companions. I would rather go through the joys and trials of life with my children than anyone else. Indeed, they are precious treasures whom the Lord has entrusted to me for a season.

It was awesome to think how God had protected us to this point. My family and I were so unworthy of His tender care. And even though I didn't know where we would go from this point, He had already given me evidence along our way that He had a plan. He was worthy of all my trust.

CHAPTER 12

Tests in Flexibility

Kay:

I emptied the drawer of clothes out on the bed and quickly stuffed them into the navy backpack in front of me. I could hear water splashing as Beverly, Grace, and Emily washed the dishes in the kitchen. Lissa called from the table where she was carefully loading our food into a cardboard box.

"Mom, Rogelio is supposed to get here in fifteen minutes."

I glanced at my watch, and saw that she was right. *It is almost four. Whew, we have got to hurry,* I thought to myself. We had been bustling around all day at top speed but still had a lot to do.

Hannah stepped into the bedroom with a broom in hand. "Mommy, I think Rogelio just got here. I heard a motor outside the door. Yep. There he is knocking. I'll get it."

I heard the metal door creaking and Hannah welcoming him in. "We will be ready in just a few minutes. I'm sorry we are not done yet."

He responded cheerfully with his heavily accented English, "Oh, don't worry. You are fine," he called out as he walked in. "Good afternoon!" he greeted each of us as he passed by the door and then stepped into the kitchen.

"Emily, I see you!" he teased, and I heard her giggle. When she had first met him, she had shyly hidden her face in my skirt, but he had slowly won her heart. He always greeted her with, "Emily, I see you!" Then he would extract a piece of candy from his pocket for her and each of the other children too. So now Emily and Rogelio were friends.

Rogelio sauntered over to the kitchen counter where Grace was drying dishes. Picking up a dish towel off the counter, he reached for a wet plate and started helping. I shook my head in amazement at his servant heart.

What a blessing that is. He and his family have already done so much for us! I thought.

As I finished packing in the bedroom, I heard laughter erupt from the kitchen. I smiled. "He is doubtless teasing the children," I said to myself.

"I am taking you to my brother Roberto's house," said Rogelio as we entered Chimaltenango. "They have an extra room where you and your family can stay."

I nodded, and asked, "Now, tell me about Roberto's family."

"Well," Rogelio began, "his wife is from the States, just like my wife Janet. Jean and Janet both came down to Guatemala as voluntary service workers many years ago. That is how Roberto and I met them. Roberto and Jean have two children. Their Lidia is seventeen, and Obed is . . . let me see . . . twelve, I believe. Here is their house now."

The truck pulled slowly up into the yard and parked near the back door. Rogelio hopped out and opened the tailgate so the girls could climb down. Isaiah and I crawled out of the cab and joined the girls who were already unloading our backpacks from the pickup bed.

Roberto came walking toward us from the barn. "Welcome!" he called heartily. Taking off his straw hat politely, he shook my hand.

Jean joined us, wiping her hands on her blue printed apron. "Welcome! Supper is almost ready. You-uns must be hungry!"

We had a wonderful supper with Roberto and Jean and their children. After we hauled buckets of water inside the house to wash the supper dishes, I excused myself to go talk to Rogelio and Janet. It was important that they know of the latest developments in our situation.

At my knock, they opened the door and graciously invited me in. After I was seated, I updated them about our big news. They listened attentively.

"I think you should call our bishop, William Bear," Rogelio said.

I called Brother William's home in Maryland, and he listened to every detail. He was deeply concerned for the safety of my family and wanted to help us in any way possible. He encouraged me to stay with Roberto and Jean until further notice. I was so grateful for their willingness to take us in during this time of uncertainty.

With one last wave, we watched the gray and white van disappear around the corner. "That van has a lot of memories for us, doesn't it?" I asked Hannah.

Hannah nodded. It was sad to watch it leave for Belize without us, but we knew this was best.

William Bear's son Phil and two other men from Belize had driven our van, loaded with our belongings, over to Guatemala when they learned we could not return to Belize. Just seeing some of the people who had done so much for us made my eyes misty. Here they were again, going out of their way to bless us.

I had decided it would be safer if the van returned to Belize rather than being kept in Guatemala, where it could help someone track us. I was certain we would learn to get around the way the common people did—by bus. Nonetheless, it still seemed strange to watch our van leave, knowing we would likely never see it again. However, I was sure this was the right thing to do and that this van had fulfilled its purpose in our lives.

I shivered as I piled twigs and newspaper into the *plancha,* a Guatemalan stove, which consists of an adobe or brick structure with an opening on one side and a sheet of metal on top. But it was more than a stove to me this morning, it was a personal enemy; daring me to try to conquer it.

Roberto's words rang in my ears. "If you could get the fire going first thing every morning, that would really help."

Because of amoebas, all the water in Guatemala had to be

boiled before it was drinkable. I remembered fondly the ease of drinking tap water in Belize, but that wasn't a helpful thought just now. Already large pots of water were sitting on the grating, ready to begin heating for the day's needs.

I must get the fire started! I thought in exasperation. I lit a piece of newspaper, but once again the little flame grew weaker and weaker until it snuffed out. I sighed in frustration. *I just don't have the touch! I had better get the hang of this.*

Again and again I tried, stuffing more and more newspaper into the *plancha,* only to watch it burn brightly for a minute or two and then extinguish without lighting the twigs. The room began filling with smoke, and my despair mounted.

Lidia came in with a pot of corn, ready to set on the *plancha.* "Do you need some help?" she asked when she saw only ashes in the *plancha.*

I set down the box of matches and sighed. "Yes, you will have to show me how to do this."

Lissa:

The fire hissed and crackled in the *plancha* as I quickly slipped my shoes on and grabbed my black sweater. I could hear Roberto already heading out to the barn to feed the chickens, and I knew the goat and the cow were impatiently waiting for me to milk them. Roberto's family was hardworking. And we had not been here long before we realized Roberto had plenty of work for all of us on his small farm.

Although the property was within the city limits, the farm was complete with chickens, rabbits, goats, a cow, and even a horse. And so we were enlisted among the work crew. I was delighted, since I had always wanted to live on a farm. This was my chance!

The cool morning air was crisp, and only the chickens disrupted the silence with their cackling. Out at the barn, I sat down on my low stool and pressed my forehead against the cow's flank, while the rich streams of warm milk flowed into the pink bucket.

Roberto passed with his hat full of fresh eggs. "Good morning!" he said.

I smiled at him over my shoulder and returned the greeting,

"Good morning! Do you want me to help take the animals out to the pasture, or do you just want the boys to do that?"

He stopped and scratched his head. "You can help," he said. "Maybe you can ask Grandfather if you can ride the mare out to the field." He laughed as my eyes lit up, and he added, "You like the horse?" I nodded and turned back to the cow, which restlessly stamped her hoof.

A large truck zoomed past, and the goat bleated, trying to run. Isaiah held her string tightly to keep her from darting into the road. Crossing the Pan American Highway with the farm animals was always a challenge, but it had to be done in order for them to graze in the fields surrounding the town.

The cow lowed, and Roberto held her tightly, looking intently at the road and waiting for the right moment. When he signaled, we would all dart across the highway.

I was so glad I didn't have to lead the cow across. The one time I did, the cow nearly pulled me into the highway.

Roberto had wisely advised me, "If the cow ever starts running into the road, just let go of the rope."

I sat high on the horse, with the reins in my hands. When Roberto shouted, "Okay, let's cross!" I nudged her into a trot. Once we were successfully on the other side, the walk to the fields was rather relaxed. We greeted other farmers who were also leading their animals to pasture. But the brown mare didn't want to saunter along leisurely, and she began picking up speed. Her hoofs pounded the hard-packed dirt road as we galloped past all the other farmers, leaving them in the dust.

I could hear the motor running long before Lidia and I arrived at the *molino*. Even down the street I could hear the "chug chug chug" of the mill.

"It sounds like it will fly into a million pieces any minute!" I exclaimed.

Lidia only laughed. "Oh, it always sounds like that," she assured me, as we stepped into the doorway.

Several other ladies were already in line to put their corn through the mill. Making tortillas was a daily routine for most Guatemalan women, and it was an intriguing process.

All morning the corn had boiled away on the *plancha* until it was soft. Once Lidia and I returned from taking the animals to the fields, she had rinsed the cooked corn in water and then brought it here to be milled. When Lidia's turn came, she dumped her bowl of corn into the top of the mill and skillfully gathered it bit by bit as it came through the bottom of the mill, ground into a sticky dough—what everyone here called *masa*.

Lidia handed the mill owner twenty-five *centavos*, and then we hurried back out onto the street.

As we made our way home, I asked, "Lidia, why is the charge for the mill just twenty-five *centavos? Does she make any profit from it?"

Lidia tucked a white cloth over the *masa* and shrugged, "I guess so."

Setting the *masa* down on the table, Lidia rinsed her hands at the *pila.* "Do you want to help me *tortillar* today?" she asked.

I smiled and shrugged. "Sure!"

"Good, the fire is just right in the *plancha,*" Lidia decided as she looked at the flame. She dipped her fingertips in a bowl of water and grabbed a wad of *masa* no larger than a golf ball, and began to *tortillar.*

I watched with keen interest as she patted and rotated the tortilla quickly forming in her hands. Laying it out on the hot grill of the *plancha,* she started another one, periodically stopping to flip the cooking tortillas. On the side of the *plancha* a stack of tortillas grew, hot and steaming. When we first came to Guatemala, my family did not care for them, but soon we grew very fond of them, especially when they were hot off the *plancha.*

———————————

Kay:

I dipped out half of the soup into a clay bowl and set it on Jean's table. I could hear her coughing in her bedroom. She had a nasty cough that she seemed unable to shake.

"Are you all right?" I called.

"Yes . . . I'm fine," she responded feebly after a pause. "I'll be there in just a minute."

I turned off the burner under the soup. "Your lunch is ready," I said, "and I'm going to take our lunch over to our side. Will the wash on the line be dry enough to take off after lunch?"

Jean's thin form appeared in the doorway, and she gripped the wall as she looked at me.

She looks so frail, I thought to myself. Her telltale cough was evidence of a mysterious lung disease. She was extra sensitive to dust, molds, and many foods, making her health a continual battle.

"Yes," she said, and then she coughed again, reaching for her handkerchief. "The wash should be ready to come in as soon as we are done eating."

I carried the steaming pot of *caldo* (soup) into our small section of the house. We had one big bedroom and a smaller room off to the side where the *plancha* stood. It was in this room that we ate our meals. I set down the soup and called out, "Children, it is time to eat."

The first ten days we had lived here, we ate all our meals with Roberto's family. But I had begun to feel that both families needed some privacy. I enjoyed having my children all to myself sometimes, and I figured they felt the same way but were just too polite to say so.

Jean did not seem at all offended when I proposed the idea of splitting up for mealtimes. Maybe she had wondered how to manage getting some family privacy too. So now my family ate in our rented portion of the house, while Roberto's ate in their side.

Yet we combined efforts on meal preparations and eventually established a routine of taking turns preparing meals. This system met the needs of both families without overloading anyone.

"Yummm . . . We are having *caldo!*" Grace exclaimed.

"Yes, and we have fresh tortillas to go with it," I added, setting a stack of hot tortillas wrapped in a bright red cloth on the small wooden table. We had all grown to love *caldo,* which was a thin soup with large chunks of vegetables and either chicken or beef.

Isaiah peered into the pot. "Good," he said, "I don't see any chicken feet!"

"I made it, so it doesn't have the feet in it, or heads!" I assured him.

Everyone laughed, as we had been very startled the first time we were served *caldo* to see feet floating among the veggies. And we knew some Guatemalans even included the head.

"The feet really aren't too bad," Hannah admitted, "but I am glad this pot doesn't have any."

The damp towels flapped in the breeze, looking bright and clean on the line. I picked up another towel, shook it out, and then clipped it up to dry.

"Hmmm. What does that clothespin say?" I asked. Leaning closer I could read a name, apparently someone Jean knew. She had written names on her clothespins as prayer reminders for herself. *What a good way to be reminded to pray for people,* I mused. I had learned a lot from living at Jean and Roberto Pichiya's.

During the dry season, clouds of dust blew in from the street, so Jean always hung her clothes inside out, so that the outside of the garment would be clean. And I had learned many ways to save money, as Jean was extremely frugal.

I had to smile. Not all the lessons had been easy to learn. Like the time there was opossum meat for lunch. That was almost more than I could stomach! But living here in Guatemala was teaching me more than that. God was using this time to show me that I had to wait on Him for our future.

I wonder how long we will be here in Chimaltenango, I thought to myself as I pinned up a yellow sheet. *Even though I really have no idea where we will go from here, I'm sure God will make it clear when it's time. He has always directed us in the past.*

Lit by one bare lightbulb, the front porch bustled with activity. The tile floor was piled high with black-bean pods, now dry and curling. Obed held a stick high over his head and brought it down with a smack onto the pile. Isaiah and Beverly helped with their own sticks, and they soon established a rhythm. After all the rigorous pounding, the pods cracked open and shiny black beans fell to the tile. Jean and I sat nearby, hulling more beans and laughing at the children's enthusiasm.

Jean coughed and continued talking. "But in order to maintain a dual residency, our family moves between the U.S. and Guatemala every few years. It is a challenge, you know, but we have to do it since Roberto is Guatemalan and I am American."

A troubled expression crossed her face, and she turned to me. "But since Roberto was in that car accident, we don't think he will be able to fly up with the children and me when we go to Pennsylvania next week. It is all those court hearings, you know . . . I guess he will just have to stay here until the hearings are over and then fly up to join us."

I nodded and wondered silently how this news would affect our stay in their home. Absentmindedly, I watched as Hannah swept the loose beans into a pile. At the supper table that night, I mentioned the problem to my children.

"I wonder if we should find another place to live before Jean and the children go. Living in one side of this house while Roberto lives alone in the other side would not be a good witness to the neighbors."

Sprinkling salt over the beans in her bowl, Hannah's eyes met mine. "Oh, I agree totally, Mommy. If they leave, I think we should go somewhere else too," she said.

Later that night after the dishes were dried and put away, I stole away to the front porch for a few minutes and peered up at the stars. Leaning against the cool block wall, I prayed silently, *Lord, please show me where we are to go now. Open the way in front of me.*

The thin bus helper turned around and shouted, "Novillero! Novillero!"

I struggled to my feet and reached for the backpack tightly wedged in the rack above my head. "Come on, children, this is it."

Hannah led the way toward the door where the impatient helper waited.

"Hurry!" he urged us.

Getting off a crowded bus rapidly was always a challenge for my family of seven, especially when the center aisle was reduced to a few inches. The people sitting on the edges of the seats stood up so that we could pass.

"Gracias," I mumbled time and time again. Finally we were all out on the street leading into the small town of Novillero, and the bus chugged away up the hill.

"It is really cool up here," Lissa said, shivering. "How high is this village anyway?"

I reached down to hold little Emily's hand. "Let's see; I think Kim said Novillero is 9,000 feet in elevation," I said. "And I believe it, with all the steep and winding roads we took in order to get here."

We slowly made our way up the cobblestone street leading into town. The road divided and we turned right, heading toward the mission house. Novillero was a picturesque little town, nestled between green mountains. A little brook gurgled through on its way to the fields.

"Mommy, who are we going to see?" Emily asked, looking up at me with her big blue eyes.

"Remember the lady we met at Dorcas and Ian's wedding?" I asked.

She looked doubtful and shook her head. "No."

"Well," I said, "she introduced herself as Kim Martin and invited us to come visit their family in the mountains. Her husband Vernon is the pastor of the Mennonite church here. She was really friendly and seemed eager for us to drop by sometime. Don't you remember her little girls: Kendra Lily, Melisa, and Tiana? They said you could jump on their trampoline when you come to their house."

"Oh, yeah. May I, Mommy?"

"Well, of course, honey." Turning to the other children, I continued, "She said this town is not too far from that beautiful Lake Atitlán. Remember? That's the lake Jean and the children took us to where they treated us to a boat ride."

"Oh, yeah, and the chocolate bananas Obed bought us that day were so yummy," Beverly remembered fondly.

"They sure were," Grace agreed.

Emily smiled at the memory and nodded happily.

"Anyway, Kim said that Novillero has a rental house available right now, and that we should come check it out, so here we are."

We spent an enjoyable day with the Vernon Martin family, and even told them our story. I felt so relaxed being able to tell Kim who we really were and why we were in Guatemala. Ever since we had crossed the border leaving the United States, we began introducing ourselves by our true names. Although sharing our history with people still made for a strange story, I was much more comfortable just being up front like this. Kim was completely unpretentious and made us feel right at home from the start.

After we had visited for several hours, she spoke up, "Hey, are you ready to go see the rental house? I think you might be interested."

I nodded. "Sure! We do need to find a housing option quickly as Jean and the children are leaving in just a few days."

Kim grabbed a light-blue sweater and opened the front door. "The house is close by, so we can just walk."

We followed Kim out the door, her children eagerly joining us. She led the way down a narrow dirt trail, speaking to me over her shoulder. "It would be so exciting if y'all moved here. It would actually be an answer to prayer. I have been wanting a family to move in here for years."

An old, shriveled-looking woman balancing a basket of fruit on her head approached us on the path. She squeaked a question to Kim, who shook her head.

"The woman asked Kim if she wanted to buy any bananas," Isaiah whispered.

I nodded. "I see."

"No," said Kim, "but will you be having any cantaloupes soon?"

The lady shook her head and quietly made her way past us.

Farther down the trail, Kim pointed to a small adobe house. "This house belongs to the witch doctor. Notice the small image on the ridge of the roof."

I examined it curiously, thinking, *I have only read about witch doctors, and one actually lives here!*

The trail turned sharply up the hill to the Pan American

Highway, which we would need to cross to reach the rental house.

Glancing in both directions for traffic, Kim said, "I just hate this highway. It scares me to have children crossing it all the time. A native boy was killed right here not long ago."

I took a step backward as a big truck zoomed past, and my blood ran cold. *I guess if we like the house, my own children will need to cross this highway routinely,* I thought.

Proceeding cautiously, we climbed the narrow, dirt trail that wound its way up the hillside through cornfields. Along the trail were three adobe houses.

As we reached the first house, Kim stepped across a trickle of muddy water and turned to face me. "The little boy who was killed on the highway lived right here," she said quietly. "His daddy is a drunk, but the mother tries to make a decent living for the family as best she can. The poor woman has a tough life."

I peered into the door as we passed and smiled at a little boy staring innocently back at me.

The second house on the spindly trail looked just as poor and humble as the first. Kim shook her head sadly and said, "Margarita, the woman here, was at one time a member of the Mennonite church, but not anymore. She has seven children from various relationships."

How sad, I thought, remembering the woman at the well in the New Testament.

Margarita's little children scurried here and there in the yard, dirty and almost naked, as though their mother were too preoc-cupied to care for them.

Just before we reached the house at the end of the trail, we passed one more house. Kim assured me this family was the most stable of the three. "They seem to live together happily, except that the father has to work during the week in Guatemala City."

"Isn't that more than three hours away from here?" I asked.

"Yes," she replied. "But, you know, it's very common around here for the men to work there and just commute to their homes on weekends," Kim explained.

This house was also adobe, with dirt floors and a tiny outhouse next to their cornfield. We had never lived in a neighborhood like this.

"Well, here we are!" Kim cried exultantly as she stepped up onto the tiled porch of the vacant house.

I stopped to catch my breath and to examine the small, basic structure. The concrete block house overlooked the Pan American Highway and the little town of Novillero.

This house looks small, I thought.

Looking around the valley with lush, green mountains in every direction, I couldn't imagine a better view. The breeze was fragrant with fresh pines gently swaying around us. It was a refreshing contrast to the dusty city life with choking bus exhaust back in Chimaltenango.

Kim explained that this flat-roofed house had an unusual layout. "It is actually two identical apartments, sharing a center wall. You see, the man who built it is from Canada, and he had hoped this house could be used for voluntary service workers who would come to help the missionaries."

Each side was identical, with two barred windows and a metal door. The two apartments shared a nicely tiled front porch, and at one end stood a closet-sized outhouse.

"I am sure," Kim said, "that you could rent both sides to accommodate your family."

The two apartments were small, measuring only 200 square feet each. I knew it would definitely require some creativity to figure out how to squeeze all of us into such a tiny place, but I knew it could work somehow.

"After all, it would be good missionary training," I said to myself, chuckling.

There was no running water in the house. The only water came from the small spigot at the coffee-colored *pila* on the porch. We had grown accustomed to using a *pila* since our earliest days in Guatemala and had come to like it. A *pila* is a huge and deep concrete sink where native Guatemalans wash their clothes, dishes, hair, and young children.

Kim turned on the faucet. "There is one problem," she said bluntly. "Vernon has worked time and time again to try to get the water to come out clear from this *pila* up here, but it just won't. No matter what he does, the water up here is always murky, for some strange reason."

I looked at the light-brown water trickling down and shrugged. "It would be an inconvenience, but one that we could live with, I suppose."

Once back in Chimaltenango, my immediate prayer focus was to determine what to do about moving. I soon felt the Lord directing that we should move right away to that little house with the murky water and the lovely view of Novillero. I called Kim and told her my decision, and she was delighted.

"But," she said, "we are just about ready to head off to the States for furlough and won't be here when you arrive. There will be some other missionaries taking our place, though, who can help you move in."

Rogelio and Janet came over to discuss the matter with us. Sitting in our little portion of the house, we discussed the best way to approach the move. They agreed the move to Novillero was a good idea.

"Would it be very hard to rent a pickup to take our belongings up to Novillero?" I asked.

Rogelio leaned back in his chair, clasping his hands behind his head. "Sister Kay," he said, "don't worry about the details. I'll take care of getting a pickup. I know someone who can do it."

And so our plans to move from Chimaltenango to Novillero began to finalize.

My alarm clock that morning was an avocado landing like a bomb on the roof at 5:55 a.m. I should have been used to this startling sound by then, since avocado trees grew tall and dangled their edible grenades just above our tin roof. The noise still got me quickly to my feet in a groggy state. And it was crucial to get up and hit the ground running, because, after all, today, May 29, 1998, was moving day.

We were all excited for this day to arrive. Hannah and Lissa cleaned our two rooms while the other children and I packed and put everything by the door to be ready when the truck arrived.

Jean and the children had already flown to the States, and so

Roberto came over and said good-bye, placing twenty pounds of black beans on the table as a farewell token.

I thanked him for his kindness and for opening his home to our family these past four months.

It didn't take long for a little Guatemalan man to load our things tightly into the bed of his small pickup, which had been hired to be our moving truck.

Isaiah, Emily, the puppy we had bought this morning, and I all crammed into the cab of the truck along with the driver.

Novillero was only an hour-and-a-half drive up the road. Hannah hailed a passing bus, and soon she and the other children were also headed up the Pan American Highway to join us.

I craned my neck to look out the window and up into the dark sky. Dreary clouds were rolling in, and it looked as though a storm was on its way.

Lord, please hold back the rain a little longer so that we can get our things under cover. I could just picture scurrying up the trail with Isaiah and Emily, our arms loaded, trying to beat the storm. The puppy in the small cardboard box whined, and I looked down at her.

"Look, Mommy, she is shivering!" Emily said sympathetically as she reached into the box and stroked the puppy's soft fur.

I nodded. "We are almost to Novillero. Maybe when we get there we can warm her up."

Isaiah, wedged against the driver, chatted easily with him. I was pleased that he was so comfortable in Spanish, but I wished I knew what they were saying.

At last the village of Novillero appeared in front of us. The dark sky and clouds looked as though they would let loose any minute. I directed the driver to the humble-looking Mennonite church building where Kim had told me we could unload our stuff. Pulling my wallet from my purse, I counted out the amount of money Rogelio had said would be a reasonable payment.

I handed the folded bills to the driver, but he smiled and shook his head. He was refusing my money! And I couldn't imagine why.

He explained to Isaiah that Rogelio had already paid him for helping me today and there was no need for me to pay him too.

Puzzled, I thought back to my earlier conversation with Rogelio. *Did he want me to think I would be footing this bill when he planned to take care of it all along?* I shook my head. Whatever the case, Rogelio and Janet had taken care of us again. I felt tremendously indebted to them. When I tried to recount all of their kindnesses to us over the past six months since we had arrived in Guatemala, I was overwhelmed with gratitude. They had certainly done everything they could possibly think of to bless the fatherless and the widow. I could only pray that the Lord would richly repay them.

Sprinkles of rain began to fall from the sky as we unloaded our things into the classroom. Having a roof over our pile of belongings was a comfort. Three young Mennonite men showed up and introduced themselves. One was the substitute missionary, Joseph Lehman, and the other two men were here to visit the Lehmans.

They set right to work and began loading some of our things into another pickup and drove it over to the trail leading to our house. We all began carrying loads up the little dirt trail to our home. Vernon had instructed them to haul the schoolteacher's refrigerator and stove up the trail to our house, since she was in the States for the summer. The Martins planned to return from furlough with a stove and refrigerator for us.

As I watched the men carefully haul the bulky stove up the narrow trail, my heart was touched knowing that people who did not even know us were so willing to be a blessing to us. Even a fourteen-year-old native girl eagerly ran to the truck and began carrying loads up the trail for us. Her name was Gloria Veronica, and we soon realized she lived in the house closest to our own. She was glad we were moving in and chatted freely, although I understood only a phrase here and there.

Emily sat on the porch, happily playing with the puppy and keeping it out of our way. She was content with her little assignment. I stepped up onto the porch with the last armful of things and panted, "We will certainly get our exercise living in this place!"

———————————————

A young, red-haired woman greeted me at the Martins' door. "Hi, I'm Charlotte Lehman, Joseph's wife," she said with a smile. "I guess you heard that we are standing in for Vernon and Kim while they are on furlough. Just c'mon in. Supper's about ready."

Two other couples were seated on the couch in the Martins' living room. "Oh, it's so nice to meet you. And thank you for having us over for supper even when you have company already, Charlotte."

"Oh, that's no problem," she assured me kindly.

Soon my children and I were seated around the long table, getting acquainted with these dear people who had all sacrificed part of their day of visiting with each other in order to help us move in and show us hospitality.

Finally, it was time for my family to make our way to our new home and bed. Before setting out, we filled a few containers with water from their kitchen.

To our unaccustomed feet the trail was quite rough, and I found it challenging, especially in the dark. As we walked single file past the witch doctor's house, I felt extra jumpy.

This is a creepy place to find yourself at night, I thought to myself.

Hannah tried carefully not to spill the valuable water she was carrying, and Isaiah walked ahead of her warning her of bumps or dips in the trail.

"Watch out, there's a big rock right here."

We continued across the Pan American Highway and up the little dirt path, groping in the dark all the way. On one side was a cornfield, level with the trail. The other side dropped several feet to a much lower cornfield. We felt our way blindly along the trail as it twisted and turned between the fields and around each little house along the hillside. Eventually we arrived at our own doorstep.

"We will definitely need to invest in some flashlights if we are going to routinely climb this unpredictable trail in the dark," I said.

CHAPTER 13

Our Home at the End of the Mud Trail

Kay:

Drawing the warm blanket tightly around my shoulders, I stepped out onto the chilly porch. Shivering in the darkness, I peered down the trail but saw nothing.

"Brrr. It's cold this morning!" I said.

I padded my way to the end of the porch and stepped onto the damp slope leading to the back of our house. The grass was heavy with dew and glimmered in the beam of my flashlight. Carefully, I walked across the wobbly plank that led onto our flat roof and peered out over the sleeping village of Novillero.

"Am I the only one up?" I asked myself, as I yawned and gazed at the little town. In the distance a rooster crowed a feeble cock-a-doodle-doo in answer to my question. The roosters in Guatemala apparently don't realize they are supposed to crow only in the morning, but rather, they crow at any hour—day or night.

I settled down onto the cold concrete and leaned against the chimney, trying to get comfortable. As I gazed up into the night sky, the stars glittered and twinkled back at me. This rooftop sanctuary inspired praise to my Maker. It was also my favorite spot to talk to God about our unpredictable life and to ask for His guidance.

A cold breeze licked my face, and I drew the blanket closer around my chin. I loved spending the early hours up here, worshiping and watching the sky grow lighter as the sun crept above the horizon and chased away the darkness.

The morning calm was shattered by a long, blaring honk as a bus rounded the corner and announced its arrival in Novillero. Neighbors hailed it and hopped aboard.

Oh, yeah, today is market day. I almost forgot. I'm glad we don't need to go to Solola today to buy produce, I thought.

I pictured the bustling market where Solola women with colorful blouses and long, thickly woven skirts would have their wares spread out attractively in front of them. We enjoyed riding the bus to market; it made us feel like we had more in common with our Indian neighbors.

I smiled as I thought about our "primitive" life here compared to our life back in the States. My eyes drifted to the houses dotting the hillside around me. Except for ours, the homes on this side of the highway were built of adobe. Their roofs were simply thin sheets of corrugated metal, and their floors were usually of hard-packed dirt.

In our small dwelling, we were learning to manage our space very creatively. My room served not only as my bedroom but also as the dining room, living room, and schoolroom. During the daytime my bed became the family couch.

There was no indoor bathroom either, but our setup was much more advanced than the natives'. We had to go only to the end of our porch to reach a nicely enclosed and roofed bathroom. The natives had to step out into the cornfield or into a cornstalk-walled "outhouse." Our toilet even flushed when we dumped a bucket of water into it.

Bathing was a lot of work. Kettles of our murky water were heated until they steamed and then carried to the tiny room at the end of the porch, where a big metal tub awaited. After the hot water was poured in, enough cold water was added until it was the right temperature. We bathed just like our grandparents did when they were children!

———————

Carefully I pushed fifteen white candles into the light blue frosting on the cake and stood back admiringly.

"It is so pretty, Mommy! I like the little sugar flowers you put on there," Beverly commented as she tilted her head sideways and studied the cake.

Summer is a season of celebration in our family, for all the females' birthdays fall within a two-month span. This was the first birthday cake of the season, and it looked cheery with its pastel icing.

A small form appeared in the doorway, and I looked up to see our next-door neighbor Inez. I hurried toward her and invited her in.

"Good morning," she said, "could you keep this piece of meat in your freezer for me?"

I smiled and nodded, taking the lumpy pink bag from her and opening the freezer door. Inez noticed the cake on the table and stepped closer for a better look.

"Oh, how nice! I have never seen such a lovely cake! I wish we could have a cake for Gloria Veronica's fifteenth birthday next week. But we don't have an oven," she said with a sigh.

My eyes met Hannah's. I felt we should offer to make a cake for her. In fact, it sounded like fun.

The expression on Hannah's face agreed, as did Lissa's. We had wished for more opportunities to participate in the work of the missionaries here. Here was our chance!

Clearing my throat, I voiced my feelings to my daughters, who conveyed the message to our friend.

"Let us bake a birthday cake for your daughter!" they said.

Inez looked doubtful and shook her head. "Oh, no!" she said. "That would be asking way too much!"

But we were adamant. "Yes, we would love to do this for you," we insisted.

She finally gave in, but confessed, "Well, actually I'm planning to have a big party for my daughter. When a girl turns fifteen here, it means she is becoming a woman. It is cause for a great celebration," she explained. "We will likely need three cakes!"

"Oh!" we said, startled. We had not figured on more than one.

After a brief silence, I glanced at Hannah and Lissa. "Tell her we can do it," I said, smiling weakly. *It will be a little more work than we had expected, but it will be all right,* I thought.

"After all, it will be a way to serve Jesus," I assured my family after she left.

Only days later Inez, looking sheepish, climbed the steps to our porch. Years before, a vehicle had sideswiped her on the highway, and ever since, one arm was almost nonfunctional, and she coddled it close to her side while her hand hung limply.

"Would you mind making two more cakes than we had decided on the other day?" she asked nervously. "I have been counting the guests, and there are more than I had realized." She rolled her eyes as though bewildered and gestured with her good arm.

We agreed to make two more cakes, but as soon as she hurried back down the trail, I began searching through my cookbooks for a recipe suitable to serve such a crowd.

Then a few days before the party, it happened again. I could tell Inez was embarrassed as she walked hesitantly toward our door. We all feared what she might say.

"I don't know how to say this," she began apologetically with downcast eyes, "but the invitation list is getting longer and longer. Can you possibly manage to bake a total of seven cakes for the party? I'm absolutely sure seven cakes will take care of it."

Smiling, we assured her we could. By now we were beginning to see the humor of the situation.

The day of the party began early for us and many of Inez's friends. Around five in the morning, when everything was still dark and quiet, we quickly dressed and silently made our way down to Inez's house, joining the hushed group gathering in the yard. Once everyone arrived, the leader broke the silence by strumming his guitar. The little crowd burst into song, and the yard rang with hearty congratulations for Gloria Veronica.

Gloria Veronica was still in bed, of course, but soon we noticed light shining through the cracks in their wooden door. Finally the door creaked open as Irene, Gloria Veronica's older sister, peered out with a sleepy smile.

Stepping back, she held open the door as we filed into the room and sang around the bed where Gloria Veronica lay, hiding under her blanket. Finally, she crawled out, feigning surprise, but obviously willing to play the role of the birthday girl. After nearly an hour of singing and munching on the sweet rolls Inez handed out, everyone wished her a very happy birthday and left.

Hurrying up the dirt path, we got right into our big project for the day.

"Seven cakes!" I exclaimed, laughing. I got down our biggest mixing bowl and set it on the table. There was a job for everyone, whether it was measuring, mixing, washing dishes, or frosting the cakes; each of us would be employed today.

Lunchtime came and went. Emily tugged on my skirt. "Mommy, I'm hungry!"

I stood up, wiping flour from my hands onto my apron. "Let's see, I think we have some crackers on the shelf. Oh, and there's some cheese in the refrigerator. That will just have to do until the party. Inez said there will be plenty of fried chicken. If nothing else, there should be plenty of cake for everyone," I said, chuckling.

Finally the last cake was out of the oven and nicely frosted. With the house smelling like a bakery, we stood around the table loaded with seven lovely cakes, admiring our work. I was relieved when they were all gingerly carried down the trail and rested safely on Inez's table.

The party turned out to be a huge success. Unfortunately, it almost got us into an unwanted business of baking cakes for the village's many happy occasions. We tried just saying "no," but discovered that answer puzzled our Indian friends who well knew we had an oven. To them it didn't seem right for us to have such a nice stove and not be willing to use it to bake cakes for sale.

To tell our neighbors we were too busy did not seem reasonable either. We had no cornfield to tend. I did not send my children off to school. We even had a maid come help us with our chores. No, they would not believe we were too busy to bake cakes for them.

Finally, God came to our rescue. Once the Martin family brought us our very own oven from the States, and we returned the schoolteacher's oven to her, we discovered ours had a problem. It could bake a cake now and then, if we watched it carefully and were willing to get down on our hands and knees and babysit the flame that went up and down without notice. But the procedure was too unpredictable and frustrating to think of supplying cakes for all the customers we would surely have.

Vernon Martin, a skillful handyman, showed up with his bag of tools time and again, but the stubborn oven refused to be repaired. Finally, I realized this was God's wonderful solution to our unwanted cake business. This was the first time I remember feeling genuinely grateful for a handicapped oven!

Now, when neighbors showed up at the door, hoping for a cake for that special someone, we pointed at our new oven and shrugged our shoulders. "This one doesn't work right. It doesn't know how to bake," we explained.

Our neighbors shook their heads, disappointed that they would have to do without the tasty treats they had recently learned to enjoy. I sighed in relief as they left.

"God," I prayed. "I know You did not bring us to this remote place in this unique season of our lives just to make us the village bakers. I believe You wanted us to have a quiet time where You could teach us some valuable lessons away from all the hustle and bustle in the States. Our dear Indian neighbors have no idea of the strange circumstances of our being in hiding. I cannot blame them for hoping we would sell cakes. But thank You, Lord, for allowing our oven to break and delivering us from this problem."

Hannah:

Leisurely I scanned the valley from our front porch, my hands submerged in a big bowl of warm, soapy dishwater. Our dog, Tammy, whined at me from the post where she was chained. She had grown from a cute little German Shepherd puppy into a big, unruly dog.

"Now don't look at me like that, Tammy," I chided, "you deserve to be chained up if all you do is tear through the neighbors' cornfields and break the young plants. And who knows how many mornings we found you on this porch, shredding to pieces the treasures you stole from our neighbors during the night!"

It was embarrassing to be considered "missionaries" and have such a wicked dog. Just last week Tammy had killed a neighbor's chicken just for sport and didn't even bother to eat it. We soundly spanked her, paid for the loss, and then followed Kim's advice to prevent such a crime from happening again.

Isaiah dutifully tied the dead bird to Tammy's neck so that she had to live with the smell of the decomposing bird until it fell off. But the pun-ishment had proved almost more terrible for us than for her. We, too, had to observe the deteriorating chicken dangling from Tammy's neck while it gave off a pungent, nauseating stench. Believe me, it was a foul, fowl odor! We were all glad when that lesson was over.

As I set a dripping plate on the dish rack, I looked down at her and scolded, "Shame on you."

The lively Central American song started up loudly, booming with a monotonous rhythm.

Oh, dear, I thought, *here comes the music again, and there goes the beautiful quietness of the morning.*

We always knew when our neighbors got up, because soon there-after the ground seemed to vibrate with music. They liked playing their radios loudly enough for the whole hillside to enjoy the music with them.

That was very gracious, except we didn't exactly share the same tastes in music. Each melody managed to land on one final, off-key note. At first we thought it was a mistake, but then we noticed that the majority of songs on the radio ended that way.

Isaiah came out the door with another stack of dishes for me. "Listen, it is that strange one again!" He mouthed the words with the song dra-matically and then rolled his eyes in mockery.

"I know. I wish they wouldn't play it."

We had unintentionally learned many of the songs on the radio, sim-ply because they were played all day long, over and over. We had not grown up listening to the radio, and it wasn't our desire to start now either. Yet, here we were, on the mission field, growing increasingly familiar with all the popular tunes. It was almost comical. We didn't know what else to do except trust that God would protect us from any lasting effects.

Tammy's ears perked up, and she jumped to her feet, barking. I looked toward the trail, where the little neighbor children, Vilma and Pedrito, stood timidly. Vilma's black disheveled hair hung loosely over her shoulders. We had given her the dress she was wearing, but now it was dirty and tattered. In her outstretched hands was a small metal plate piled high with steaming *tamalitos.*

"We just wanted to bring you a little something," her small voice quavered. They were scared of Tammy.

"Oh, don't worry; the dog is chained," I assured them.

The two children crept up the steps, eyeing Tammy warily. I accepted the warm plate.

"Just a moment and I'll be back," I said, smiling into their innocent faces before darting inside. I emptied what they had brought us into another bowl, grabbed a handful of candy, and dumped it into their plate. As I stepped out onto the porch, the children's brown eyes gleamed as they stared wide-eyed at the colorful candy.

"Gracias," Vilma murmured, and they quickly retraced their steps off the porch.

As soon as their little brown feet touched the dusty trail, they took off running, eager to show their mother Margarita their treasure.

Kay:

The straps on my heavy backpack cut into my shoulders, and the ten pounds of potatoes pressed into my back. Each of the children was carrying some kind of bag filled with produce we had carefully selected and bartered for at market.

"Isn't it funny how we shop now that we live in Guatemala?" I said to Lissa who was hurrying up the trail ahead of me, cradling a watermelon. "The way we decide whether or not to buy a watermelon is to ask ourselves if we are willing to carry one home!"

She nodded. "Yeah, I never realized how heavy produce really was until we had to physically carry it!"

We were still smiling about it when we reached the top of the trail and wearily climbed the steps up onto the porch. Suddenly, we noticed an Indian woman nervously waiting for us in the yard. Staring at her feet, she motioned toward the line of trees that framed our yard.

". . . and the tree fell on your electric line. I am so sorry," she said. "We already sent for the repairman to come." She pointed in the direction of the accident.

Sure enough, there lay a tall tree, flat across the electric line.

I stared at it for a moment in disbelief, a wave of irritation rising within me. They had chopped a nice tall tree very close to our house; a tree I assumed was ours.

Did she purposely time cutting our tree down to coincide with our trip to market? To my shame, I found myself judging her. *Sometimes it's a blessing not to know much of the language,* I thought in frustration. I know it is moments like these that determine what the villagers think of us Christians.

Oh, Lord, help me to pass the tests You send my way, I prayed, as I looked into her troubled face and managed a weak smile. "Oh, it's all right," I assured her before easing my heavy backpack down onto the gray tile.

I knew our Indian friends depended on their *plancha* more than we did ours because it was the only way to cook their food. They routinely combed the mountainsides looking for firewood. Picking up bundles of small tree limbs, they carried them home in neat bunches, balanced on their heads or tied to their backs. That was work for the women and children.

We used our *plancha* only when we wanted to heat up the house, but our neighbors needed to have it going all the time. Some neighbors occasionally ordered a truckload of firewood to be dumped by the path near the highway. Others were too poor to purchase wood. In desperation, they sometimes chopped down trees in places where they should have first asked permission.

This experience provided an opportunity to practice the character of Jesus. I was disappointed in myself, because I knew that, at least in my heart, I had failed this time. *Lord, please teach me to love people unconditionally.*

The washing machine chugged systematically on the porch. Irene bent over the *pila,* faithfully scrubbing a stain out of Isaiah's jeans. She looked up at me with her dark brown eyes and smiled, using the back of her wet hand to brush a strand of dark hair out of her face. She was so helpful to our family.

We had not lived very long in Novillero until I discovered I simply could not school my children, cook our meals, and stay on top of the cleaning and laundry. Eventually I had asked our next-door neighbor Inez if her oldest daughter Irene could come to our house several days a week to help us out.

We enjoyed having her; she was a quiet, very hard worker. She was also very patient when we flipped through our Spanish dictionary to find the word for "mop" or "sweep" or "clothesline" and other terms we had yet to learn.

During their furlough, Vernon and Kim had purchased a washing machine for us, so we no longer spent hours at the *pila* scrubbing our clothes. Irene quickly learned how to run the washing machine, even though she had never used one before. We did not have water hooked up to the machine, so for every washload she filled buckets of water and dumped them into the washing machine. It was rather primitive to us, but quite advanced for her.

Experience soon taught us it was common for the electricity to go off unexpectedly. If it happened when Irene was doing the laundry, she finished out the load in the *pila,* the way she did her own laundry.

Lissa lit a match and held it to the burner, waiting for it to light. *Click, click, click,* but the burner refused to catch.

"Mommy," she wailed, "I think the propane tank is empty. The burner won't light."

She bent over the small tank and picked it up. "The tank doesn't weigh much; I think it's out."

I sighed and got up from the table where I had been explaining a math lesson to Beverly. Joining Lissa at the stove, I sniffed. "Well, I can smell propane, but that is not unusual. You are right; the tank seems empty."

I tipped the gray tank and set it back up with a clang. "Where is Isaiah? He and I will have to run down to the blue *tienda* to exchange it for a full one. I knew it would run out sometime, and I guess today is the day!"

Lissa nodded and dipped her finger into the cold water in the pot on the stove. "I guess we get to wash dishes with cold water this morning."

Isaiah shouldered the empty tank and headed down the dirt

trail. I followed and watched his feet going quickly, one after the other, ahead of me.

"Hey, son, remember I'm not nine years old like you are," I said, trying to keep up with his youthful pace.

He looked back and grinned.

"Isaiah," I panted, "remember how we exchanged propane tanks when we lived in Chimaltenago? All we had to do was take the empty one across the street to the little business there, pay the price, and then roll the full one back to the Pichiyas. This will definitely give us better exercise. But how will we get the full one up to our house? This hill might feel more steep if you're carrying a loaded tank."

He shrugged his shoulders. "I don't know," he answered, continuing at a good pace. I was almost forced to jog in order to keep up.

At the bottom of the hill, we crossed the Pan American Highway and took the winding trail leading into town. Minutes later we stepped out onto the cobblestone road and walked the last hundred yards toward the blue *tienda*.

Suddenly we stopped in alarm, and Isaiah set the tank down with a thud. In the open doorway of the store, two big German shepherds had stationed themselves as guards. They barked viciously, daring us to enter. The look in their eyes assured me that they took their job seriously, and I was afraid to step past them.

"Nice doggie, nice doggie," I said softly in a trembling voice. Smiling nervously at them, I tentatively stretched out a friendly hand.

Suddenly the dog nearest me lunged and snapped at the sleeve of my sweater. I screamed and jumped back in terror.

Instantly the stout *tienda* owner appeared and flew toward the dogs, scolding them severely and leading them away. When he returned, he assured us that his dogs hadn't meant to scare us.

"Sure," I tried to agree, but my heart was still thumping wildly.

He rolled our empty tank into the courtyard for us and went to find a full one. A parrot sat swinging from his perch and squawking loudly. In the corner stood a *molino* for grinding corn.

Finally, the owner returned and, with a loud bang, set a big, heavy tank on the floor beside us.

"Here you are," he said, grunting. I handed him the money and thanked him while Isaiah attempted to pick up the full propane tank.

Isaiah set it back down heavily, and looked up at me. "Mom, I can't pick it up," he whispered.

"Are you sure?" I whispered back.

"Mom, you try it. It's heavy."

"Oh, yeah, I see what you mean. Ugh! I can't even lift it at all."

Isaiah and I stared at each other, trying to think of what to do. "How will we ever get this thing home?" he groaned.

"Well, Isaiah, do you think we could carry it together if we try really hard?"

"Up the hill, Mom?"

Glancing at the hill, I was barely able to see our little block house hidden in the cornfield. "Hmmm. I don't know, but we have to get it up there somehow. Hey, Isaiah, I've got it! Let's walk down to the hardware store and buy a wheelbarrow and haul it home that way!"

Minutes later we returned with a nice orange wheelbarrow, quite pleased at our ingenuity.

Just then we spied a native woman carrying a propane tank on her head, just like the one we were trying to lug home.

"Isn't it a bit humiliating to have to use a wheelbarrow to haul ours home?" I asked.

He nodded.

"Oh, well, Isaiah," I said, "there's no use chiding ourselves about how strong the natives are and how weak and puny we Americans are."

"Okay, Mom, are you ready?" he asked.

Working together, we barely lifted the full tank into the wheelbarrow.

"Why does one tank of propane have to weigh so much?" I asked my son, realizing he had no idea either.

I grasped the handles of the wheelbarrow and pushed with all my might, but the tank flipped to one side, and the wheelbarrow immediately toppled over. The tank landed with a heavy thud onto the cobblestone road just outside the *tienda*.

"Oh, dear!" I rolled my eyes and stifled a laugh at Isaiah who quickly righted the upset wheelbarrow.

"This is embarrassing," he groaned.

With pure determination and all of our combined strength, we wrestled the tank back into the wheelbarrow and somehow got it moving forward again. This time I decided to trot alongside to steady it while Isaiah pushed the wheelbarrow. But once again the propane tank rolled to one side, causing the wheelbarrow to overturn, dumping its contents. *Thud!*

This time we both laughed out loud, partly from stress and partly from the sheer humor of the moment. By trial and error, we managed to improve our method, slowly hobbling in the direction of home.

"Mommy," Isaiah said excitedly, "what if we take the path through Marta's yard where the slope isn't so steep. Then we could get home more easily!"

I paused for a minute, resting. "Oh, I'd hate to bother them by going through their courtyard like that," I disagreed. "Yes, it would definitely be more level. And it would be a shortcut to the path we usually take. Well, maybe they wouldn't mind too much, since we are pretty desperate at the moment. Okay, you're right. Let's head that way!"

As we stepped into Marta's courtyard, I smiled and said, "Excuse us. Do you mind if we cut across your courtyard to get home?"

Marta quickly wrung out the skirt she was rinsing and flung it over the wash line. "Yes, of course you may come through here." Drying her wet hands on her apron, she added, "Why, that tank must be heavy. Just a minute and I'll run inside and get Juan to help you with it."

Minutes later her husband emerged from the kitchen, smiling and nodding respectfully. Then he effortlessly pushed the wheelbarrow across the highway, up the hill, and all the way to our house, more quickly than we normally walked the trail empty-handed!

As Isaiah and I followed him, I realized he was using the wheelbarrow only to be polite. He could just as easily have carried the tank with one hand. At the top of the trail, he hauled the tank up onto our porch and even carried it inside, insisting he was glad to do us the favor.

As my children and I watched his white cowboy hat bob down the trail toward his home, I said, "The Guatemalans are such a gracious and hospitable people! God was so good to provide that dear man to save the day for us. However, there has to be some way to get a propane tank to our house without imposing on people like that."

CHAPTER 14

Novillero, an Interesting Life

Lissa:

Gloria Veronica pulled the belt tighter.

"I . . . can't . . . breathe!" I gasped.

Gloria tucked in the end of the belt and squealed with laughter at the look on my face. "The belt has to be tight so the skirt won't fall off, you know!"

I looked down at my pinched waist and asked, "This tight?"

She flipped her dark braid over her shoulder and sighed. "I guess we can try it more loosely, but you'll have to get used to it being tight. That is just how we wear *cortes!*"

I shook my head and murmured, "I don't know if I'll even be able to walk with this thing on."

Gloria Veronica busied herself with my belt. "Oh, yes," she said, "you'll learn. It just takes time."

I studied Gloria Veronica's skirt and blouse as she knelt in front of me, adjusting my belt. The native women in Novillero wore beautifully embroidered, loose-fitting blouses and thick woven skirts that hung to their ankles. The *cortes*, as the skirts were called, was a long piece of beautifully woven cloth, which they wrapped around and around themselves.

"Many of the women wear eight yards of material in their *cortes*," Gloria Veronica explained.

It was true; sometimes the skirts were bulky, but they were modest. Wearing *cortes* made a lot of sense to me. For one, it was just so cold here in the mountains with an elevation of nine thousand feet. And not just that, but simple, cotton dresses were often impractical.

The native women's skirts were thick and sturdy, and stood the dirt much better than cotton. Plus, a *corte* was actually longer than most of our dresses, and we felt we should be at least as modest as they.

Mary Beth Bentz, the schoolteacher for Vernon Martin's family, had been a real inspiration to our family. When she had first come to Novillero, she decided to connect with the natives as much as she could. So she began wearing a *corte* over her dress and set about learning the native dialect, *Quiche*. She was always learning something from them, like *tortillando*, or weaving. Mary Beth became a welcome and frequent guest in the homes of the natives, and they loved her teachable spirit. She quickly won her way into their hearts.

We decided to follow her good example and buy *cortes* at the market for ourselves.

We hurried to church dressed in our new skirts, pleased to look more like the natives. The white adobe church house in Novillero with its simple green roof was quite a contrast to the elaborate Catholic churches nearby. Regular attendance at our church was about thirty, and most of the members were older people. We slipped inside and slid quietly onto the third bench.

Salvador stood, walked slowly forward, and turned to face us with his eyes toward the floor. He was so short that we could just barely see him behind the pulpit. "Good morning, brothers and sisters. Let's pray," he mumbled quietly, covering his mouth.

I fought a smile. *Dear Salvador,* I thought. *He is rather self-conscious about his missing front teeth.*

Salvador was as consistent as the clock; he always wore his bright green sweater and a white cowboy hat, which he methodically hung on the same peg in the back of the room.

I looked around the small chapel at our church family. Salvador's wife, Juana, sat next to me with a colorful cloth wrapped around her shoulders and tied in the front. Her eyes twinkled at me, and she nodded happily. She spoke almost no Spanish, so we could exchange only simple greetings and hugs and could say no more.

Right behind me was Vicenta, the oldest member of our church. She was ancient, but no one knew exactly how old she was. Kim had told us Vicenta had no birth certificate, and there was no way her age could be determined. With the exception of one tooth, she was completely toothless; but that didn't keep her from gumming a sweet smile. She was always barefoot, and her toes were crooked and disfigured. We were told that long ago her feet had been beaten and crushed and had then healed this way; she could not have worn shoes if she had any. I couldn't imagine who would want to beat such a dear old lady as Vicenta.

As we were singing, Emily sneezed and patted me on the knee. "Please!" she whispered desperately, holding her hand to her nose. "Have Mommy pass some toilet paper! I need to blow my nose."

I passed the message to Mommy who promptly bent down and dug through her purse, pulling out a roll of pink toilet paper. For some reason, pink seemed to be the standard color in Guatemala. While passing the roll, it slipped from her fingers and hit the floor, rolling swiftly forward under the benches. It came to a final rest, bumping into the platform at the front of the church, leaving a long trail of pink paper behind it.

Sister Dominga, on the other side of Mommy, turned toward us and cracked a smile. Usually stoic, she could not contain herself this time. She shut her eyes and her shoulders began heaving with silent sobs of laughter.

Mommy leaned over and whispered, "It's worth the embarrassment just to see Dominga laugh!"

Hannah:

During our time in Novillero, news about our case was very scarce. Only a few times did we hear anything or sense any danger. Once an American man working with another mission went into the American Embassy and was asked if he knew Kay Evans. He replied that he did not meddle in other peoples' personal business. He had never met us, but he sent a message to us through other missionaries alerting us to be careful.

Then we had a message from Sharon Eby. Lissa and I sat on the floor next to Mommy's bed and asked her about it.

Mommy looked concerned. "It was really strange," she said, leaning against the cool block wall. "Sharon radioed Kim and said that our landlady in Belize wanted to talk to me."

I grimaced. "Why would she need to talk to you?"

Mommy shrugged. "Her message was that a friend of hers needed to go to a doctor in Guatemala City, and we were the only people they knew in Guatemala."

Lissa groaned. "I smell a rat. Maybe her 'friend' is Grandmom herself!"

I nodded. "What are you going to do, Mom?"

"Nothing!" she said. "I prayed about it, but I feel very uneasy about the whole situation. I sent a message back to Sharon to tell our landlady that we are unable to come."

I sighed in relief. "Good. Let's play it safe."

She nodded but continued, "Hannah and Lissa, I know God has led us here, and I know His guiding hand is on us. I just feel that something is going to happen. I don't envision us just being here, hiding in the mountains of Guatemala, for the rest of our lives."

I gasped. "Mommy, it's funny you said that, because I feel the same way."

Lissa looked at us incredulously. "Me too!" she exclaimed.

One question was on our minds. Lissa voiced it: "I wonder what will happen?"

My mind was bursting with questions. *Will Granddad and Grandmom repent and decide to stop hunting us? Will we somehow be allowed to go back to the States?*

The future was shrouded as if by a curtain blocking our view. But God knew all about it. He knew that our days in a quaint little Guatemalan town nestled on a mountainside were numbered. He knew everything that lay ahead, and He was even using this time to prepare us. He was getting us spiritually equipped for what lay ahead.

Kay:

I will lift up mine eyes unto the hills, from whence cometh my help. My help cometh from the LORD, which made heaven and earth. He will not suffer thy foot to be moved: he that keepeth thee will not slumber. Behold, he that keepeth Israel shall neither slumber nor sleep.[1]

---

1. Psalm 121:1-4

I looked around at my children as we sat on the bed for evening devotions. It had been a long day, and we were all tired. Emily was already nodding off. I pulled her onto my lap, and we finished reciting Psalm 121. We enjoyed reciting Scripture after reading and praying before kissing each other good night.

"Good night, Grace. Good night, Beverly . . ."

Later, I stepped outside. The metal door clicked shut behind me, and I stood shivering in the cold night air as I looked out over the village of Novillero. "I wonder why the gymnasium is all lit up. Oh, they must be having a big dance," I groaned.

I could hear the deep pulsing of the music. The sheer noise and volume that went along with a community dance had become all too familiar to us when we had heard it back in Chimaltenango. There the gymnasium had been right next door, and our walls and floors had vibrated from the loud music, sometimes throbbing until 2 a.m.

Well, I thought, *at least here in Novillero we are across the highway and up the mountain a ways from it all.*

I pushed open the door to the kitchen and hurried to bed. Sometime during the night, I half awoke and heard Tammy barking loudly. She kept racing up the hill above our house and then back onto the porch. But I just turned over groggily and drifted back to sleep.

The next morning dawned bright and clear. Our neighbor Inez hurried up the hill with a worried expression on her face. "Are you all okay?" she asked.

"Sure," I said, nodding.

"You were not harmed at all in the night?" she asked, insistently.

I scratched my head. "We are all just fine and we slept well," I assured her. "I faintly recall hearing our dog barking but that is all."

She sighed in relief. "My whole family was scared!" she said. "During the night we heard some drunks make their way noisily up the hill and bang loudly on your metal door numerous times." She shook her head incredulously. "I can't believe you didn't hear it! I suppose they must have come away drunk from the dance."

We were stunned.

Isaiah looked at her with wide eyes. "Are you sure that it was *our* door?"

She nodded emphatically. "Oh, yes! We all heard them!"

Hannah shook her head in disbelief. Our house was so tiny that we surely would have heard such banging on a metal door in the middle of the night, yet we had not. God must have prevented us from hearing the noise, and had used our dog to scare the intruders off. How grateful we were for God's protection! Someone had intended to do us harm in the night, and we had never known it!

I thought of two passages we recited every day from Psalm 91:5, 6. *Thou shalt not be afraid for the terror by night; nor for the arrow that flieth by day; nor for the pestilence that walketh in darkness,* and also Psalm 4:8, *I will both lay me down in peace, and sleep: for thou, LORD, only makest me dwell in safety.*

God had even kept us from a frightening experience, since He prevented our ears from hearing the noise. Our God and our only source of protection was far mightier than any sophisticated security alarm system available in the United States. What wonderful and unsurpassable security we have in Jesus!

Lissa:

I bent over the table, trying to finish up a letter.

"*¡Buenas tardes!*" someone called into the dining room.

I glanced up and saw one of our neighbors standing at the doorway. "I was just wondering if I could borrow a Bible. You see, it's almost time to go to the evening service."

Putting down my pen, I nodded. "Um, let me see. Yes, I think I can find you one. Just a minute."

I scanned the bookshelf and pulled off a Spanish Bible we did not use often. I smiled and handed it to her.

She looked disappointed. "Oh, I'm sorry," she said. "I was hoping I could use that one." She pointed at a smaller Bible.

The smile on my face suddenly felt plastic, but I swallowed the lump in my throat and went back to the bookshelf. Carefully I pulled down my favorite, well-worn Bible and handed it to her.

She thanked me profusely and ran merrily back down the trail.

I watched her go, and wished my heart were more kind toward her. *Why is it that people here see no need to buy something if they can just as easily borrow it? Neighbors come to our door daily asking to borrow nearly anything: an umbrella, flashlight, wheelbarrow, sweaters, money, Bible, chicken bouillon, shoes . . .*

At devotions I voiced my feelings. Mommy smiled at me and agreed. "I know what you mean, but don't you think we need to be Jesus to them?"

I nodded and looked down, ashamed.

Mommy opened her Bible. "Let's read what Jesus said for us to do," she said. "Let's see, here it is in Luke 6:30. 'Give to every man that asketh of thee; and of him that taketh away thy goods ask them not again.' "

I could just imagine my favorite Bible being carried down the trail never to return.

" 'And as ye would that men should do to you, do ye also to them likewise . . . . But love ye your enemies'—now children, our neighbors are not our enemies, but still catch Jesus' heartbeat here—'and do good, and lend, hoping for nothing again; and your reward shall be great, and ye shall be the children of the Highest: for he is kind unto the unthankful and to the evil. Be ye therefore merciful, as your Father also is merciful . . . . Give, and it shall be given unto you; good measure, pressed down, and shaken together, and running over, shall men give into your bosom. For with the same measure that ye mete withal it shall be measured to you again.'[1]

"Okay now, this is where giving up our rights becomes practical. We need to love our neighbors even when they do things we don't like. We need to let God do His pruning work in our hearts. Also, let's remember that borrowing is more commonplace in their culture than it is where we came from."

Thus, we slowly became more flexible and cheerful whenever neighbors knocked on our door wanting to come in and use our blender to puree their cooked black beans into smooth ones for refried beans. Or when they wanted to put some of their meat into our freezer or to retrieve meat put in previously. Or when they asked to borrow any number of things they knew we had.

---

1. Luke 6:31-38

After all, wasn't it the least we could do for them since we did have things they didn't? And, as it turned out, we found we were even blessed in return. Our neighbors were delighted to teach us how to make some of their delicious Guatemalan specialties. We found they were wonderful cooks, patient teachers, and very pleasant company as well.

"It is starting to rain!" Grace squealed from the front yard. She pranced into the kitchen where Mommy and I were making lunch.

"Quick," Mommy exclaimed, dropping the wooden spoon onto the stove top, "we need to get the clothes off the line before they get wet!"

Everyone dashed out to the clotheslines strung between the trees and began pulling off the laundry.

"Mommy," Hannah called with her arms loaded with towels, "shall I hang all of these on the porch?"

Mommy grabbed the last washcloth off the line and darted for the porch. "Yes," she panted, "but we will try to hang up all the clothes inside the house where they will dry more quickly."

After everything was hung, we sat around the table eating hot soup. "Does the U.S. have a rainy season?" Emily asked.

I passed a bowl of crackers. "No, Emily, it doesn't," I answered.

Beverly jumped up and said, "A drop of water just dripped on my head!"

We all looked at the ceiling. "Sure enough, there is a drip," Isaiah announced with an upward glance.

"Well, get a bowl and set it where the water falls. Here, you can sit by me now."

Beverly burst out laughing. "We can honestly tell people we have no running water inside our house except for what comes through the ceiling!"

I smiled, and Hannah added, "And we grow our own carpet too!"

Mommy shook her head. "I really don't know what to do about the mold growing on the floor and walls. It does look like white carpet, doesn't it? I just cleaned it up yesterday, but it's already coming back today."

"Mommy," Hannah said, smiling as she smeared avocado onto a

tortilla with a fork, "I think this is the most interesting place we have ever lived."

Kay:

Official permission to stay in Guatemala was granted in 90-day increments, which meant that every three months we left the country and reentered. Now, once again, our time had dwindled away, which meant another trip to the border.

Another option was gathering our courage and walking boldly into the immigration office in Guatemala City and presenting our passports. Only rarely did we do that. Going there was scarier because they scrutinized us more closely than the officials at border crossings.

We much preferred just crossing a border and visiting missionaries in a neighboring country. Kim had told me about a Mennonite mission in El Salvador that would welcome a visit from us.

As the bus rumbled down the highway, I thought about the next few days. I had made arrangements to stay with the Eli Glick family in El Salvador. We were excited about getting a glimpse of the missionaries at work in another Central American country. The closer we got to El Salvador, the warmer the climate. We had long since peeled off our sweaters and rolled up our sleeves.

But my stomach knotted at the thought of the border crossing. My nerves were on edge, and my mind drifted to countless questions. *What will this border crossing be like? Do they have a computer? Have they been alerted that an American family is hiding somewhere in Central America?* On and on went the questions. Finally I stopped myself and shook my head. *Lord, You have directed and protected us so far; surely You will continue to do so.*

Standing at the window of the little office building at the El Salvadoran border, an official took our documents and examined them thoroughly. Finally he nodded, pulled out his black stamp, and pounded it onto a page of each passport.

Looking at me expressionlessly, he told me how much it would cost to cross into El Salvador. It sounded expensive to me, so I had Hannah calculate it before finally counting out the money.

"He certainly must think highly of his country to charge so much just for the privilege of stepping over the border," I whispered teasingly to my children.

I handed the money through the window. The man took it methodically and counted it twice to make sure it was exactly right. With a thankful heart, I breathed a sigh of relief as we left the office and stepped into El Salvador.

"God is good, children. He allowed us to get through another border crossing without problems."

The street was lined with brightly painted school buses. Streaks of color were splashed across each one in wild, crazy patterns.

"It looks like each bus is trying to outdo the last," Isaiah commented as he gazed at the pieces of artwork before us.

"We should find out which bus we need," Lissa reminded me.

A driver leaned leisurely against the side of his bus, dangling a cigarette between his fingers. Hurting for business, he watched us hopefully.

"Let's ask him if he knows which bus we need," I said quietly.

As we hurried toward him, a sickening feeling washed over me. "You know what? I can't believe the mistake I made!" I confessed weakly. "I forgot to jot down the Glicks' address! I don't know where to ask the bus driver to take us."

My children stared at me in disbelief.

"Mom, you're kidding!" Lissa groaned with wide eyes.

I felt overwhelmed, but it was all too true; my mistake presented us with a real problem. Here we were, in a foreign country, and we did not know where we were supposed to go, nor did we know how to contact our hosts. I hadn't been given a phone number, and I had forgotten the paper with their address.

What should I do? Such a dumb mistake; I can't believe it, I scolded myself. I prayed desperately that God would help us, but I was full of doubts.

We walked slowly up to the bus driver. "We have a problem," I began feebly. "We want to visit the Eli Glicks, but we don't have their address and don't know which bus to take!"

The bus driver smiled one of those happy Central American "I-can-handle-this-little-difficulty" smiles and motioned us onto his bus. "Do you want me to drop you off at the school or the clinic?" he asked calmly.

I could hardly believe my ears! This man knew not only where they lived, but also that they ran a clinic next to their house. The fact that I had forgotten the information didn't even matter. Suddenly I felt more ashamed of my lack of faith than I had felt over forgetting to bring the address. It was humbling and yet wonderful to know we were so tenderly cared for by an incredible God who makes allowances for human mistakes. We took our seats, thankful and rejoicing.

What a strange bus this was, though! Fake red fur lined the dash, and dangling beads framed the inside of the windshield. And as the bus rumbled on and on, so did the loud, sleazy music the driver played.

After a long while, the bus driver motioned to me. "Here you are!" he said, pointing to a house. "The Glicks live there."

I thanked him, and we quickly gathered up our bags and stepped off the bus.

As the bus roared away, we crossed the street. Approaching the house, we noticed a small pickup pulling into the driveway. A young American woman wearing a white veiling like ours climbed out, along with her small children.

As she unstrapped her baby from his car seat, she looked at us curiously. Then holding her little one, she walked up to me and introduced herself. "Hi. I'm Judy Glick," she said and invited us sweetly into her in-laws' home.

Verda Glick met us at the door, and I introduced my family. Both Judy and Verda seemed strangely puzzled, and it began to dawn on me that somehow they had not gotten the message that we were coming. Nonetheless, in true Mennonite hospitality, Verda invited us warmly into her home.

"Now tell me about yourself," she encouraged, handing each of us a cold drink of lemonade and sitting down next to me on the couch. Her kind face and motherly way put us all at ease.

I briefed her on who we were and why we were there, giving her the quick version of our story.

She listened with keen interest and sympathy. "Hardships draw us closer to the Lord, don't you think?"

I nodded.

Verda continued, "My husband Eli was once kidnapped here in El Salvador and was in serious danger for a time. We have such a burden for the lost souls of this country, but it remains a hostile land to the message of truth."

It was fascinating to hear the struggles other followers of Christ had been through. I found it comforting that the Lord had been faithful to them as well. Our times with the Christians in El Salvador, though brief, were always a boost of encouragement, inspiring us to be more committed to Jesus.

CHAPTER **15**

"How Long, O Lord?"

As dusk settled over El Chal in northern Guatemala, the town was settling for the night. Candlelight flickered through the windows of small homes dotting the roadside. I stifled a yawn. It had been a long but enjoyable week.

Once again we needed to cross the border in order to have another ninety days stamped into our passports. This time we gathered courage to boat back to Belize and visit our first missionary friends in Central America. Nancy Stutzman met us at the shore and took us wading in the beautiful ocean near her home before feeding us a delicious Belizean meal. Then we were off again to visit Tim and Rhoda Miller and all our friends serving in northern Belize.

Time went by too quickly because they were such an enjoyable group, and before we knew it, it was time to hail a bus for Guatemala. On the way home, we stopped in El Chal to spend several days with our friends Mark and Norma Gingerich and their family. But now it was time to catch the bus and head toward our little home in the mountains.

Norma's voice broke into my thoughts. "I wonder if the bus will show up tonight."

"Yeah, it is starting to look a little hopeless," I returned, looking at my watch again. Our families sat by the roadside, awaiting the arrival of the only bus that ran through this desolate area to the capital city. From there we would catch another bus for our home in Novillero.

For the past two nights we had waited by the road for hours, hoping in vain for the promised bus. Twice, after the scheduled time had come and gone, we had laughed, loaded our backpacks back into the van, and returned to Mark and Norma's home to spend another day.

The visit had stretched out longer than I had planned, but it had been wonderful to get a glimpse into the life of the Gingerich family. These past few days had been such a treat for us, and my children weren't minding the wait. Our family loved to sing, and we quickly discovered they did too. And Mark's family was made up of lively storytellers. Time had flown as we listened to one fascinating story after another.

I chuckled under my breath, recalling an incident at the dinner table yesterday. Just as we were eating the last bites of a wonderful meal Sarah had made, a voice called from the yard. Mark got up from the table and paused at the door.

"Oh, it's a salesman," he said, quietly slipping to the front gate.

"What kind of salesman?" Norma asked as she rose from the table and stepped to the door, squinting her eyes. "It looks like he's selling dishes."

We all followed her outside and listened as the vendor gave his sales pitch.

"These beautiful green dishes are of the very finest quality. Notice the exquisite craftsmanship," he boasted, holding out a plate for Mark to examine. "And besides their beauty, they will not break or chip if you drop them. Just watch!" He lifted a plate from the box at his feet and flung it into the air.

How strange, I thought, *to watch a grown man earning his living by throwing plates!* I was skeptical as the shimmering plate sailed to earth with a clank. To our surprise it didn't shatter on the gravel.

"You see?" the salesman exulted as he stooped, picked up the plate from the gravel, and proudly handed it to Mark. "They are just the kind of dishes every house should have!"

I guess Mark was pretty impressed, because he bought a set for Norma. After all, green was her favorite color.

As Mark settled back into his chair at the table, he had turned to Norma. "Happy anniversary, honey," he said, with a twinkle in his eye just for her.

At last the distant rumble of a bus was heard, and I looked quickly down the road. Mark stepped into the street, signaling for the bus to stop. With a great hiss, the large bus stopped in front of us.

The helper opened the door and jumped out. "Guatemala City?" he called.

Mark nodded and turned to help us with our bags. Giving Norma a quick hug, I took Emily's hand and helped her up the high step into the bus. Cool air washed over me as we climbed the stairs and hurried down the aisle. Hannah quickly stowed our backpacks in the rack, and we slipped into soft seats. And then, with a jerk, the bus was off. We smiled and waved at the dim silhouettes of Mark and Norma and their children.

As the bus swayed around curves and the black jungle flew past us in the night, I thought back over our time in El Chal. *The Lord has blessed us with friends that are such godly examples,* I thought gratefully.

Watching Mark preach to the small group gathered in the humble building on Sunday, going with Norma to give a bundle of clothing to a new and needy mother, and seeing how their family interacted so lovingly with one another and their fellow villagers were all such an encouragement. My family and I relished the memories of time with these new friends. But more importantly, I knew my children's appetites had been whetted and a fresh zeal stirred within their hearts by observing this family who delighted in serving Jesus together.

We all gathered eagerly around Hannah and watched her rip open the thick envelope.

"Is it from the Magees?" Emily asked excitedly.

Isaiah nodded, intently scrutinizing the stack of letters Hannah pulled out of the envelope and handed to me. The little piece of paper on top had "Beverly" scribbled in a childish hand, and I handed it to her. She beamed with delight. Mail was a rare and precious treat.

We had no mailbox or address for our hillside home in Novillero. But since things had grown so quiet about our situation, I had given the main address used by all of the M.A.M. missionaries to our friends, Kevin and Laura Magee. From time to time, they sent us wonderful packets of mail, including hand-drawn pictures and letters from their children and even a cassette tape of their family singing. Proverbs 25:25, *As cold waters to a thirsty soul, so is good news from a far country,* became quite true for our family.

But today amidst the usual letters, I noticed a note attached to an envelope bearing my name. "Kay," the note stated, "enclosed is a newspaper clipping about you from your hometown paper. We strongly encourage you to spend time in prayer before opening this envelope to make sure you have clearance from the Lord to do so, and if so, that He might prepare your heart."

Though bursting with curiosity, I quietly slid the envelope into my pocket to read later when I was alone. That night, after praying and seeking the Lord for direction, I gingerly tore open the envelope.

It was a good thing I had taken their advice. On the front page of the article was a photo of my in-laws. They peered at me with sorrowful faces, seated on a bed that the article said they had purchased for my children. Another picture displayed the brand-new stuffed animals and dolls that would belong to my children whenever they might be found. My mind reeled as I read the slanderous article about me. It made my in-laws sound like wonderful people only trying to "rescue" their mistreated grandchildren. The article went on and on.

How many people have read this article and believed its contents? I wondered, my face growing hot. I fell to my knees and poured out my discouragement and frustrations to the Lord.

As I knelt by the bed, baring my soul, the Lord began to impress one thing very strongly on my heart. *Kay, your reputation is totally unimportant. It really does not matter what people think of you, whether it is true or false. The only reputation you need to be concerned about is Mine.*

Peace washed over me, and I suddenly felt free, realizing and accepting that my reputation truly didn't matter. I only needed to focus on Jesus Christ. What a relief!

Beverly skipped into the kitchen through the open door. "The Martins are coming, the Martins are coming!" she said happily.

I pulled the sizzling turkey out of the oven and set it on the table. "Good, everything is ready now. Beverly, go get the other children and tell them it's time to eat."

Hannah slid the last steaming rolls into the basket and tucked a woven cloth over the top to keep them warm. "What else would you like for me to do?" she asked.

I closed my eyes and thought. "All we lack is the cranberry sauce. Can you get that out?" I asked.

She nodded and hurried to the refrigerator.

Tammy yapped, and I heard Melisa Martin giggling outside. Poking my head out the door, I called, "Hello, everyone! Just come on in!"

Vernon stepped onto the porch with baby Lavina in his arms and nodded. "Thank ya," he said.

Kim set a bowl of mashed potatoes down on the *pila* and caught her breath. "My, that trail is something!"

I laughed, agreeing. Everyone crammed tightly into our little house long enough for prayer.

Vernon cleared his throat and said, "Well, let's thank the Lord for His provisions."

We all bowed our heads as he prayed. ". . . In Jesus' name. Amen!"

Tiana pranced around her daddy's feet and said, "Please, can I have a roll now?"

Vernon looked down and smiled. "Just a minute, little girl! Mommy will get your plate soon."

It was Thanksgiving Day, 1999. We thought it would be fun to invite the Martin family to our tiny house for this special day. Since we couldn't all fit inside, we decided to take advantage of the beautiful weather and have the children carry their plates outside. Our families had enjoyed sharing meals together once a week, but usually we gathered at the Martins' more spacious house.

"Kay, do you have a serving spoon for the green beans?"

"Oh, yes, of course!" I pulled open the top drawer and dug through the big spoons. "Will this one work?" I asked Kim as I handed her a large metal spoon.

"That looks great."

Benji and Marv followed Isaiah outside, their plates piled high with turkey, dressing, mashed potatoes, green beans, and rolls. As they passed Tammy on their way to the flat roof, she barked and whined enviously, confined to her chain. After the children had all filled their plates, Vernon, Kim, and I dished heaps of steaming food onto ours and sat down in the dining room.

Our year and a half of living on this hillside and getting to know the Martin family was a blessing. It had been a rich season of our lives, and we felt grateful to God and to them.

After all the plates were scraped clean and the dishes were washed, we relaxed on the grassy slope behind our house. The little children ran in the yard, happily playing, while the older ones sat around us talking.

Kim turned to me. "I have a concern about your life of hiding. What will you do when your children want to marry? How will you manage the legalities of it?"

I shared her concern. This was not a new thought for me. I had asked God that question a few times myself. Frankly, I didn't know the answers to such perplexing questions.

Hannah broke the silence. "Mommy and Lissa and I tend to think we will not always be in hiding."

Lissa nodded emphatically. "Even though we can't see into the future, we feel our circumstances are going to change. I just can't see us hiding in the mountains of Guatemala until Emily is eighteen!"

It was true. All three of us had an unexplainable peace about whatever God was planning to do.

"But you know, Kim, we certainly do understand that familiar restlessness rising within us, impatient to know what God has in store for us," I said. "All we can do right now is wait."

CHAPTER 16

Surrounded

Lissa:

I shivered as I waited outside Mommy's door. Behind me the sun was just peeking over the mountain and casting its bright rays into the valley. Mist was rising from wet cornfields, and wisps of smoke curled slowly up from neighboring chimneys. It was a beautiful Sunday morning in Novillero.

I turned and knocked again, and Mommy opened the door. A wave of humid air hit my face as I stepped into the kitchen. A big pot of steaming water sat on the stove boiling away—our day's supply of drinking water.

"We have an hour until church starts," I said. "Does your Sunday veil need to be ironed?"

Mommy pulled hot apple cake from the oven and nodded. "Yes, I think it's hanging on the line, along with yours and Hannah's, out on the porch."

I peered out and saw that she was right. "How could I have missed them? They were right there the whole time!" I unclipped the white veils from the line, hurrying back to the bedroom.

As I turned the dial on the iron to "silk" and waited for it to heat up, my gaze drifted to the calendar on the wall, "November 28, 1999." *How time flies*, I thought.

Laying the veils out in front of me on the ironing board, I carefully pressed each one, making sure I did not scorch them. They scorch easily and making veils was not my gift.

Suddenly, the door burst open and Hannah darted in, her face white with terror, "They are coming here! A whole string of them, and there is an American with them! Pray!"

I stared at her. "Who is coming here?" I demanded. "What is going on?"

She waved helplessly out the door. "I saw them from the porch. In single file on our trail is a long string of police officers, and they're coming here right now! And there is a white man with them!"

My heart skipped a beat. "You're kidding!" I whispered.

Setting down the iron, I ran to the door and looked. Sure enough, there was a whole line of men in dark-blue uniforms hurrying up the trail toward our house. "Have you told Mom?" I asked desperately.

"Yes. She is still getting ready. I'd better go help her. Pray, Lissa!" she urged frantically. With that, she turned and vanished out the door.

I stared intently at the men as they drew closer. "Why all the guards? And they have such *big* guns!"

It was as if a fog enveloped me, like the haze that often drifted over the mountains. This couldn't really be happening to us! This was the moment we had feared for so long. I remembered those talks our family had had, believing God would change our circumstances; even begging Him to change them. Of course, we did not want to live in hiding forever. Now suddenly the moment of reckoning had come.

We knew God had supernaturally protected us these three and a half years in hiding. God couldn't want us to be found . . . could He? *This just can't be happening!* I wanted to pinch myself and discover this was merely a bad dream, a very bad dream. But no, it was too real.

Running away didn't even cross our minds. Slowly, our family gathered on the porch. Tammy was barking uncontrollably, and Isaiah quickly ran to chain her up. Our situation wouldn't be helped if Tammy bit one of these visitors.

Solemnly, we observed the approaching men. The large machine guns in their hands demanded respect. Each man had extra ammunition hanging over his shoulder. As they approached our home, they fanned out all around our house to ensure that we could not escape. A chill crept down my spine.

Three people stepped forward and climbed the steps onto the porch, facing our stunned family. A Guatemalan man in civilian clothes and a short female official faced us, both clutching clipboards. Behind them cringed a tall American man in Western clothes and snakeskin boots, peering at us uneasily from behind his glasses. When his eyes met mine, he dropped his gaze, jamming his hands into his pockets.

The woman looked around and boldly addressed us. "Are you the Evans family?" she asked in Spanish.

Hannah translated softly for Mommy.

Suddenly appearing small and defenseless, Mommy nodded slightly.

The woman plunged ahead. "Are you Kay Evans? Is Emily Evans here?"

Mommy nervously answered both questions affirmatively.

The woman explained. "I am a member of the National Civil Police." The shiny badge on her uniform agreed with her statement. "Someone in the States is concerned about the welfare of your children and is sending us to find them and to make sure they are safe."

After several minutes of questioning, Hannah asked the woman, "Why is this American here?"

The lady explained, "He is our interpreter."

So far he had said nothing but only stared blankly at his boots as if he wished he weren't here.

Hannah and I exchanged glances, guessing he must be a private investigator rather than an interpreter.

"Why isn't he translating, then?" Hannah ventured to ask.

The woman ignored the question and explained further. "We need to take you up to Santa Lucia to the courthouse. There a judge will be able to look the children over and verify that they appear healthy and sound. Then you can come home."

Though she made it sound like a very simple procedure, I had my doubts.

Almost as an afterthought, she added, "Oh, your mom doesn't even need to come; just the children."

Mommy raised her eyebrows. This was out of the question. She would not let us out of her sight with these strangers.

"Do you want me to try and sneak away and tell Vernon and Kim what's happening?" I whispered to Mommy. I desperately wanted them to know. I was sure they could help. Besides, Vernon's Spanish was much better than ours.

"Yes, go!" Mommy whispered back.

Heading toward the backyard, I planned to slip down through a deep ravine and make my way to the Martins. *Just maybe*, I thought, *I can get away without anyone noticing.*

But I had taken only a few paces into the backyard until I realized this plan was impossible. Armed men toting machine guns were everywhere—behind our house and on top of our flat roof, giving them a great lookout. There was no way I could slip away unnoticed.

Returning to Mommy I whispered, "The whole house is surrounded. I will have to leave in plain view. There is no other option."

Her eyes met mine, and she nodded slightly.

Taking a deep breath I started down the porch stairs and onto the trail. For a moment everyone watched in silence as I started down the path.

Suddenly shrill whistles pierced the air, and my blood ran cold.

"You can't go!" an officer shouted angrily.

"What? Am I not even allowed to go get our pastor?" I asked in a very shaky voice.

Two of the people whispered to each other and then nodded that I could go, but only with a uniformed escort. Isaiah came along too, and he was also given an escort.

My feet pounded down the familiar path, but my head felt light and dizzy. I followed the trail to where it ended at the Pan American Highway, and then I led the way across the road and down the path winding its way to the Martins' house.

What will I tell Kim and Vernon? I wondered again and again.

I heard Vernon's van chugging up the highway. It made a tremendous rattling noise, and I turned in despair only to see it disappear around the bend, heading away from us.

"Oh, no!" I moaned and then turned to the guard. "Our pastor drives up the highway to Nahuala every Sunday morning to pick up some of our church members. I just heard him driving his van up the highway."

"Well, let's turn around and go back then," she said quickly.

"No," I told her, "I want to at least tell his wife Kim."

She looked undecided for a minute but finally agreed. We started back down the trail, and with each step the question burned in my mind, *How will I tell Kim?*

Before I had a chance to knock on the Martins' door, twelve-year-old Marv pushed it open. Seeing us with the officers, his eyes widened in alarm.

Suddenly I wasn't strong anymore, and tears flooded my eyes. We hurried inside with the officers close behind us. The family quickly gathered around, stunned, and listened to my story.

I was so distraught I could hardly talk. "The officers came this morning," I sobbed. "There is a whole mob of them over at our house. And they want to take us up to Santa Lucia. I am sure that Granddad and Grandmom sent them!"

None of us could believe this was really happening. Once Kim made sense of my blubbering, she and Benji rushed across the highway and up the mountain to our house. Susana, the Martins' oldest daughter, decided to seize a golden opportunity by hurrying back to the kitchen and carrying out their extra breakfast to share with the officers. Then, filled with dread, we slowly retraced our steps homeward.

Kay:

After watching Lissa and Isaiah and their two guards hurry down the trail, my eyes drifted to the officers surrounding us. *Lord, it's hard to believe this is really happening. Help me trust that You will work even this for good.*

Hannah laid her hand on my shoulder, and I turned toward her.

"Mommy," she said softly, her eyebrows furrowed, "this seems like a perfect time to do good to those who hate us, doesn't it? I was just thinking; we have that extra pan of apple cake that I made earlier. It's sitting in the kitchen and probably still warm. Do you want me to cut it and serve it to the officers? Beverly and Grace could help me."

I nodded, a smile forming on my lips.

Each officer gratefully accepted a piece of cake from my daughter's hands. Despite the crisis of the moment, it was almost comical to see the guards casually sling their machine guns over their shoulders and reach for the treat. Only the tall white man refused Hannah's offer. Instead, he paced back and forth like a mouse in an imaginary cage, smoking one cigarette after another. He was the picture of guilt and seemed very uneasy about the whole situation.

Glancing down the hillside, I saw Kim and her fifteen-year-old son huffing up the trail, dressed for church. Benji strode over to the officers with his hands on his hips, his face red with indignation.

"What are you doing here?" he demanded. "Do you need something?"

Dissatisfied with their evasive answers, Kim came over to the steps where Hannah and I stood, her face a picture of concern. "I think we should pray," she said.

While Benji continued to question the officers, we huddled together in quiet, urgent prayer. It was reassuring to be reminded that God was in control.

"Vernon left already to go up to Nahuala," Kim sighed, adjusting her glasses. "He has no idea what we are facing just now. Oh, I wish he were here!"

The plainclothes officer walked toward us, and we looked at him with dread.

"Well," he said with authority, "it's time that we escort your family to the courthouse in Santa Lucia." There was no doubt in his voice—we were going with him.

Hannah:

Margarita was scrubbing clothes in the *pila* as we hurried by on the trail. Taking in the puzzling scene before her, she flung a wet blouse haphazardly on the line and rushed toward me, her eyes begging me to tell her what was going on.

I gave her a quick hug before I was rushed on down the trail. "Pray for us!" I called over my shoulder.

Margarita nodded speechlessly and stood with wet hands hanging limply at her side, watching us go.

Once we reached the bottom of the hill, we were escorted alongside the highway toward the parked vehicles awaiting us. On the other side of the highway were gathered Kim's little girls—Kendra, Melisa, and Tiana—hoping to see us before we left.

With them was Joanne Gingerich, a young lady from Canada, who lived with them and served as their cook. She had become a friend of ours since her arrival here. Sobbing, she cupped her hands around her mouth and called out, "I'm going to call my mom in Canada this morning. Canada will be praying for you!"

We looked back at her gratefully, with tears running down our own cheeks. Her words shook me. Suddenly I realized we might not be allowed to come back here!

"I think I'll roll down the window a bit," I said.

Mommy sighed as we sat waiting for the officials to organize the caravan. They stood in a cluster several feet from the car, discussing plans. My sisters and brother and I, plus Kim, were tightly packed into the backseat of this little car, with Emily and Grace sitting on laps. Mommy was in the front passenger seat, a gearshift separating her seat from the driver's.

Kim looked at the police cars parked around us and tapped her foot. "Oh, where is Vernon?" she said. "I am sure things would go better if he were here!"

"I wish he were here too," Lissa mumbled. "Oh, look, here comes Inez."

We peered eagerly out the window as our next-door neighbor rushed toward us, tears streaming down her beautiful brown cheeks. She reached her hand through the open window, clasping Mommy's hands tightly. "You are good people! You haven't stolen anything! Trust in the Lord. God will take care of you even though what these people are doing to you is horrible!"

Just then, we heard the familiar rattling of Vernon's van. At the sight of the police cars, he pulled off to the side of the road and jumped out to investigate. We had been stalled long enough for Vernon to make it back in time. God's timing was perfect.

Vernon talked for a few minutes to the officers in his typical calm, unruffled manner. Then he came over to the car to talk to us.

Kim opened her door. "Oh, Vern," she said, "I'm so glad you got here. What do you think they want to do?"

"We'll just have to wait and see," he said. "I'll drop off this van load of brethren at the church house and then drive up to meet you at the courthouse in Santa Lucia," he assured her, patting her shoulder. Then he turned and strode toward the van, nodding politely to the guards.

The driver revved up the little car and pulled onto the road winding its way around the mountain, circling all the way up to Santa Lucia.

Mommy opened her Bible, slowly turning the pages. "Oh, children, listen to this Scripture. It is so fitting right now!"

> *He that dwelleth in the secret place of the most High shall abide under the shadow of the Almighty. I will say of the LORD, He is my refuge and my fortress: my God; in him will I trust. Surely he shall deliver thee from the snare of the fowler, and from the noisome pestilence. Thou shalt not be afraid for the terror by night; nor for the arrow that flieth by day. Because he hath set his love upon me, therefore will I deliver him: I will set him on high, because he hath known my name. He shall call upon me, and I will answer him: I will be with him in trouble; I will deliver him, and honour him.*[1]

Together we quoted the comforting words of the familiar passage. Though we had recited it daily, it suddenly had more meaning than I ever realized before.

It was 10:30 a.m. Only an hour and a half had passed since our peaceful Sunday morning had been interrupted so abruptly. Just an hour and a half ago, our lives had been normal. How quickly things had changed! Now we were captives, escorted by police cars with flashing red and blue lights. Seeing the number of people involved in our capture gave us an idea of how seriously this was being taken by these officials.

Santa Lucia was crawling with people. Sunday was the big market day when natives flocked from nearby villages to buy and sell. The driver carefully wove his way through the crowded streets and brought the vehicle to a stop in front of a dreary building I had never noticed before.

"This is the courthouse?" I asked incredulously.

All I got in reply was a brisk nod. People stared at us as we were hurried toward the door. Stepping inside, I blinked in the dim light. Glancing around the dusty and poorly furnished room, I saw only a couple of

---

1. Psalm 91:1-3, 5, 14, 15

policemen and the American man who was busy making calls on his cell phone. We sat on a simple wooden bench to wait.

The American man sat anxiously in a wooden chair, then suddenly stood up and headed outside. Through the window we could see him pulling out another cigarette.

"There goes the American man again," Isaiah whispered. "What shall we call him? If we give him a secret code name, he won't know when we are talking about him!"

Lissa agreed, "Yeah, what about Cochlaeus, the shady character in the book we've been reading as a family. You know, the book we borrowed from Kim?"

Mommy nodded, and so it was decided; the tall American man would be dubbed "Cochlaeus."

"He must be really nervous," Kim whispered. "He leaves to smoke a cigarette between every phone call."

Cochlaeus had tried all morning to avoid eye contact with us, and now he began staying outside the dreary building for longer and longer periods of time.

Kay:

"Mommy," Hannah whispered, "do you see that official over there? He has a paper with our pictures on it."

I stared intently at the papers in the man's hand, and nodded, "I wonder if they are copies of the same pictures that were posted in Wal-Mart."

"Hmmm. Could be," she responded as the door creaked open and Vernon walked in.

An officer beckoned for Vernon to come to his desk, so he sauntered toward him, pulling up a chair. They spoke quietly, looking intently at the papers spread before them.

Nodding, Vernon turned toward me and said, "Kay, could you come over here? They have some questions for you, and we need to fill out some paperwork. I'll interpret for you."

I stepped to the desk and stared at the forms in front of me. "What am I supposed to write here?" I asked.

Vernon leaned closer to the forms. "Oh, here they want to know where you were born. And on the line under it write the date of your birth."

I nodded and bent over the paper, grateful for Vernon's help. He was so fluent in Spanish. My hand shook as I tried to write. The morning's events were very distressing.

What will happen to my family over the next few hours and days? I thought wearily.

Vernon pointed to the next line on the paper. "Here they want to know if you will promise not to flee."

I hesitated. "Well," I admitted, "if I thought the conditions for fleeing were just right, I am not totally sure what I would do. We've fled before. How can I absolutely promise we won't again?"

Vernon bit his lip and looked at me thoughtfully. I knew it was not rational to consider fleeing. We were clearly caught, and with guards standing by with machine guns, I knew our chances of running away were very slim. Our circumstances had changed so drastically in just one morning that my mind hadn't had time to process everything. Surely this wasn't happening to us—yet it was.

"Ma'am, may I see all the passports, please?" The questioner interrupted my thoughts.

I pulled the stack of blue passports out of my purse and handed them over. He opened them and began typing the information on a big clunky typewriter.

"Is this the last form?" I asked, placing them into the hands of the woman who came to collect them.

"I think it must be," Vernon declared as he stood up and stretched before strolling to the other side of the room to join his wife.

I motioned for Isaiah to scoot over on the bench, so that I could sit down next to Kim.

She leaned close to me and whispered, "Kay, Vernon and I need to go back to Novillero. He needs to take the van load of brothers and sisters from Nahuala back home, and I need to nurse the baby. We'll leave Benji here to be with y'all. Do you want Hannah to come with us so that she can get some stuff from your house? You probably have no idea how long it will be until you can go home again."

"Yes," I answered quickly. Turning to Hannah I said, "Since you are not a minor, you are the only child of mine who can leave here without being under guard. Go back with Kim and Vernon and gather up whatever you think we might need from the house. It may be a while until we go back home."

Hannah listened carefully and nodded. "I'll be back as soon as I can. I love you, Mommy," she said, giving me a quick hug.

CHAPTER 17

"Is There No Mercy?"

Lissa:

I watched Hannah disappear out the door and longed to go with her. *But of course they won't let me out*, I thought in frustration. I could see a guard through the window gripping his M16, carefully watching the door. *Oh, but I want out!*

The large clock on the far wall ticked slowly. Everything was eerily quiet, except for the sound of Cochlaeus pacing in the next room. Occasionally, we could hear him talking on his phone. I strained to catch any word. *Just maybe we can figure out what is going on!* I thought. Hours passed, but nothing happened.

Once Cochlaeus poked his head through the door. "Are y'all hungry?" he asked. "I can go get you something to eat."

Mommy looked at us, but we all shook our heads. How could we think of food when our family was in the middle of such a huge crisis?

The stress and the monotony of the situation had taken its toll on everyone. We were finally allowed to run in the courtyard to stretch our legs, but not until the guards had examined every wall that enclosed us.

"They want to make sure there is no way we can escape," I said in a low tone to Mommy.

"Hey," Isaiah called, "let's play freeze tag!"

Mommy joined in the game too. It was fun, but the horrible knot in my stomach reminded me why we were here. Looking upward, I noticed the beautiful blue sky and delicate clouds floating by.

How can such a beautiful day be so terrible? I thought.

A shriek of laughter startled me as Grace darted by behind me with Isaiah close at her heels. I laughed and cheered. "Run, Grace, run!"

As we were being ushered back into the waiting area, Beverly whispered, "The judge is in the other room. I saw him."

"Really?" Mommy's face showed both excitement and dread. "I wonder what he will say?" None of us knew.

The door swung open, and we all looked eagerly to see who might be coming. It was dear Inez. She rushed toward us and fell into Mommy's arms, and then stood back to look deeply into her face. Her eyes reflected the sorrow and pain we all felt.

Behind her, Irene stood quietly. She stretched out her hand and took my cold one.

"How are you? What is happening?" she inquired.

I shook my head. "Nothing is happening," I replied. "I don't understand it."

Inez was speaking vehemently, ". . . and when all of the neighbors heard what had happened, they were mad. They said if they had known, and if the police hadn't moved in so quickly, they would have come out with their guns to defend you and the children. But they didn't have time."

My heart was warmed at their loyalty, but I knew it was the Lord who had kept them from doing anything. Fighting would only have made things worse.

Again the door opened, and Vernon and Hannah hurried in.

"Oh," I sighed. "I'm so glad you are back."

Hannah nodded and sat down, and opened her backpack. "Here is your Bible, Lissa. And Beverly, here are your little dolls."

The next time the door opened, a female officer entered. "Please follow me," she said, "the judge wants to speak with you."

We walked quietly into the adjoining room where the judge sat behind a metal desk. Looking up from the papers spread out in front of him, he motioned for us to sit down on the bench facing the desk.

His eyes peered into ours. "We need to find a place for you all to spend the night," he said, breaking the silence.

Mommy interrupted, "But I was told all you needed to do was look at the children to see if they were safe, and then you would send us home!"

He leaned back in his chair and shook his head grimly. "I'm sorry

that is not possible. You see, there is another judge with more authority in the capital. He will need to see you before you can be released.
That will not be possible until tomorrow, so we need to keep you
overnight."

His words fell heavily, and my heart sank. Mommy's face mirrored
the dismay I felt.

The woman officer picked up the phone and began calling different facilities, looking for a place for us to stay.

"We will be able to stay somewhere together as a family, won't
we?" Mommy pleaded.

The officer nodded, her curls bouncing. Covering the receiver she
assured us, "Don't worry, we will make sure you all get to stay
together."

After several minutes, she hung up the phone and said, "All right,
one of the facilities has given approval for your family to come spend
the night. But it's in Guatemala City, so you have a three-hour drive
ahead of you."

I stole a glance at the clock. It was already late. "It will be dark by
the time we reach the capital," I said.

"Come," the judge said as he stood to his feet. "Follow me outside. We have a vehicle ready to take you."

As we were ushered toward the front door, I heard Vernon talking to the judge. "Yeah, I think I'll go into the City as well, just in case
I can be of help."

The judge agreed. "Yes, that would be fine. In fact, I think the vehicle the Evans' family is going in is full, so maybe I can ride with you."

Vernon smiled widely. "Sure, you're welcome to come along."

Soon we were in a yellow van, rattling down the Pan American
Highway. When we rounded the curve that passed through
Novillero, I pressed my face against the window and strained my
longing eyes to catch a glimpse of the small, block home up on the
hillside hidden in the cornfields.

"There it is!" I cried. "Oh, I wonder if we will ever walk that trail
again."

Sweet memories of life there for the past year and a half flooded
my mind. Our house quickly slid out of sight, and I turned, sadly
watching as the familiar town of Novillero disappeared behind us.

Kay:

". . . And we searched Solola all of last night and finally found you this morning." The female officer was turned in her seat and talking incessantly.

Beverly, Grace, and Emily sat wide-eyed on the seat beside me, shocked at this woman's bold manner, thick makeup, and gaudy jewelry. Her hair was pulled up into a high, short ponytail that consisted of tight ringlets bouncing in every direction as she shook her head.

Will she ever run out of things to say? I wondered wearily.

Cochlaeus was seated in the front passenger seat, absorbed in his own thoughts. The Guatemalan driver and officers in the van sat like statues, with no opportunity to speak, as this woman gushed on and on.

Once when the woman took a breath, the officer next to her turned and asked, "Could you and your children sing for us?"

I stared, stunned, and wondered if I had heard correctly. Leaning over, I whispered to Hannah, "Doesn't this remind you of the Psalm that says our captors asked of us a song?"

She nodded in amazement.

"Do you remember exactly where that is?" I asked.

Hannah began flipping through her Bible. "Okay, here it is, Mommy, Psalm 137:2, 3, 'We hanged our harps upon the willows in the midst thereof. For there they that carried us away captive required of us a song; and they that wasted us required of us mirth.' "

So we began singing, at our captor's request.

> Like a river glorious is God's perfect peace,
> Over all victorious in its bright increase;
>
> Perfect, yet it floweth, fuller every day,
> Perfect, yet it groweth, deeper all the way.
>
> Stayed upon Jehovah, hearts are fully blest;
> Finding, as He promised, perfect peace and rest.
>
> Hidden in the hollow of His blessed hand,
> Never foe can follow, never traitor stand;

Not a surge of worry, not a shade of care,
Not a blast of hurry, touch the spirit there.

Stayed upon Jehovah, hearts are fully blest;
Finding, as He promised, perfect peace and rest.

Every joy or trial falleth from above,
Traced upon our dial by the Sun of Love;

We may trust Him fully, all for us to do —
They who trust Him wholly find Him wholly true.

Stayed upon Jehovah, hearts are fully blest;
Finding, as He promised, perfect peace and rest.

This song had become a favorite during our years of hiding. *It just fits so perfectly,* I thought, as warm tears streamed down my cheeks. It amazed me how the Lord cheered us and encouraged us anew as the miles sped by, taking us farther and farther from our mountain home.

On and on we sang, both English songs and Spanish. Sometimes when we sang in Spanish, the officer who had requested that we sing closed his eyes and joined us.

We stopped at Solola, where our family usually went to market, and dropped off the woman officer. After she left, we waited in the van, guarded by the singing officer.

"Thank you so much for singing for me," he said gratefully. Then he pulled a scrap of paper out of his pocket and busily scribbled something. When he was finished, he handed it to me.

He had jotted down a Scripture verse for us. *Have not I commanded thee? Be strong and of a good courage; be not afraid, neither be thou dismayed: for the LORD thy God is with thee whithersoever thou goest.*[1]

"I know the Bible says that in the last days the church will be persecuted," he said sympathetically. "Your family is being persecuted for the cause of Christ right now. I want to urge you to stand strong and trust God through this fiery trial you are facing."

I looked at him quizzically. *Why has he taken it upon himself to give us this uplifting little sermon?* I wondered.

---

1. Joshua 1:9

Though it was puzzling to get a pep talk from one of our captors, we nodded in agreement. But we dared not look at one another and had to stifle a few grins. Whose side was this man on anyway?

Eventually he noticed our expressions, and seemed to catch the irony of it himself. "You know," he said, "I'm a Christian too. And I don't enjoy this aspect of my job, but it cannot be helped. I do not choose the assignments that are given to me."

Before the others returned to the van, he jotted his name and business address on another scrap of paper and handed it to me. "Hey, if you ever need anything, just give me a call."

How could we ever be in greater need, I wondered, *than right now?* Yet I knew the true source of our help was not man but God. I thanked the officer and politely tucked the information in my purse, determined to discard it later.

Cochlaeus ducked his head into the open door of the van and handed us several welcome bottles of purified water. "Do any of you have health problems or need any sort of medication?" he asked. There were numerous pharmacies in this bustling town.

I shook my head. "No, we're fine," I replied. "Thank you for the water."

"No problem," he answered before quickly looking away. Somehow, despite his role in all this, there was a hint of something gentle and kind in his manner. He seemed to wish he could somehow make our ride more pleasant. Maybe underneath that mask of duty Cochlaeus had a soft heart.

Hannah:

Darkness had fallen, and Emily lay asleep in Mommy's lap. In the light of the street lamps I could see tears glistening on Mommy's cheeks. My heart felt as if it were breaking. I wanted to pull the little girls into my arms and protect them from whatever would happen. I was emotionally drained.

The van turned off into a residential neighborhood. I strained my eyes to see the homes lining the street. The van slowed to a stop in front of a large white building surrounded by a high block wall topped with coils of barbed wire. A big white sign in the yard stated in bold letters, *Ayudando con el corazón,* or "Helping with the Heart."

"Look, the street is lined with cars! Oh, there is Vernon's van," Isaiah announced.

A crowd of fifteen or more people had gathered on the front lawn waiting for us. As we climbed stiffly from the van, an embassy vehicle drove up rapidly and parked in the long line of cars. Three white men jumped out and quickly strode over to the group gathered like a swarm of bees. They all appeared to be embassy personnel, private investigators, or other individuals interested in our discovery and capture.

Armed guards were posted near the large, metal gate leading into the home. Men paced back and forth, staring at us suspiciously and speaking into walkie-talkies or conversing in low tones. A chilly wind blew mercilessly.

"I'm terribly cold!" Lissa chattered, visibly shivering.

We were shocked when Cochlaeus sauntered over, took off his leather jacket, and placed it around her shoulders. "Here," he said.

Mommy looked up into the dark sky. "How do we know they will let us stay together tonight?" She groaned, obviously ill at ease. "You know they lied to us earlier today. I don't think I can trust them."

As if in response, the officer who had given us the sermon on trusting God came over. "You know what?" he explained apologetically, "this place is actually an orphanage and accepts only minors under the age of eighteen. Only your five younger children are going to be able to stay here."

Mommy glared at him, speechless. "We are *not* going in there!" she whispered to me. "If we go through those gates, I'm as much as signing over all of my rights as a mother."

The group on the lawn huddled together, watching us closely and conferring in low tones.

Mommy was adamant, and I firmly agreed with her. We could not comply with them, or they would take the children away from her.

Finally a large, bald white man, whom we later learned was another private investigator, sidled up to Lissa. "You'd better tell your mother that if she doesn't cooperate, she will spend the night in a Guatemalan jail," he announced quietly.

Lissa's eyes grew wide with fear. She had heard the horror stories about Guatemalan jails. No one ever wants to go there.

"Please just do what they say, Mommy," Lissa urged, "or you will be hauled off to jail!"

Mommy closed her eyes. "But as soon as we step onto their property, you and the other children will be snatched away from me!" she whispered desperately through clenched teeth.

Vernon walked over. "I think it would be best for you to just comply with their wishes," he said softly. "You really have no choice. Kay, it is pointless to postpone the inevitable."

Mommy bowed her head, and after a moment of silent agony, she sighed deeply and surrendered. After all, we were already in their hands. "Okay, we'll go in," she whispered.

We entered the orphanage compound, followed by the embassy crowd and other interested bystanders. The large metal gate clanged shut with a ring of finality, and a feeling of dread rose within me. We were ushered quickly across a dark patio toward an open door, where a woman directed us into a small office.

What is going to happen next? I thought, my heart beating wildly. Deep down I knew they intended to tear our precious family apart.

"Please have a seat, ma'am," the lady said, pointing to the couch.

White plywood walls rising halfway to the ceiling on two sides of this makeshift office partitioned this small corner from the rest of the orphanage. Beyond the walls were rows and rows of sleeping brown babies in institutional metal cribs.

How many babies and children are contained within these walls? I wondered sadly.

All seven of us squeezed onto the couch together. Tears dripped from Mommy's chin as she held Emily on her lap, desperately wanting to protect her from what was about to happen.

The crowd had followed us from the yard and squeezed through the door, pressing against one another, competing for the best vantage points. Glancing up, I caught sight of a young white man with a cruel, sinister grin, eagerly taking in the whole scene. Perhaps this was his first chance to observe a mother and her children being ripped apart.

I was grateful to see Vernon in the crowd. It was comforting to see someone familiar. And I knew he was praying.

After a few moments of awful silence, a young woman marched in and glanced down at the clipboard in her hand. "Emily Evans," she read systematically, "come with me." She held out her hand to Emily. "I'll take you to where the five-year-olds go."

Mommy drew Emily tightly to herself. *Is that woman going to take my little sister from the arms of her loving mother?* I thought wildly.

Emily clung desperately to Mommy and began to sob uncontrollably, burying her face in her chest.

Surely, I told myself, *this woman has never known the bond a mother feels with her child.*

This place was an institution, even a business. Our hearts were bleeding, and those in authority didn't even care. There was no way Mommy was going to let Emily be led off and filed away with a room full of unfamiliar five-year-olds if she could prevent it. What cruelty! Mommy glanced through the crowd as though searching for some face that might have pity on our family and help us. But, with the exception of Vernon, this did not appear to be a merciful crowd!

Desperately, Mommy turned to Vernon. "Is there no mercy here?" she cried out in anguish.

Vernon looked at her helplessly, unable to say anything in this horrible moment. No one here could help us. But in spite of what was going on, I knew Someone else was present, and He did have mercy, and He was helping us through this. His heart was even bleeding and crying with ours. I knew He was able to use even this horrible night to accomplish something good, though I could not imagine what.

"Why don't you have one of the older children accompany Emily?" the woman with the clipboard suggested. At this, Mommy took courage, knowing it was pointless to prolong the agony. She hugged Emily tightly and then looked into her innocent, young face wet with tears.

With a trembling voice, Mommy tried to console Emily. "Emily, I love you dearly; you know that. Let's pray every day that God will bring our family back together soon. Okay?" Emily nodded sorrowfully. Mommy continued, "I want you to go with Lissa now. Hannah and I hope to come and see all of you just as soon as we can."

Then Mommy tenderly hugged and kissed each of the children. "I love you," she assured each one in a shaky voice. "You are very precious to me."

I hugged and kissed each one too, as we said good-bye. *This is so hard!* I screamed inside.

"Please," Mommy begged me, "ask the lady if the children may all sleep in the same room."

I quickly turned and asked the question in Spanish, but the lady slowly shook her head. "No, we cannot allow that."

The children were all crying. "Ask her again," Mommy whispered.

I pleaded with the woman. "It is very important that my siblings be kept together," I insisted. "Please!"

Finally, she nodded indifferently and turned to lead them away. Lissa, wearing the backpack, carried Emily and followed the woman. Just before she rounded the corner, she turned and looked back with longing eyes. Emily was still crying, her head buried in Lissa's neck. Isaiah, Beverly, and Grace silently followed Lissa through the gate and between the long rows of cribs.

"God is faithful!" we called after them. Mommy and I held each other and wept as they disappeared from view.

CHAPTER 18

"I Will Be With Him in Trouble . . ."

Hannah:

Julio continued, ". . . Standing in the shadows, I overheard the guards saying something about the grandparents flying in tonight. I guess that's your in-laws, Kay."

Silently we pondered Julio's words. He was from the church in Novillero and had come along with Vernon. The van sped quickly along the dark streets, heading toward the Mennonite Air Missions headquarters where we would spend the night.

"But it doesn't make sense to me," Mommy said slowly, "why the people at the orphanage did not take me into custody. They have the children, but they let me go! I wonder why . . ."

I touched her arm. "Maybe they know that if they have your children, you will not venture far from them."

She looked at me quizzically, and then nodded. "They are right."

Vernon slowly pulled the van into the courtyard of the mission compound. "Well, whatever the case, God has this whole situation under His control," he drawled. Vernon was such a calming influence.

The light from the kitchen shone brightly through the window, warmly inviting us in. I pushed open the door and found the kitchen lined with serious faces.

Someone asked the question on everyone's mind. "What happened?"

"Well, the children are in the orphanage now," Vernon began, and then retold the events of the evening.

When he finished, one seasoned missionary cautioned Mommy, "If I were in your shoes, I would be concerned that my children would be whisked off to the airport during the night. I would go and park where I could watch that orphanage."

Mommy's nerves were still on edge from our extremely stressful day, and her eyes grew wide with concern. Her mother-heart was fully attuned to anything that would further threaten the welfare of her precious children, so she didn't need to be cautioned twice.

Vernon and a couple of other men drove us back to the orphanage. We parked down the street, just out of view of the guards posted at the gate. Time slowly ticked by, but nothing happened, so in the early hours of the morning we wearily drove back to M.A.M. and fell into our beds, totally exhausted.

In the night I awoke to the sound of soft weeping. Under the warm blankets, I wondered where I was. *Oh, yes, I remember now,* I thought, as I slowly sat up and rubbed my eyes.

Mommy was sitting up in bed, with her head buried in her hands, her elbows resting on her knees. I could hear her quietly praying, "Dear Lord, please restore to me the gift of motherhood."

The verse in Jeremiah 31:15 flashed into my mind. *A voice was heard in Ramah, lamentation, and bitter weeping; Rachel weeping for her children refused to be comforted for her children, because they were not.*

I sat up and scooted next to Mommy, joining her in prayer. How our hearts ached for our family to be reunited.

We wondered what was going on with the others. Were they being treated well? Had they been allowed to stay together? What would the days and weeks ahead hold for each of us? In the stillness of the early morning, we brought all of our concerns to the Lord.

———————

Lissa:

I lay wide awake in a sagging metal bunk bed with Emily curled up next to me, sound asleep. Everything was silent, except for the whimper of a baby now and then. My eyes stared unfocused at the red exit sign glowing over the door as my mind replayed the previous day's events.

A warm tear slid down my cheek and onto my pillow. I felt keenly responsible for Isaiah, Beverly, Grace, and Emily. They would depend on me to be strong and encouraging. I was their "mother" for the time being. But now, awake and alone, my pent-up emotions broke loose. I cried, "God, I can't handle this without You!"

Slowly the children began to stir, and I quietly got up, shivering, and slipped into my dress.

"Good morning!" I whispered to Isaiah who sat up sleepily in his top bunk.

"Morning," he mumbled, looking around the room curiously.

Two orphanage children still lay in their beds asleep. The place looked quite different than it had late last night.

"Aren't you glad the director let us all stay together?" I asked Isaiah. "I mean, they could have divided us into different rooms."

He nodded. "When will they let us see Mommy?" he asked.

"Oh, Isaiah," I said with a sigh as I leaned up against his bunk and looked into his face, "I really don't know, but I hope it will be today. Girls," I turned and called to them, "it's time to get up and get dressed. I will read a chapter to you from the Bible before breakfast, okay?"

———————

"Here you are," announced the worker, as she set a steaming bowl in front of me. I looked down to see a boiled plantain surrounded by soupy refried beans sliding pathetically all over the plate. As I pushed at them with my fork, a feeling of disgust rose in my stomach. But I tried to smile and forced myself to say, *"Gracias."*

Glancing around the table I saw orphans hungrily shoveling the food into their mouths.

Isaiah looked at me pleadingly and whispered, "Do we have to eat this stuff?"

I swallowed. "At least try," I said. "Surely we can eat some of it!"

Beverly took her fork and cut into the plantain, which turned into mush. She scooped it up with her spoon and nibbled a little. "Yuck!" she moaned.

After managing a few bites myself, I told them, "Let's eat as much as we can. I know it's gross, but let's at least try!"

Emily looked down at her plastic bowl and carefully scooped up another spoonful of the runny beans, determined to do her best. Once we had eaten as much as we could, we were escorted back to our small room.

Grace crawled into a lower bunk and said, "What do we do now?"

I looked around. "I don't know." Peering out the window, I could see a swing set. "Maybe they will let us go outside."

I poked my head into the nursery where a woman was bent over the railing of a crib, changing a baby's clothes. "Excuse me, but I was wondering if we may go outside?"

The lady straightened and replied, "Um, let me ask the supervisor, and I'll get back to you."

We sat down on the beds to wait, hoping desperately she would agree.

Minutes later the lady hurried through the door, smoothing her white apron. "You may go outside for an hour, but we don't want you to get sick. Wear your sweaters!"

Gleefully the girls grabbed their sweaters, and we darted out the back door into the yard, where we played freeze tag and hide-and-seek. The older orphans taught us how to play a game similar to war ball. After a while, I sat on a swing and watched the children play.

Only a few of the orphans were old enough to join us in outside play. One of the nurses had told me there were around sixty children housed in this one building. "We get a lot of our babies off the streets," she said. "Some are found on doorsteps, while others are discovered in trash cans. Most of them are adopted by people from the States."

The glass door slid open, and the worker hurried toward me.

Oh, dear, I thought, *she is going to tell us to go inside.* But her words surprised me.

"Your mother and sister are here," she said. "They want to visit you, and we can let them in for half an hour. However, they may not enter the building, so you will have to visit with them here in the yard."

My face lit up, and I jumped to my feet. "I am so glad they are here! Isaiah, Beverly, Grace, Emily, listen!"

They stopped their game and stared at me, wondering why I was so excited. "Mommy and Hannah are here!" I cried joyfully.

Just then Mommy and Hannah were let into the yard, and we raced toward them. "Hi, Mommy!" Emily squealed.

Mommy dropped to her knees and wrapped her in a huge bear hug. "It is so good to see you again."

I sighed happily.

"Uncle David and Aunt Sue Beth are flying in tonight," she said. "They will be here to help with whatever needs to be done. Oh, and guess what? We have been told that we should be preparing for a Guatemalan court hearing, so Hannah and I have been busy filing papers and trying to find a lawyer to represent us. Oh, children, so many people are sacrificing time to bless us. People all over are praying for us, and they said to tell you they love you. Here are some letters they sent."

We eagerly took the pile of envelopes she handed us.

"Lissa, did the guard hand you a note today?" Mommy asked me.

I looked at her quizzically. "No," I said. "Did you give him one?"

"I didn't," she said, "but Dorcas Alperez Pichiya came by to see you, and they wouldn't let her in. So she left a note for you with the guard, but I guess you never got it."

My heart sank to hear that a friend had come so close but had not been permitted to see us.

"Oh, and here are some notebooks I got for you to write or color in. And here are some snacks," Mommy added.

Isaiah eyed the snacks gratefully. "Thank you so much, Mommy! The food here is horrible, but we can live off these snacks if we have to."

It was wonderful to hear about life on the other side of the big block wall, but the best part of the visit was just to see Mommy and Hannah. We huddled in a circle as Mommy embraced us and, with a trembling voice, committed us again to God's care.

It seemed like only minutes until an armed guard was walking toward us. "Ma'am, your visiting time is over. Please come with me to the front gate."

Time had flown by too quickly.

Lying on my bed, I reread a letter Mommy had brought that afternoon from a good friend. *Oh, I am so grateful for friends and the encouragement they give,* I thought. I was interrupted when the director of the orphanage rushed into our room.

"I want all of you children to come to my office immediately," she announced.

A deep dread filled my heart, but I slowly got up and took Emily by the hand.

"What does she want?" Beverly mouthed.

I shrugged my shoulders. "I don't know but let's just go."

The director led us into her office, marked by a big sign that read "Private." Several staff members greeted us and pulled out some Legos for the children to play with.

I sat on the couch and watched, feeling extremely uneasy. *What is going on here? Something feels wrong.*

The director hurried out of the room, but within several minutes she burst through the door again. "Okay, Evans children, come with me," she ordered.

Warily I got up, and the children left the Legos. The director hurried us into the big room and toward the little corner office where we had said good-bye to Mommy and Hannah last night. Over the top of the plywood partition, I could see the top of someone's head. Then it struck me—it was Grandmom!

My stomach did a total somersault. I wanted to turn and run the other way. We had not seen our grandparents in three and a half years, and I had no desire to see them now. A wave of anger flooded me as we were marched toward that little office to be "reunited" with our grandparents.

"Hel-lo, Lissa!" Granddad exclaimed, feigning shock and smiling from ear to ear. He stood, wrapping me in a big hug, exactly the way I had remembered him.

I sat woodenly on the couch while Grandmom gushed over us.

My heart thumped wildly, but I plastered a smile on my face. If I wasn't careful, things would go harder for us here at the orphanage. The director was obviously on my grandparents' side.

Sitting on the desk and silently observing the whole conversation, was the bald private investigator that had threatened Mommy with being thrown into jail if she failed to cooperate.

How long will we have to endure this visit? How can they expect us to be happy to see them? I thought as the minutes dragged on and on. *Lord, I know I should love them with Christ's love, but it seems impossible!*

Finally they gave us a last hug and walked out the door. By then, I was frustrated and discouraged.

After Granddad and Grandmom left, the bald investigator turned to me. "You were a good cowboy for talking nicely with your grandparents," he said. "I know you are only sixteen, but you need to act like you are thirty-two. You know, my boss admires you for having guts." He chuckled and winked, flashing a wide, wicked smile.

I fought a feeling of disgust, and turned to leave the room.

"You may go to your room now," said the director, holding open the door.

As we went, a nurse stopped me. "You were wonderful with your grandparents," she said. "It was good of you to be so congenial to them."

I smiled at her halfheartedly. *Am I being watched that closely?* I wondered.

All the staff seemed extremely cordial that evening, so I gathered the nerve to ask for an iron. They immediately granted me permission.

As I ironed, I thought back over the visit. *Does Mommy know that Granddad and Grandmom are in town? I wish I could talk to her!* On a sudden inspiration, I set down the iron and said, "Maybe they will let me use the phone."

Once I finished ironing, I hurried back to our room and peeked into the director's office. "Excuse me, but I have a question."

From behind her computer, she raised her eyebrows. "Yes?"

"Umm, " I murmured, scrambling for the right words. "I was wondering if I could make a phone call."

She nearly laughed, and suddenly I felt dumb standing in front of her. "No!" she said, resuming her authoritative tone. "That is not permitted."

My eyes dropped to the floor. "I see. Thank you," I mumbled, and fled back to our room, very dejected. *Of course, I should have known . . . I must remember that I am a prisoner here.*

Kay:

Victor Ovalle's deep voice rose and fell as he prayed. "And dear

Lord, we ask that You go ahead of us as we enter the courthouse. Guide and direct the hearts of each one we talk to. And thank You, Lord, for Your faithfulness. We love You, God. In the wonderful name of Jesus we pray. Amen."

As we made our way up the sidewalk to the court building, I turned to Vernon and Victor. "Thank you so much for coming in here with us. I will never be able to thank you enough for all you are doing for our family."

Hannah nodded emphatically. "Yes, thank you both so much!"

Victor turned and smiled. "It is my privilege to serve the Lord Jesus in this way. It is a blessing for me to be able to do this!"

Vernon held open the heavy glass door, and we hurried in and followed Victor up a flight of steep stairs. Minutes later we found ourselves in a small office where several secretaries sat, busy at their typewriters.

"Good morning," Victor called warmly. "I need to find some information about a certain court case . . ."

Victor was a dear, God-fearing Guatemalan whose friendly and respectful manner won him instant rapport with every class of people.

One of the secretaries paused from her typing to answer his questions. She got up, thumbing through a big stack of papers. "You say the name is Evans? I am sorry. I do not seem to have any file by that name."

Victor's face fell, and we climbed the next flight of stairs to inquire in another office. Again we were disappointed. We followed Victor and Vernon through the dingy hallways, poking our heads into various rooms and soliciting the help of every secretary we could find. Still, we could not locate any files bearing our name.

Retracing our steps to the first offices we had entered, Victor pleaded with the secretaries to look once more. Finally, the files were discovered, and we were able to begin preparing our court case. Not knowing the first hearing date, we were doing our homework immediately in case the hearing would be very soon.

———

A knock sounded on the door, and I set my Bible on the bed and hurried to answer it.

"I'm sorry to disturb you," Starla Groves, the mission secretary, said quickly, "but I thought you might want to see all the faxes that came in since yesterday."

She handed me a stack of papers, and I studied the one on top. "Important!" it said in bold words. "Character Reference for Kay Evans."

My mouth fell open in amazement. "Are they all like this?"

Starla nodded, smiling at my astonishment. "I need to run to the office; if you need me, I'll be there."

"Thank you!" I said, returning to my room, still staring at the words on the paper. "Hannah, can you believe this? Look," I said flipping through the pages, "character reference after character reference. Why, some of these people I haven't seen in years, yet they still want to help." It was hard to believe.

Our friend, Verda Glick, had called from El Salvador and asked if she could gather some character references, as they could prove useful if presented to the Guatemalan judge. I had asked some of the men who were giving me advice, and they encouraged me to accept her offer.

She immediately set to work, and character references started pouring in by the dozens. Several of my friends in the States helped make contacts too. Old friends of mine wrote a few lines about how they remembered me as a parent, stating why they thought I should be allowed to keep my children. Missionaries we had met in El Salvador, Belize, and Guatemala took time to write their impressions of me as well, hoping to convince the judge that I should have my children back. That so many people rushed to our aid was a heartwarming balm.

Lissa:

"Ohhh, look!" Beverly cried and pointed over my shoulder to the photo in my hand. "I had that doll when we lived in Houston."

I peered closer at the picture and nodded. "Sure enough. And notice how small you were here, Grace."

Uncle David and Aunt Sue Beth had thoughtfully tucked into their suitcases a box of our old photos, and so Mommy and Hannah had brought them along for their visit with us this morning.

Holding the box in my lap, I held up the pictures one by one for all to see.

"Oh, Mommy, look at this sweet picture of Daddy holding Emily when she was a baby!" I exclaimed.

"It is so nice to see pictures of Daddy again!" Isaiah piped up. "Mommy, did Caleb, Timmy, and Drew come with Uncle David and Aunt Sue Beth?"

"No," said Mommy sympathetically, "but I do have their family picture in my purse somewhere." Digging through her big blue purse she continued, "Actually, David and Sue Beth and a whole van load of people are waiting outside hoping to get to visit with you."

"Really?" we all cried excitedly.

"Oh, but Mommy, the director is gone for the day and extra guests will not be allowed inside the compound." I moaned sadly.

"Well, maybe you can visit with them through the little window in the gate," she consoled me.

After our visit with Mommy and Hannah had flown by, we followed them to the gate and watched as the guard locked them out.

"May we please speak to our friends outside through the little window?" I asked hopefully.

He smiled and shrugged his shoulders. "Why not?" He unlatched the little metal door covering the small window and stepped aside so we could peer out. The window was about four inches square, with a bar running through the middle of it.

Do they think anyone would try to climb through such a small opening? Or why else is that bar there? I wondered.

It was funny trying to shake hands or talk to our visitors through a four-inch window. Having a whole van load of people come to the orphanage just to encourage us was so special. We were certainly encouraged!

CHAPTER 19

Behind Walls and Barbed Wire

Lissa:

We sat somberly on the bottom bunk as the social worker pulled out a folding chair and sat down facing us. She forced a smile and tried to act relaxed. "So you hadn't seen your grandparents in years until the other night?"

I nodded slightly, and she plunged on.

"Well, that's too bad. All grandparents should be able to spend time with their grandchildren. And you poor children have been living back in the mountains in a small village. My!" She shook her head and clucked in disapproval. "Well, I am here to talk to you about your situation. You see, in Guatemala, in a custody case like yours, children over the age of seven are allowed to choose whom they want to live with."

She smiled cordially, as though we would think this was wonderful information. But her words were no comfort. From what she had just said, Emily would be required to live with Granddad and Grandmom, and that was not good news. In fact, it scared us.

The social worker had spoken Spanish, assuming Emily did not understand, but she did. And suddenly, Emily burst into tears, clinging tightly to me and hiding her face in my shoulder.

This is so cruel! I thought, taking her into my arms.

Seeing Emily's tears, the lady quickly changed tactics. "Here, let's go up to my office," she said.

We followed her up the winding stairs and stepped into a beautiful private office. The carpet was thick and lush.

"I haven't seen carpet like this since we left the States!" I whispered to Isaiah.

He nodded, and looked slowly around the room. One wall was a solid mirror. Grace made a face at herself and giggled.

"Now," the social worker continued, "I want each of you to draw a picture for us to show the judge. Draw a picture of one person, okay?"

When Isaiah finished his drawing, she leaned over him for a look. "You draw very nicely," she said. "Please tell me about this picture. Who is that lady?"

Isaiah rolled the pencil back and forth between his fingers. "That is my mom. See, she is holding a Bible. And that is God's protection over her," he said, pointing to a large wing stretched over her head. A terrible storm raged in the sky and lightning flashed and evil eyes were peering out of the darkness.

The lady grew concerned but kept her tone even and controlled. "Now whose eyes are those?"

Isaiah quietly put down his pencil and looked away.

"Will you tell me?" she probed.

He stole a peek at his picture and slowly shook his head.

"And Mommy, most of the food is gross!" Grace said, grimacing.

"We have had beans for every meal but one so far," Beverly added in disgust.

Hannah smiled. "But you are used to eating beans at home."

"Yes, but not like this," Grace assured her. "These slide all over your plate like water!"

Mommy laughed to see Grace's dramatic expressions.

"Mommy, at first I had the children try to eat all their food, but I've given up on that. We discovered the orphans love it when we give them most of our food, and we just eat a little. Plus, Mommy," I lowered my voice, "if I don't make the children eat all of theirs, I don't have to eat all of mine!"

I laughed as Mommy's smile grew wider. "And with all the wonderful snacks you bring us," I said, holding up a bag she had just given us minutes earlier, "we really don't go hungry!"

Mommy sighed happily. "You know, I really miss hearing your voices. But it is wonderful to see you now and touch you," she said, her eyes brimming with tears.

Hannah rebraided Beverly's hair and turned to me. "There are four people from the mission outside in the car, hoping they'll be allowed to come in and see you. Can you ask the director if she will let them in?"

I frowned. "I don't think she will say yes," I said, "but we can at least try."

The director was talking with the social worker when I cautiously approached. "May I ask you a question?" I ventured.

She leaned forward and smiled. "Of course," she said.

"Well, several of our friends are outside, and I was wondering if they could come in and visit for just a minute?"

Her smile froze, and she slowly shook her head. "No, I don't think so."

My heart sank. *To think, our friends are this close, but we cannot see them!* I thought.

The social worker watched my face fall and spoke up. "Exactly how many are there?" she asked.

Hope began to rise. "Four!" I answered quickly.

She nodded firmly. "Yes, they may come in for just a few minutes."

I looked to the director, who also nodded in resignation.

"Thank you so much!" I exclaimed, my heart bursting with gratitude.

How we rejoiced when our four friends came through the big metal gate! We hugged and cried, but mostly laughed and enjoyed a few minutes of sheer happiness.

"Just outside the big metal gates are two guards from the American Embassy, heavily armed and holding machine guns!" our wide-eyed visitors told us.

We laughed to think we were being guarded with such vigilance. That night I went to bed lighthearted and grateful that God had caused the director and social worker to allow us that visit. God was so good to us.

Kay:

Hannah and I walked along the dirty, narrow sidewalk toward

the bus stop. I glanced at my watch and shook my head. "I had no idea it was this late! I was hoping to get off early this morning, but all those phone calls . . ." My voice trailed off.

We waited at the corner until a big orange bus screeched to a stop, and we climbed the steps. I sat on a bench by the window, and Hannah slid in next to me.

"This sounds kind of scary, but I'm glad we are trying it on our own," Hannah said over the roar of the engine.

I nodded, thankful for the carefully written directions on the yellow paper in my hand. I reread all the directions and bus numbers we would need for our morning adventure. The bus halted briefly while passengers hurried on and others jumped off. It was a typical business-as-usual kind of day in the heart of Guatemala City.

The first few days the children were in the orphanage, friends had volunteered to drive us over to see them. We were very grateful for such kindness and for the fellowship it provided. But usually those taking us were not allowed inside to visit. This was a disappointment to our friends and to my children, who wanted very much to see them.

Hannah and I began feeling bad for imposing on people to drive us so far across town, knowing they might end up sitting and waiting while we went inside. Yesterday I had asked the missionaries how we might be able to get to the orphanage by bus. The directions sounded complicated because of bus changes and watching for unfamiliar landmarks. But we decided to try anyway.

I prayed silently. "Lord, please help us to do this right. You know how confusing Guatemala City can be. And all those bus changes we need to make concern me. We really need Your help."

On one of these quick bus stops, a Guatemalan man with a backpack hopped aboard. I stared at him intently, hardly believing my eyes.

Hannah elbowed me. "Mommy, look, there is Mario!"

Mario Vasquez was one of the native brothers from our very own little Mennonite church back in Novillero. We knew Mario did business in the city, and here he was!

"Hannah, he will know exactly when we should get off this bus to meet the next one. Ask him if he can do that."

When Mario saw us, he smiled brightly and made his way down the aisle. "Oh, don't worry at all," he assured us after he heard our request. "I'll get off with you and escort you to your next bus."

I was very grateful for his kindness and humbled that he rearranged his plans to help us. "The next bus stop is a hard one to find," he said, "and you might miss it. So I'll just show you exactly where it is."

A couple of minutes later we were waiting for our next bus, and Mario was returning to his errands. As he waved good-bye, he flashed a big smile, revealing his teeth outlined with gold.

We waved back, thanking him heartily.

Looking over his shoulder, he assured us again it was *por nada* (nothing) and that he was very glad to help.

We were so thankful God had placed Mario in our path that day. We had been late catching our first bus. Then, out of the hundreds of buses zipping in and out all over Guatemala City that morning, Mario had emerged from among thousands of people and stepped onto our bus in our very moment of need. Sometimes the little things God does for us mean every bit as much as the big ones. At the time, finding the right bus connection did not seem a little thing!

Busing to the orphanage on our own was going to become a daily routine for Hannah and me, so it was important that we learn the route.

"Lord," I prayed gratefully. "Once again I stand in awe of You and Your ways."

Hannah:

In the late morning sun, the orphanage looked almost cheery with bright pink bougainvillea curling over the top of the high barbed-wire wall. But in spite of the beautiful flowers, the sight of this place reminded us of the heaviness in our hearts.

"It looks so different in the daylight than it did that first night we were brought here, don't you think?" Mommy asked as we hurried down the sidewalk toward the building.

I nodded. "Yes, it actually looks like any of the other houses along this residential street, except for the big white sign in the yard." I hated that my sisters and brother were being tightly guarded behind these high walls.

We are all part of one happy family. Can't we be together? I thought. *I am their sister. The only thing that prohibits my staying with them is my age. And Mommy . . . Well, she is their mother, and she loves them!*

It didn't seem right that she should be prevented from being with her own children.

"Mommy," I said just before we turned up the wide driveway leading to the orphanage gate, "you know how we long to have the children with us again but aren't allowed to?"

"Uh-huh," she answered, stepping up on the curb.

"I wonder if this is how God feels sometimes about mankind. He created us. He loved us and bought us with His own blood. And then people allow sin into their lives and are snatched away by the devil and taken into his fortress."

We stopped in front of the large black gate. Mommy knocked hard on the metal door; the pounding resounded hollowly. She knocked again. We waited.

"I see what you mean, Hannah. God's heart longs and aches and bleeds for His children."

"But they are on the other side of the wall . . . in bondage," I continued. "And the only thing that can free them is the power of God. And what can free my brother and sisters?"

"Only the power of God!" Mommy answered.

A cool morning breeze rustled the bright flowers above us, sending a few petals floating down lazily.

"I don't think the guard heard me knock," Mommy said. "I'll try the doorbell." She pressed the small glowing button, and a shrill ring sounded in the courtyard.

"I hear footsteps," I whispered.

Mommy nodded. The little window in the door swung open, and a guard peered out at us through the four-inch square opening.

"We would like to see the Evans children," I said.

"Just a minute," he said, "I need to ask the director."

Minutes later, he swung open the gate, and Mommy and I stepped inside. The guard was a slender man with a thin black mustache and armed with a gun slung over his shoulder.

"Follow me around back," he said. "You will visit with the children in the yard."

Lissa:

Emily and I raced to the tree, glad to reach base without getting caught. "We're safe!" I called to Beverly who was "it" in a big game of "hide-and-seek."

Beverly sighed and shook her head. "But where is Isaiah? I can't find him!"

Emily and I exchanged glances and laughed. "I won't tell," Emily mouthed to me.

I grinned. "Good!"

Grace peeked out from behind a sprawling lemon tree, and Beverly caught sight of her. "I see you, Grace!" she called, and the chase began.

Grace shrieked as she zigged and zagged through the yard with Beverly at her heels. Around the bushes and through the swing set they came. Just feet from the base, Beverly's fingertips swiped Grace's back. "Got you!" she shouted.

"Awww, too bad," Grace panted.

A huge roar erupted behind us, and we all screamed and scattered as Isaiah dashed to the base.

"Now come on," Isaiah grinned, fully rewarded. "Beverly, aren't you supposed to chase me?"

She rolled her eyes. "I guess, but where were you hiding? I looked all over for you."

He flopped on the grass to catch his breath. "Not *all* over," he said, laughing, "because you didn't find me. I was down in the ravine."

The grassy yard sloped downward into a sharp ravine, creating splendid hiding spots. But even there, the high block wall topped with razor wire lined the property.

"There is no way I'd ever want to get caught in that," Isaiah confided as he lay on his back, peering up at the sky.

"Niños," the familiar orphanage guard called, rounding the corner and sauntering toward us, "your mother and sister are here to visit."

Isaiah leaped up from the ground, our game forgotten.

Mommy and Hannah hurried toward us, their arms outstretched. "Hello!"

The guard smiled and returned to his post near the front of the compound, leaving us to ourselves.

Hannah:

"So I hid down there." Isaiah pointed toward the bottom of the hill where the rugged sidewalk ended abruptly. "And Beverly never found me!"

Mommy and I peered down the steep trail. "Looks like fun!" I said, grinning at Isaiah's enthusiasm.

"Mommy, you can see our room through the glass," Emily said, leading Mommy by the hand to their room's sliding-glass door.

We cupped our hands against the glass, looking inside.

"The bottom bunk is where Lissa and I sleep," Emily explained. "The one above it is Beverly and Grace's. Isaiah's bunk is over there," she added, pointing. "But we get so tired of being in there," she said, screwing up her face sadly, "especially when all that the other children do is watch TV. Playing outside is what I like best."

It was wonderful to see the sweet faces so dear to us. We listened eagerly to every detail of their lives behind these walls, and they anxiously quizzed us about the "outside" world. The time we spent with them was just too short.

The guard reappeared. *"Señoras,"* he announced, "your time is up. Please come with me to the front gate."

Lissa:

"Children, look outside!" I called, with my face pressed against the cool glass. We watched, intrigued, as Baldy stalked into the backyard. Behind him marched a string of guards, all wearing dark-blue uniforms and matching hats, cocked jauntily on their heads. Baldy halted at the edge of the ravine and motioned downward, talking rapidly.

"I wish we could hear what he is saying," Isaiah whispered.

"Me too," Beverly added.

One by one, the guards trotted down into the ravine with their walkie-talkies.

Grace patted me on the arm. "What are they doing?"

I tore my eyes away from the exciting scene and glanced at her. "I wonder if they saw us motioning down there when Mommy and Hannah were here. Remember when Isaiah told them about the wonderful hide-and-seek spots down there?"

A grin spread across Isaiah's face. "Maybe they think we're planning to escape!"

We all burst into laughter. "This is just too good! To think, they are that worried, and we have no plans at all to escape!"

As the hours passed and the guards lingered, we decided they had come to stay, posted to watch around the clock.

A worker slid open the heavy glass door to our room. "You children may go outside and run around a little bit before supper. But don't go down into the ravine!" she said, glaring at us as we slipped out the door.

The guards looked rather out of place, standing fully armed in our playground. After a rather subdued game of freeze tag, Isaiah sidled up to a guard.

"Why are you here?" he asked.

The guard rested his hand on a pistol tucked into his belt. "Well," he said casually, "some prisoners escaped into the valley behind the orphanage." He waved his hand over his shoulder. "And we are looking for them."

"Oh, I see," Isaiah said, nodding.

We knew it was all a fabrication. But it certainly made for a better story and for broader smiles on our faces. We could hardly wait to tell Mommy and Hannah.

Once during the night, the curtain hanging over the large glass window in our bunk room fell, rousing me from sleep. Groggily I glanced out the window and spied a guard wearing a ski mask to keep warm and holding a machine gun, peering back at me.

It was startling at first, but as the nights went by, we soon grew accustomed to it. Late one evening, I noticed a weary guard, holding his M16 and sitting on one of the swings, trying to catch a nap. What a job!

Grandmom reached into the paper bag and carefully pulled out a hamburger. "Here you are, Lissa. And here are some French fries."

"Thank you," I said. "They smell wonderful."

Granddad eased onto the chair beside me. "So how are you?"

I looked into his face, nervously wondering what to say. To say I was doing well would be a lie, but I wasn't doing terribly. So I just smiled and said, "Fine, but I have one question that has been bugging me."

Granddad nodded. "Well, then ask it," he said.

I set my warm hamburger on the napkin in my lap. "Granddad, why are you pursuing our family and trying to take us away from Mommy? Is there some Scriptural reason for doing what you are doing?" I was tired of all the sweet talk and wanted an honest answer.

Granddad sighed and looked away. Finally he said, "Lissa, I'll tell you what. Let me get back to you on that, okay?"

"Fine," I said and picked up my hamburger again. I sensed my bluntness made Granddad uncomfortable.

On their next visit, Granddad tried again. "Lissa," he said, "it's hard to explain this, but try to understand. The Bible says to take good care of your family, and so we are trying to do that."

I stared in disbelief. *How can this be taking good care of the widow and the fatherless?* I wondered.

CHAPTER 20

Lifted by Hands of Grace

Kay:

Fingering the railing carefully, I tiptoed up the metal stairs leading to the flat roof of the mission. Reaching the top, I ducked under the wash lines, laid my Bible on a chair, and peered over the wall into the dark, silent street below. I felt so much at home here on the roof.

"This reminds me of my little prayer nook back in Novillero, Lord. How good You are to provide me another private place to talk to You," I prayed.

The hush and solitude of the mornings beckoned me. It was during the hours before sunup that I paced back and forth, crying out to God for grace to face the bleak day ahead. Finally, as the sun rose, I would sit down and open my Bible.

This morning I turned to 1 Samuel and began reading: *And David was greatly distressed; for the people spake of stoning him, because the soul of all the people was grieved, every man for his sons and for his daughters: but David encouraged himself in the* Lord *his God.*[1]

I paused, looking into the brightening sky. *Lord, I, too, will need to strengthen myself daily in You to be able to endure these difficult times.*

"Riiiiing!" The sound of the phone cut into my reverie. *Who is calling so early in the morning?* I wondered. After three and a half years without a telephone, the daily bombardment of phone calls at M.A.M. headquarters was a strange adjustment. The

---

1. 1 Samuel 30:6

247

mission was swamped with calls about our situation. When we
came in from lawyers' appointments or from visits at the orphanage, I was usually handed stacks of faxes and e-mails from people wanting to encourage us. Many of them I did not even know.
Some of them shared Scriptures and insights God had brought to
mind as they prayed for us.

I felt very lifted up in prayer through this unbelievable trial.
How thankful I was for everyone interceding before the Father on
my behalf.

Olga Hernández peeked through my open doorway. "Excuse
me, Kay, but your dad is on the phone."

"My dad?" I asked, startled. I dashed across the courtyard, my
mind racing. *What will I say to him?* It had been three and a half
years since I had heard that familiar voice.

During those years of absence, I had written him many
vaguely worded letters with no return addresses. These letters
had been difficult for me to write, and they must have been frustrating for my dad and stepmom to read. I had been careful not to
disclose our location or any pertinent information about our life
in hiding.

Each envelope bore a different U.S. postmark, for very often,
kind visitors volunteered to mail my letters when they returned
to the U.S. from Central America. I was grateful God had provided a way to at least let my folks know we were all right. But it
was not a normal, two-way communication, and my dad had felt
cut off from us.

Leaning against the wall, I held the phone to my ear, absentmindedly watching Olga mop the kitchen floor. Hearing my dad's
voice, loved from my earliest childhood, brought a lump to my
throat. The kitchen blurred before me, and I covered my mouth so
he wouldn't hear my sobbing.

His first few words confirmed my suspicion that my dad felt
deeply wounded. I feared I had lost his respect and approval,
which had always been very precious to me. I stared numbly at
the floor thinking back over my life. I could recall only a few
incidents when Dad had expressed his disappointment in me. I

forced my mind back to reality. I could feel his disapproval keenly. I was grieved, especially because of the heartache he had been through.

"Kay, I just don't know what to think anymore," my dad said in exasperation. "This whole matter is so senseless. I still can't believe my own daughter just dropped out of society. I truly cannot believe it! You have prevented me from seeing you and my grandchildren for these three and a half years, and I feel cheated. I have worried and fretted about each of you every day. My health has even suffered because of this."

His frustration poured through the phone lines from Texas to Guatemala. How could I blame him? This was my dad. But he wasn't through.

"I've read all the newspaper articles about you, and I don't know who's right anymore. Of course, I am extremely relieved to hear that you and the children are alive and safe. But I'll be honest with you, Kay; I don't understand why you didn't just do things the normal way. Why didn't you just let Walter and Jan have the visiting rights they insisted on? You surely could have avoided this huge mess you've gotten yourself into."

"But Daddy," I sobbed, "I did what I believed was . . ."

"Surely, Kay," he interrupted, "you could have worked out some sort of compromise to give them at least a little time with the kids now and then. And you would have saved yourself having this whole thing blow up into a legal case. Yes, things would have gone a whole lot smoother for you if you had just done things right. But now, well . . . now everything is a huge mess. What you have done makes absolutely no sense to me!"

How could I argue? He certainly had a right to say everything he did. And it was true—he was painfully affected by everything that had happened and had done nothing to deserve it. I bit my lip as I groped for words, and tears fell unchecked from my cheeks.

After a long pause he spoke again. "Kay, you'd better c'mon back home and get things straightened out."

"Dad, if I come back home, I will likely be jailed. Do you realize that?"

"No, surely they would not do that to you."

I sighed heavily. "Well, good-bye, Daddy. I love you. I'm so sorry I have hurt you."

"I love you too, sugar."

Slowly I hung up the phone. *Will he ever be able to forgive me for the heartache I have caused?* I wondered.

Hannah and I tried to visit the orphanage twice a day. Sometimes the guard would say we couldn't visit the children until later. Sometimes he said the children were eating. Or they were at the doctor's office, and we should return in an hour or so. Occasionally, we were just told we couldn't come inside, period.

Since we depended on bus transportation, we couldn't easily come and go, so if we weren't granted admittance, we usually just sat on the curb until the guards eventually let us in. This was irritating at first, since we were always eager to see the children. Yet it provided us with prayer time together, away from the constantly-ringing telephone at M.A.M.

One day as we approached the orphanage, we saw Cochlaeus pacing the sidewalk.

"He is likely waiting for his ride," I said quietly to Hannah.

By the time we reached the driveway, he looked up, and his face grew tense.

He is obviously uncomfortable to be here while we are, I thought to myself. I did not want him to think we hated him, so I decided to strike up a conversation.

"It is a nice day, isn't it?" I said, breaking the silence.

He gulped and looked away. "Yep, real nice day."

It must have been unnerving to chat with the very people he had captured. But as the moments passed and we were still stuck in the yard together, he began sharing sketchy information about himself. We learned that, although he was American, his wife lived in Colombia.

"I travel all over on jobs similar to this, but I don't always enjoy my line of work," he confessed. Pausing, he glanced around. "This assignment has been especially unpleasant. My work often involves reclaiming children, but it's usually taking them from their father and returning them to their mother. This is the first time I have been actively involved in separating children from their mother. It bothers me," he admitted, dropping the remainder of his cigarette and grinding it into the pavement with his boot.

Lissa:

We sat stiffly in the minivan, feeling out of place. Cochlaeus had taken us to a doctor's office to get "physicals," which had amounted to little more than a short conversation with a doctor about our health.

Now the minivan sped rapidly down the busy road, dodging slower vehicles and honking in disapproval. Two armed guards sat importantly in the front seat, proudly holding their machine guns. Sitting next to the driver, Baldy snapped his cell phone shut and slid it into his pocket. I watched small homes with well-kept lawns flashing past.

Isaiah nudged me and whispered, "Look in that car next to us. There are about five Americans!"

I peered eagerly into the car to see if we knew them, but we didn't. Watching with interest as the car passed us, we smiled when the lady in the backseat looked up and waved.

"I wonder where they are from?" Beverly asked.

Our driver hit the brakes, and we leaned forward in our seats, wondering what the problem was.

"Do the people in that car know these kids?" the driver asked Baldy with concern.

Baldy stared angrily at the Americans and shook his head. "No, they don't, but let's go to the orphanage the back way, just to be safe." He grabbed his cell phone, punched in a number, and vented his frustration to someone.

The minivan surged forward, and the guards held their guns drawn and ready.

I gripped the seat in front of me and whispered, "Do you think they would actually shoot if something happened?"

Isaiah stared at the shiny gun held by the guard in front of him and said, "I don't know."

Hannah:

Verda sighed. "I just don't understand why they permit so few visits with the children. You say people have been turned away from the orphanage several times, even their own mother and sister on occasion?" She shook her head in irritation.

Mommy and I nodded. It was very frustrating.

"Yes, everyone is eager to see the children, but they seldom allow anyone in," I asserted.

Eli pulled a suitcase from the trunk of his car and set it down with a thud on the concrete. Turning to Uncle David, he said, "Surely there is some way to see those children. I'd like to talk to them."

"Well, join the club!" Sue Beth chimed in. "It's almost a miracle if you're selected to enter the gate. We got a brief visit through a tiny hole in the front gate. I just wanted to jerk the children through that hole and give 'em a big hug."

"What's the earliest they would consider visitors if we go over there tomorrow?" Eli inquired.

"Well, let me see . . . Tomorrow they're supposed to meet with the judge of the minors at the juvenile courthouse. I think they'll be going over there first thing in the morning," Mommy answered.

Verda clapped her hands together in excitement. "Oh, then I think we should all show up at the juvenile courthouse too," she proposed. "We would be away from the orphanage and its restrictions. We could all see the children and let them know we're thinking of them!"

We all studied Verda's face, a sudden wave of hope rising within each of us.

"Hey, I'm for that. It couldn't hurt to try," Uncle David added.

We smiled in anticipation of the coming day and then headed off to our rooms.

Kay:

Bending over the washer, I pulled out the small load and tossed it into the dryer. *It is so strange to be doing laundry for only two. I wonder who is doing the children's wash now.* My thoughts drifted to the orphanage. I leaned up against the washer. "Lord, I feel so overwhelmed at the enormity of this situation."

I heard quick steps on the sidewalk. Verda appeared, hurrying toward me. "Oh, I'm glad to catch you all alone," she said, wrapping me in a warm embrace. "I've been so eager to talk to you. I trust the Lord is pouring out His grace richly upon you."

Knowing the trials Verda had endured made her testimony more meaningful and her encouragement sweeter to my aching heart. I knew this older, wiser sister in the Lord understood.

"Kay," Verda said suddenly, "let's just kneel to pray right here."

So we knelt together on the cold tile, the two of us alone, right there by the dryer. She enfolded me in her comforting arms and prayed earnestly for me and my children. It is a tender memory I will always cherish.

Lissa:

I yawned and peered out from under my covers. Light streamed in through the window, illuminating the room with a warm glow. I rolled over and reached under the bed, pulling out my Bible.

"Lord," I prayed quietly, "You know what we will face today. We are going to be taken to the courthouse to talk to the judge of the minors, and I am nervous . . ."

The bed creaked as I leaned on my elbows and opened my Bible. Red letters jumped out at me amidst a page of black words, *Be of good cheer, Paul: for as thou hast testified of me in Jerusalem, so must thou bear witness also at Rome.*[1]

I reread the whole verse, and the verses around it. I wanted to block out the message of the verse, but in my heart I knew God might be telling me to be prepared.

"Lissa, be prepared to return to the States," a still, small voice seemed to say.

Oh, but surely not! I assured myself. *God wouldn't let that happen . . . would He? Lord, don't You want our family to be together?*

I shut my Bible and twiddled its ribbon marker with my finger. *What if we would be taken back to the States to live with Granddad*

1. Acts 23:11

and Grandmom? I closed my eyes and shook my head. That was just too much to think about.

———————————

K ay:

"Good morning, Kay." Norma Gingerich stepped out of the car parked in the M.A.M. driveway and hugged me tenderly. "You have been on my heart and in my prayers so much. How are you doing?"

"This morning we are excited at the possibility of seeing the children at the juvenile courthouse. The judge wants to question them today, and some of us have decided to go, hoping to catch a glimpse of them when they file in or out of the building," I answered.

"Oh, really?" Norma exclaimed.

"That sounds like a very good idea," Mark Gingerich commented as he joined us and shook my hand. Turning to his wife he said, "Norma, why don't you go along with her? I could probably spare you for a day if you would like to stay and be here with Kay."

She looked thoughtfully into his face. "Yes, Mark, I think that would be good. I would like to stay if you're sure you don't mind."

Mark glanced at his watch. "I need to be in San Bartolomé in time to preach later, but I think I have time to take you, Kay, and Hannah to the courthouse first."

———————————

H annah:

I peered up at the inconspicuous brown building.

"This is the courthouse?" Norma asked.

"I know, it isn't extremely impressive, is it?" I replied.

Uncle David, Aunt Sue Beth, Norma, Mommy, and I hurried toward the door. Suddenly Mommy stopped, and I nearly bumped into her. "Look, there is Cochlaeus standing near the entrance," she exclaimed.

There was the tall American leaning against the wall, smoking a cigarette.

Norma hesitated. "Is something wrong?" she asked.

Just then Cochlaeus noticed us, and a shocked look flashed across his face. Jerking the cigarette stub from his mouth, he threw it down and began walking briskly toward us. "Hello!" he chirped in a forced manner. "I wasn't expecting to see you here."

"Yes, I know," Mommy began. "We were just hoping to catch a glimpse of the children this morning. That's all."

"I see," he said as he studied our little group briefly. Then he walked down the sidewalk past us, attempting to appear nonchalant.

Glancing at Mommy, I noticed the look of determination on her face, and I knew she was not going to get this close to her children only to be turned away.

"Well," Mommy said, "let's go in and see if we can find them."

Uncle David pushed open the glass door and held it open for us. Inside, we hurried through the metal detector and started tensely up the dark stairway.

What if Granddad and Grandmom are up these stairs? I worried. I haven't seen them in all these years, and so much has happened . . . Will I be able to pardon them? Surely God will give us the grace to be forgiving.

Mommy had asked several people to especially pray that we would respond lovingly when we first saw them. Vernon had told us he was praying that we could forgive them. I was grateful for everyone's prayers.

Step after step, upward and onward we climbed, hoping to see the children. On a landing, Mommy paused and drew in a breath sharply. I peered over her shoulder to see what surprised her.

Through a glass we saw several people gathered in a small, narrow room. Although part of the glass had been covered with brown paper for privacy, we could see the tops of my grandparents' heads, with their backs to us.

"Yes, that is Grandmom's hair, all right!" I gasped.

The lawyers and my grandparents were so engrossed in their conversation that they never noticed us.

"Whew," I sighed, my heart thumping, "that was close!"

We had seen no sign of the children on the first five floors of the building, so we headed up to the sixth and last story. As we ascended the final steps, an armed guard appeared and blocked our way.

"You cannot come up here!" he said firmly.

Mommy glanced at me. "Hmmm, this must be where they are," she concluded.

Turning around, we retraced our steps to the bottom floor.

"We should wait near the entrance," Norma suggested. "There is no other way for the children to leave the building, so sooner or later they'll have to come out this door."

Sue Beth agreed. "Yes, then we should be in a good spot to see them!"

As we took our positions against the wall just inside the entrance, Eli and Verda appeared in the doorway.

"Kay," Verda announced, "we've decided to head over to the American Embassy and see if we can find out anything. We'll be back."

"Oh, that would be great," Mommy responded.

The rest of us waited, our eyes turning to the stairway every time someone descended.

After a while, Uncle David glanced at his watch. "What could be taking so long up there?" he asked impatiently.

Through the glass doors we could see activity in the street before us. Curious, Sue Beth stepped closer to the window. "What is going on out there?" she asked, turning to me with a puzzled expression and pushing a strand of hair behind her ear.

Norma and I joined her.

"I've seen streets blocked off for parades in this country, but the juvenile courthouse seems like an odd location for a parade," Mommy commented.

"It certainly does," Norma agreed.

Police cars arrived and parked strategically to cut off traffic. Guards jumped out of vehicles and took positions, speaking into walkie-talkies. Cochlaeus paced the sidewalk, puffing a cigarette, looking more nervous than ever.

I felt uneasy and turned to Mommy. "This doesn't look like a parade to me."

She looked at me with concern on her face. "No, it doesn't. From here it's hard to tell what's going on. I'm stepping outside for a closer look," she decided, opening the glass door.

As we followed her, Baldy emerged from the crowd of officials and hurried toward the entrance with another man. I turned the other way, hoping he would overlook us and rush past. But he strode briskly up to me and waved a piece of paper in my face.

"Hannah, look!" he said in his thick British accent. "Here is a plane ticket with your name on it. Your grandparents have been kind enough to pay your way to fly back to the States with them. It was very good of them, you know."

I stepped away. "I'm not interested in going back to the States with my grandparents," I announced icily. "I want to stay here with my family."

Baldy smiled arrogantly and leaned toward me as he stuffed the ticket back into his pocket. "Don't be surprised if you change your mind," he said in a sinister voice. He nudged his buddy and winked before they disappeared inside the building.

CHAPTER 21

"Where's Mommy?"

Lissa:

"All right, children, now that I have written down what you have each said, I would like you to step into the next room." The judge rolled back her plush chair and stood. "Thank you so much for talking with me," she said, smiling as she opened the door at the back of her office.

I grabbed Emily's hand, and we all followed her into the room.

"I need to talk with a few other officials about this case, and then I will get back with you, all right?" she asked.

I nodded, and she stepped back into her office and pulled the door firmly shut. We turned and surveyed the small room. A screen saver stared dully back at us from a computer in the corner.

"Well, I guess we can have a seat," I said, plopping onto an over-stuffed couch.

Light streamed in from a huge window overlooking the street below. Grace stood up on the couch and peered down. "I see the minivan that brought us here. And look, the guard is still standing there holding his gun."

We all looked down at the people and cars below.

"Whew!" Isaiah whistled. "It sure is a long way down. How many floors up are we?"

"At least four, I think," I answered, resting my head on the soft back of the couch.

This morning before we left the orphanage, Cochlaeus had told me what we could expect. "We are taking you and your siblings to meet with the judge of the minors today. The judge will ask you questions and write a report that tells how you feel about your situation."

I was grateful for a bit of an idea about what was going to happen. We had arrived at the juvenile courthouse early in the morning and had been briskly escorted up several flights of stairs before being ushered into the judge's office. She had asked each of us whom we wanted to live with and why.

As we waited in the quiet little office, I wondered what the judge and the officials were deciding about our case.

Suddenly Beverly grabbed my shoulder, jarring me from my thoughts. "Lissa, look down there on the sidewalk. I see Sister Norma!"

"What?" I cried in surprise. Whirling around, I squinted my eyes at the small form on the sidewalk far below.

"Sure enough, but how did she get here? How did she know we're up here?"

Soon we saw more people we knew, and finally we even saw Hannah and Uncle David. They walked out across the street and peered up in our direction, using their hands to shield the bright sunlight from their eyes.

"Wave, guys, wave!" I encouraged the children, and we waved until our arms ached. But our friends below could not see us through the dark, tinted window.

"Oh, I wish they could see us," Beverly said, sighing.

"I do too, but at least they are here. That is so exciting!" Isaiah exclaimed, as he carefully climbed onto the windowsill for a better view.

Hannah:

Our eyes scanned up and down the street.

"I can't figure it out. They certainly seem ready for something, but what?" Mommy mused. "Do you suppose someone important is here who requires a lot of security?"

"It's possible," Norma replied.

The crowd of officials seemed to be closing in tighter. Several officers stood alertly nearby, when suddenly a Guatemalan man approached Mommy with an air of authority.

"Excuse me, ma'am, but I need to see your passport," he said confidently.

Mommy looked at him in surprise and then glanced helplessly at Norma. Norma came immediately to interpret.

"Sir, we don't make a habit of carrying our passports any more than necessary, because they can get stolen," Mommy explained.

Norma translated what Mommy said.

But the man was very demanding. "You must present your passport to me at once," he insisted. He wasn't about to take "no" for an answer. "It's illegal here for a foreigner not to have his passport with him at all times," he snapped, glaring at Mommy.

Norma looked at him skeptically. "I have never heard of such a law, and I have lived here for years."

The man ignored Norma. "Show me your passport!" he demanded again.

Norma tried to reason with him, standing her ground to defend Mommy. "I don't have my passport with me either," she said desperately. "Am I in trouble too?"

The man shook his head. "No, you are okay; it's just this other woman I'm concerned with."

I sighed in exasperation. He was being extremely unreasonable!

Mommy turned to Norma, "Maybe someone could go back to the mission and pick up my passport if it's so important. It looks like we need it quickly."

I turned to Uncle David standing next to me. "Can you run with me to find a pay phone?" I asked. "We need to ask someone at the mission to bring Mommy's passport . . . fast!"

Uncle David nodded and led the way through the crowd. As soon as we crossed the street, we broke into a run.

Desperately I fumbled with the phone, trying to make the call, but I couldn't get it to work. Finally, I just gave up. "Uncle David, this phone doesn't work."

"I guess we should go back then," he said uncertainly.

When we returned to the group at the courthouse, Mommy was gone! Norma was wringing her hands in bewilderment.

"What happened?" I asked, fearing the worst.

"The man insisted that since your mom didn't have her passport with her, she must come immediately with him to the immigration office,"

Norma answered. "I offered to have someone bring it right away, but he said that wasn't good enough. Then he just grabbed your mother by the arm and put her into the back of a car. They let your aunt go along, and then they sped away."

Speechless, I studied Norma's face. "What should we do?" I finally managed to ask.

David glanced toward the door. "Let's not leave until the children come down," he said. "Then we can decide what to do."

I nodded in agreement.

Kay:

By now it was obvious why there had been so much commotion out on the street. The squad cars, security, and official-looking people were gathered because of us! I felt my eyes smart with tears. Sue Beth looked at me tenderly, putting her hand on my knee in consolation. The car flew down the street.

Where is he taking us? I wondered. After a brief silence, I ventured to use my limited Spanish. Leaning forward, I asked the driver, *"¿Dónde va?"* (Where are you going?)

There was no answer from him or from the guard beside him. I watched the driver's expressionless eyes in the rearview mirror. Soon we arrived at the familiar immigration office, and the car screeched to a halt. The guard jerked open the door, and we were ordered out and hastily escorted up the stairs.

"Sit here until we return for you!" the man barked. The door slammed shut, and Sue Beth and I stared at each other in silence.

"What do you think they will do with me?" I asked Sue Beth eventually.

"Kay, who knows? We just have to trust God and pray."

The wait was agonizing. "What can they be doing to take so long?" I wondered.

After some time, the men burst through the door again, urging us to come with them immediately. They hurried us down the stairs. "Go faster!" they said.

Getting back into the little car, we sped away again. I tried my question once more. *"¿Dónde va?"* I asked.

This time the driver turned toward me. *"El Aeropuerto,"* he said.

Okay, I thought, *so now we are heading for the airport.* Somehow I had suspected that. "Sue Beth, I get it! I think I understand what is going on. They must be planning to fly me to the U.S. today. Suddenly, everything makes sense. Why else would they have stopped off by Immigration except to push through the paperwork?"

"Yeah, I bet you're right." She nodded.

I leaned back against the seat and closed my eyes. Even though the driver had not given me the news I had wanted, it was somehow comforting to at least be told the truth.

Lissa:

The door opened and the judge stepped into the office, followed by a tall, slender American ready to interpret if necessary. I spun around from my view out the window and tried to swallow the lump in my throat.

The judge must make the final decision, I remembered.

In her hand was a yellow sheet of paper. Glancing at it, she took a deep breath and started reading in Spanish. I stared at her, listening carefully to her words. "Since you are American citizens . . ."

She spoke long, official words, followed by our names and ages, leaving my mind weary and confused.

"Do you understand?" the judge asked, pausing and looking intently into my face.

I jumped. "Understand what?" I asked.

The judge sighed. "As I read, since you are American citizens you must be judged in the United States of America. Tomorrow morning you will fly home with your grandparents to the States. A court there will hear your case. Do you understand what I am saying?"

Her words crashed in around me like a wave of doom. "Oh, uh, yes, ma'am," I answered numbly.

You are returning to the U.S., she had said. Tears filled my eyes, and spilled onto my cheeks. All I could think was, *We don't want to leave Guatemala and go live with our grandparents! What is going to happen to our family?*

The children sat quietly on the couch, listening to the judge and watching me dab my eyes with a tissue.

Beverly leaned over and whispered in my ear, "Why are you crying?"

Sadly, I whispered back, "Because, Beverly, the lady just said we are going back to the States tomorrow with Granddad and Grandmom."

Her eyes grew wide as she fought back tears. "What about Mommy?" she asked.

"I don't know," I replied, and a fresh wave of tears flooded my eyes. The judge's form swam in front of me, and I barely heard her voice as she continued speaking. *What will happen to Mommy?* I thought desperately.

The door opened again as Cochlaeus entered. "Everything is ready," he announced to the judge and the interpreter.

The interpreter looked at his watch and then at us, "Okay, kids, it is time to take you down to the car; and then we will be driving you over to the American Embassy. Now, listen very carefully. You are not allowed to speak to your friends waiting downstairs to see you, except to tell them good-bye. All right," he said, motioning for us to follow closely behind him. "Let's go!"

I stumbled blindly down the steps, holding Emily's hand and wiping my eyes with the wadded tissue. *Why did he tell us we can't talk to our friends?* I thought as we tried to keep up with his long steps.

As Cochlaeus and a string of guards escorted us out of the building, we were met by a crowd of dear faces. I could see Hannah reaching out her arms and smiling, and Norma was right beside her. I saw Eli and Verda Glick and Uncle David. As we were rushed past them, Hannah gave me a quick hug.

"Hannah," I cried, "they said we're going to be taken to the States tomorrow!"

We were not allowed to stop walking. I wanted so badly to stop and speak with these friends of ours, but I couldn't. The guards shoved me on.

"God will take care of you!" Hannah called.

The tall American interpreter turned and gave Hannah a scornful glance. "Yeah, He certainly will!" he sneered.

We were hurried into the minivan, and the guards piled in after us.

As the van began moving, the little huddle of friends stood with their arms outstretched toward us. The precious group became a blur through my tears as we sped away.

Even though we were separated, we knew we were loved and supported by our family in Christ.

Cochlaeus led us past the long line of people waiting to get into the Embassy.

"Don't worry," he said, "we have special passes and will be able to go right in."

We stepped into the beautiful lobby, and an attractive secretary seated at the desk welcomed us. "The grandparents are waiting in the private conference room," she said, pointing down the hall.

Slowly following our escort, we stared at the glistening marble floor and exquisite mahogany furniture. I suddenly felt like I was in the States again, visiting some prestigious hotel.

"They should be in here," Cochlaeus said as he pushed open a door and peeked in. "Yep, this is it." He held the door wide and waited for us to enter.

Granddad and Grandmom were seated alone at a long, beautiful table. "Hey!" Granddad called out in his typical friendly voice, pushing back his chair and standing to his feet. Grandmom hurried over to us and hugged each of us tightly, sighing happily.

Turning to Cochlaeus, she said, "Children, let's thank this man for the wonderful job he has done. Soon, you will be back in the United States with your natural family!"

I looked into her face, hardly believing my ears. This was the strangest comment she could have made. *They are taking us away from our most "natural" family member, Mommy!* I thought.

Grandmom chatted incessantly about how wonderful this was, but I sat stoically at the table, not daring to express the angry feelings burning in my heart.

Hannah:

Outside of Immigration, the conversation suddenly stopped as I joined our small group of anxious friends, eager to hear what I had learned.

"She isn't here," I told them breathlessly. "I have looked upstairs, searched every hallway, and asked different people if they have seen a lady with a thing on her head like mine, but no, nobody has seen such a lady. I don't think she is here. I don't know what to do, but we just have to find her!" I said fearfully.

A vehicle honked and approached the curb near us. It was the mission vehicle.

"Oh, they must have brought your mother's passport," Norma announced as she hurried over. After talking briefly with the driver, she nodded, and accepted Mommy's passport. Turning to us, she said, "Darrell says he can take us to the American Embassy to look for her."

"Hey, that would be great!" Uncle David agreed, hurrying over to open the door for us.

As we sped toward the embassy, I was overcome with emotion. Laying my head on Norma's shoulder, I cried.

At the embassy, we took our places in the long line snaking its way into the building. When we finally stepped into a waiting room and found seats along the wall, a side door opened and a tall man strode in.

He looks familiar, I thought. *Haven't I seen him before? Oh, yes, he is the man who mocked me about God taking care of the children.*

The tall man approached me and shook my hand, pretending to be cordial, as though he were a friend wanting to help.

"Mommy was taken somewhere this morning, and we are trying to locate her," I said. "Do you know where she is?"

He smiled. "Yes," he said, feigning sympathy. "I have an idea where she is, but I cannot tell you. Only she will be able to tell you."

I stared at him in disbelief. *What a ridiculous answer,* I thought. There he sat, calmly and graciously telling me he wouldn't give me the information I needed. I restrained myself and tried to remain calm, but oh, the turmoil within! *Doesn't he get it? This is an emergency situation!* Surely he must have known how desperate I felt, yet there was not a trace of genuine concern on his face.

As the man continued speaking in circles, I noticed Norma hurrying toward me. "Come, Hannah!" she exclaimed. "We have to leave RIGHT NOW!"

I jumped up and muttered a token "thank you" to the unhelpful man as Norma and I dashed hastily toward the front door.

"I just phoned the mission," Norma explained, panting. "They said Sue Beth just called with an update on your mom."

My ears perked up to catch every detail.

"Your mother is now at the airport and about to be flown out of the country."

"Oh, no!" I gasped. "We have got to get there before her flight takes off!" My steps quickened.

As we rushed down the hallway, an office door opened, and out stepped Granddad.

"Hiiiii," he said in his hearty "glad-to-see-you" fashion and gave me a hug.

I tried to smile, but thought, *Oh, this is so bizarre! This is the awkward moment I dreaded. How can my granddad act as if there's nothing strange about our bumping into one another in the American Embassy of Guatemala after all these years?*

He said something else, but I only remember not being thrilled to see him.

"Excuse me," I said, "but we really have to go."

Once outside, we ran to the street and flagged a taxi. Climbing in, Norma leaned forward. "Please drive as fast as you can to the airport," she begged the driver.

The driver gave a quick nod, and we were off. The small car darted in and out of traffic, dodging people and buses. As we sped down the street, I bent over my lap and tried to jot my dear Mommy a quick note.

Lissa:

After a hectic day, we were back in the orphanage for what was to be our last night. If everything went as the judge said, we would be traveling back to the States tomorrow with Grandmom and Granddad. *Oh, how I dread tomorrow,* I thought. *Will we see Mommy and Hannah before we go? When will this ever end? When will we be a normal family again?*

Emily patted my arm, and I looked up from my journal.

"I want to see Mommy and Hannah. When will they come to visit?"

I wished she hadn't asked. I had been trying to ignore the same nagging question myself for hours. "Oh, Emily, I don't know. But they have come every day since we were put in here nine days ago, so I imagine they will try to come tonight."

She nodded soberly, but I could tell she sensed my anxiety. The other children sat on the floor playing a game with Enrique and Lluvia. These two orphans slept in our room as well, so they spent all day, every day, with us.

"It is getting too dark in here," Lluvia proclaimed loudly as she hopped up and switched on the light.

I glanced out the window. "Sure enough, it is getting dark. Where, oh where, are Mommy and Hannah? They have come faithfully every day, but it is so late now!"

I snapped my journal shut and crawled stiffly off the lower bunk. "Children," I said, "I am going to talk to the director. I'll be back in a few minutes." I slid open the heavy glass door and hurried toward the office. Knocking lightly, I pushed on the director's door. "Excuse me, ma'am," I said.

The director glanced up from where she sat busily filling out a paper. "Come in. Have a seat."

I sat on the edge of the couch and watched as she finished writing. At the bottom of the page she signed her name with a flourish and then laid down the pen.

"Is there something I can do for you?" she asked.

I ran my foot along the edge of the blue rug. Taking a deep breath, I finally began.

"We went to the courthouse today and spoke with a judge. She told us that tomorrow we are going to be flown to the States with my grandparents."

I tried to be strong as I explained this, but tears welled up unbidden. *Oh, dear,* I thought, *here I go again!*

But as I talked, I saw a miracle take place before my eyes. The director, who in the past had been curt, was suddenly very sympathetic. Her expression softened, and she even tried to comfort me.

"Why, I had no idea this was going to happen." She grimaced and put her hand to her forehead. "Had I known, I would have allowed your mother and sister more time to visit you."

Until now, she had assumed my grandparents were in the right and had routinely allowed them longer visits with us than Mommy and Hannah. She left her chair and joined me on the couch.

"Be strong for the little ones' sakes," she said gently. "Never give up."

I wiped my eyes. "Mommy and Hannah have not come to visit us yet today," I said, "and I am worried. Do you think you would be able to call the mission and see if they are coming?"

"Of course," she said, reaching for the phone. "What's the number?" After several attempts without success, she turned to me. "I'm sorry, but the line is busy. I've tried several times."

I nodded dully. Mommy had told me that many people were calling, faxing, and e-mailing the mission.

"But I'll keep trying, okay?" she said tenderly.

I nodded and got up from the soft couch. "Thank you!" I said gratefully.

She shrugged. "Oh, it's really nothing."

Late that night I lay awake in bed, wondering where on earth Mommy and Hannah were. *What will happen to us?* I thought.

One of the nurses paused at the door. Hearing me crying, she tiptoed to my bunk and wrapped her arms around me. "You must trust God," she murmured kindly. "He will take care of you."

It was as if an angel had whispered sweet encouragement in my ear while I longed for sleep to come.

CHAPTER 22

Unlikely Companions

Kay:

"Flight 327, Guatemala City to Miami, departure in ten minutes," a lady's voice announced over the loudspeaker.

The gate just in front of me was bustling with activity. Flight attendants rushed about making last-minute preparations.

Ten minutes . . . I glanced at my watch. Sue Beth and I had been brought to the airport only moments before, where I had been turned over to Baldy.

I sat down and tried to concentrate. *I have so little time; what should I be doing?* I thought. Quickly pulling some paper and a pen from my purse, I jotted a note for Sue Beth to give Hannah.

Hannah, my dear:

This will make a good day to record in your journal. I'm leaving you with some options of what you should do. Just pray about it. God will lead you right.

Option #1: Fly out with Lissa, Isaiah, Beverly, Grace, and Emily tomorrow.
Option #2: Fly out with Uncle David and Aunt Sue Beth in a few days.
Option #3: You could take Uncle David and Aunt Sue Beth to Novillero since they wanted to see our home there.

You could either fly out with them or schedule an earlier flight if you don't want to wait that long to join the others.

Things for you to do:
- *Jump for joy! We are being counted worthy!*
- *Contact Laura and Kevin to tell them what has happened.*
- *Pay Starla (the mission secretary) for our phone usage.*
  - *Collect things that would soon be critically important for us; especially things for a court case.*

I love you!

God will be with you–and me–and Lissa, Isaiah, Beverly, Grace, and Emily.

Stay close to Him.

I miss you!

Mom

Sensing that my flight was about to board, Sue Beth reached into her purse and gave me nearly all of the American money she had.

"Here, Kay, you might need this."

I wasn't sure why I would need it. After all, do prisoners need money? But I accepted it gratefully. Sue Beth had witnessed yet another eventful moment of my life, but it was time to part again. We embraced tearfully, and then she turned and left to phone someone to pick her up.

I had pondered this moment before. If I were flown to the U.S., one of the private investigators would probably escort me to ensure that I was handed over to the proper authorities in the U.S. In such an instance, I had hoped it would be Cochlaeus because of his almost gentle, apologetic manner. I had not even let myself think about being stuck with Baldy, that mountain of a man who was so arrogant, rude, and obnoxious!

Now the moment had come, and I was placed with none other than Baldy himself! We eyed one another warily. It was clear Baldy was just as unhappy with this arrangement as I was. This was an assignment we would both have to endure.

I sat waiting for Baldy's instructions. Rushing me out of the country against my will and without my passport made for a major hassle, requiring a lot of spur-of-the-moment paperwork. I couldn't board the plane until everything was approved.

Finally, after a lengthy session talking forcefully with the attendants and the manager at the counter, Baldy said it was time for us to run and catch our flight. And I nearly did have to run in order to keep up with his long, brisk strides, even though my only baggage was my purse.

As we sped to our gate, someone called my name. I glanced around.

"Kay, the Lord bless you! Be strong! May the Lord go with you!"

I turned toward the source of those beautiful English words. At the end of the hall were friends from M.A.M. They had learned what was happening and had rushed over, hoping to tell me good-bye before I boarded the plane. How sweet! It meant so much and was just the boost of encouragement I needed.

As they waved and called out to me, my heart was deeply moved, and tears spilled down my cheeks. This was such a painful way to leave, yet God had sent friends to strengthen me. Though I saw them for only a few seconds, that beautiful scene was forever etched in my memory, and I will always cherish it.

As Baldy and I took our seats toward the rear of the airliner, I breathed a grateful prayer for having been given a window seat. From a security standpoint, the window seat made sense, to ensure that I would not escape down the aisle. But from my perspective, a window seat would provide my only hope of "escaping" Baldy. This way, I could at least look out the window and fix my gaze elsewhere without having to look past him.

As soon as I was seated, a Guatemalan stewardess appeared at the end of our row and handed me a note. I could feel Baldy watching me out of the corner of his eye. I was grateful he at least had the decency not to look on and read the cherished words my daughter had written.

Dearest Mommy,

God is in control! This is part of His perfect will. "All things work together for good to those who love God, to those who are the called according to His purpose. For whom He foreknew, He also predestined to be conformed to the image of His Son, that He might be the firstborn among many brethren. Moreover, whom He predestined, these He also called, whom He called, these He also justified, and whom He justified, these He also glorified."

Please read more there in Romans 8. God is so good! I love you very much!

(Psalm 91 and Isaiah 54) God is stronger. I hope to fly out tomorrow with the children.

Love, Hannah

Holding the note tenderly, I savored every word before slipping it into my purse. It was a timely note, which I needed right then, encouraging me to be strong in the Lord. Hannah must have arrived at the airport right after I boarded the plane. I imagined her and the cluster of well-wishers inside the airport, praying for me and my family.

––––––––

Hannah:

My friends and I peered through the window at the 737 taxiing slowly into position for takeoff. Then, with engines roaring, it gathered speed and rushed down the runway. In moments it lifted into the sky.

My eyes were glued to the aircraft becoming smaller with every second. I wiped tears from my cheeks. That plane held the dearest person on earth to me, but it was taking her farther and farther away.

How I wish I could have done more than send a hasty note with the flight attendant, I thought. *But at least I was able to do that much. I looked at the little group gathered with me. What a comfort to have these precious friends here so I'm not experiencing this terrible moment alone. Thank You, Father!*

Heading to the pay phones on a nearby wall, I reached into my purse for the slip of paper with the phone number where I could reach Grandmom and Granddad.

"Yes, Granddad, I've decided since the children are flying out tomorrow, I'll take you up on that offer for a ticket with them. Yes . . . and thank you. Bye."

Turning from the pay phone, I noticed a very familiar Guatemalan man striding swiftly toward me.

"*¿Qúe está pasando? ¿Está Kay aquí todavía?*" he asked breathlessly.

I looked intently into his kind face. "No, Dr. Casares, her plane just took off."

Glancing toward the window, his shoulders sagged and a sigh of frustration escaped his lips. Someone had notified him about Mommy's situation, and he had dropped everything and rushed over, hoping to influence the authorities not to send Mommy to the States. He was too late. But what an encouragement that even our Guatemalan family physician cared enough to come.

Slowly our group drifted out to the parking lot, many of us in tears. There was no longer any need to hurry. Mommy was gone. As we got into the van, Vernon led a heartfelt prayer, and then Sue Beth handed me the note Mommy had written just before her flight. As the van wove its way through the thick city traffic, my eyes looked out the window, but my mind was on the note in my hands.

Jump for joy . . . We are counted worthy . . . I shook my head. *What an awesome thought!*

Kay:

Making small talk with someone you don't care to get acquainted with can be a challenge. A mutual lack of appreciation for each other may well have been the only thing we had in common.

Kay, I thought to myself, *this could be a pretty miserable day if you don't at least try to talk to him.* So I gathered enough courage to say something.

I started with a simple question. "So, where are you from?"

He turned toward me and said, "London, but I live wherever my work takes me. All over the world, ya know!"

He responded defensively to nearly every question I asked. Finally I dared to ask a few questions about our discovery and capture, but he always shook his head.

"I cannot give you an answer for that," he'd say in his thick British accent. "It is privileged information, ya know." Then he would look smugly away.

He pulled a note from his pocket and proceeded to quiz me

about certain things from it. I quickly realized it was a note Lissa had intended for me. How it had ended up in his hands instead, I couldn't imagine.

In the note, Lissa had used our secret code names, Baldy and Cochlaeus, as she referred to the two private investigators. He had rightly figured out that Baldy referred to him, since he so obviously fit the description. He grimaced as he read the name.

"Why did you refer to my coworker as 'Cochlaeus'?" he asked.

It really bugged him to not know the background on this name, but I didn't see any point in letting him in on our little family secret. I looked into his hard face. "I can't tell you that," I said. "That is privileged information, you know."

He looked away, irritated, and then tried another approach. Throughout the evening, he attempted to get me to answer this question, but I remained resolute. I could play this game too.

Our little outing was not getting off to a very good start. The thought of being Baldy's prisoner for the trip annoyed me. *Lord, why didn't you allow Cochlaeus to be my escort instead of Baldy? There seemed to be at least a hint of compassion in Cochlaeus, whereas Baldy appears to have none. It might ruin his "tough guy" image. And Lord, this flight would be so much more tolerable with Cochlaeus. He would at least leave me alone with my thoughts about my children.*

Nonetheless, I had to come to grips with reality. God had clearly chosen for me to spend this time with Baldy. I could hear Baldy telling a stranger in the aisle seat about how he had to break his date with the most beautiful girl in all of Guatemala in order to escort this prisoner back to the U.S.

I looked out my small window and thought, *Oh, how can I tolerate this man all day long?* Then a mischievous thought came to me. *Kay, you thought you were stuck with him. Well, he is stuck with you too. He can't get away from you anymore than you can get away from him! Just maybe something good can come out of this. He obviously needs the Lord. His abrasive personality has made that apparent.*

I decided I should use this rare opportunity to witness to him. After all, the Bible says, *Go ye into all the world, and preach the*

---

1. Mark 16:15

gospel to every creature.[1]

What should I do? I wondered. *I don't want to step out of the place God has chosen for me as a woman. The New Testament has instructions about how women should relate to men. I certainly want to be careful, but I also don't want to miss the opportunity to witness to this man, either, if that is why God has put him into my path today. Hey, what if I just read Scripture to him? That's it. I'll read the Bible to him.*

Being from England, Baldy would have no language barrier. "Do you own a Bible?" I asked him.

"No," he retorted. "I don't *need* one because I am *not* a sinner. 'The Big Guy Up There' and I are doing just fine."

After asking a few more questions, I launched my plan. Bracing myself, I said, "I'm going to read my Bible, and I think I'll just read out loud."

He gave me a "You-have-got-to-be-kidding!" look, but I proceeded nonetheless, pretending not to notice his irritation. I pulled my little tray down from the seat in front of me and carefully laid my Bible on it, turning to the Gospel of John. I thought I would begin reading the first chapter and see what happened.

At first he tried to ignore me, probably thinking I would eventually stop. I overheard him commenting to the stranger next to him, ". . . and this prisoner of mine has now taken it upon herself to read the Bible to me! Can you believe what I got stuck with?"

Loud laughter followed, but I fixed my eyes on my Bible and kept reading. After their laughter and joking dwindled to a stop, Baldy sat quietly seething. Eventually the other man got up and left to find another seat.

Baldy interrupted me. "Look," he fumed, "you have driven off a passenger by insisting on reading aloud."

Twice more he hinted that I stop this nonsense, but I just ignored him and continued. By now I had read four chapters. Eventually, the thought struck me that I was enjoying this too much and would probably not receive any reward in heaven for forcing the truth onto someone in this manner. God showed me that my little mission outreach program had a flaw—my heart was not right toward Baldy.

Closing my Bible, I sat silently, gazing out the window at the hazy patches of brown land and blue water far below. *What should I do?* I silently asked God. *You know, I really should ask Baldy's forgiveness for my pushiness,* I thought. *If I don't, God may not be able to use me at all to reach him with the truth he so desperately needs.*

Welcoming the silence, Baldy turned to me. "You really need to go to court right away so a judge can iron out all these legal problems between you and your in-laws."

I paused, wondering how the Lord wanted me to answer. "Yes, I do have a lot of problems that will have to be addressed before a judge," I agreed. "But someday you, I, and everyone else will have to face the Judge of all judges. Each one of us will be required to give an account of our lives. And that Judge will be the One who will judge your soul. Are you ready for that?"

He looked away.

Before long we would be landing, and I felt it was time to make my apology. Looking up at him I said, "Would you please forgive me for trying to shove the Bible down your throat when it was obvious you weren't interested? It wasn't right for me to read the Bible to you against your wishes."

He studied me for a few seconds. "Well, uh," he muttered in his gruff British accent, "you're going through a lot right now . . . It's all right."

Just as we were landing in Miami, Baldy turned and said, "Hey, stick close to me, do you hear? I have to handle a lot of paperwork so that we can make our connecting flight."

Once in the terminal, we went into a little office where Baldy explained our situation to an officer and showed him papers with signatures. The man leaned back in his swivel chair, sighing deeply as he checked them over carefully. Then he nodded casually and told Baldy where to go next.

We were soon assigned to an attractive lady officer who escorted us to the gate for our connecting flight to Houston. As we walked briskly along, Baldy talked nonstop, as if trying to impress her, hardly giving her a chance to say anything.

"Hey, ya know what?" he said, digging his hand deep into his shirt pocket and pulling out a small notebook. "I've got to make a phone call."

As we waited, I turned to the lady officer. "Could you please take me to the ladies' room?"

"Of course," she said and led the way.

As soon as we rounded the corner out of Baldy's sight, the woman looked squarely at me and said, "What are your charges? I mean, what did you do?"

Standing by the long metal sink in the restroom, I gave her a nutshell version of our story.

She was extremely sweet and sympathetic. "You know," she said, "I am a Christian, too, and I really think this kind of thing will be happening more and more to Christians as time goes on."

I heartily agreed. Rejoining Baldy, who was by now waiting for us, we hurried on to the boarding gate. After checking in, it was time for the woman to leave us.

"God bless you," the woman said, kissing my cheek and embracing me tenderly. She was such an encouragement to me, and I found my eyes suddenly filling with tears. "I'm going to be praying for you," she said. Then turning, she walked briskly past Baldy, not even acknowledging his presence.

Baldy's eyes bulged with anger. "You made me look bad in front of her," he snarled through clenched teeth.

"I'm sorry," I replied, "I didn't mean to. It's just that she is a Christian and she understands."

I sat down to wait near our gate, wanting to be alone. I opened my Bible, but the words seemed to swim across the page as tears flowed steadily.

Baldy didn't know what to do with me. He kept offering to buy me snacks or drinks. I had refused the meal on the plane, and perhaps he was worried I might faint, and he would be held responsible.

"Hey, don't worry about me," I assured him. "I'll be fine." I continued reading my Bible. God was changing my heart toward Baldy, and I was determined not to force Scripture on him anymore. He was definitely acting nicer toward me. He even sat down next to me while we waited and asked what I was reading in my Bible. I showed him and shared briefly what it meant to me, but I was careful not to say too much.

Once we boarded the plane for Houston, he asked, "Hey, where are the Ten Commandments in the Bible?"

I looked them up and pointed them out to him. He read silently and asked a few questions. I answered them as simply and accurately as I knew how.

On the flight from Guatemala to Miami he had asked me some trick questions about the Bible. I wondered if he would do so again, but he didn't. Then he asked where the Bible teaches about the end of the world. I looked up some of those passages, and again he read. There was definitely a different manner—a seriousness—that hadn't been there before. As we began the long descent into Houston, he got up and left his seat for a long while.

I took this opportunity to write him a letter, for I knew we would soon be parting ways. I wrote out some key verses for him, since he had no knowledge of the Bible. After he returned, I handed him my letter.

"I want you to know God loves you very much and has a purpose for your life." As I spoke, his eyes grew moist, and he looked away thoughtfully.

It would be a miracle for such a man to humble himself and surrender his life to Jesus. The Holy Spirit was doing something in his heart. But how Baldy would respond, I may not know until eternity.

CHAPTER 23

"Line Up Against the Wall!"

Kay:

As I gazed at the tiny lights glittering everywhere in the city below, a nostalgic feeling arose within me. This is where I had been the busy wife of a trauma surgeon. I had given birth to two babies here, watched my husband dying, and fled out a back window with my six children three and a half years ago.

But now, I thought, *I am returning as a prisoner, and most likely I'll be jailed shortly. What a change in circumstances.*

The stewardess's voice came over the intercom. "Please buckle your seat belts as we begin our final descent into Houston. Thank you."

I pressed my nose against the cool Plexiglas window. Below us, the blue lights lining the runway were quickly rising toward us. Leaning back in my seat, I closed my eyes. *Lord, I don't know what they'll do with me once we touch down. Please give me the grace I need!*

As soon as we stepped off the plane and into the jet-way connecting the plane to the terminal, two unfamiliar women were waiting for us. Seeing Baldy with me, the shorter one spoke.

"Hello, Kay," she said in a cheerful yet professional tone. "Do you understand that you are being taken into custody?"

"Yes, ma'am."

"And I guess you know I will need to put you in handcuffs?"

"Yes, ma'am."

"Did you have a good flight?" the other woman asked Baldy.

He shrugged nonchalantly. "Rather uneventful, except for all the hoops we had to jump through to get the paperwork done."

The woman nodded. "It's always irritating when that happens."

"Tell me about it," he grunted, hardly looking at her. The cool, metal handcuffs cut into my wrists behind me as we walked briskly through the Houston Intercontinental Airport. I felt conspicuous and ashamed, as if the word "Inmate" had been stamped across my back for all the world to see. I had been through this airport before, but never as a prisoner. I was glad that tonight the corridors were nearly empty, and even more grateful that I did not recognize any of the lone travelers seated at departure gates. I did not wish to be seen like this.

Keeping up the rapid pace, the woman who had handcuffed me turned to Baldy. "It's good you're here because a lot's going on. I think they want you back tomorrow when the children fly in."

"Yeah, I figured as much," he retorted gruffly. "You girls would never guess what I had to forfeit in order to make this little run today."

He turned impressively to the women. Readjusting my wrists in the handcuffs, I sighed. *Oh, no, here we go again.*

". . . so my date with the most beautiful girl in all of Guatemala had to be canceled."

I wish I had kept count of how many times he had told that story today. The women ignored his boast.

Once we were in the car, I leaned forward in my seat, trying not to put pressure against the handcuffs. *This ride will not be comfortable,* I told myself as we pulled away from the curb, *but at least it should be short.*

The woman who had handcuffed me flipped on the overhead light and began rummaging through my purse. Pulling out a photo of the Magees, she asked, "Is this the Duane Eby family that work at the mission in Guatemala City?"

"No," I answered simply. I turned my face toward the window, hoping to avoid further questioning. Remembering detective movies I had seen growing up, I decided not to freely give out information to strangers working with my in-laws.

"And why did you and your children get off the bus after leaving the Solola market only to catch another bus back to your house in Novillero? Did you know you were being watched? Were you trying to throw us off, so that we wouldn't find your house?"

"No," I answered, surprised that they had seen us at the market.

She laughed. "Then you probably had no idea we took pictures of some of your children at the market, did you?"

"No," I returned curtly.

"After a thorough investigation, we finally narrowed our search down to the area you lived in, but it still took all of Saturday night and part of that Sunday morning before we actually found you."

"I see," I heard myself saying. Looking out the window again, I added these new pieces to the puzzle of how we were captured.

The driver slowed as we neared what appeared in the dim streetlights to be a tall, dreary building. As she turned from the downtown street, the headlights lit up the entrance to an underground parking area.

This must be it, I decided as we pulled in.

The slamming of the car doors echoed off the cement walls as I got out of the backseat and was escorted toward the receiving section of the Harris County Jail.

Tucking in his shirt, Baldy grinned at the ladies. "Man, I'm ravenous. Are there any decent food joints around here at this time of night?" he inquired, as we neared the entrance.

The driver rattled off a few options as she held the door for us.

When we reached the counter, Baldy handed a stack of papers to the officer in charge. Scrutinizing each one, the officer nodded and walked around to release me from my handcuffs. I rubbed my wrists, which now felt wonderfully free. The driver handed the officer my blue purse and Bible.

"Here is her bag and a book. I guess it must be her Bible."

"Yep," the officer answered. "We'll take care of her."

Baldy and the two women promptly retreated outside. I couldn't blame them for leaving so quickly. No one would stay in a place like this unless they were required to.

"Line up against the wall!" a female officer barked.

I joined two other women standing a few feet from the dirty wall. The female officer stepped from behind the counter to frisk each of us newcomers.

"Put your hands up on the wall, and spread your legs," she ordered.

I imitated the others as they stood as far from the wall as they could, their legs outstretched, and placed their hands on the wall. The officer checked us over methodically from behind. I had never been frisked before, so this was totally new to me. I was very grateful that at least a lady officer was assigned to the job.

Several male officers were busy behind the counter asking questions, stamping papers, and collecting wallets and purses. A tall policeman fished through my purse, very carefully examining the contents. Finally he dumped it on the counter and dug through everything item by item: my wallet, a pen, a notepad, a small bottle of hand lotion.

"You'll have to take that handkerchief thing off your head; I'll put it with your other things here."

I touched the white veil on my head. "Can't I keep it on? I'm wearing it for religious reasons."

He frowned. "Nope, rules are rules," he said grimly. "Just put it right here. Maybe you can get permission on down the line to wear it, but I don't have any authority to let you."

Slowly I slid the pins out of my veil and removed it from my head. Tenderly I handed over the round piece of white cloth. *The keepers of the walls took away my veil from me.*[1]

But the officer still wasn't satisfied. "The barrettes in your hair too. Nothing is allowed in your hair."

One by one I took them out and handed them over. My rights were being taken away. I was now an inmate.

My eyes drifted to my black Bible. "May I keep my Bible with me?"

The officer looked up and studied me for a minute. "Well, all right," he said finally. "That's probably okay. But I'll need to go through it and take out any bookmarks or extra things you have in it."

He fanned through my Bible, pulling out bookmarks and dropping them into my purse. His rough hands slid my Bible into a brown paper bag, folded the top of the bag carefully, and stapled

---

1. Song of Solomon 5:7

it shut.

"Now don't open this bag at all until they put you into your cell. Do you understand?"

I took it gratefully. "Oh, yes, sir. I'll make sure of that." I had no idea it would be seventeen hours before I would finally arrive at my cell.

"Go sit over there," the officer said, pointing to a slab of concrete on the far side of a foreboding room. Warily, I eyed the other people on the bench. Three rowdy teenage boys sat laughing at the far end. An older Hispanic man sat quietly by himself, his shoulders slumping, and his eyes staring blankly at the concrete floor.

What a picture of dejection, I thought, as I sat down on the cold bench, clutching my brown paper bag.

An attractive young woman sat down beside me. She bent over and hid her head between her knees, completely unaware of me.

"Hello," I called quietly. Slowly she sat up, pushing her long blonde hair back out of her face.

I shuddered as she stared toward me, for her eyes were distant and unfocused.

She turned away, looking straight in front of her. "Aaaaaaa!" she shrieked, striking the air. She cursed and railed angrily at some imaginary person in front of her. A cold chill crept down my spine. Burying her face in her hands, she moaned, "Déjà vu." Soon she was again jabbering senselessly. "Aaaaaaa!" she sobbed. "Déjà vu, ohhhhhh . . . Déjà vu."

I guessed by her one comprehensible word that she must have seen this dreary place before. It was eerie to hear her talking on and on to her imaginary enemy. *Apparently she's here on drug charges,* I surmised.

"Hey, you . . . ," the guard yelled an obscenity at the young man before the counter.

I sat on the hard, concrete bench watching the officers fill out the papers necessary for processing new inmates. Their language was shocking to me. They spoke cynically to one another and to those being jailed.

"Look, inmate, go sit over there or I'll . . . !" he bellowed and uttered a vile threat.

The head officer delighted in saying every vulgar word that popped into his head.

"Ha, ha! That was a good one," he would congratulate himself.

This man was clearly the leader in this nasty trend. I wasn't surprised that the inmates used bad language. But I had expected better of the officers.

The most profane officer must have noticed my horror, for he suddenly strode from behind the counter and came toward me. I shuddered as he slid onto the bench next to me and put his arm around my shoulders.

"I want to apologize for my buddies here," he said sarcastically.

I froze to my seat, repulsed by his behavior.

"You see," he continued, "they just don't know how to talk nice. You'll have to excuse them for their language."

How absolutely absurd, I thought and looked away, speechless.

He got up and resumed his duties behind the counter. It was a sick joke that officers such as these were responsible for keeping law and order. The counter merely separated one group of sinners from the other.

What kind of justice is this? I thought to myself.

The metal door clanged shut behind me, and I heard the lock click into place. About twenty-five women looked up at me, the newcomer. A metal bench lined three sides of the room, very similar to the dismal room I had just left. A young woman scooted over on the bench and patted the spot next to her. I managed a smile as I slunk down beside her. Due to overcrowding, some women sat on the concrete floor. One woman with matted, curly hair was lying in the corner drooling and apparently drugged, oblivious to her surroundings.

This room, I later learned, was called a "holding tank." Made of concrete floors, walls, and ceiling, it had no windows except for the glass pane in the door, through which an officer making his rounds could look in on us. In the corner was a commode. Occasionally a woman leisurely made her way to it and attended to her needs in front of everyone, as if it were totally normal.

Angry voices rose and fell as women swapped stories of unjust charges and unfair treatment. Vile language gushed from the women's mouths at a shocking rate. Terms I had never heard flew back and forth about drugs and drug paraphernalia and drug possession. What a strange place this was!

During a pause in the conversation, the most talkative woman studied me. "What'd you do?" she finally asked.

I didn't really want to go into it with her, but I found myself saying, "Well, I was charged with six counts of interference with child custody. You see, I have six children. And after my husband died a few years ago, his parents pursued me in court for visitation rights with their grandchildren." She frowned, but I went on. "I never showed up in court because I didn't want them to have visitation rights. So my children and I fled the country to run away from them. But they eventually found us in Guatemala. So, here I am."

She cursed vehemently. "And you were just trying to protect your own kids! Don't that just stink?"

The thought of my children, and being separated from them, flooded me with a sudden wave of emotion. Tears filled my eyes, and the room full of women swam before me.

An excited buzz filled the room as my story passed from one little group to another, the women turning to examine me as the interesting newcomer with the strange story.

Soon they returned to sharing their own thoughts, arrests, and fates, bringing a new flood of angry conversation and cursing.

Lord, I prayed silently, *please protect me from the corrupt conversations all about me.*

I had never heard such a high concentration of filthy language. I had thought I would have one advantage here over being in Guatemala, assuming in prison we would all speak the same language. But from what I was hearing, English seemed to be the second language for most of these women. Profanity was clearly their native tongue.

How long will I have to sit here in agony, not knowing what to do? I wondered. *Suddenly the thought struck me: I could sing hymns like Paul and Silas did in the New Testament. Perhaps that would help drown out the vile language and encourage me as well!*

Mustering my courage, I put my fingers into my ears, closed my eyes, and put my elbows on my knees. *If only I could detach myself from this horrible place, Lord.*

Finally, I took a deep breath and started singing in a shaky voice. "Amazing Grace, how sweet the sound . . ." Singing aloud in a crowded jail cell was sure a stretch for me, taking me far out of my comfort zone. But the familiar words struck chords of hope in my heart, and my voice grew stronger. "Lord, the light of Your love is shining, in the midst of the darkness shining . . ."

I sang every hymn I could think of, each song lifting my spirits, giving me new strength, and reminding me of the Lord and His love.

"Ink your thumb on this pad and then press it here."

I pressed my thumb firmly in the center of the indicated square.

The officer nodded briskly. "Now step up onto these scales."

My weight was scribbled onto the form, and then I was sent on to the next station.

Various times throughout the night we had been corralled to different stations, which was all part of being processed into the jail system. We had been thoroughly questioned and were even given chest X rays. Jail admittance was much more involved than I had ever dreamed. The worst part of the night for me was when a female officer led us into a long room.

"All right, inmates, strip off your clothes, and then walk over to the shower wall there," she ordered, pointing to a wall with a row of shower nozzles. I stared at her in shock, but she rushed on, hardened to what she was asking of us.

"Give your clothes to me, and I'll mark them. You'll get them back when you are released."

I slowly unzipped my dress, wishing this weren't really happening. It was so humiliating. I remembered Corrie ten Boom's experiences in concentration camps. I could at least be grateful no male officer was present. Nonetheless, I was mortified. I handed my clothes to a policewoman, and she stuffed them into a bag, scribbling my jail identification number on it.

"Next," she called as she tossed the bag into the crate now piled high. The line moved on.

About fifteen women and I stepped dripping wet from the open shower area. A short female guard walked down the line, handing out our new jail clothes. Roughly folded orange scrubs were shoved into my hands.

Such a terrible color, I thought, but right now any covering was welcome, so I quickly slipped them on. The pants were baggy, the legs dragged on the bare floor, and the shirt's V-neck was too low. Nevertheless, I was grateful to have something, anything, to wear.

"Line up, inmates!"

We shuffled over to the wall and waited for our next order.

"Tell me about your charges. Why are you here?" The woman officer seated behind the window spoke almost kindly.

Briefly and as accurately as I knew how, I explained what had happened in the past few years.

The officer nodded and marked something on the paper in front of her. She looked up, smiling. "I'm going to put you on our quietest floor," she said. A word of kindness or a smile meant so much.

"Thank you!" I said gratefully.

"Now, go and get a sheet and blanket off the stack over there. You will need to carry them to your unit."

"You four, come over here!" a male guard shouted from the elevator door to three other ladies and me.

He pushed the button, and when the doors opened, he motioned for us to step inside. After the doors closed again, the elevator shuddered and began its slow climb.

I looked around at the women, freshly clad in their new orange outfits. Two of them looked hard and calloused, indifferent about being incarcerated. But the third was a young girl, and her large brown eyes reflected fear.

She must still be in her teens! I thought, noticing her hands shaking as she clasped the rough blanket close to her chest. *I guess this is her first time here too.*

I lifted my wrist to examine the plastic bracelet I was now wearing, which bore my jail identification number. It was hard to imagine I was now an official inmate with my own inmate number.

The elevator chimed, and the doors opened methodically. When we stepped out, a female officer was waiting for us.

"Follow me!" Her voice was gruff, and her manner masculine. She ordered us into a large empty dining room. "Okay, inmates," she growled, pacing back and forth as if she were a marine drill sergeant, "in case you don't know, from time to time we do what we call a 'strip search.' We're to make sure none of you have smuggled any drugs or weapons in here. So, let's get on with it. Line up against the wall. C'mon. Get over there, on the double!" she barked.

This was routine for her, I suppose, yet it was a horrible, new experience for me—so humiliating, so dehumanizing!

Once the search was over, she led us back into the hall and pointed to a stack of blue plastic bed mats.

"Each of you will take one to your allotted unit."

I bent down and grabbed one of the thin mats. Tucking my sheet and blanket under one arm along with my treasured brown bag, I dragged my flimsy bed mat with the other. I fell into line behind the other women as we followed the officer down the long, bare hall.

"You!" the officer said, nodding at me. "Go in here!"

I peered through the bars into the unit. Some women sat at a round metal table playing dominoes, while others stared blankly at the television.

"This is Cell Block 4A3," the officer said. Pushing a button, the officer stepped aside and the barred gate slid open. I stepped into the unit, dragging my mat behind me. The gate closed after me with an awful slamming noise, metal against metal.

As I entered the room, the women looked up suspiciously. One young woman pointed to an empty cell, saying, "That's yours."

Never having seen inside a prison cell before, I looked around my new room with wide eyes. In one corner was a tiny metal sink. Just to its left was a metal shelf meant to be a desk, attached to the wall. A metal stool was securely attached to the floor. The bed was simply a low metal table. I tossed my mat onto the bed and then sat down and looked around.

On the far wall was even a touch of luxury—a built-in radio. *How odd,* I thought. *If this is a jail, why would they provide prisoners with TVs in the dining rooms and radios in their private cells?*

In the opposite corner was a metal toilet that faced an automatic door. I soon learned that this door stayed open throughout the day. At bedtime an officer pushed a button in the hallway to automatically close everyone's cell door, making sure we were confined to our little individual rooms.

The door slid out of the wall somewhat like an elevator door. I set my paper bag on the desk and studied the little bed and mat.

So, how do I make a bed like this? I asked myself.

Just then, a fair-skinned inmate with long, flowing red hair appeared at my door. "Hello, I'm Jessica. I'll show you how to make up your bed," she said as she unfolded the sheet. "There's really just one way to make it come out right."

Skillfully she knotted each corner of the sheet and tucked the knots underneath every corner of the mat for a makeshift fitted sheet. I was surprised at her ingenuity and grateful for her expertise.

"Thank you for taking the time to teach me!" I said.

She shrugged. "You really need to be careful what you say around here," she said under her breath. "Keep details of your case to yourself. There's a lot of talk in here, and it's hard to know whom you can trust."

I nodded slowly. "Thank you for the advice. I appreciate it."

She carefully educated me on other important little details of jail life that I would need to know. "Always make sure you are at the appointed spot for head count. You must stand in front of your automatic door several times a day whenever the officers show up. You know, they want to make sure we're all accounted for. You'll get the hang of it soon."

I was grateful she let me know what was expected.

Just before Jessica stepped out of my cell, she said, "Oh, today you can order what you need from the jail store. Did you have any money on you when you came in?"

I nodded.

"Good," she said. "If you want anything, order it today. We can order only one day a week. Come, I'll show you where the order sheets are kept."

She led the way to a metal table where an African-American woman was bent over a paper, filling out an order.

"Here is one," the woman said, handing me a paper.

I slid onto a metal bench and studied the list. "Stamps, envelopes, notebook paper, pens, undergarments, snacks—and even a King James Bible." It was a surprising list: the African-American ladies in here could even buy a special product for their hair called "Afro Sheen."

A few medications could be purchased, such as Milk of Magnesia, since the jail diet was notoriously low in fiber. Looking over the list of basic items, I realized Sue Beth's money would come in handy for shopping! I could buy a few things I needed.

"Look," I whispered to myself, "here is a thermal long-sleeved shirt on the list." Feeling immodest and cold in this bright orange scrub suit, I quickly checked the appropriate box to order the shirt.

An inmate appeared on the hallway side of our cell block and called my name. I looked at her quizzically, wondering what she could want. Although clad just like me, she had obviously earned enough respect to be granted limited freedom and to serve as a volunteer. As I approached her, she reached her hand through the bars and handed me a note.

I looked down curiously and read that someone was here to see me. *Why, who could possibly even know I am here?* I asked myself. *I just got here today!*

Closely examining the note, I recognized the name of the visitor. It was the lawyer I had contacted for information after we had first gone into hiding.

"Oh, thank You, God!" I whispered excitedly. I had jotted down this lawyer's name and number back in Guatemala City so that I could contact him after arriving here, but I had either misplaced it or it was on one of the papers the officer had taken from my Bible. But according to this note, he was here, and I hadn't even been in jail twenty-four hours. It did not matter that I had lost his contact information. God was still able to send him, because He knew I needed a lawyer.

The expressionless guard opened the door and nodded for me to enter a special room provided for prisoners to talk privately with their attorneys. As she closed the door behind me, the key turned in the lock, and I could hear the ring of keys clanking on her belt as she headed back down the hall.

Wearing these hideous bright orange scrubs, I felt embarrassed to be seen by anyone, especially a man. I felt about as presentable as if I had answered the door of my home in pajamas.

But the lawyer stood up briefly from the stool on his side of the bars and greeted me as if I looked normal.

"Hello, Kay," he said graciously.

I smiled nervously at him through the bars separating us and quietly took my seat on the metal stool facing him. His portion of the room looked identical to mine, though he had the freedom to leave through the door behind him when he chose. Resting his elbows on a metal shelf between us, he looked down at the papers in his hands.

"How did you know I was here?" I asked curiously.

"Your brother, David, contacted me from Guatemala City and also your friends, Kevin and Laura Magee. They said I would find you here."

He gave me some of the basic facts: some of which I knew, and some I did not.

"Kay," he said seriously, leaning forward, "since you did not show up in court when your in-laws first pursued you, through a default judgment they eventually obtained full legal custody of your children, assuming, of course, that you would eventually be found. You have been charged with six felony counts of interference with child custody since this case is regarding your six children."

Describing the severity of my charges, his face grew grim.

"Each indictment has been given a worth of $500,000 which means that you have a $3,000,000 bond on your head."

My mind reeled at the thought. "Are you serious?" I exclaimed.

He nodded grimly. "Quite serious. What you need now is a defense attorney who specializes in criminal law. I am not that kind of lawyer. This case has grown very complex, and I cannot help you anymore."

He stopped and began again, as if a new thought had come to him. "Let's see, I will be in court this Friday, and I could try finding a lawyer for you then. Yes, I'll try to do that. I should tell you, though, a good defense attorney comes with a high price tag, and you'll likely emerge from this court case penniless."

"I just want to be reunited with my children," I said earnestly, "no matter how much money it costs. I know God can provide."

"Oh," he said, "do you remember the social worker who interviewed you and the children after your husband's death? She worked for Child Protective Services."

"Yes, of course," I returned, remembering that long-ago day.

The lawyer's eyes sparkled as he peered at me through the bars. "Well," he said, drumming his fingers on the metal desktop, "she no longer works there. And she says she wants to testify for you in court."

I raised my eyebrows, grateful to hear she would be willing to do such a thing. "That would be very kind of her," I said, grasping the one ray of hope in an otherwise bleak report.

Finally, I asked what was weighing on me most of all. "How soon can I get out of here and be back with my children?" I asked. I was desperate and anxious to see them again.

A look of compassion crossed his face. After all, he had children of his own. "Oh, I could not even venture to say," he said, leaning back on his stool. "That's something you'll need to discuss with your defense attorney. I would have no way of knowing. But I should go, so I can help you find that lawyer." He stood up and grabbed his briefcase.

"Thank you for your help," I said, rising to my feet.

"No problem," he replied as he opened the door and stepped into the hall on his side.

I turned and pressed my face against the glass window in my

door. *Where are the guards?* I wondered. I knocked firmly, over and over, the sound echoing again and again in the small concrete room.

Finally, a lady guard's face appeared in the window, and I heard her keys noisily clank together. The heavy door swung open and I stepped out into the hall.

"Since you met with your lawyer you will need to be strip searched," she said dully.

My heart sank. *Oh, no, not again,* I thought. *Dear Lord Jesus, I can see how living here without You could eventually harden a person. Help me ever to be tender to Your voice . . .*

CHAPTER 24

Going *Home?*

Hannah:

I paused at the door, not wanting to enter. My eyes wandered from the bed to the nightstand where my Bible lay. This was the room I had shared for the past ten days with Mommy at the Mennonite Air Missions headquarters in Guatemala City. I would always remember the sweet and sad times that drew our hearts together here.

Several mornings I had awakened in this room to hear Mommy sobbing. We had knelt together by the bed and prayed. But now Mommy was gone, and I didn't want to be here alone.

Taking a deep breath, I stepped inside and sat on the bed. Flopping onto my side, I replayed the events of the day in my mind. *I can hardly believe Mommy is already in the States and likely in jail.* I shook my head as if to wake myself from a bad dream. But it wasn't a dream.

"I feel so alone!" I said to no one at all. My voice bounced off the wall, and the words came back at me.

Yet, I knew in my heart I wasn't alone. *I will never leave you nor forsake you!* The words flooded my heart with a wave of reassurance. *Lord, I thank You that You know me even better than Mommy does. Thank You for being here with me. And thank You for the grace You are pouring out on me.*

I looked at the clock on the nightstand and yawned. It was late, and tomorrow morning I would be flying out with my younger brother and sisters. While I was eager to be reunited with them, I dreaded saying goodbye to all our friends here.

My emotions were so mixed up about flying the next day that I didn't even want to think about it. Pulling back the covers, I crawled into bed and eventually drifted off to sleep.

Spread out on the bed were several stacks of papers, a few of my journals, and pictures and letters Kim had brought from our house in Novillero. My clothes were already packed, and now I had to figure out what to do with these things.

Oh, I want to take them all, but what if Grandmom and Granddad could use any of it against us in court? I thought.

Picking up my journal, I flipped through it, scanning the pages. *I'd better not take it,* I decided. I quickly shoved all the personal things into a grocery sack and set it on the floor. *I'll just have Kim send them to us later.* I zipped up the bulging suitcase and lugged it out the door.

The mission courtyard was bustling with activity. It seemed everyone from the mission was going to the airport. I smiled to myself. It felt good to be so cared for. I dragged the suitcase to Vernon's van where he lifted it into the back.

Just before I crawled into the van, someone called out, "Let's get a few pictures before we leave!"

So we gathered, and I tried to smile for the cameras, but my heart was heavy.

Lissa:

I sat in the restaurant booth trying to eat my hamburger, but my stomach was in knots. I kept glancing at my watch and tapping my foot.

"When do you think we'll be going to the airport?" I asked Granddad.

"Oh, maybe in a few minutes," he said, smiling.

I was very eager to get to the airport, not because I wanted to leave Guatemala, but because I wanted to see Hannah and our friends from the mission. I expected them to be there, but I wasn't sure if we would be allowed to see them.

"Isaiah, eat your hamburger. We will need to leave as soon as you are done," Grandmom said to Isaiah, who looked up from his play with a Happy Meal toy.

"Hurry!" I begged Isaiah. I could hardly wait.

Finally, we got into the van and drove the few miles to the airport. After Cochlaeus had parked the van near the entrance, Grandmom opened the side door. "Now, children," she said, "you all need to stay right with us. Don't scatter—even to greet any friends that might be here. You must stay by Granddad or Grandmom's side at all times! Do you understand? And here, put these tags on. See, they have your name and social security number on the front, and our address and phone number on the back, just in case we would happen to get separated."

I rolled my eyes. *How humbling!* I thought. *Like requiring identification to be pinned on prisoners, or attaching information to toddlers' clothing so they'll be returned if they wander off!*

But we dutifully pinned on the tags and tried not to be annoyed.

"Look, here comes Hannah!" Grace squealed excitedly. We had been waiting in the airport for Hannah to arrive, and now we finally saw her coming. I was delighted to see the host of friends accompanying her.

"There are Kim and Vernon and the children," I exclaimed. "And some of Mark and Norma Gingerich's family, Eli and Verda Glick from El Salvador, Sharon Eby and the children, Victor and Anita Ovalle, Lamar and Beulah Hurst, and others. Why, even Olga, Starla, and Kayla came!"

My smile grew wider as these dear friends surrounded us. In this traumatic time, each handshake and warm hug was so reassuring. It was just wonderful to be with all these dear people, but it was also sad, because we were saying good-bye, something I really did not want to do.

Norma Gingerich handed me a bouquet of beautiful red roses, and wrapped me in a big, tender hug.

"How can we leave Guatemala now," I said through my tears, "when you all have become so dear to us?"

She held me close. "God will give you the grace," she whispered.

I nodded and dabbed my eyes with a wet tissue.

Grandmom uneasily scanned the group of people around us and then looked at the numerous Guatemalan guards hired for the occasion. She whispered something to Granddad.

"I wonder if they think our friends will try to abduct us?" Hannah asked.

I shrugged my shoulders and grimaced. "Who knows?"

I noticed Norma coming up behind Grandmom and touching her on the shoulder. When Grandmom turned, she was startled to see Norma's smiling face.

"Um, hi," Grandmom stammered. "I'm Jan Evans." She extended her hand to shake Norma's.

"Yes, and I am Norma Gingerich. We just wanted to give you these roses," she said, and handed her a bouquet.

I watched, wide-eyed. In my heart I knew the Lord had a lesson in this for me. *Lissa, even if your grandparents aren't treating your family justly, I want you to bless and love them with MY love.*

"Hey, children," Kim called, "we want a picture of you before you go."

I looked at Hannah and saw that her face was red and swollen from crying, just as I imagined mine was.

"Oh, well," I said, "I don't really feel ready for a picture, but that's okay."

We tried to smile, but it's hard to look happy when you aren't. Cameras flashed, and then Granddad said, "Okay, kids, it's time to go."

After quick, last-second hugs, we turned and started down the corridor, away from all those precious friends. Then they did a beautiful thing—they began singing. The words swelled and flowed sweetly over us. "God be with you till we meet again . . ."

A lump grew in my throat, and tears coursed down my cheeks. Just as we entered the gate for our flight, we looked back at the crowd gathered at the end of the corridor. One last time we waved to the throng of tearstained faces and the waving sea of hands. It was a scene I'll never forget. I wished I could have stood there longer, but we were being hurried on.

"Come on, kids, we need to board the plane," said Grandmom.

We walked somberly into the gate area . . . and began a new chapter of our lives.

———————————

"Please keep your seat belts fastened until the seat belt lights go off. We hope you enjoy flying with us today," the intercom announced.

As the last passengers took their seats, I peered longingly out the window. Granddad was seated to my right, and Grace was on the other side of him, next to the window, kicking her feet against the seat and looking bored.

The engines whined shrilly, and slowly the plane taxied to the runway. Very soon we were lifting off. Grace peered out the window to the ground dropping away below us. The plane climbed abruptly, and then banked sharply to the left. The view below us was spectacular. We watched as the Guatemalan mountains and volcanoes faded into the distance.

How ironic, I thought. *We had not wanted to stay in Guatemala when God closed the door for us to return to Belize. But now that we're leaving the country, it's so hard to say good-bye. Life in Guatemala wasn't always easy. I remember well longing for the freedom to return to the States. Although we had been in hiding, we definitely had a peace knowing God had directed us to Guatemala. And now, God is again making His will for us clear. Lord, help me trust You even when I don't understand Your ways.*

I stared at the pen in my hands, and reread what I had scribbled in my journal. *It just doesn't sound right. How can I possibly put into words what I am feeling?* I leafed through the pages I had filled while we were at the orphanage, and then returned to the page I had started half an hour ago.

Oh well, I'll write later. I slid the journal into my backpack and leaned back in my seat. *So much has happened in the past ten days. I wonder where Mommy is right now. Jail? Oh, what an awful thought . . .*

Time crawled, and even though I normally enjoyed flying, this flight seemed endless. I closed my eyes and tried to sleep.

––––––––––––

Hannah:

"We will be landing in Houston in ten minutes," the voice on the intercom announced. "Our flight is on schedule, and landing time is 4:16 p.m. Thank you for flying with American Airlines."

I shifted and looked at Emily, who was slumped over in her seat, sleeping.

"Emily, sweetie, wake up. We will be landing in a few minutes. So get your things together."

I gently shook Emily's shoulder. She sat up, rubbing her eyes, and stretched. Peering out the window, I thought, *I wonder if anyone we know will be waiting for us. It would be nice to see our old friends again.*

The ground was getting closer, and by now I could see cars snaking swiftly along the endless maze of freeways. The city looked just as massive as I remembered.

Very soon we were on the ground, entering the terminal.

"Are these all the passports?" questioned the official behind the immigrations counter.

"Yes, this is the Evans group," Cochlaeus answered. "And here are their documents." He showed her a stack of official papers.

The woman glanced at them. "Oh, you are the Evans group. You're fine. Go on." And she waved us on without any further questions.

I looked over at Lissa and shrugged. "I guess the staff here was informed about us."

"Yeah, I guess so. She didn't even look at the papers!" Lissa said in a low voice.

In the baggage claim, Isaiah pulled our last suitcase off the conveyor belt. "Look!" he hissed. "Here comes Baldy and a bunch of policemen!"

I turned toward the entrance, and coldly watched them approach. My past experiences with Baldy had not been pleasant, and here he was again, and this time with police officers.

"I wonder what he wants," Lissa groaned.

"I don't know," I mumbled, "but I'm not happy to see him."

Baldy towered over us. "You weren't expecting to see ole Baldy here, now were you?" he chortled. Laughing, he slapped his knee at his own joke, but we were not impressed. Seeing our disfavor, he turned to Grandmom and said, "We'll take you out through a back way to avoid unnecessary meetings. I'll show you the way."

With that, he turned and led us to a door marked "Private." Holding it open, he motioned us through. We followed an officer down a long hall. At the very end, he pushed open a door, and we stepped, blinking, into bright sunlight.

"Right this way, folks!" the elderly officer chirruped as he led us to two police cars parked by the sidewalk. "Now, you won't all fit in one vehicle, so you'll have to split up. Mr. Evans, you can go in this one, and Mrs.

Evans, you may go in that one," he said, waving to the second car.

"Thank you so much for all your help," Grandmom gushed. "Now, children, thank this man for his kindness, and then get into one of the cars. Hannah, you and Lissa and Beverly go in that car with Granddad, and the rest of us will go in this one."

Lissa:

As the big silver clock on the wall ticked loudly, I absentmindedly watched the second hand go around and around.

Isaiah yawned and slumped down in his chair, wishing for something to do. We had been driven to the police headquarters from the airport and now sat around a big table in this conference room, waiting. Grandmom was speaking with the district attorney who had been assigned to our case.

The meeting seems to be taking a long time, I thought. I scooted the cold Dr. Pepper can back and forth in front of me, and looked over at Hannah, who looked as bored as I felt.

The door opened and we all looked up to see Uncle Leo come striding in.

"Hello, kids!" he spoke loudly, with a big grin on his face. "Long time, no see!"

It was typical Uncle Leo, always teasing and fun to be around. But as he tousled Isaiah's hair and tweaked Beverly's nose, I could tell things were different now. We had not seen him in three and a half years, and a lot of things had changed.

He gave me a big hug, and I hugged him back, although I wasn't especially happy to see him. *For one thing*, I told myself, *he has sided with Grandmom and Granddad.*

He seated himself next to me. "I have something for y'all," he said. He watched our eyes grow wide with interest, as he pulled a stack of notes from his pocket and set them on the mahogany table. "There was a group of people waiting to see you when you got off the plane, but because you went the back way, you didn't see them. When I told them you had already gone, they sent these notes with me."

Anger burned within me to think we had not been allowed to see our friends. But we eagerly read the notes, and our hearts were blessed to know they cared and had taken the time to come see us, even if they were prevented the opportunity.

Uncle Leo chitchatted a while, and then things grew quiet again. Finally, I asked him the question on all of our hearts.

"Where is Mommy?"

He looked away and sighed. I could tell he didn't want to say. After all, he was our uncle and didn't want to hurt us.

Though he tried to evade my question, I was adamant. "Where is Mommy? Do you know?"

He nodded seriously. "She has been arrested and taken to the Harris County Jail."

I was not surprised. In fact, it was good to finally get a definite answer. Grandmom and Granddad seemed to feel the less we knew, the better.

But I was very glad to know. And I wanted to know more. "And why did you and Grandmom and Granddad pursue us when you knew if we were found, we would be separated from Mommy?"

He said, "Your mom's actions showed some insecurity. She needs some time to get her problems fixed, and then you will probably be reunited."

I was angry. Leaning back in my chair, I folded my arms across my chest. *Mommy is NOT an insecure person,* I thought. *But even if she were, why am I experiencing all this separation, questioning, and extreme anxiety at the hands of the "secure" people? Is this how "secure" people act? If so, then I don't think I even want to be "secure." I have never in my whole life felt so insecure as right now.*

But I didn't say anything. Instead, I picked up my Dr. Pepper and took a big gulp. I needed to calm down.

Granddad's chair squeaked as he leaned forward and put his hand on the table. "Now, girls, to change the subject a bit, I would like to know why you are dressing the way you do now?"

I stared at him, inwardly groaning. That was the last thing I wanted to talk about right then.

But he spoke on, with the air of a counselor. "You see, I want to assist you in any way I can."

Not believing him, we just looked at him with forced smiles.

Hannah spoke up, "Well, Granddad, we just want to be modest."

I followed Grandmom up the stairs and paused behind her as she inserted the hotel room key. She pushed open the door, and we stepped into the cool room. I dropped the two pillows on the bed, and headed toward the door.

"No, Lissa, wait!" Grandmom said. "You have to be with one of us at all times, do you understand?"

I sighed. "Yes, ma'am."

It had been an exhausting day, flying out of Guatemala and then the questioning that Hannah, Isaiah, and I all had at the police head-quarters. It had been so confusing. The district attorney who was working for my grandparents had been so friendly, but I didn't trust her and tried to guard each word I said. Her questions had droned on and on:

"Do you know your mother is in jail now? Where did you go while you lived in hiding? Whose house did you stay in? Which of your grandparents do you trust more? Do you want to be with your grandparents?"

My head still ached, and now all I wanted was to go to bed.

Grandmom came up behind me and said, "Okay, let's go back to the van now. There is plenty to bring in. We have two adjoining rooms here. Granddad, Uncle Leo, and Isaiah will have one room, and the rest of us will have the other. It will work fine."

I nodded and headed down the steps, passing Uncle Leo coming up the stairs with a suitcase and a backpack in each hand.

Grandmom said, "Leo, we have Rooms 258 and 259. You fellows will have the first room, and we ladies will have the second."

"All right," he mumbled as he continued his way up the steps.

Before long all our luggage was in our room, and we were getting ready for bed.

"They're afraid we're going to try to run away. It's clear they don't trust us," said Hannah. "But at the same time, we should try to understand their perspective to some degree."

I nodded.

Hannah went on, "They've gone to great lengths to do what they consider best. You have heard their view: They have just 'rescued' their grandchildren from a third-world country and brought them back so that they will grow up to be 'normal Americans.' They have spent much money, time, and energy just to find us, and now we don't even want to go with them!"

I squirted toothpaste onto my toothbrush. Glancing in the mirror, I saw Grandmom busy making a pallet on the floor by the door. Hannah and I spoke in hushed tones.

"Yeah," I said, "but it's irritating to be guarded so closely. I would love to have some elbow room!"

Hannah gave me a weary smile. "I know," she said. "Just try to be understanding. I mean, we need to be loving to them."

"Girls," Grandmom said as she settled onto the pallet, "my back is bothering me tonight, so I will sleep here on the floor. Lying flat like this should help."

Hannah and I exchanged glances. It was clear what she was doing. With her feet up against the door, no one could leave the room without her knowing. Later, when the lights were snapped off, we laughed silently into our pillows. Our poor grandmother was going to extremes to keep us from escaping.

The next morning we laughed even harder when Isaiah told us Uncle Leo had slept on the floor, too, with his feet propped against the door!

Riding in Granddad and Grandmom's van we heard our grandparents' view of our condition.

"You children are suffering from something called "Post Traumatic Stress Disorder," and consequently you need professional help," explained Grandmom. "This morning I made appointments with the highest-ranking pediatric psychologists available in the Houston area. They will evaluate each of you and provide the assistance you need.

"Walter, they said they are full for a little while, but they will get back to us when they can work us in. It might be a week or two."

Granddad nodded as he slowed the van and exited the highway.

"Children," Grandmom spoke up again, "we will be seeing your Aunt Elaine and Uncle Allen and their children."

Elaine was Daddy's sister, and her family lived on the outskirts of Houston in a suburb known as Katy. I was a little apprehensive about how this visit would go after not seeing them for so long.

"And we don't know whose side they are on. How do you think that this will go, Hannah?" I asked.

Hannah shook her head. "I really don't know," she whispered. "But look, here we are."

Granddad parked the van by the sidewalk, and we peered out at the two-story home.

"It looks just like I remember it," Isaiah said in a low voice.

I held Grace's hand as we walked up the pebble sidewalk. Grandmom rang the doorbell even though we could see my cousin Bryan peeking through the window.

Aunt Elaine threw open the door with a shriek of delight. "Ahhhhhhh! You're here! Come in! Oh, it is so good to see all of you."

She proceeded to kiss each of us, and then stood, wiping her eyes, not knowing whether to laugh or to cry, so she did some of both.

She hasn't changed a bit, I thought gratefully.

It was good to see them again. Lauren and Elizabeth eyed me and smiled shyly. We hugged, but I could hardly believe how much they had changed since we were last together.

"I can't believe it's really you."

"Well, well, well, you don't all have to stand at the door." Elaine shooed us into the house. "Come into the kitchen, and I'll get you all a drink. We have juice and water."

Memories flooded over me as I looked around. We had celebrated the Evans' family Christmas here, as well as Daddy's last Christmas. I smiled as I thought of the time we had played "hide-and-seek," even before they had officially moved in. There had been no furniture then, only big, empty rooms.

The three "little" boys—Aaron, Jay, and Bryan—were not so little anymore. I had to laugh at them now, because they had already warmed up to Isaiah, explaining their newest GI Joe set to him.

"Come on upstairs and see it!" Jay urged, and all four went traips- ing up the steps.

Beverly and Grace soon followed Miriam, who was just a little younger than Beverly, up to her room to play. In the kitchen, Elaine bustled about, filling cups and commenting on how much each one had grown.

"My, I can hardly believe the change in Isaiah," she exclaimed. "Why, he was a little boy when you left, and now he is a young man."

Aunt Elaine had such a wonderful way of putting us at ease.

Lauren came over to me and whispered into my ear, "Lissa, I want to hear YOUR side of the story for myself. Would you like to come up to our room to talk?"

"That sounds great to me," I said, setting my cup on the counter.

As I followed Lauren and Elizabeth up to their room, I thought, *Just maybe they aren't on Grandmom and Granddad's side after all.*

Once inside Lauren's room, Elizabeth securely shut the door, and I began our story. They sat listening, completely engrossed, until I finished.

"Oh, I feel so much better to know all that!" Lauren confided. "You see, all we've been hearing about y'all was what we got from Grandmom. And so you see, we got HER version of things. But I am glad to hear you speak for yourself."

We sat on the bed and talked and talked until we had made up for the years of absence.

I'm so glad I have not only cousins but friends! I thought to myself.

Hannah:

Aunt Elaine called from the foot of the stairs. "Lunch, everyone. It's time to eat, so come on down!"

From the kitchen I could hear feet thumping on the steps as the children headed toward the kitchen. I continued filling cups with water, with Emily beside me, holding onto my skirt.

Poor thing, I thought, *so much has changed so quickly for her.*

Everyone gathered in a circle to pray. I hoisted Emily onto my hip and bowed my head for the prayer.

"Hannah!"

I jerked my head up, and Grandmom repeated my name.

"Hannah, Emily does not need you to hold her. She is just fine, so put her down."

"But, Grandmom, she is still kind of scared. May I please hold her?"

Emily clung to me, wrapping her arms around my neck and whimpering. It nearly broke my heart, and the thought that I might not be allowed to hold my sister was frightening.

Again I pleaded with Grandmom. "Please, may I hold her?" I begged.

Grandmom noticed everyone was watching to see how she would answer. "I guess, but Emily, you need to stop crying. There is no need to cry. You are perfectly all right."

The map was spread on the table, and Uncle Leo was explaining where the jail was located.

"It is really quite simple," he said. "It is smack in the middle of downtown, you know. I would be happy to take you to see your mom, if you would like." Then he cleared his throat and continued, "But I'm not sure she would want to see me."

I looked up. "Well, even if you have hurt her, I know she will try to forgive you."

Suddenly, something inside me snapped, and the tears that had been threatening all morning flooded my eyes. I simply couldn't hold them back any longer. Wiping my eyes with my sleeve, I struggled to control my emotions.

Aunt Elaine rushed over and hugged me, while others crowded around.

"Hannah, I need to talk to you," said Aunt Elaine. Taking me aside into the living room, she and Uncle Allen tried to explain where they stood. "Please don't think we are on Granddad and Grandmom's side just because that is what you are told."

I looked at them skeptically.

"Really, Hannah, believe me, we do not agree with what my parents have done. We have tried to be neutral, but I don't think we'll be able to much longer. Please believe that, Hannah!"

I nodded and wiped my eyes.

"And, Hannah, there is one more thing I want to say. I don't know for sure, but I think my parents may have their home phone line tapped so that every conversation will be taped. To be on the safe side, you should just assume they will have the ability to play back every phone conversation."

My eyes grew big as she spoke. *This sounds just like a detective story, yet it is real!*

Unfolding a piece of paper, I glanced at the number I had jotted down in Guatemala. Our friend Laura Magee had told me she would come from Mississippi to her mom's house in Houston to make herself available to us. I dialed the number and held the phone to my ear, listening to it ringing. *Oh, I hope she is there!*

Someone picked up and spoke. Instantly I recognized the voice. "Laura, this is Hannah."

"Oh, Hannah, it is so good to hear from you! I've been wondering what is going on. After your phone call from Guatemala, I realized I had failed to get a number where I could call you here."

"Yes, we are here at my aunt's house for a few days. It has been pretty rough so far. I really want to see Mommy again." As much as I tried, I couldn't keep from crying.

"Oh, Hannah, are you okay? Would you like me to pick you up and take you to the jail to see your mother?"

I didn't want to impose on her, but found myself saying, "Yes, Laura, that would be wonderful!"

When I climbed into the car that afternoon and shut the door behind me, I looked over at Laura. "Thank you so much for doing this for me," I said. "I can't tell you how much it means to me!"

She smiled as we pulled away from Aunt Elaine's house and said, "Hey, this is why I came down here. I just wanted to help you all. I want to be available for anything you need me to do."

I was grateful to God for this dear friend. Even though she and Kevin and their family had moved to Mississippi, she had driven all the way here just to help us.

"Now, Hannah, I have a surprise for you. I have scheduled an interview with a lawyer. As much as possible we need to keep this a secret, so don't mention it to your grandparents."

"Oh, of course not!"

"We need to find a lawyer who will be able to work toward getting your mom out of jail. If your grandparents found out, I think this would be explosive information."

"I agree totally, Laura."

I shuddered as I looked up at the dismal building towering above us. Laura pushed open the heavy door, and we stepped into the gloomy lobby and joined the long line leading to a counter at the front of the room. I looked around, feeling very out of place. The room was huge, but dingy, and the people waiting in this unwelcoming place were of a totally different culture than my own. They had all come to visit some inmate friend of theirs.

Inmate, I thought. *What a strange label for my own dear mother!*

Uncle Leo and the lawyer we had just met with had prepared me for this visit and for what I might see.

"You won't get to touch your mother; she will be behind glass. She will be wearing an orange outfit and will most likely look tired."

I was grateful for the briefing, because otherwise I would have been hit even harder with the "culture" shock.

"Next," barked the officer at the metal counter.

"Yes," I said timidly. "We are here to visit Kay Evans."

"Identification, please," he growled.

Laura showed him her driver's license, and I held out my passport. After copying down our names and ID numbers, he handed us a piece of paper.

"Just go through the metal detector and then through that door. Take the elevator to the fourth floor and give this paper to the officer at the window up there."

At the window, a female guard held out her hand, and I gave her the paper.

"Ummm, Kay Evans . . . " She flipped through some files and pulled out a paper. "No, she has not had any visitors today. Okay, ladies, just go sit at one of those cubicles over there. The inmate will be out in a few minutes."

Laura stepped over to the visiting area, and I followed.

"Look how all the prisoners have to talk through the little mouthpiece in the glass to be heard!" I exclaimed quietly.

Laura nodded and peered through the thick window into the prisoners' side where several women, dressed in a sickening orange, sat in booths, talking through the glass.

I had just set my purse on the metal counter when Mommy came into view. She was wearing the same ugly, orange scrubs the other prisoners wore. Her hair hung limply around her shoulders and was grayer than I remembered. I had heard she was not allowed to wear her veil here, but nonetheless, it was a shock to see her without it. But it was still my own dear Mommy, and tears flooded my eyes at the very sight of her dear face.

" . . . so, Laura and I went by the lawyer's office just before we came here, and I paid him to handle the first hearing. He told us to tell you it is imperative that you do not share the details of your case with anyone other than him. It is just safer that way."

A man from the next booth overheard me, and responded, "You got that right!"

I hadn't realized anyone was listening. I lowered my voice and continued, telling her all that had happened till now.

"The officer at the window told us we have only fifteen minutes to talk with you, so I need to talk fast. The children are all at Aunt Elaine's right now, but we are leaving for Amarillo in the morning."

The visit went far too quickly, and before I was ready, the guard motioned that our time was up. Mommy stood, blowing me a kiss as she turned and walked back into her unit. Wiping tears from my cheeks, I grabbed my purse and followed Laura back to the elevator.

"It was so very good to see her again!" I found myself saying to Laura. "What a blessing."

CHAPTER 25

An Altar in Jail

Kay:

Sitting on my bed with my Bible across my lap, I could hear the TV and the usual din from the dining room. Women chatted and milled about, busying themselves in this world behind bars. How I wished I could block out the endless droning of foolish talk and TV commercials.

"Kay Evans, you have a visitor!" a voice shouted above the chaos.

I jumped up, smoothed my hair, and strode quickly to the barred area where the volunteer handed me a little slip of pink paper. The scribbling simply stated, "attorney visit." I waited near the entrance until a lady guard appeared in the hallway and pushed the button, opening the gate to release me.

As I entered the visitation cell, the lawyer stood. Something about him instantly demanded respect. He was a tall man with glasses, curly black hair, and a neatly trimmed beard.

"Hello, Kay. I'm Alex Azzo," he said, seating himself again. "I met with your friend Laura Magee in my office, and she gave me some idea of what you are going through . . . I'm sorry."

He didn't try to impress me with his credentials but showed a genuine interest in me and the predicament I was in. I sensed a deep compassion for my being painfully separated from my children.

For a few minutes he just talked to me as a potential client, giving us a chance to get acquainted with each other. A lawyer doesn't have to take on a new client, and a client doesn't have to

310

retain a certain lawyer. Eventually he pushed a stack of papers in my direction.

"Kay, would you please read over this during the next few days to make sure you understand the lawyer/client responsibilities we would have to one another? Then you can decide if you want to retain me as your attorney for this case. In the meantime, I will go ahead and represent you at tomorrow's hearing."

After he finished, I couldn't hold back my question any longer. "There is one thing I really want to know. How soon can I be reunited with my children? I mean, how long does this kind of problem take to resolve?"

He studied me thoughtfully and slowly ran his fingers through his dark beard, realizing my naïveté in legal matters.

Choosing to prepare me for the worst, he began, "Well, technically, for each of your charges, you could be jailed for up to two years. With six separate charges, you could be in prison for up to twelve years."

He must have read the horror that flashed across my face, for he quickly continued, "But I think they might be willing to reduce your charges and jail you for only two years total."

My mind reeled under the terrible news. *Is two years supposed to sound like a bargain?* I thought. I had seldom been away from my children at all, and he was telling me we could be apart for two whole years and possibly more! This was horrible!

Unsuccessfully I fought back the tears. *Oh, I am so tired of terrible news!* I thought. I wanted to get away somewhere all by myself and have a long, hard cry.

Cry I did, once I returned to my little cell. How I wished I could close my door and be alone! But I was now a prisoner, and the door to my room opened and closed at the will of someone else. Nonetheless, I threw a blanket over myself and poured out my woes to God.

"God, surely You can do better than two years. I miss my children terribly!"

Later, Alex Azzo visited again and introduced me to another attorney named Jim Lindeman.

"Kay, because of the complexity of your case, I would like your permission to enlist the help of my friend . . . "

I felt God was leading me to approve their working together on my case.

"Okay, inmates," the guard shouted, "grab your breakfast bag from the table when I call your name and then get back into your cell! Fast!"

The bright fluorescent lights lit up the room with a bluish hue. *It must be about 4 a.m.*, I thought sleepily, rubbing my puffy eyes. *What an early breakfast time!*

Before my cell door had opened, I had heard other metal doors and barred gates clanging open up and down the corridors, the noise growing louder as it came closer to our unit. Hearing metal clanging against metal was a very unpleasant way to wake up. The officers' loud, gruff voices shouted through every set of bars, scaring each inmate to her feet.

"Evans!" a guard finally called.

I dashed from my doorway, snatched up one of the little brown bags and darted back.

Slam! The doors of every cell shut simultaneously, securely enclosing every inmate. I set my bag down on the tiny metal desk, and opened it to peek inside.

"Jail-style room service is so blah," I said, yawning. "A carton of juice, a boiled egg, and a packaged cinnamon roll. It seems terribly early to eat. I think I'll just wait until later."

I picked up my Bible and crawled onto the bed, scooting up against the wall and wrapping the thin, tattered blanket around my orange prison outfit. My best prayer time came just after this first head count of the day when I could enjoy a couple of quiet hours alone after the other inmates crawled back into bed. A few hours later the doors would automatically open for the day, and the unit would spring into its monotonous and noisy routine.

"Lord, what do You want to say to me now that I'm in jail? You definitely have my attention," I prayed.

I sat with my Bible in my lap, staring dully at the tiny, colorless room enclosing me. I looked down at my Bible and marveled that God had made a way for me to have it here with me.

"Thank You, Lord . . . But, I must confess I'm feeling shut out of my children's lives right now. Oh, God, this is so painful. I miss them. You are my only link to my children."

My eyes grew misty as I struggled before the Lord.

How long I sat there feeling sorry for myself, I cannot say. "Okay, enough self-pity," I scolded myself. "Lord, what do You have to say to me while I'm in this strange, new environment?"

I closed my eyes and sat still, waiting. Impatiently, I opened my Bible, clueless as to what I should read. I just felt numb. I took off my glasses and wiped away tears with my shirt before putting them back on.

Focusing on the passage before me, I sighed deeply and began reading. *And he said, Take now thy son, thine only son Isaac, whom thou lovest, and get thee into the land of Moriah; and offer him there for a burnt offering upon one of the mountains which I will tell thee of.*[1]

Is that verse for me, Lord? I read it again. Then I read the entire story through and then started over again. *Yes, Lord. You want me to lay each of my children on the altar before You, don't You? It's true. They belong to You and not to me.*

I climbed off the bed and knelt before the Lord on the cold floor. "Father, I give You Hannah. I give You Lissa. I give You Isaiah. I give You Beverly. I give You Grace, and I give You Emily. I love these children whom You have given me. Thank You for letting me be their mother. But they are Yours, Lord. Let me never lose sight of that. Please shield them from evil as Your own children. God, You know my children are now in the very environment I tried so hard to protect them from. Yet, I know You have allowed this. Please, somehow use this difficult time in their lives to accomplish Your good purposes. In Jesus' worthy name. Amen."

After surrendering my children, I felt able to focus on whatever ministry God would give me here in jail. I remembered how useless I used to feel in Guatemala. I had always desired to be a missionary, and yet once I was actually on a foreign mission field, I was unable to communicate with the native people. My progress with their language was slow and clumsy. It was frustrating. My children had caught on to the language quickly. Why hadn't I?

But now my circumstances were totally turned around. I had

---

1. Genesis 22:2

been brought back to my homeland and plopped into quite another mission field . . . an American jail! Here, I was completely fluent in the language. Sometimes I even wished I did not understand everything I heard. Yet, I was able to communicate very refreshing news to a few ladies who had never known or understood the truth about Jesus Christ.

I soon noticed there is an unusual kinship in jail. Everyone has a story, and each one has a pain in his heart for one reason or another. After a few days Jessica shared with me that she had a daughter.

"Oh, really?" I asked.

Children held a soft spot in everyone's heart here in jail, and Jessica beamed as she told me about her nine-year-old, Beverly.

"Jessica, my nine-year-old daughter is named Beverly too!"

We smiled at each other. But when I tried talking to her about the condition of her soul, she bristled and said, "Kay, you're all right, but keep your religion to yourself. I don't want nothing to do with God."

Jessica usually displayed a tough exterior. I could only pray Jesus would prepare her heart to want to know Him somehow, someday.

Jessica, I learned, wasn't even her real name. She had been incarcerated under one of her aliases. She and her husband had been ringleaders in a motorcycle gang and had gotten into a fight with the police. In the fight, she had reportedly slashed an officer's throat. Now she and her husband were both incarcerated and beginning what could become lifetime sentences. She had run with a bad crowd and was now paying a heavy price.

Though she could talk as rough as the roughest of these hardened women, Jessica had a heart that bled for those who were hurting. Often she found me in tears in my room trying to write letters or draw pictures for my children. She would steal into my cell and hug me, attempting to console me as best she knew how.

She had an appreciation for art too, and one day brought me a collection of tattoo artwork. "You can use this for pictures to make for your children if you want," she said. She had little to offer me, but it warmed my heart that she wanted to give what little she had.

I could never have imagined myself browsing through a tattoo portfolio, but I accepted the booklet from her hands to let her know I appreciated her kindness. Flipping through the collection, I was shocked by almost every drawing.

Watching the horror on my face, she broke in, "Oh, I know some of them are terrible, aren't they? But you might find something you like."

I seriously doubt it! I thought. Yet I did not want to appear ungrateful, so I continued turning the pages. Finally, I spotted the Chinese word for "joy" and copied it onto one of my letters to my children. I thanked Jessica and handed the awful collection back, determined never to pick it up again.

"And remember you can call me collect while I'm staying at my mom's house, anytime."

I smiled at Laura's familiar face through the glass. "I know. Thank you so much for serving me in so many ways."

She just smiled and tucked her notepad into her purse. "I'm glad I can do it."

I looked forward to Laura's regular visits. For a little while, Hannah was permitted to communicate with Laura, which meant Laura could relay to me savored news about my children. She also ran countless errands and made important calls for me, both of which I could not do from jail.

At Kevin's suggestion, Laura set up a special bank account for my legal expenses. She also took care of contacting people from whom I needed advice. She was a major go-between for many things happening with my case that I couldn't deal with from jail.

"Laura, I know you have six little children in Mississippi who are surely missing their mommy, and yet here you are, seven hours away, laying down your life for me."

"Well," she assured me, "Kevin insisted I come help you. And since he is working at home right now, it seems to be working out okay. Besides, his mom drives over to help him whenever she can."

I nodded, sobered to think that so many were sacrificing to help me.

"They say you are allowed one fifteen-minute visit a day," Linda Stevenson informed me, scooting the chair up closer to the window between us. "But I'm telling people who call to sign up that if any of your kids come to town they get first priority. I'll just bump off whoever was scheduled."

"Oh, Linda, I appreciate that. I am grateful people want to visit, but I would be very disappointed if any of my children were in town and could not get in to see me."

Linda took off her glasses and began cleaning them with a handkerchief.

"Linda, you have no idea what a blessing all these visits have been. Why, just yesterday, Doug Meyers was such a boost to me."

Fresh in my mind was the kind face of the elder from the church we had attended when Ron was alive. Doug's words rang in my ears, "Kay, I want you to know something. If I had been presented with the circumstances you faced, I would probably have fled too."

And a word spoken in due season, how good is it![1] I thought.

Linda had volunteered to schedule jail visits for me, seven days a week. It was truly a labor of love, not knowing how long this could last. Often, these visits provided me with refreshing exposure to life beyond the prison walls; and often God provided just the encouragement I needed.

Linda and her husband, Errol, graciously cared for friends who flew in for my court hearings. They even picked some of them up at the airport and provided hospitality, opening their home and their hearts to strangers. Several times their home was filled to capacity with friends of mine.

"Well, Kay, before the guard says my time is up, let me read off the list of people coming to see you this week. Oh, and I'll be sending out an e-mail update tonight. Is there something you want people to specifically pray for?"

"Well, let's see . . ."

---

1. Proverbs 15:23

Lissa:

"Couple's grandchildren home from Guatemala after three years on the run," was printed boldly across the page of the Amarillo newspaper in Granddad's hands.

"And Walter," Grandmom gushed, "did you see this?"

She pointed to a paragraph, and he nodded.

"Walter and Jan Evans received the best Christmas present ever a few weeks early, or three years late, depending on how you look at it," the article began.

I peered eagerly over Granddad's shoulder, trying to read the fine print. The journalist had a slanted opinion about our case, which I had expected.

After buying the paper early this morning, Granddad promptly had the article laminated.

The article is done very attractively, I thought, *even if its content is not all true.*

In the corner, a small map of Guatemala showed where we had been when we were "rescued in a remote, mountainous village."

I tried not to smile, but it sounded so dramatic! When I came to the last line that read, "It is a real love story," I nearly snorted, but quickly caught myself.

"Well," Grandmom sighed contentedly, "we will have to keep this article in the van, to have it handy, you know."

I held my Bible on my lap and rested my hand on the arm of the thick couch. It was Sunday morning, and we were having "church" in my grandparents' living room.

"Children, we feel you need some time to adjust to life here before we take you out into the public, to church, for example," Granddad had told us.

I was glad, because we were going through some major adjustments—"culture shock" it could be called. Everything had changed so suddenly, and we now found ourselves in a completely different environment than the one we had known for the past several years. Almost everything seemed to be diametrically opposite—the people, the surroundings, the conversations.

This has been one of the most stressful weeks of my life, I thought, as I listened to Granddad expound out of his Bible. *And I guess it has been a strain on Granddad and Grandmom too. But what can I say?*

I tried to concentrate on what Grandmom was now saying. "Now, children, you know we have done all this for your good. We want you to grow up and live normal lives. You have been emotionally and psychologically disturbed, and we want to assist your recovery."

My mind flashed to the quote in one of the Amarillo newspaper articles stating that Grandmom and Granddad wanted to "integrate us back into society." I caught myself lost in a whirl of my own thoughts, but Grandmom was still talking.

"Granddad and I are concerned about you. All of you insist your mother has done the best thing for you. However, she is getting what she deserves, and now you need to support Grandmom and Granddad. Do you understand?"

I bit my lip and fought back the anger boiling within me. *Why are they brainwashing us? They're forcing their opinions on us, and we don't want them. How can they expect us to love them when they ripped us away from the dearest person on earth to us?*

After lunch, the doorbell rang. Trixy barked and ran to the door, toenails clicking on the tile. Grandmom hurried to the door, and from the dining room I could hear her exclamations of delight.

"Oh, Sarah, it's wonderful to see you! Won't you come in? Oh, you brought us supper. Thank you so much! Children, come meet this wonderful friend . . ."

The woman beamed and nodded slightly. We stood, silent and embarrassed.

"Oh, Sarah, wouldn't you love to hear the children sing?"

My heart sank, but it was too late.

Granddad came up behind us and agreed. "Yes, the children sing beautifully, like the von Trapps. What song will you sing, kids?"

These situations were extremely awkward for us. We knew these people had heard a very sad story about the poor, deprived Evans grandchildren living in a remote location in the dangerous country of Guatemala. Yet we felt we had been taken from a happy life and were now imprisoned in a high-security jail.

But we learned to plaster smiles on our faces and to continue shaking the hands of our many sympathizers. Many people's hearts were touched with pity for us. The local fire station brought us a big box full of toys. Sunday school classes took up collections. And families brought meals.

It was early, and Hannah was still sleeping soundly beside me in bed. I turned over and lay awake for a few minutes. After a bit, I sat up, threw back my covers and tiptoed to the door. Pushing it open, I stepped out onto the cold tile of the hallway. As I rubbed my eyes, I nearly collided with Grandmom, hurrying the other way.

"Good morning, Lissa," she chirruped loudly.

"Mornin'," I mumbled sleepily.

She stopped and faced me critically. "Lissa, you should not walk around with a smile on your face if you don't mean it. In doing so, you are being a hypocrite!"

I stared at her, trying to get my sleepy brain to comprehend what she was saying. After a pause, I yawned and said, "Well, do you want me to wear a frown?"

Her eyes grew wide in horror, and she said, "No! Of course not."

"Oh," I said, and turned into the bathroom. I shut the door behind me and studied my reflection in the mirror.

"Lissa," I said to the pajama-clad girl peering back at me, "you will just have to be a 'hypocrite' then!"

Emily wiped her eyes and ducked into her room, throwing herself onto her bed. Hannah and I rushed to the door, peering in after her.

"Emily, are you okay?" Hannah asked quietly.

With her face buried in her pillow, we could hear her sobs. "I . . . miss . . . Mommy!"

Hannah and I looked at each other and then toward the living room where Granddad and Grandmom were talking.

"Dare we go into the girls' room?" Hannah asked.

I shrugged my shoulders, still angry about the latest rule. Sitting erect in her chair, Grandmom had spoken up at supper last night. "Children, Granddad has made a rule that you may not go into the other children's rooms unless you have special permission from

Granddad or me. Do you all understand? If you want to talk to each other, it can be done in the living room and not behind closed doors."

I had stared at my plate, hoping she couldn't detect the fire raging within me.

I heard Grandmom walking quickly toward us in the hall.

"Girls, what is going on? Why is Emily crying?"

She rushed past us into the room and bent over Emily. "What is wrong, dear?" Emily only cried harder. Grandmom picked her up, and swept past us into her room, securely shutting the door behind her.

Hannah and I glared at the door. If only we could see through it, and see what Grandmom was doing with Emily.

What is she telling her? I wondered. I shuddered to think.

This was the hardest thing about being at Granddad and Grandmom's. They were preventing us, in many small ways, from interacting as brother and sisters. That greatly concerned Hannah and me. We felt responsible to keep all the children reminded that we were a family. Even if Mommy was in jail, we were still a family.

First Mommy had been taken away from us, and now it seemed our own sibling relationships were being taken away too. We wanted time together without our grandparents being involved in our conversations. They wanted the exact opposite.

Another difficulty was the drastic switch in authority. We suddenly found ourselves in a home where the authority did not support Mommy. So, in order to follow what we knew Mommy would want, we had to cross what our grandparents wanted.

The issue of sibling time was one Hannah and I felt we could not compromise. But what were we to do? *Dear Lord, You see our problem*, I prayed. *Somehow help us, please!*

CHAPTER 26

A Light in My Cell

Kay:

I stood by my cell door as the guard droned out each name during roll call.

"Guthrie" . . . "5589, here." . . . "Evans" . . . "7492, here." . . . "Oliver". . . "9032, here." . . . "Smith" . . . "4178, here." . . .

I clutched the rough blanket tightly under my chin. This morning the inmates in our unit resembled Indian squaws, wrapped in our sheets or blankets. Last night, just before being locked into our individual cells, we had been instructed to turn in our uniforms so they could be laundered.

Finishing roll call and turning to a clean pile of orange scrubs, I joined the ladies rummaging through the pants and shirts on the table. I grabbed the last scrubs as the other ladies shuffled back to their cells clutching theirs.

This will be an interesting fit, I thought, raising my eyebrows as I held up a giant-sized pair of pants. The shirt was no better, being several sizes larger than the one I had last week.

"Evans!" the guard shouted, "you're the only one in here who goes to court today. Be ready when the guard comes for you."

I nodded before slipping into my cell to get dressed. Considering that Harris County Jail is one of the largest county jails in the world, housing around 13,000 prisoners, the organization and efficiency are remarkable.

I breathed a sigh of relief when I saw the guard who came to escort me. Guards were often rude and tough to the inmates, making us feel less than human. But this was one of the few women guards who acted like a lady.

She ushered me from behind my world of bars into the long, cheerless hallway. When we were alone, she eyed me curiously. "Why are you in here?" she asked.

I knew she would drop me off at the end of the hall, so I gave her a very brief version of my story.

She shook her head. "That stinks!" she grumbled with a sympathetic frown.

Word about my case had circulated among the guards, possibly because of newspaper articles they had read and the volume of mail I was receiving. I knew guards were not permitted to befriend a prisoner, yet her response showed compassion. It was her way of saying, "I'm sorry you are in this awful place." And it warmed my heart to think a guard would care.

The heavy door clanged shut behind me, and around thirty faces glanced up dully.

There must be quite a few hearings today, I thought as I sat on a concrete slab bench and looked around. Court days meant long hours of sitting restlessly in holding tanks; we were often herded from one holding tank to another before finally being escorted one by one into the grand courtroom to face judgment.

But until then, the women sat by the scores on the cold concrete floors, swapping shameful stories. Some of them prided themselves in loud swearing and coarse jesting. This place seemed like the lobby to hell, if there could be such a thing. There was a toilet in the corner in plain view, for anyone who dared to use it.

This morning one woman's loud swearing and endless stream of obscenities became the focus of everyone's attention. I tried shutting it out, but after a while I felt I could not take any more of her mind-polluting crudeness.

Finally, I raised my voice above her cursing. "Excuse me, but can we just be ladies in here, or must we act like animals?"

A hush fell upon the room. The loud woman shot a fiery glare in my direction. If looks could kill, that would have been the end of me. But she only shrieked louder and began hurling all kinds of insults directly at me.

What if she comes over here and beats me up? What would I do? I wondered frantically.

I realized my error and tried to apologize. "Hey, I'm sorry, but can I just tell you about Someone named Jesus Christ who cares a whole lot about you? He's made a big difference in my life and . . ."

But she wasn't listening and continued to scream filthy accusations. She was outraged that I had belittled her before her audience. By one brief insult, I had lost any opportunity to witness to her.

What a shame, I thought. *I cut her off before she even heard one word of truth.*

As we were being herded down the corridor to the next holding cell, I was still chiding myself for my failure. A shy young prisoner caught up to me and unexpectedly tapped me on the shoulder.

"I heard what you said in there," she whispered. "Could you pray for me?"

"I'll be glad to pray for you," I said in a hushed tone.

Through her, God was encouraging me that He could still use me in this dark, vile place. I must simply learn from my failures and move on.

"Okay, you with felony charges, line up over here!"

A male guard pointed to the wall, yelling above the din of prisoners. I made my way toward the wall and lined up with four male prisoners. I looked around in surprise, discovering that only one female inmate stood with me.

Where did these people come from? I wondered.

Chewing a wad of gum, the guard approached us, carrying chains and handcuffs.

"I'll have to chain y'all together because we've got to walk across the street to the criminal courthouse," he said as he worked with the keys and chains in a routine manner.

I shuddered to think of being seen in public. He strode to the door and led us through the first floor of a parking garage and out onto the sidewalk, noisy with traffic. I squinted in the bright sunlight. The downtown street was full of cars waiting at the stoplight, but I turned my gaze away from the drivers' faces.

It is so humiliating to be seen dressed in bright orange prison clothes, chained to other prisoners, and escorted by an officer, I thought, shivering as we stepped up onto the curb.

Despite the embarrassment, one of the male prisoners looked up and said, "Oh, the sky! It is so good to see the sky again!"

His words helped divert my attention upward. He expressed something we could all appreciate.

Oh, that is so true, I thought. *Just to be outside and to actually feel the breeze across my face. To catch a glimpse of the blue sky and the white clouds floating overhead is marvelous.*

It was wonderful therapy indeed for prisoners starved for the loveliness of nature, after being penned behind bars. Listening to my handcuffs clank against the chains, I mused, *Could this be how Jesus felt when He was brought before Pilate? I'm sure this is only a small glimpse of what Jesus went through for me and all of mankind.*

We entered the criminal courthouse and crowded into an elevator heading up a few floors. After the elevator doors opened, the deputy escorted us down a narrow hallway. He stopped before a door, fidgeted with a dangling ring of keys, and unlocked the door.

Unchaining the men, he announced, "Okay, all male prisoners, step inside."

As he locked them inside, I watched through a little window in the door as the men seated themselves on the concrete benches. The other female prisoner and I were led farther down the hall and through a doorway into a large, empty courtroom. The deputy silently led us to empty jury chairs facing the judge's seat, in full view of anyone sitting in on this hearing.

Quickly and skillfully he fastened chains to our ankles and then secured them to the floor in front of our chairs. Neither of us would be able to go anywhere. His job required few words but a great deal of locking and unlocking and chaining prisoners together to lead them to their next destination and then unchaining them again. Now that we were secured, he left us alone in the cold and empty courtroom. The sound of his keys jangling against one another faded away as he left the room. It would be a whole hour or more until we were scheduled to see the judge.

I glanced around. Darkly stained furnishings gave this courtroom an impressive appearance. It was refreshing to see a clock on the wall again.

The young prisoner seated next to me told me she was facing drug charges. This was a familiar scene to her; she looked bored with the routine. After talking a few minutes, she slumped in her chair, her head drooping lower and lower as she drifted off to sleep.

How can she be so indifferent? I wondered. This was all scary and new to me. I felt embarrassed to be seen dressed like this, in a bright orange scrub shirt and pants. And even though I had only begun wearing a veil on my head since my husband's death, it was odd how naked I felt without one now. As I sat in the empty room with the woman slumped over and oblivious to everything around her, I decided I would rather not waste my time.

I had no idea what to expect once the court proceedings began, so I prayed aloud with all my might in that short hour. It was good for me to sit there, facing the empty judge's seat.

"Oh, Lord, my Eternal Judge," I prayed, as if He were sitting right there in that seat. "I am asking You to direct the heart of the earthly judge who will soon enter this room."

As the widow in Luke 18, I begged God for justice. It was comforting to know that the outcome of this hearing was ultimately in the hands of the Higher Judge, to whom I was speaking now.

I began wondering who might show up for this hearing. As the time drew near, I noticed my sister-in-law, Elaine, briefly looking in through the window of the door at the opposite side of the room. She smiled at me but wasn't allowed to enter yet. After a while, my lawyers entered, and the courtroom began filling up. Court personnel entered in their professional outfits, shuffling papers, making small talk among themselves. This was just another workday to them—business as usual. Everyone seemed dressed in his best except for me and the woman beside me, who was now fully awake.

As I glanced over the audience, I spotted Hannah, and tears

came to my eyes. I had not realized she would be coming. So much had happened over the past three days, and we hadn't even been able to talk things over as was our custom.

She gave me a beautiful smile, as if to say she was proud of me. That look meant so much. I knew how awful I must look at the moment.

Elaine; her husband, Allen; my brother-in-law, Leo; my dad and stepmom; and several friends who had traveled a distance had also come for the hearing.

The bailiff's loud, droning voice broke into my thoughts, "All arise!"

Everyone stood up respectfully as Judge Belinda Hill entered the room. Inmates reported that this woman was a judge to be feared. The attractive, yet stern-looking, African-American walked in confidently in her flowing black judge's robe. Seated on the judge's bench above all the others, her appearance was impressive and commanding.

A rustling sound swept across the room as people sat down again. The tense courtroom proceedings were at last underway, and the judge began dealing methodically, yet carefully, with each case on her docket.

From time to time my lawyer, Alex Azzo, or his associate would walk over to me, bend down, and quietly explain what was happening.

"Kay Evans, you may approach the bench."

The bailiff stooped and unchained me. As my attorneys accompanied me to the bench to face the judge, my mouth went totally dry.

Will I be asked to speak? I worried. I was grateful for my lawyers' guidance in this critical moment. Mr. Azzo spoke first and addressed the issue of the bond. We had hoped the judge would lower the preposterous bond that had been set for me.

"No," the judge said, shaking her head decidedly. "Kay is a flight risk. She fled the country with her six children and was missing for three and a half years . . . "

From the judge's perspective, I had not complied with the rules when I had been summoned to court at the time of my husband's death. Not showing up to defend oneself in court was simply inexcusable in the eyes of the judicial system. The only thing that came out of this disappointing hearing was that another court date was set for the following Thursday, December 16. I returned to my cell just after noon, feeling discouraged and missing my children terribly.

Lord, this is a horrible nightmare. Would You help me? I prayed. *I want to believe the promises I find in Your Word. I desire to walk in victory and faith, even when things look hopeless! And, to be honest, they do look a little hopeless right now.*

My dad found the court proceedings extremely difficult. Throughout our years of hiding, he had neither seen nor talked to me. To see his daughter now, at last, seated in a courtroom in orange scrubs, a prisoner, was humiliating and painful! He had invested so much as a father. What kind of fruit was this after all the labor and sacrifice he had made to raise me properly? No one in my family or among all my relatives had ever been thrown into jail. I couldn't imagine his grief and distress.

Although my dad was now retired, he had worked many years as a well-respected optometrist. I remember the pride I had always felt in telling people I was his daughter. Together, he and my mom had provided for me one of those rare and happy childhoods few people are blessed with. I have always looked back upon my upbringing with fondness and gratitude.

I was the fourth-born as well as the last child, and the only girl. My dad had been an elder in a local church for many years. He enjoyed hard work and had always invested his time showing my brothers and me how to enjoy working hard too. In his spare time, he and my mom always found a way to minister to needy people.

He was greatly loved and appreciated by everyone, as far as I knew, before my beloved mother died back in 1982. The community loved him just as much now that he had married a well-respected widow. I greatly admired my dad and the consistent integrity of his character.

Now as I seated myself across the Plexiglas window from him and my stepmom, I saw my dad as a terribly distraught, ashen-faced man in his late seventies. These years had been hard on him. New lines were etched across his face, and his hair had turned much grayer. I looked into his sad eyes and felt responsible for his anguish.

Just now, with the morning's court scene fresh on his mind, he was angry.

"Kay, I cannot believe that my own daughter is in jail. It just doesn't seem possible. Do you see now that you have messed up? Well, do you?"

"But, Dad, I did exactly what I . . ."

"Here you are, in jail!" Dad interrupted. "Just look at you! I can't believe this!"

I had seldom ever seen my dad angry. I hated to think he was unhappy with me now and that I was the source of his frustration.

"How could you have robbed me of these three and a half years of being a grandparent?"

As my dad voiced his hurt, I could tell that my answers were not satisfactory, nor did he want to hear them. In spite of having often used poor judgment since my husband's death, I still felt strongly that God had directed me into hiding for my children's protection. But I knew that would not make any sense to him now, particularly in this setting, and especially while I was wearing a prisoner's uniform.

As our conversation continued to spin in unproductive circles, I felt this meeting was not accomplishing anything positive. Instead, things were heating up. My stepmom just sat there weeping with her hand over her mouth, observing the pitiful scene between father and daughter.

We all faced each other in excruciating anguish. None of us were in a frame of mind to talk through the issues of the recent years.

I abruptly ended the conversation by saying, "Daddy, I love you, but I'd better go."

Then I stood and turned around, relinquishing the balance of my allotted visiting time. I walked slowly and dejectedly back to my unit. Never in my whole life had I walked out on my dad when he was talking to me. It felt horrible to do so now, yet it was too painful for us all to sit there any longer. I hoped I could still please him and ease his later years, rather than burden him or be a thorn in his flesh.

Yet I was developing an even stronger desire to learn how to please my heavenly Father. It was my commitment to Him that had prompted our escape from everything familiar to us in the first place. How intensely I needed my heavenly Father just now.

As I returned to my unit, my heart was very heavy. I longed for the moment when my cell door would bang shut for the night. I desperately needed time alone to sob into my blanket and ask my Eternal Father for new strength to go on.

A Light in My Cell

And a light shined in the cell,
And there was not any wall,
And there was no dark at all;
Only Thou, Immanuel.

Light of Love shined in the cell,
Turned to gold the iron bars,
Opened windows to the stars;
Peace stood there as sentinel.

Dearest Lord, how can it be
That Thou art so kind to me?
Love is shining in my cell,
Jesus, my Immanuel.
~Amy Carmichael[1]

---

1. From page 341 of *Mountain Breezes* by Amy Carmichael. Copyright © 1999 by the Dohnavur Fellowship, and published by CLC Publications, Fort Washington, PA. All rights reserved.

CHAPTER 27

"We ARE Your Authorities!"

Hannah:

"And Hannah, although you will not be psychologically evaluated since you are no longer a minor, we will need you to provide some background," Grandmom explained grimly.

I nodded in agreement. Looking out the big office window I prayed silently, *Lord, I am really dreading this. You know how we have always been leery of psychiatry and psychology. And here we are now at the most reputable pediatric psychiatric office in all of Houston! Please guard and protect us in the name of Jesus, and keep us from saying anything that could be twisted or taken the wrong way.*

My grandparents are highly educated people, and Granddad himself had long been a "certified counselor," so it was obvious to them what we needed. They had informed us with all gravity that we were suffering from "Post Traumatic Stress Disorder."

We had learned that laughing when we were alone was a great stress reliever. This diagnosis was one thing we laughed about until we cried. Nevertheless, I was really dreading these sessions. I knew we were probably a bit different from most of our peers. Would these professionals decide we were "unstable"?

Each of us children was interviewed individually by a trained staff member. Being uneasy that I might say something that could be used against Mommy in court, I was very guarded with my answers.

"Did your religion change much after your dad died?" the lady asked.

"No," I said. That was an easy question. "We had always believed that Jesus is the Son of God, and that He loves us."

As she continued to probe, I relaxed a little. It didn't seem as bad as

I had imagined. Nevertheless, I was glad when it was over. Weeks later, the test results came back saying the children were fine.

"Oh, praise God! He watched over each result, making sure it would all be used for His glory. The tests we sweated over were no problem for Him!" I exulted. My heart overflowed with gratitude.

I sat at the breakfast table, folding my napkin again and again. We were in the middle of a heated discussion about authority. Breakfast was long since over, but the conversation was not.

"Hannah and Lissa," Grandmom stated firmly, "it is time you understand that you are no longer in charge of Isaiah and the three girls."

In charge! I thought to myself. *I didn't have a lot of authority over them anyway. I never spanked them; that was Mommy's job. I guess it's my influence that is unwelcome.*

Lissa and I were allowed to choose what we wore, but we were sternly informed that we had no jurisdiction over the little girls.

"Don't even give them the impression it is wrong to wear what we choose for them to put on," Grandmom commanded, her eyes flashing.

"And girls," Granddad added, "as far as the way you and Lissa are dressing, do you realize it is un-Scriptural? In fact, it is prideful for you to dress that way."

For the first several weeks, grueling talks like this happened regularly. They always left me feeling drained.

Later, when I was alone in our bedroom, I knelt by the bed and cried. "Lord, it was easy to forgive Grandmom and Granddad while we lived faraway in Guatemala. But now that we live with them, it is quite another matter! I know this is the real test, and I want to pass this test, Lord."

I paused and thought of what God was teaching me in this trial. I had to praise Him. "Father, You know this is the very situation I worried about and feared during the years we were in hiding. I didn't think I could endure this, God. But You ARE pouring out daily Your portion of grace, which I need so terribly. You are here too! You have not forsaken us. Your faithfulness in this trying time reveals how compassionate You are."

Granddad stirred the oatmeal and then turned off the burner.

"Shall I go ahead and set the table for breakfast, Granddad?"

He nodded. "That sounds wonderful. Thank you!"

As I set a stack of plates onto the beautiful wooden table, he spoke up again. "Hannah, I would like for you and Lissa to go with me this morning to pick up some quilts we ordered for Christmas presents. They're at a little country store about forty-five minutes away, and I thought we could eat lunch out too."

"That sounds fine," I agreed. "What time do you want us to be ready?"

He shrugged. "Oh, in half an hour or so."

Grandmom walked briskly into the kitchen. "Yes, Hannah," she said, "you and Lissa really should go with Granddad. The children will be just fine, yes, just fine."

Going with Granddad hadn't bothered me until Grandmom started pressuring us to go with him, and then I grew suspicious. My mind went over every possible scenario as I poured milk into the glasses at each plate.

Why is she so eager for us to go with Granddad? Is she going to do something with the younger children while we're gone?

After prayer we passed the oatmeal and brown sugar around the table and began eating.

"Isaiah, Beverly, Grace, and Emily, this morning Granddad, Hannah, and Lissa are going to do a few errands for us," Grandmom said. "While they're gone, you all will go with me to the hair salon so I can get my hair trimmed."

I was immediately skeptical. "Are you the only one getting a haircut?" I asked with concern.

Grandmom glared at me. "Why do you ask?" she said coldly.

Stirring more milk into my oatmeal, I gulped and plunged ahead. "Grandmom, we have told you how we feel about getting our hair cut. I was just worried you might cut the girls' hair."

She sat rigidly in her seat, staring at me intently. "Hannah, remember you no longer have any authority over the children. You need to let Granddad and me make the decisions around here. This kind of thing is in OUR jurisdiction now." She spoke with such an air of hostility that I almost shivered.

Everyone had stopped eating and just sat in their seats, feeling very uncomfortable. Grace began to cry.

"Hannah, look, you made your sister cry!" Grandmom said shrilly.

"No, we will not cut the girls' hair. Grace, dear, you don't need to cry."

The rest of the meal was miserable, and I tried to eat as quickly as possible so that I could be excused. After we were finished eating and had taken our dishes to the sink, I saw Emily crying silently. I felt so sorry for my little sisters, and seeing one of them cry nearly broke my heart.

"Here, Emily, come." I stretched my hands out to her and quickly grabbed her up into my arms. She hid her face in my shoulder.

Grandmom seemed especially irritated to see Lissa or me holding Emily, and this was no exception.

"Hannah, put Emily down right now!"

"Grandmom," Lissa's voice broke in pleadingly, "you won't even let us hold our sister anymore! Please let us be a sister to her!"

Tears filled my eyes.

"All right," Grandmom said quietly, "you may hold her this time. But she is getting too big to hold!" She turned and quickly left the kitchen.

Uncle Calvin marched into the girls' room with Grandmom at his heels.

"Good morning, my nieces!" he announced dramatically. "This is that wonderful day we have all looked forward to, when all your cousins and aunts and uncles will be coming for Christmas! Wake up and take a look. I have personally picked out the clothes you get to wear today!"

Beverly, Grace, and Emily began to stir, rubbing their eyes groggily. One by one they sat up and stared, wishing it were just a bad dream. Uncle Calvin, our bachelor uncle, had arrived yesterday. Grandmom held up three of the donated dresses in her hand.

"That's right, girls; today you will be wearing these lovely dresses!" she announced triumphantly. "Just this morning Uncle Calvin has been browsing through clothes people have donated, and he has personally selected these for you, so I want you to jump right up. Run along to the bathroom and slip them on at once."

Tears formed in the girls' eyes. There seemed to be no choice. Finally, Beverly swallowed hard and said, "But Grandmom, I don't think those dresses will work very well for us."

Grandmom's mouth formed into a hard line. "Grandmom did not ask you what you thought," she scolded. "Now, get up right now, each one of you! Take the dresses and go put them on!"

Tears and appeals availed nothing. The decision was firm. It was an unhappy morning in my grandparents' home.

Grace pulled her dress on and looked in the mirror unhappily. "I can't wear this thing in front of other people!" she protested, shaking her head. In a final attempt to resist wearing the dreadful outfit, she came out with it deliberately on backwards.

Grandmom and Uncle Calvin frowned disapprovingly. "You march right back in there and put it on properly, or we will put it on you ourselves," Grandmom threatened.

The battle was lost, and my sisters began wearing clothes my grandparents selected for them.

I stood by helplessly, observing what appeared to me to be cruel treatment of my little sisters. I wanted to run to their rescue or comfort them in some way, but I couldn't. I wasn't allowed to. All I could do was pray for them.

I had to keep in mind that God wanted to use these very circumstances to create something beautiful in each of their hearts as well as in my own. I had to remind myself that Granddad and Grandmom wanted to do what they perceived to be the right thing for us. They didn't want us to be social misfits, so they were trying to change us, so we could blend in with society.

My grandparents eventually worked out a rotation for my little sisters' clothing selection. They ruled that the girls could choose their clothing two days a week and on all the other days, they would wear whatever Granddad or Grandmom selected.

Masses of community people had furnished us with many bags of used clothing. As bag after bag was hauled through the door, the garage had been fixed up with a clothing rack that stretched its entire width. After friends sorted through all the clothes, shoes, and toys, the rack was heavily laden with hanging clothes. There were also containers full of clothes stacked along the wall. The garage resembled a thrift store.

Grandmom browsed for dresses that would fit Beverly, Grace, and Emily. At first my grandparents allowed my sisters to wear dresses to replace the ones we had made for them. But gradually they began to require them to wear blue jeans and fashionable tops.

I sat Indian style on the bed, staring at my open Bible in front of me, but my thoughts kept going to the heated discussion that had occurred at the breakfast table this morning. Behind me I could hear Lissa typing furiously on the computer. I smiled as I remembered what she had told me, "Hannah, keeping this computer journal helps me blow off some steam."

"Lissa," I spoke up, and her typing paused.

"Yes?"

I turned on the bed and faced her. "There is something I think I should warn you about."

She screwed up her nose and waited for me to go on.

"Sometimes I get this feeling that Granddad and Grandmom will not let me stay here much longer. You know they think I am a bad influence on the rest of you, especially the younger ones."

She nodded. "What would we do without your influence though?"

"Well, God will give you the grace for whatever happens," I assured her. "But anyway, Grandmom drops a comment here and there about me needing to cooperate in order to be able to stay here. After all of the trauma our family has been through, I want to be here to encourage you and Isaiah and the girls. But I feel my contact with you all is slowly becoming more limited. For example, every time I am caught talking alone with one of the younger ones, we both get into trouble."

Lissa left her chair by the desk and sat on the edge of the bed, listening intently.

"I want you to know, I think eventually Granddad and Grandmom might tell me to leave," I whispered. "I just didn't want you to be shocked or devastated if that happens."

Lissa's face was very serious as she looked into my eyes. "You think they would really kick you out?"

I nodded sadly.

———

"Dingdong!" The doorbell rang, but I didn't pay much attention. The doorbell rang a lot around here, especially with all the meals and gifts people brought over.

I was back in the study watching a National Geographic video with Grace and Emily. Lissa burst through the door.

"The mailman is here," she said breathlessly, "and I think you got some mail, Hannah. But I'm not sure if Granddad and Grandmom are going to let you accept it."

I studied her and then quickly got up from the couch. Moments later I arrived at the front door where Grandmom and Granddad stood talking with the mailman. I peered over Grandmom's shoulder and saw a big manila envelope with my name on the front. It was certified mail to me from Alex Azzo.

Looks important, I thought.

Granddad also held a package in his hand, and it looked exactly like the one Grandmom held, except it had their names on the front instead of mine.

"May I have my mail, please?" I extended my hand to Grandmom. She made no move to give it to me. Frustrated, I spoke up again, "I am an adult, and I think I should be allowed to receive my own mail."

Grandmom raised her eyebrows at Granddad, neither of them knowing what to do. It was clear they did not want me to have this package. The bewildered mailman looked on. He was only trying to do his job.

With sudden resolve, Grandmom spoke up. "I'll call Leo and see what he thinks we should do."

Grandmom disappeared around the corner, leaving Granddad, the mailman, and me staring at one another. Minutes later she returned with an important look on her face.

"Hannah, you have two choices," she announced. "You can let the package go back to the post office, or you can sign to accept it, but if you do, then you'll have to pack your bags and move out of our home."

I listened to her words in agitation. I glanced at Granddad to see if he agreed with this cold verdict, but he stood by passively.

Is moving out the only way I can receive this package? I wondered in disbelief. *What a difficult choice!*

Suddenly I was the one who needed advice. *I should call Kevin and Laura Magee,* I decided. *They might have some wisdom on what I should do.* Turning to the postman, I asked, "Could I catch up to you in a few minutes and give you my decision?"

He nodded kindly and said, "No problem." Then he turned to leave, no doubt wondering what was going on in this household.

I hurried into our room to find the Magees' telephone number. Lissa noticed my flushed face and figured out what was going on.

"You're leaving, aren't you?" she asked abruptly.

"I think so," I answered, trembling, as I dug through my purse searching for my little notebook. "Oh, here it is. "

I snatched it up and flipped through the pages until I found the Magees' phone number. In the kitchen, my hands shook as I dialed the number. Kevin Magee answered right away. Nervously I told him the situation and the options I was suddenly facing.

He suggested we pray about it right then, over the phone. He prayed for wisdom so that I would know what to do. After the prayer, he asked, "Do you need to make this decision today or can it wait?"

"I don't really know," I confessed.

After we talked a minute or two, he said, "Well, Hannah, it sounds to me like the wisest thing to do would be to let the package return to the post office for now. You should be able to retrieve it later when things are not so hot."

I nodded. "Thank you so much for your input. We'll talk to y'all later. Uh-huh, bye."

I hung up the phone feeling much more settled. Now I knew what to tell the mailman.

Kay:

"Laura, how do people know about me? I am getting stacks of mail every week!"

Laura smiled, leaning close to the Plexiglas barrier between us. "Oh, didn't I tell you? Kevin and his brother Mike set up a Web site for you, and they are sending out regular e-mail updates so that people will know how to pray for you and the children."

"Oh, tell them thanks. It's amazing to think that so many people care enough to sit down and write me a letter and tell me they are praying. I had no idea I could be so encouraged while confined behind bars. You know, Laura, this is really a gloomy, depressing place. Yet I know God is using the prayers and uplifting notes of all these people to help me avoid the depression that plagues so many of the prisoners in here."

As Aaron and Hur bore up the hands of Moses when the battle grew long and his arms became weary, so the Lord was now using the encouragement of His servants in different places to strengthen me in the middle of my trial.

"Mail call!" the deputy yelled as she appeared at the little caged area in the hallway. This had become a bright spot in my day. Mail never came on Saturday or Sunday, so seven in the morning on Monday through Friday was definitely something to look forward to. I listened attentively to the names she called.

"Oliver . . . Evans . . ."

I quickly fell in line with the women waiting to be handed their prized mail.

Mail call had become a laborious task for the deputy who delivered our unit's mail. She studied me briefly when it was my turn to step up to the horizontal slit in the bars.

"Okay, Evans, looks like we have another sea of mail to sift through for you, so let's get started."

I tried to hide my delight as I eyed the thick stack she shuffled through on the little metal shelf. I looked forward to spending time in my cell, reading and rereading what each correspondent had to say. What a wonderful way to pass away the dreary hours behind bars.

"*All* of that is my mail?" I queried.

"Yep. You sure must know a lot of people."

"Well actually, I've been getting a lot of mail from people I don't know at all. But they are Christians, and they just want to encourage me right now."

She looked at me above her glasses, uncomprehendingly. There was no way she could understand the love I was experiencing from my sisters and brothers within the body of Christ. How could I explain to her that there were people out there I had never seen who just wanted to help lift the load I was carrying? It was hard for even me to comprehend.

I tried making out the name signed neatly at the bottom of the letter she held. The guard didn't bother reading it; she just checked it for suspicious items that could be slipped in somewhere. It was so strange to watch someone else go through my mail, turning each page over to inspect it before handing it to me. Carefully, she sorted through the letters, tearing into each envelope, deftly fingering the contents. Satisfied that no contraband was being smuggled in with the letter, she ripped the stamp and return address off the envelope and then handed the letter and what remained of the envelope to me.

"Here," she handed me the letter methodically, "you can have this one."

I took it gratefully, but I watched as she tore off the return address sticker on the next envelope.

"Um, excuse me," I asked timidly, "would you mind telling me why you have to tear off all of the stamps and return address stickers?"

Her eyes never left her work as she returned dully, "Well, some people smuggle drugs in here underneath the stamps or stickers."

Done with that envelope, she handed it to me, and turned to the next one on the stack beside her. "It's our job to make sure nothing like that makes it in here. And make sure you tell your friends not to send you stamps, envelopes, money, gum, sharp objects, or anything extra. Only simple letters are permitted."

"Oh, yes, ma'am," I said, gathering my courage. "Umm, I have a question. Would I be permitted to keep the return address stickers just long enough to jot them down for my own record?"

She nodded her approval, watching out of the corner of her eye as I walked to the closest table to copy them off.

Later, as I slipped off to my cell with the treasured mail, I thought about how these letters were often just the word I needed at the moment. Children colored pictures to put with their mommies' letters. It warmed my heart to see the brightly-colored pages, and I tried to envision the little ones who had so carefully drawn them for me. How precious to know that even children were praying for my family.

The pictures reminded me of my own children's artwork. I carefully hung up the colored pages, wedging them tightly between the radio and the wall. Guards, who often inspected each of our cells, soon noticed this resemblance of home, and promptly ripped them off my wall, tossing them into the trash. Yet even the memory of artwork from children comforted me, reminding me that children and families—some of whom didn't even know us, cared enough to pray. I was so grateful to God for providing me this unexpected avenue of encouragement in such a cheerless place.

CHAPTER 28

A Mission Field Behind Bars

K<small>ay</small>:

It was 2:00 p.m. and time for head count. We stood at our cell doors, waiting. It seemed to be taking longer than usual for the deputy in charge to arrive and count us. Finally I heard the familiar commotion in the hallway—barred doors clanging open and slamming shut as each unit, all down the long hallway, had its turn. The noise was growing louder, until it was time for our unit to get the same treatment. Today, the sergeant was along, with two deputies and an inmate volunteer besides. That could mean only one thing—every unit was getting a thorough shakedown.

Like a pack of hunting dogs on the first day of hunting season, they marched swiftly in to inspect us. How many violations of jail rules would we be charged with? How many contraband items would they find among us? We would soon know.

With stern faces, they stepped briskly past us. An appointed inmate followed them, swinging a clear plastic trash bag containing bottles of medicines and other items collected from other units. Bottles would be searched out from among us and tossed in too. Seven perfect oranges left over from lunch were snatched up from our dining table and pitched into the bag. Lists of daily duties and activities were ripped dramatically from the wall where we had taped them, along with a newspaper clipping someone had posted about "Santa."

"NOTHING, NOTHING is to be put up on these walls!" the sergeant shouted at us, making us feel very small and ashamed.

Yes, we must remember not to post anything on the walls. The sergeant and deputy grimaced as they filed by impressively. I almost got the feeling we might be shot; they acted so serious. They considered us lowly criminals with "no-telling-what" stashed away in our cells.

Then, one by one, they entered our cells and overturned every bed mat, looked into every container, and grabbed up any leftovers from previous meals—packaged Twinkies or a hot dog bun—saved for a little snack in this dreary place. They were also checking for any sign of drugs or stolen medicine. It was a grave moment on this floor of the Harris County Jail.

From time to time the deputy or sergeant would openly interrogate a prisoner, perhaps asking the reason for stocking so many rolls of toilet paper in her cell. I held my breath, hoping desperately they would not interrogate me.

The team worked quickly, filling their large, clear bags with our personal stashes of leftover packaged snacks and other findings. It was the Christmas season, but the deputy was the very opposite of the world's "Santa Claus." Rather than bringing gifts, he grabbed up everyone's meager treasures.

As they prepared to leave, the sergeant studied the arrangement of napkins on our clean dining table and checked underneath them for any evidence of something hidden. Then the sergeant was gone just as quickly as he had come, undaunted by any spirit of Christmas. His silent, joyless subjects followed close behind, careful to show no expression on their faces.

We all let out a deep sigh of relief. The raid was over.

Rebecca came to our unit the same way everyone else did. As the bars banged open, the young Hispanic woman with shoulder-length black hair stepped inside, glancing around blankly. Women looked up from their games of dominoes or the TV to eye the newcomer.

Without bothering to introduce herself, she gazed at us and without any change of expression announced, "I'm pregnant."

I thought it was a strange way to address a crowd of staring women, yet it is hard to know what to say when you are the new inmate and all eyes are on you. With such an announcement, we scrutinized her more carefully.

Well, she is kind of plump, but I wouldn't have known she was actually expecting, I thought.

When I asked when her baby was due, she said, "Next month."

Hmmm, I thought, *she hardly even shows!*

There had been no mistaking my condition when I was that far along. Yet I reasoned that all women are different, and occasionally you hear stories of women who keep it hidden for nine months. *Who knows? Maybe Rebecca is just one of those.*

Rebecca was entering a unit full of mothers. There were ten or eleven of us in here on most days. We all felt for her.

"Imagine, expecting a baby in a place like this!" we whispered.

We began giving her our extra cookies, bananas, that extra carton of milk or tiny container of peanut butter, or the meat patty we could just as easily do without. She needed it more, we reasoned. I tried to think what it must be like trying to "eat for two" on prison food. I noticed many of the ladies beginning to sacrifice here and there. It made everyone feel good. After all, we were helping feed an unborn baby!

"So, is this your first child?" I asked one day.

"Yeah, the first," she beamed, as she patted her tummy and smiled proudly. But later someone said Rebecca had mentioned having three other children already.

Puzzled, I shook my head. "I must have misunderstood," I said.

Her crime sounded so small. We all thought she would be out in a flash. The story went like this—she and her husband had gone into a convenience store. But when she came out of the ladies' room, her husband was missing, and she was taken into custody for his theft. How awful! It seemed that a simple explanation might fix her up, and she could be free. But when she returned from court, she had been given thirty days.

How strange, we thought.

One day, the lab technician came to our unit to give us all pregnancy tests. Only 73-year-old Marie escaped having one.

Oh! This will be neat, I thought. The pretty girl taking samples had lined up all of our tests together. When I had done home pregnancy tests years ago, I could watch only my own results. But today would be different, seeing about ten ladies' tests at once. We would all get to observe ours slowly indicating negative, and Rebecca's would show positive.

It was certainly something different from our usual routine, so we watched with interest. But the most disappointing thing happened. As we all peered over Rebecca's shoulder and studied her results, we saw it turn out just like everyone else's—negative!

"Hey, Rebecca, you *are not* pregnant!" one of the women said in a condescending tone.

Rebecca flew to her room and threw herself on her bed, sobbing bitterly. Imagine, being about to deliver your first (or fourth) child, only to discover you don't have one after all. She had reason to be upset!

I went into her room, attempting to console her, but it was no use. She talked of how mean everyone in our unit was. She talked of suicide. I left her cell, shaking my head.

"Kay," a volunteer called, handing me a slip of pink paper through the bars, "looks like you have an attorney visit."

On my way to meet the attorney, I passed the deputy. My mind was still occupied with thoughts of Rebecca, so I turned to her.

"One of the inmates, Rebecca in 4A3, is talking about harming herself. She's upset that she flunked her pregnancy test."

"Really? I'll check things out," she assured me.

When I returned from my lawyer visit, the deputy and several other staff had moved Rebecca out of the unit and had come behind bars with us for a frank talk. This deputy had a man's haircut, carried herself like a man, and talked with a very authoritative, masculine manner.

"Listen up, ladies!" she announced very sternly. "I want all of you to just leave Rebecca alone. Do not tease her. Do not argue with her. If she wants to be pregnant, then you just *let her be pregnant!*"

A few snickers were stifled among our otherwise silent little group, but we all nodded our consent as the deputy turned and stamped out through the barred gate.

When Rebecca was brought back, we smiled and welcomed her warmly. Before this, we all had regarded her as a young mother.

But now we saw a child, or rather, a woman with a childlike mind. And along with all these mothers missing their own children, I hoped Rebecca would be well taken care of.

The large dining room was empty as I sat near the open doorway across the table from a man whom I had never seen. This was my first visit with a chaplain. I learned it was an unusual visit because, generally, a male chaplain was permitted to minister only to male inmates. Female inmates were generally ministered to by female chaplains.

"But," Robert Bottoms slowly explained, "I was granted special permission to visit you because your former pastor, Rod Hovey, is a personal friend of mine. He asked me to check up on you and see if you need anything."

I nodded gratefully. "Actually I have had a question on my mind ever since I was admitted," I said. "Do I have the freedom to hold Bible studies with other ladies while here in jail?"

He leaned forward in his chair. "It's interesting, but you will find you have more religious freedom inside these walls than you would outside. There should be absolutely no problem for you to hold Bible studies as long as you do not infringe on the rights of others. In fact," he leaned over and lifted his briefcase to the table, "I have a paperback King James Bible and some good study guides here that will help you get started."

He pulled them out and stacked them on the metal table in front of me, as I eyed them gratefully. "I will be back again to see if you need anything else," he said, smiling.

"Oh, what a blessing these will be," I said with a sigh.

Robert became a regular visitor, providing me with fresh supplies for my Bible studies and praying for me. How gracious God was to bless me with this brother's steady encouragement and a source of materials.

Early one Thursday I sat alone in my cell, relishing time alone to read in my Bible. The words seemed to jump right off the page, blessing the very core of my being. The precious Word repeatedly proved to be my source of strength and encouragement. This morning I had turned to Jeremiah 31:15-17.

> *Thus saith the LORD; A voice was heard in Ramah,*
> *lamentation, and bitter weeping;*
> *Rachel weeping for her children*
> *refused to be comforted for her children,*
> *because they were not.*
> *Thus saith the LORD; Refrain thy voice from weeping,*
> *and thine eyes from tears:*
> *for thy work shall be rewarded, saith the LORD;*
> *and they shall come again from the land of the enemy.*
> *And there is hope in thine end, saith the LORD,*
> *that thy children shall come again to their own border.*

To me, this passage was a beautiful promise from my God, who was not only watching over all the circumstances of my family but was actually directing my family's course. My heart was filled with a tremendous hope. I grabbed a notebook from my desk and scribbled the passage down in my notes to read when I needed encouragement.

A few days later, I received a letter from Hannah. She wrote that God had shown her a beautiful Scripture passage on Thursday morning. It was Jeremiah 31:15-17! I believed it was a confirmation of what the Lord planned to do. "Thank You, Lord!"

I stood carefully on the metal stool and peered through the narrow band of glass high on the far wall. Just above the roof of a nearby building I could see a delicious sliver of blue sky. It was bright out there.

"I wonder what time it is."

"Miss Kay," Debbie said, scowling, "You better get yourse'f down, girl. Dem guards wouldn't like to see you up deh like dat."

"I just wanted to see the sky. It looks like it may be noon."

Our unit had no clock, and everyone's watches had been taken away upon entering jail. Guards grew weary of being asked the monotonous question, "What time is it?"

Debbie motioned toward the TV. "Come on, girl, you can tell what time it is by checking the shows that come on. In the paper, you know, you can see what shows come on and when. Let's see . . ." She bent over the paper, scanning the TV schedule. "It must be around one o'clock."

A friendly face peered through the bars and called, "Is Kay Evans in here?"

Startled, I made my way toward the gate. "I am Kay," I said.

The lady reached through the bars and shook my hand. "I am Carol Williamson, and I'm a chaplain on another floor. A friend of mine told me about you, and I read about your situation on the Web, so I decided to come meet you."

Her eyes sparkled as she spoke. I recognized the joy of Jesus Christ flowing from her. We bonded instantly. It was a blessing and an encouragement to hear how she touched the lives of other inmates with the hope of Jesus. God was giving both of us a heart for these ladies. She was reaching into their hearts from the free side, whereas I was on the inside with them. Carol stopped by weekly, and we prayed together as two friends on opposite sides of the bars.

The exhausted woman stepped into our unit dragging her thin plastic mat. She looked up with a distant gaze as the gate clanged shut behind her.

Poor thing, I thought, *she looks so confused.*

The day I had arrived in this awful place had been ordering day; consequently, I had been able to acquire basic necessities quickly. But it was not so for some inmates. Not everyone had a friend like Sue Beth, who had slipped me money so I didn't arrive here penniless. Some of these women came into jail with no money at all.

God had given me an idea of how to reach out to newcomers. After each new jail-mate found her cell, I would slip into her room and introduce myself.

"Hi, I'm Kay. I sleep in the cell right over there. I know what it's like coming in here without shampoo, deodorant, or anything. If you need something I have, feel free to come borrow it. Okay?"

God used this small deed to open up my little jail ministry. Word began spreading quickly that I also held Bible studies in my cell. Some women were clearly not interested. Yet, enough were interested that I had my hands full with usually one—and sometimes two—Bible studies a day.

I started out trying to study the Bible with interested ladies individually. I thought it would be easier for them to open up and be honest this way. But eventually one of them came to me with a suggestion.

"Miss Kay, rather than having separate Bible studies, why don't you just lead a group Bible study for us each day? That way, we can all learn from each other. Don't you think so?"

I decided it was worth a try. And indeed, it was exciting to hear the women openly share with one another and pray. I was discovering that the jail ministry God had blessed me with was very fulfilling.

"Lord," I prayed one day, "You know how I miss my children and how I long to be reunited with them. But until then, I just want to thank You for giving me something so fulfilling to do. I love working with these ladies. They listen to me better than they do the jail chaplains, since I am on the same side of the bars as they are. And some of them, Lord, are beginning to see You really do want a relationship with them. I feel so privileged that You have allowed me this opportunity to be a part of Your work here in this mission field."

A volunteer slid a tray through the slot in the bars. I grasped it and walked toward the round metal tables. I slid onto a stool next to Christina, a new prisoner with long black hair. She was a slender girl with fine features. I smiled and introduced myself.

"Hello, I am Kay."

She nodded back at me as she emptied a package of Kool-Aid into her Styrofoam cup of water, stirring it with a plastic spoon.

"So, where are you from?" I asked, ripping off the plastic around my disposable fork and spoon.

"I'm from Italy," she explained, as she dabbed margarine from the tiny packet onto a slice of bread and began smearing it around. Between bites she filled me in on her history. "I have made it my goal to experience life to the full," she said. "I do not want to be deprived of anything life has to offer. I want to learn everything I can, whether good or bad."

I forgot about my lunch as she talked on and on, speaking unabashedly about the lesbian lifestyle she had chosen.

"Lord," I prayed, "how will You be able to direct this conversation if I can't even get a word in edgewise?"

Finally she wound down a bit, and I sensed God whispering, "Kay, here is your opportunity."

So I began. "Christina, you said you want to learn about everything you can in this life, and you don't want any opportunity to pass you by. Isn't that what you said?"

I paused and looked into her dark eyes. She nodded convincingly.

"Well, it just so happens that I lead a Bible study in my little cell over there every afternoon." I pointed in the direction of my room. Then I leaned forward before emphasizing my next point. "This might be one of those opportunities you spoke of—a way to learn more about what life has to offer you. Other ladies will be coming to my cell too, after the next head count. Will you come and join us, Christina?"

She nodded without hesitation. "Yes, I would love to come."

As soon as the afternoon head count was over, women began drifting into my cell. Since meeting Christina, I had looked up a few specific Scriptures and jotted them on a sheet of paper, which I slid between the pages of my Bible.

I was amazed at how God enabled me to quickly find the very passages I needed. It was not like me at all. Before jail life, I had often leaned on Hannah as my "quick reference" for Bible passages, and if she did not know, of course there was always our trusty concordance. But here, neither of those helps was available. Yet the Holy Spirit was supplying my every need for this work He had given me.

True to her word, Christina came, hesitating at the door before slipping in and seating herself on my bed. She had told me she was ignorant about the Bible. As I read, it was clear this was indeed a new book to her. She listened attentively, and when I read the Scriptures on homosexuality, she took it all in thought-fully.

After about forty-five minutes in the Word, I wondered at her silence. "Christina, do you have anything to say?" I ventured to ask.

She appeared deep in thought. "Well," she responded, "I believe what you said is true. And I would like to have this new life you talked about. But I just don't know how to get out of the lifestyle I am caught up in."

I was touched that she was so honest in front of the other listening prisoners. Christina was bailed out of jail that very afternoon, and I never saw her again. But I pray that a seed of truth was planted in her heart, and that God will send someone else to water it.

I shook her shoulder and spoke loudly, "Get up! It is head count time; wake up!"

The young black woman rolled over in bed and groaned. The other inmate and I looked at each other with concern.

"She's gonna get in big trouble if she don't get up now," my fellow inmate worried out loud.

The sleeping woman had been brought in off the streets sometime during the night.

"We will just have to pull her to her feet then," I said.

I grasped one hand, and she grabbed the other, and we both pulled. The small woman stood to her feet groggily and made her way outside her room. I dashed back to my position by my door. Being asleep over head count was a serious offense. No one wanted to get shouted at by the guard.

The guard stood by the bars, taking roll. "Jones" . . . "5861 . . . here," "Thompson" . . . "6617 . . . here." As the new woman stood with her head bowed and eyes closed, we watched to see what would happen as her turn approached. "Hobgood". . . "8993 . . . here," she mumbled groggily without even opening her eyes.

My, she's good, I thought. I still had to glance at my wrist bracelet in order to quote my number correctly. Later, when she was heading for the shower, she poked her head inside my door.

"My name's Evelyn. I'm headin' for the shower. Are you sure you don't mind me using your stuff?"

"Oh, no, not at all. Here you go." I placed the shampoo and deodorant into her hands. She smiled at me shyly.

After her shower, she returned the shampoo and deodorant to me gratefully and seemed to want to talk. I scooted over on my bed and invited her in to sit beside me. When she was seated, she asked, "Is it true you have Bible studies with some of the ladies here in your room?"

I nodded. "Yes, it is. And I would be very happy to study with you."

Without hesitating she responded, "I would like that."

We visited a few minutes, and I found out she had been in jail about six times before, which is why she had her prisoner identification number memorized. It reduces paperwork for the jail staff to let repeat offenders retain the number they were issued when they were first incarcerated.

Evelyn had a winning smile. She claimed to possess a master's degree in education. But for whatever reason, she had slipped into living a shameful life on the streets. Out there, beyond these walls, she was known as "Little Bit," since she was a tiny woman, about my height. I was surprised that she spoke so openly about her sinful lifestyle. I was impressed by her honesty, though, and indeed, it helped me know her better.

Before she left I said, "I would like to spend a few hours studying by myself to see what the Lord would have me to share with you."

She nodded soberly as she got up from the bed and headed toward her own cell.

When she finally came into my room ready for the study, she plopped herself on my bed and began to sob bitterly. I found myself stifling a laugh at this unsolicited outburst.

"Evelyn," I said incredulously, "I haven't even begun to read out of my Bible yet, and here you are crying already."

She smiled at me through her tears. She seemed so hungry for truth; it was a beautiful thing to see.

As I turned the pages of my Bible, I told her, "I just want you to sit back and notice the character of Jesus as I read to you about

Him. These true stories will help you see how Jesus feels about you, Evelyn."

I read various stories from the New Testament such as the woman at the well, John 4:5-42; the woman caught in adultery, John 8:3-11; and the woman who washed Jesus' feet and wiped them with her hair, Luke 7:36-50.

Evelyn wept silently all the while I was reading.

After I finished, I merely told her, "Evelyn, I want you to contemplate the character of this man, Jesus, overnight. That is all."

When she returned the next day, I found she was more than ready to surrender her heart to the tender Saviour, about whom she had meditated late into the night.

CHAPTER 29

Life as an Inmate

Kay:

I spread the newspaper out on the table and eagerly scanned the front page. "Ah, there it is," I said, leaning closer for a better look.

Articles about my case showed up from time to time in the *Houston Chronicle,* and of course I was always interested to read what the media had to say about it. I wasn't the only one interested though. The other ladies in the unit couldn't restrain their curiosity and talked openly about my case.

"Is dat one 'bout you?" Debbie asked as she peered over my shoulder.

I nodded and handed her the paper. As she read the article and realized I was in jail on a $3,000,000 bond, she looked me over carefully, her eyebrows suddenly moving higher on her forehead. When I explained that my six felony charges represented each of my six children and that each charge was valued at $500,000, her eyes grew large.

Laying aside the paper, she exclaimed dramatically, "Girl, you got yoursef some perty special chiddren! Ain't none of MY children worth $500,000. Yes, indeed, I'd say you got yoursef some perty special chiddren!"

Patty was in the cell right next to mine. She was so kind and polite to everyone. I wondered why she was in a place like this.

She showed genuine concern for me, worrying about me on

days I spent fasting, as if she wanted to make sure I wouldn't wither up and die.

"I won't say anything to anyone about how many meals you're missing," she said, "unless you start looking bad. Then I will tell on you out of concern for you. Do you understand?"

I felt the pressure was on. But I knew God could sustain me. These were such serious days that I needed to spend them in prayer and fasting at least some of the time.

Every food tray came with a Kool-Aid packet. Patty began saving hers for me so that I could have some flavor to stir into my water.

I fell into line behind Evelyn, my flat bedsheet ready to be tossed into the growing pile at the guard's feet. What I failed to notice was that all the other inmates had unknotted the corners before turning them in. After Evelyn had dropped her sheet onto the growing pile, I dropped mine and headed back toward my cell.

"Hey, inmate!" the woman guard barked gruffly. "Get back over here! Just what do you think you're doing? Don't throw that sheet onto the pile without untying the corners first!"

I stooped over the sheet and, with shaking hands, hastily began untying each knot.

"You'd better be ready next time. Don't you make me have to wait on you!" She scowled.

"Yes, ma'am," my voice quavered as I struggled with the last knot. "I'm very sorry."

I was not accustomed to being shouted at. My sheets would certainly be ready next time.

I looked at the little calendar I had drawn on my notepad. *It is Isaiah's birthday,* I thought as I stared down at the block marked January 5. *I want so badly to call him, but there is only a slim chance, since I'd have to call my in-laws' home collect.*

I doubted they would accept the charges of a collect phone call from *me* in the Harris County Jail. But I took a deep breath and decided to make the attempt anyway. "If they say no, at least I'll have tried."

Our unit was quiet that morning, as most of the women had gone back to bed after the second head count. I was glad because I did not want anyone overhearing my conversation.

One ring, two rings. "Hello, this is Walter Evans."

"Hello, Walter, this is Kay. Could I please speak to Isaiah?" I paused. "Uh, it's his birthday."

"No, Kay, I don't think that will be possible. We were just about to walk out the door to take him to the doctor."

There was a long pause. "Couldn't I please talk to him?"

Suddenly Jan was on the phone. "Kay, Isaiah is ill, and we need to leave with him right now in order to be on time for his doctor's appointment."

"Jan, could I please speak with Isaiah? It's his birthday! I haven't gotten to talk to him for a month. I won't keep him long. I just want to hear his voice again."

"No, Kay, I really don't think that will be possible."

"Hi, Mommy!"

"Oh, Isaiah!" My voice broke with emotion.

"How are you?"

"I'm fine, Mom. I miss you!"

"Oh, I miss you too, Isaiah! Happy Birthday! I love you!"

"I love you too, Mom!"

"Isaiah, did you get the letters I sent to you?"

"No, Mom. What letters?"

Walter broke in and said, "Well, we have to be going now."

"Thank you so much for letting me talk to Isaiah! I really appreciate it. Good-bye."

The phone clicked. Even though they both had told me it was not possible for me to speak to Isaiah, somehow God had intervened. Oh, it was such a joy just to hear Isaiah's voice!

I had not dared to ask if I could speak to my daughters too, even though I desperately wanted to! But God had given me a wonderful gift in allowing me to speak with my son on the morning of his birthday. What a precious blessing!

As I hung up the phone, I ran to my cell and threw myself on my bed in a flood of tears. I couldn't believe I had actually gotten to hear my son's voice! Even though I was disappointed and agitated that Isaiah, and I'm sure the other children, had not received my letters, that could not squelch the joy I felt at hearing his voice on his eleventh birthday.

Patty entered my room and gently put her hand on my back. I got up and she gave me a much-needed bear hug. She just held me for a while, letting me sob on her shoulder. Neither of us said anything. The moment was too intense for words.

———————————

Sitting alone on my bed, I felt grateful for the time away from the other inmates. The automatic metal doors to my cell had finally closed, giving me some precious solitude. I was extremely burdened tonight. I had called Laura earlier this evening, and she had given me the crushing news.

"Kay, did you hear that your in-laws are putting Isaiah, Beverly, Grace, and Emily into public school?"

"No! You have got to be kidding," I gasped.

"It's true. They'll be starting tomorrow. I hated to tell you, but I thought you should know," she said sympathetically.

This was a blow and very upsetting to me. Each of my children had been homeschooled from the beginning. When Hannah had been ready to enter first grade, our preacher back in Phoenix had suggested I homeschool her. Since then, home education had become a way of life for our family. Yet here my children were going off to public school tomorrow, January 10, against my wishes.

I found it hard to believe this could actually be happening. "Dear Lord, I don't understand the way You do things. I have tried so hard to protect my children from worldly influences, and now, besides being with their grandparents, they are being placed in public school. I can't even let them know I'll be praying."

I was too stunned to cry, but the anguish of my heart was intense.

I opened my Bible to see what comfort the Lord would offer. For some reason I found myself reading in Lamentations and was very blessed by the verses I found.

It is of the LORD's mercies that we are not consumed,

*because his compassions fail not. They are new every morn-
ing: great is thy faithfulness. The LORD is my portion, saith
my soul; therefore will I hope in him. The LORD is good unto
them that wait for him, to the soul that seeketh him. It is
good that a man should both hope and quietly wait for the
salvation of the LORD.*

*For the Lord will not cast off for ever: But though he
cause grief, yet will he have compassion according to the
multitude of his mercies. . .*

*I called upon thy name, O LORD, out of the low dungeon.
Thou hast heard my voice: hide not thine ear at my
breathing, at my cry. Thou drewest near in the day that I
called upon thee: thou saidst, Fear not. O Lord, thou hast
pleaded the causes of my soul; thou hast redeemed my life.
O LORD, thou hast seen my wrong: judge thou my cause.*[1]

I reflected on God's mercy and faithfulness to me and my children, and suddenly my heart filled with an unexplainable joy.
Although things looked discouraging, God's Word reminded me of
His promises and of His might. I was safe in His care, and my
children were too.

Even with strong reservations about the public school environment, my greater concerns were about them being in my in-
laws' home. Perhaps going to school was God's way of protecting
them from a greater danger.

I had to smile when I remembered my children would be
attending the very same school I had attended as a child. This
would become one more thing my children and I would have in
common. Even while being separated from my children, God was
overseeing every detail in such a way that the bond of love and
common ground we shared was actually being strengthened.

That night, as I stretched out on my jail bed, I fell asleep
thinking about my tender heavenly Father.

———————

My fellow inmates liked to keep the television in our unit blaring loudly, perhaps to drown out painful thoughts of being

———————

1. Lamentations 3:22-26, 31, 32, 55-59

trapped in this life behind bars. I found it frustrating not to be able to separate myself from the constantly droning noise and evil. Since I couldn't shut my cell door, there seemed to be no way of escaping it. I could not understand why there would be a TV in jail anyway.

"Isn't jail supposed to be a punishment?" I grumbled. Nonetheless, TV was a reality here, just like the offensive language and the steel bars. It was just one more thing I could not get away from. I soon learned that in order to reduce arguments among the ladies there was a system for how TV programs were selected each day.

Someone had organized a cleanup duty rotation. The one whose turn it was to be in charge of the early morning cleanup was also granted the privilege of choosing which TV programs everyone would watch that day.

I was informed of this arrangement on my first morning in charge of cleanup duty. I resisted immediately.

"I don't even like television. Can I just bow out of this 'privilege' and let someone else choose today's programs instead? Or, better yet, can I just say that since I'm in charge of cleanup, we will all take a 24-hour break from TV?"

The inmate who had been explaining things to me protested. "No! If you don't choose the TV programs to watch, a fight will break out in here. Chaos will rule."

I hadn't thought about that. So, I walked slowly to a table and sat down with the newspaper, leafing through the pages until I found the TV schedule. It felt so strange to be planning out a day of TV programs. I settled on the news and old serials I thought would be the least offensive to my own ears. In any case, it would be a nice break from the vile conversations on the talk shows.

Afterward, still disgusted by the TV assignment, I poured out my frustrations to God. "Lord, the TV is such an irritating distraction in here. It makes it hard for me to concentrate when I study the Bible on my own, and it interferes with the studies I have with the other ladies too. And Satan uses it to lure some women away from coming to the Bible studies at all. It is just a monotonous intruder throughout the day. Would You please do something about it?"

Soon after voicing my complaint to God, a wonderful thing happened. The television broke—yes, it completely broke. A repairman came and attempted to fix the mysterious malfunction but was unsuccessful. As he gathered up his tools from the floor, he shook his head.

I praised the Lord, rejoicing quietly over this victory. I considered it to be one of the ways God was letting me know He was attentively listening and overseeing my every need. I was so grateful to Him.

The TV remained in disrepair for close to three weeks until one of the deputies took pity on the ladies in our unit and had it replaced. In the meantime, I was grateful for the respite. I could be more effective in the ministry God had given to me in jail.

In my distress I called upon the LORD, and cried unto my God: he heard my voice out of his temple, and my cry came before him, even into his ears.[1]

Lissa:

The mail lay on the table, and I eyed it longingly. Right there on top I could see a letter addressed to me. I wanted to pounce on it and take it to my room to read in blessed privacy. But rules were rules, and I knew Granddad or Grandmom would want to peruse the contents before I got it. Granddad sat at the table, methodically going through his own mail. I could bear it no longer.

"Granddad, could you please scan this letter of mine, so that I can go read it? It is a note from a good friend."

Granddad looked up and smiled. Then taking the envelope in his hand, he slit it open and handed me the letter, without even bothering to read it as they usually did. I thanked him profusely and then nearly danced off to my room to enjoy my mail. Sitting on my bed, I laughed and cried my way through the letter. Proverbs 25:25 had come to have a real meaning in my life. *As cold waters to a thirsty soul, so is good news from a far country.*

Guatemala was indeed a far country, but not all our mail came from that far away. I sighed happily and glanced at the stack of letters

---

1. Psalm 18:6

on my desk. It was incredible how much mail we were getting. Something came nearly every day, and oftentimes there was a pile addressed to "The Evans Children."

The mail was always refreshing and lifted our spirits. People from many places wrote us—old friends we had not seen in years and friends from Guatemala, as well as people we had never even met. More than once, I got letters from complete strangers encouraging me to be faithful.

My grandparents seemed convinced we were going to be "abducted" again. As a precaution, they arranged for two officers from the police department to come and fingerprint us the *official* way. The officers came in uniform, complete with guns and bullets. From a tube they squeezed a small dab of dark ink onto a clean piece of flat metal and evened it out with a roller.

Then they took each one of us by turn and pressed our fingers, first onto the inked metal, and then onto the square on the card bearing our name. Once the procedure was complete, the cards were given to Granddad and Grandmom, who filed them away. My poor grandparents were trying everything they could think of that might help authorities locate and identify us in case we were "abducted" again.

A security system was installed in their house. "Friends of ours from church donated it," they explained. Now all the doors and windows were monitored. If a door or window was opened when the system was on "lock," the alarm would scream its terrible shrill beeping all throughout the house. If the beeping went on for more than a minute without being timed out by Grandmom or Granddad punching in the secret code, the police would call to see if they needed to come.

All this seemed hilarious to us; we had no intentions of escaping.

My alarm clock beeped annoyingly.

"Is it morning already?" I moaned, glaring at the clock.

I crawled out of my nice, cozy bed, flipped on the light, and turned off the alarm. "Oh, it is four instead of five! I must have accidentally set it an hour early. Well, since I am up, I might as well stay up."

After a hot bath, I carried my dirty clothes out to the garage where Grandmom sorted all the laundry. But the moment I opened the door into the garage, I realized my mistake. The security system was still on. As the alarm shrieked through the house, I stood helplessly by the door, staring at the little red light flashing on the security system.

What should I do? I thought desperately, but of course I did not know the code. Grandmom rushed into the laundry room, hastily wrapped in her bathrobe, and quickly punched in the password. Suddenly the whole situation struck me as funny, and I struggled to keep a straight face.

Grandmom sighed in relief as the flashing and beeping stopped. Her face reflected the irritation she felt.

Clearing my throat, I asked half in jest, "Wouldn't it make more sense for you to show me the secret code, so if this happens again, I can just turn it off myself?"

She stared at me incredulously. "No, that is not an option!" she snapped.

I nodded soberly, and escaped to my room.

"Lissa!" someone hissed under the door. I looked up from my homework and heard my name again. I slipped off my bed, tiptoed to the door, and opened it silently.

There stood Beverly. She quickly slipped into my room, and I swung the door shut behind her. Beverly was smiling mischievously.

"How are you doing? How was your day?" I asked.

"Oh, it was all right, except I got into trouble at school." A concerned look crossed my face, but she quickly responded, "No, I mean I wouldn't do this dance the P. E. teacher had us all do. So she took me to the principal's office."

The children being in public school caused extra stress in our relationship with our grandparents. Issues came up in class, and the children came home with stories that deepened our concerns.

One evening Isaiah had come home with a troubled expression. "Lissa," he said, "I hate school! Everyone there is on Grandmom and Granddad's side. Today I got into trouble in class. Every morning the class recites the pledge of allegiance to the flag, you know? Anyway, I decided I wasn't going to, because it's not true. It says something about 'liberty and justice for all,' but that is a lie. Mommy is not getting liberty or justice, so I refused to say it. My teacher sent me to the principal's office. He talked to me sternly about my lack of patriotism, but I just don't care. Oh, Lissa, I hate school . . ." His voice had trailed off sorrowfully.

Now it was Beverly who had visited the principal's office. I sighed wearily. "I'm sorry, Beverly. What did they say to you?"

"Well, he said if I felt it was wrong, I didn't have to. But he wasn't very happy with me."

We both heard steps in the hall, and they were coming our way. I frantically looked around my room.

"Quick, Beverly, into the closet," I said. "Grandmom would not be happy to find you here. Hurry, and be quiet!"

She jumped behind my dresses just as I heard a knock at the door. My heart filled with dread as I opened the door. Grandmom stood there looking seriously at me. I smiled weakly.

"Lissa, do you know where Isaiah is?"

"No, ma'am, have you looked in the study?"

"Oh, no, I haven't," she said. With that, she turned and headed the other way.

"That was too close," I said, sighing with relief. I scooted my dresses apart so Beverly could emerge. "We have to be really careful. And don't come in here unless you really have something important to say, because we could both get into big trouble if we get caught."

She nodded. Seconds later, when the coast was clear, she scurried back to her room.

CHAPTER 30

"Mommy, Is It True?"

K_{ay}:

Closing my Bible, I looked into the earnest faces in my cell. "Well, that's all for now, I guess. Thank you all for sharing."

I hesitated for a few seconds before Evelyn broke into my thoughts. She looked directly at me and asked, "Sista' Kay, you are worried 'bout that court hearing tomorrow, aren't you?"

"Well, I must admit I am."

"Thought so. Girls, let's gather 'round Sista Kay and pray fo' her. She needs duh touch of duh Masta."

All five women huddled around me and knelt on the hard floor to pray. Evelyn's strong voice led out.

"Dear Lord Jesus, we come to You just as humbly as we know how. We is prayin' on behalf of our Sista Kay. Lord, we ask You in de name of Your darlin' Son, Jesus, to reunite her with her six precious chiddren and let dem be a family agin."

I never felt so prayed over as when Evelyn prayed for me in her dramatic yet precious way. I wondered why my own white culture tends toward such predictable phrases and lack of emotion. Everyone should have the rich privilege of praying with brothers or sisters from other cultures. It added to fellowship a depth and meaning I had never known.

Within our little Bible study group, Evelyn quickly became my strongest encourager. After our prayer times, we enjoyed spirited song services. Evelyn often took the lead. She had dreamed as a little girl of being a singer, and now her rich voice echoed throughout our unit, singing beautiful songs for Jesus. I marveled at the flair and trills she could add to a simple line of music.

Sometimes the prisoners who didn't attend our Bible study became annoyed with her unabashed singing because it drowned out their TV programs or domino games. But Evelyn sang on, her eyes closed, tuning out everything else. I admired her uninhibited worship.

"Thank you."

I accepted the pink slip and instantly looked to see who my visitors were. My dad, stepmom, Hannah, and Lissa were all here together to visit me. Walking down the corridor, I bit my lip. I was worried about this visit.

Inmates are permitted, at the most, two adult visitors at a time and two children, I thought. *What will happen this time, since three of my visitors are technically adults? Will they permit my dad and stepmom to visit me but bump off my daughters?*

I shook my head and prayed, "Lord, please don't let that happen."

As I drew closer to the visiting area, I had mixed emotions. While I desperately wanted to talk to Hannah and Lissa, I was afraid of what my dad might say. At our last visit, he was very frustrated.

I decided to plead with the guard in charge. Rounding the corner, I noticed it was the gruff, bulldog-looking one, the hardest to appeal to. *Oh, no!* I groaned inwardly. Nonetheless, I would try my best to explain my desire to see my daughters.

As I expected, he appeared unsympathetic and immovable, hardly looking at me as I spoke. I had hoped to sense at least a trace of mercy in him. But guards aren't trained to practice mercy.

My appeal was from the depth of a mother's heart. But like a stone statue, his face was expressionless, giving neither a glimmer of hope nor any indication of what he might do.

Apprehensively, I seated myself at the window where my dad and stepmom were already waiting. Taking a deep breath, I prayed silently. *God, please give me grace to withstand whatever my dad might say.*

I didn't want a repeat of our last visit and, frankly, I was nervous. I had tried unsuccessfully to write my dad a letter since then, but nothing had looked right on paper. Consequently, each letter had been crumpled up and tossed into the trash.

I guess the girls were bumped off, I concluded, my heart sinking. Looking awkwardly from my dad's face to my stepmom's, I didn't know what to say. But I noticed my dad wore a different expression than when he had been here last. I decided to begin the conversation.

"Dad, I never meant to hurt you through all that has happened and . . ."

He shook his head. "You don't deserve to be in a place like this," he said. "It's not right that they put you in here."

I couldn't believe my ears. *Is Dad sympathetic toward me now? What changed his mind? What has softened him?*

As we talked, he assured me of his love for me. I felt greatly relieved.

Before long, the guard nodded that my visiting time was up. My dad and stepmom stood up and filed out into the hallway. And then, to my great surprise, Hannah and Lissa quickly replaced them at the window and sat down.

What is this? I thought with a surge of joy. *Am I going to get a visit with both of my daughters too?*

I glanced at the guard in disbelief. I thought I detected just a hint of a smug grin on his broad face as he sat at his post, his thick arms folded in front of him, pretending not to notice me. He was busy monitoring other visits going on in the visitor station.

I looked back at my girls. It was so good to look into their fresh, young faces again, which were so beautiful to this mother. How grateful I was to have even a brief private visit with them.

Lissa:

It was so good to see Mommy again. Although it had to be in the county jail, and even if we couldn't have that hug we longed for, there was so much to catch up on.

"Friends called us at Granddad and Grandmom's and said a whole lot of them are coming to the hearing tomorrow. We knew the phone conversations were taped, but it was sweet to talk to them again. I wanted to come here so badly, Mommy, but we really didn't think Granddad and Grandmom would let me come down here for the hearing tomorrow, but they did!"

Mommy smiled back at me and said, "Praise the Lord; I am so glad they did."

I nodded and continued, "Hannah and I rode down with Grandfather and Mimi, and we are staying at Aunt Elaine's."

But there was something else I needed to talk to Mommy about. It was the troubling lies we had been hearing about her. Our grandparents were constantly telling us children things about our mother that were really confusing.

One night recently, Hannah and I had slipped off to our room, and she had asked me, "Are they right? Do you think what Granddad and Grandmom are telling us is true? I mean, they sound so convincing."

My answer was sharp. "Of course not! Don't believe what they say when it doesn't match up with what you know is true!"

Her face relaxed, and I could tell she was relieved. But it was confusing to live in our grandparents' home; I had to admit it myself. We heard wild accusations about our mom over and over and over again, day in and day out. A trace of fear was creeping in, confusing us, despite what we knew to be truth.

Could it be that our own mother really is different from what we thought her to be? we found ourselves wondering in our weakest moments. *No, it doesn't add up,* we reasoned. *Our grandparents are just wrong. Maybe after speaking about it so much, they're deceived into believing those things. Whatever the case, we must dismiss what they're saying as untrue and not allow ourselves to dwell on it.*

As long as Hannah and I were together, we could remind one another that we knew our mommy was truthful. That certainly helped.

But now, in this jail visit, just one look into her dear face reminded me that she was everything we knew her to be—truthful, loving, and dependable. But just to prove wrong what we had been hearing, we asked her about specific, terrible accusations. We were relieved to hear from her own mouth what we had known all along. We had no reason to doubt our mommy. She was not perfect; none of us are.

She had often confessed to us that she was far from perfect. But neither was she the person my grandparents were painting her to be. How those jail visits encouraged us! We were still a family, even if miles and people, court cases and glass barriers, separated us.

Mommy wanted to know everything about how things had been going for us. She could tell our lives had been quite stressful. But there was little time to get into specifics.

"Tell me how Isaiah, Beverly, Grace, and Emily are coping with life with Grandmom and Granddad. Oh, ever since Beverly was allowed to come along and see me several weeks ago, I have missed her all the more."

The three of us talked hurriedly to exchange as much information as we could before the guard would call a halt to our timed visit. But the guard, who had seemed so uncompromising and gruff, ended up giving Mommy an extra-long visit with us.

"I can't believe he's giving us all this time," she whispered to us. "He could have denied me the privilege altogether of having this chat with my daughters, declaring that 'rules are rules.' What a blessing!"

Our hearts were full of gratitude to God for turning the heart of a callous guard and causing him to have compassion toward us.

CHAPTER 31

"Order in the Court!"

– January 11, 2000 –

Hannah:

The elevator chimed, and the number *17* flashed in the little display screen near the ceiling. When the metal doors slid open, Lissa, Aunt Elaine, and I hurried into the hall. Our steps resounded loudly as we walked down the corridor. Since no hearings were in session this early, doors to the courtrooms were locked.

In spite of the early hour, several of our friends had already gathered, waiting at the very end of the hallway. I had not seen some of them since we left Guatemala. Their presence was a boost to my spirits!

Lissa and I greeted each one, hugging the ladies tightly and giving the men hearty handshakes. Although seeing our friends was exciting, a cloud of nervous anticipation hung over us.

"Lissa," I whispered, "does the courthouse ever remind you of the hospital? You know, here we are, in these quiet halls, eagerly waiting to hear what Mommy's outcome will be. It reminds me of how a family paces the floor, trying to stay calm while their loved one is in the operating room.

"I wonder what the judge will decide today. I am just grateful that the judge's heart is held by God's hand, to guide it in the direction of His choosing. What a wonderful reminder for today."

At last the door to the 312th District Court was unlocked, and we streamed in and found seats on the long, padded benches. I looked around the large courtroom, tastefully furnished with dark polished wood. The room had a royal, awe-inspiring air about it that made me feel small and insignificant. Its very nature provoked fear. Facts were facts in this solemn place.

In this room some people learned they would spend the rest of their lives in prison. Others heard that their lives would be ended. Chills went down my spine. This was not a place where one easily found mercy.

The purpose for today's hearing was to again see if the judge would consider reducing Mommy's bond.

Oh, Lord, I prayed, *please cause Judge Hill to bring the bond down!*

On the far wall above the judge's bench hung a clock. The second hand seemed to mock my eagerness for the proceedings to begin as it slowly made its way around the clock's face. Lawyers, court workers, and secretaries spoke quietly as they prepared for the session. To the left of the judge's bench stood the bailiff. He always seemed to be grouchy, and this morning was no different.

Suddenly the door by the judge's bench swung open. The bailiff croaked, "All rise!" as Judge Belinda Hill strode in.

We stood respectfully.

"You may be seated," the judge announced and sat down behind her high desk.

One of the court secretaries stood and began calling the names on the day's docket. Unlike a school roll call, here it was imperative that everyone be present. For example, if someone out of jail on bond failed to show up, his bond would then be claimed by the state, and he would be returned to jail. I was slowly learning how important this was.

"State versus Smith," the secretary's voice called out.

"Here!" a deep voice responded from somewhere to my right.

"State versus Johnson." After a three-second pause, the secretary said, "The State moves for forfeiture of the bond."

Just like that! And Johnson would be jailed again. I gulped.

Once roll call was over, the judge began hearing cases. From a door on the left, an inmate was led into the courtroom. He was wearing the typical bright orange prisoner outfit, and his hands were securely hand-cuffed behind his back. With two lawyers accompanying him, he shuffled toward the judge's bench. One lawyer represented him and the other represented the state.

The judge peered down sternly. "How do you plead?"

"Guilty, Your Honor," he mumbled.

Judge Hill removed her glasses. "Are you pleading guilty because you are guilty, and for no other reason? No one has forced you or coerced you, but you are pleading guilty freely and voluntarily?"

"Yes, Your Honor," he mumbled again.

Then he was led back through the door, and the next prisoner was brought out.

Kay:

I shifted again on the cold, metal bench, trying to find a more comfortable position. I had sat here for hours and was eager for a change of scenery.

I wonder who all is out there? I asked myself for the umpteenth time. Earlier Alex Azzo's face had appeared in the window of the holding cell where several prisoners and I sat waiting our turns to enter the courtroom. Before the day's sessions had begun, he was excited, and his words had rung like music in my ears.

"Kay, you won't believe this! About fifty people are out there, all here to see and support you. I think some of them are friends from Guatemala."

"Really?" I had cried, wide-eyed. "Oh, when can I come out and see them?"

"Kay, I don't know. I am still waiting on the district attorney to show up. I really should go now, but I'll be back when I know more."

I had watched him turn and head back to the excitement of the courtroom, leaving me still waiting and wondering.

What could be taking them so long? I thought impatiently. I felt like a horse, eager to bolt through the gate and onto the racetrack. My mind drifted back to this morning when I had been herded through the underground tunnels with hordes of other prisoners and then deposited into one frigid holding tank after another. I assumed that eventually I would emerge from the "catacombs" into the grandeur of the courtroom to face the judge.

With the brand-new criminal courthouse now completed, my journey was now mostly through underground tunnels rather than crossing downtown streets as we used to have to do to reach the old courthouse. Though I missed seeing the glorious sky, I was thankful for the change. I did not miss having to cross the street as a prisoner—a spectacle for all to see.

Hannah:

Finally it was time for Mommy's case. The lawyers, Alex Azzo and Jim Lindeman, were called forward, but Mommy was not brought out. Around forty or fifty people in the audience were anxious to hear what would happen to Mommy. We did not even know some of the people who had come to support her, but having them there was very encouraging! Their presence made the state's lawyer nervous.

A hushed silence fell over the courtroom. Everyone strained to hear what was being said between the lawyers and the judge, but their voices were so low that I caught only snatches here and there. Finally I heard the state's lawyer say something about another appointment. When the conversation ended, the lawyers came to speak to us.

"Come out to the hallway," said Mr. Azzo. "We'll talk there."

Aunt Elaine, all our friends and supporters, and Lissa and I stood and made our way to the door en masse. Looking behind me, I noticed the judge's eyes following us. The courtroom was left nearly empty.

Once in the hallway, we all crowded around Mr. Azzo, who explained articulately what had just happened. "The prosecuting attorney informed the judge he has another case today, so he won't be able to handle ours. So it has been postponed until tomorrow," he said matter-of-factly, attempting to hide his own disappointment.

A silent groan swept through the crowd as his words sank in. These people had gone to tremendous efforts to be here. Fighting traffic in downtown Houston was no easy feat for the local folks, and some of these people had driven or flown from other cities or states. And now the hearing was postponed.

We were learning, to our dismay, that this happens repeatedly in the court system. I tried to console myself that God allowed this, so I should rest assured that He would use it for good. Nonetheless, looking around at the disappointed faces of our friends, I felt frustrated, knowing the trouble and expense they had gone to in order to come. It was a good time for all of us to remind ourselves that God was in control.

Kay:

I was jolted out of my scattered thoughts when Mr. Azzo tapped once again on the low window through which we could talk. I jumped up and ran over eagerly. He was shaking his head apologetically.

"Kay, your hearing has suddenly been rescheduled for tomorrow. You'll not enter the courtroom at all today. I'm sorry."

I stared at him, stunned and speechless. He had to be kidding! I had just gotten all worked up about going into the courtroom only to learn it was not to be. What a letdown!

Lissa:

We stood close to the glass in the jail visiting area, grinning widely. Mommy smiled back through her tears, and put her hand on the glass, the closest thing to a hug she could give us. Although I had been terribly disappointed about the canceled hearing, it was wonderful seeing Mommy again. Though her bright orange outfit was simply hideous, her sweet face was just as dear as it had ever been, even with her hair down.

"They still won't let me wear a veil in here," she said. "But I have learned I can wear one at the courthouse. Once I'm back on jailhouse property, I must take it off."

"That's odd," Hannah and I agreed.

"Mommy, you would not believe all the people that came for the hearing today: Phil and Connie Bear, Joe Lehman, Wesley and Alice King, Arthur and Ruth Shirk, Nevin Good, and many others! Mom, a whole bunch of people—some of whom we don't even know flew down for this hearing!"

She shook her head in disbelief as Hannah and I listed all who had flown in to show their support.

"I just can't believe people would do that for us! Isn't God good?"

"Yes, but their return flights leave before your hearing tomorrow. They were all terribly disappointed they couldn't see you."

Mommy glanced uneasily at the guard supervising the inmates visiting with their guests. We knew our time was almost up.

Hannah glanced at her watch and said, "Hey, Mommy, he is letting us have more than fifteen minutes this time."

"Really?" she said. "What a blessing! Thank You, Lord!" After we had nearly thirty precious minutes of talking with our mother, the guard motioned that we should bring our conversation to a close.

As we reached the lobby on the main floor, Hannah and I were discussing the miracle God had worked in allowing us an extra fifteen minutes with Mommy. We excitedly told Aunt Elaine, our cousin Lauren, and Laura Magee about our visit. Pushing open the heavy doors of the jail lobby, we nearly bumped into Mr. Azzo and Mr. Lindeman.

Both of them were speaking on their cell phones. When he saw us, Mr. Azzo paused and whispered, "Hey! Stay right here. We need to talk to you, NOW! Just let us get off the phone."

I looked over at Aunt Elaine and shrugged my shoulders. "What could they want? It sounds important."

The lawyers paced back and forth on the dirty sidewalk while we waited, eager to know what was going on.

Mr. Azzo ended his conversation. "Yes, and have that paper faxed to my office ASAP! Understand? Good." He snapped his phone shut. "You will not believe what just happened," he said excitedly. "This is simply incredible. We just got out of a meeting with the judge, and she agreed to lower the bond to one percent of the original amount. Did you catch that? ONE PERCENT! I have never seen this happen before."

Hannah and I joyfully hugged each other, our hearts bursting with gratitude. This was a miracle from God!

"But," Mr. Azzo said soberly, "there are some restrictions. Your mother will have to stay within Harris County, wearing an ankle monitor. And she will not be allowed any contact with her minor children."

I grimaced when he said "minor children" because that meant me.

Mr. Azzo went on to explain. "Hannah and Lissa, I want you to be very careful to help your mom keep the restrictions of her bond. You must not do anything that would even look like a violation of these restrictions. Your mom isn't supposed to have any contact with her minor children, so you must be extremely careful. Don't even tell the younger children, 'Mommy loves you.' That could be mistaken for passing messages. Understand?"

I listened carefully, slowly becoming aware how drastically these restrictions would affect me. I wouldn't be able to talk to Mommy until the restriction was lifted. *That will be hard,* I thought, but I knew God had a plan in this.

"And just think, Mommy can get out of jail now! Thank You, precious Father, for allowing us to meet with the lawyers *after* our visit with Mommy rather than before. You blessed me with one last, wonderful visit with Mommy."

Kay:

Only minutes after returning to my unit from my visit with the girls, I was notified that my defense attorneys had just arrived to see me. *This is not unusual,* I thought. *They come frequently, though not often together, to inform me of new developments in the case or to have me sign something.*

I retraced my steps down the hallway, hoping they might explain why the hearing had suddenly been rescheduled for tomorrow. Court proceedings were such a puzzle to me. I was grateful God had provided lawyers who could help me make at least some sense of it all. And I was thankful for their dedication. It seemed that they were eating, drinking, and sleeping this case.

When I walked into the conference cubicle, my lawyers were wearing huge smiles. They reminded me of two boys about to burst with something terribly exciting, and both wanting to be the one to say it. But since they were dignified men, they exercised good manners and looked at each other with gracious restraint while I waited.

Finally, Mr. Azzo blurted out, "Kay, you are NOT going to believe this, but we have just come out of a meeting with the judge, and we have some VERY encouraging news! She has finally agreed to lower your bond! She is willing to lower it to $30,000!"

"Are you serious?" I responded. "OH, PRAISE GOD!" I was thrilled.

Usually in these lawyer/client meetings, we sat as we talked through the bars to one another. But this meeting was so exciting that none of us even thought about sitting down.

"And furthermore," he continued, "an older couple, Arthur and Ruth Shirk, who flew here for your court hearing, have volunteered to pay your bond. They are arranging right now to have the money wired. They said you could reimburse them later."

"Really? Oh, thank God!"

Mr. Azzo scratched his head. "Kay, I don't understand. You hardly even know this couple, and yet they are putting out this kind of money for you!"

I smiled, wondering how to explain that in the body of Christ we all look for ways to help one another. *And whether one member suffer, all the members suffer with it.*[1]

My heart was overflowing with gratitude that these people were willing to pour out their resources before the Lord, that I might be delivered from jail. *God, please richly reward them,* I prayed silently.

"However," Alex Azzo continued, "the judge has some restrictions you'll have to agree to before the bond will be reduced. But, Kay, if you ask me, I think it's worth it!"

"Well, what are the restrictions?" I asked.

"Okay, listen carefully. Number one, you cannot leave Harris County; number two, between the hours of 5:00 p.m. and 8:00 a.m., you cannot leave the house where you will be staying. Oh, and by the way, Laura Magee's mother, Ann Montagne, has volunteered to let you live at her house, so if that is agreeable with you, we will arrange for you to live there."

"Oh, how kind of her!" I exclaimed.

He continued reading the list from his yellow notepad. "Number three, you must wear an ankle monitor at all times; number four, you may have no contact whatsoever with your minor children; and number five, you may not have any contact with your in-laws."

Well, it sounds like I'll be on a pretty tight leash, I thought soberly. *Yet there is so much I need to do that I can't do from in here, I can hardly argue the point.*

My mind flashed back to the sweet way Evelyn and a few of

---

1. 1 Corinthians 12:26

my jail comrades had specifically prayed over my hearing just yesterday. This was an answer to their prayers, and the prayers of many other people too. In fact, the whole group of people who flew in for the hearing had been praying and fasting on my behalf for this very purpose. God was definitely listening to His people who were crying out for my family and me.

Yes, this was an answer to many people's prayers. In my heart, I thanked the One who had brought about such a wonderful miracle today.

I looked back at Mr. Azzo and Mr. Lindeman. "I'll accept the judge's proposal," I said.

They looked extremely pleased and nodded approvingly. Mr. Azzo informed me that the purpose of the next day's court proceedings would be for me to stand before the judge and agree to the terms of the bond.

"So, when do I actually get to leave this place?" I asked eagerly.

"I'm guessing they'll dismiss you sometime tomorrow," he answered as he shuffled the papers before him. Then both lawyers prepared to go.

I floated out of the room and all the way back to my unit, it seemed. My mind was spinning with exciting details of being set free. Yet my thoughts kept returning soberly to the restrictions being placed on my freedom. *Why will I not even be allowed any contact with my own minor children?* I mused. *That seems especially harsh and stings the most.*

After thinking about it, though, I realized it was because I had fled with my children years before. That fact had caused the judge to consider me a flight risk. She was just trying to make sure I wouldn't find a way to vanish with them again.

But in spite of the restrictions, hope swelled within me as I thought about the God I served. He could easily lift that restriction and all the others as well, whenever the time was right.

———

Lissa:

As the miles flew past, Hannah recounted to me the events of the second day's court proceedings. I hadn't been allowed to be there because the bond restrictions required that I not see or speak to Mommy.

"After Mommy was brought to the judge's bench, Judge Hill read to her the restrictions of her bond, and then asked methodically, 'Do you understand?'

"Mommy said, 'Yes,' but her voice broke. Lissa, it was so sad and happy at the same time. I mean, I'm very glad she is getting out of jail today. Hey, she might even be out right now! Anyway, it was sad though, because I know it will be so painful to not be able to communicate with the younger children. That will be the most difficult restriction for her to keep. After the procedure was completed, Mommy smiled at me as she was led out."

It was dark when we reached Granddad and Grandmom's house. Grandfather and Mimi helped us pull our suitcases out of the trunk and carry them to the porch. Soon Isaiah, Beverly, Grace, and Emily streamed out of the house, attacking us with hugs. It was good to see them again. Hannah went inside with them and put our suitcases in our room. I stayed on the porch with both sets of grandparents, where a heated discussion had begun.

My Evans grandmother spoke up, "But the restriction says Kay may not have contact with the minor children, and Hannah is no longer a minor. Consequently, she may not stay here, because Kay could contact the children through Hannah!"

Mommy's dad protested. "But Jan, you know Hannah wouldn't do that! If necessary, Hannah could even cut off all contact with Kay, if that's what it takes to honor the restrictions of the bond."

Grandmom shook her head decisively. "No. She may no longer stay here. That is our decision," she announced with finality.

By then, Hannah was back on the porch. We listened to the conversation with sinking hearts. We had known this might happen, but I had fought against even the thought.

"Go gather your things, Hannah," Grandmom ordered sternly.

Touching Hannah's arm gently, Grandfather said, "Sugar, you can come home with us tonight."

Hannah looked down and tearfully made her way to our room.

I followed, seething with anger. "Hannah, how can they be so heartless? The restrictions did NOT say we couldn't stay together, and can't Grandmom and Granddad see we need to stay together?"

"I guess not, Lissa, but we need to love them, even if they are unloving."

"Unloving," I muttered through clenched teeth. "This is more than unloving . . . Oh dear, I know I shouldn't feel this way."

Catching sight of my angry face in the mirror, I sighed. "You're right, Hannah. I must love them even if it's the last thing in the world I feel like doing!"

Hannah gave one last round of hugs. Then grabbing her bags, she headed out the door with Grandfather and Mimi. After the door closed behind her, I again found myself the oldest of our little family.

That night I went to my room, which was all my own now. I sat on the bed and read my Bible and prayed, "Lord, please, please let us be a family again! And help me to forgive Grandmom and Granddad."

CHAPTER 32

The Opening of the Prison to Those That Are Bound [1]

K ay:

Standing on the dusty sidewalk in downtown Houston, I waited for Laura to pick me up. I relished the breeze on my face. It was Wednesday, January 12, 2000, a beautiful day. I tried to comprehend the reality that I was free—no longer an inmate, no longer just a number, no longer behind bars! I had been delivered from all of that, only moments before, by an amazing Deliverer.

Here I was, at last, standing in what inmates call "the free world." How fitting that I should have these first few moments outside those grim walls all alone with God! Once again I admired the beauty of His creation. Clouds floated effortlessly above me, painted by the orange sunset. Birds fluttered heavenward. I could relate to the freedom they possessed. Oh, it felt so good to be outside! I couldn't get enough of it!

Only yards away, I noticed the bridge over a murky river coursing its way through the city. I walked closer for a better view. Even a dirty river was refreshing to my eyes after staring at concrete walls for so many days.

I looked back at the dingy, brown brick structure known as Harris County Jail, rising from the pavement like a gloomy monument of shame. I let my eyes follow its height upward, counting each floor of the great, depressing building.

---

1. Isaiah 61:1

I knew what went on in there. I had friends in there. God had taught me important lessons within those walls over the past thirty-seven days. But once again wearing my own dress and Sunday shoes and clutching my purse, I anticipated the future.

"Lord, I praise You for all You have done, and for getting me out of jail! How can I thank You for the mighty ways You have moved on my behalf to set me free? I am unworthy of having a Rescuer like You. It is true that You are the Defender of widows. You have just proved that to me. But, Lord, You know my heart. You know to be free without my children will afford me very little pleasure. And for You—it will afford You only a portion of the honor You deserve. I believe the mighty thing You have done is merely the first step toward my being reunited with my dear children. Lord, I trust You. You are the same God who moved the judge to reduce my bond from $3,000,000 to $30,000. And I trust You will not stop until my children are fully restored to me."

Laura and I headed straight for her mom's patio home on the outskirts of Houston. Her neighborhood was comprised of small, attractive homes packed tightly together, each with a miniature yard. Ann Montagne had come to visit me in jail, and I remembered seeing her in the courtroom, so I knew what she looked like.

Ann opened the door and welcomed me warmly. "Hello, Kay! I'm so glad you finally got out of that jail!" She wrapped me in a warm hug.

I nodded. "Yes, I am very grateful to be out."

Ann motioned for Laura and me to step inside. "Please come on in."

She showed me to my room and then led Laura and me to the kitchen where supper was cooking.

"Something smells wonderful," I exclaimed.

Stirring the steaming pot on the stove, she looked at me cheerily. "I hope you're hungry. I thought you might enjoy a real meal for a change."

Lining her kitchen counters were neatly stacked boxes of specialty crackers and gourmet cookies for easy access. It reminded me of a grocery store aisle.

When she noticed me eyeing the display, she encouraged me, "Help yourself anytime, Kay." It was certainly tempting.

As we sat around the dinner table, Ann listened keenly to every detail of my release. She had faithfully attended my hearings even though she limped on a bad leg. Sometimes she had had to hobble a distance to the courthouse after finally locating a parking spot. The meal that night was quite a contrast to jail cuisine, and I helped myself to seconds, and contemplated thirds.

———————

Ring! The telephone rang shrilly.

Ann casually picked it up. "Hello? Oh, yes, she is. Just a moment."

I hadn't even been at Ann's a day, and already someone was calling for me.

"It's Hannah," Ann whispered, handing me the phone.

I knew Hannah and Lissa were riding home from Houston with my parents, affectionately called Grandfather and Mimi by their grandchildren. They lived only a five-minute drive from Granddad and Grandmom Evans in Amarillo.

"Mommy, they won't let me live with them!" Hannah said, her voice cracking with emotion.

"What!"

"Granddad and Grandmom," she repeated, "they won't let me live with them anymore!"

I was perplexed, wondering what could have happened. "Hannah, where are you calling from?" I asked in consternation.

"I'm at a grocery store with Grandfather and Mimi," she blubbered. "They are taking me home with them after they get some groceries. When we arrived at Granddad and Grandmom's house, they said they had decided I shouldn't live with them anymore since I'm not a minor. They said it could jeopardize the restrictions placed on your bond."

"Oh," I said, trying to take it all in. Holding the receiver firmly against my ear, I repeated Hannah's words back to her. "They won't let you live with them anymore?"

Ann and Laura stepped closer to hear better, their eyes fixed on my face.

"Hannah can come live here with us," Ann mouthed to me dramatically.

Ann had no idea how much she would sacrifice by welcoming me into her home, yet she sacrificed, and very graciously. When I told Hannah that Ann had invited her to join me, she was very relieved.

We immediately tried to think of ways to get her to Houston. Laura offered to drive several hours through the night, right then, to pick her up. I was not surprised, because that is the type of friend she is. Yet I could not allow it, because I knew Laura was already tired and stressed enough. I arranged for Hannah to ride with my brother David and Sue Beth, who would drive from Amarillo to see us on Saturday.

After supper dishes were cleared away, Ann got comfortable in her favorite chair and was soon absorbed in a well-worn novel. Laura took this opportunity to call her husband, so I slipped away to familiarize myself with the bedroom I would sleep in. Moments later, a shriek of laughter resounded from Ann's chair, and I couldn't help but investigate. Ann sat thoroughly engrossed in a book she was obviously enjoying.

As I moved a pillow and sat down on the couch near her, she closed her book with a quiet chuckle and looked up at me thoughtfully.

"Ann," I said, "you have been very gracious to open up your home to me, and I appreciate that. Please let me help you with the bills while I stay here."

She smiled and shook her head, unconcerned. "We can work that out later."

A gentle hand touched my shoulder, and a soft voice called, "Kay, good morning! It's five o'clock."

What a change this was from waking to shouting guards and clanging steel doors. Laura's voice was such a sweet sound.

Nonetheless, there is no time to lose today, I recalled, pushing back the covers and sitting up. I needed Laura to drive me downtown to the civil defense building first thing, where I was required to arrange for my ankle monitoring device. It would be specially delivered and placed on my ankle later in the day, but first I had to sign forms and pay for it.

Each week I would need to report to the same office so that they could verify that I was still wearing it. *I wish they would just trust me not to take it off. It would save both of us a lot of hassle,* I grumbled silently.

Nonetheless, I needed to play with grace my part of "guilty until proved innocent." It was good for me to have Laura around. She was a quiet servant. And she reminded me to whom I was anchored while I was facing great demands and many questions.

Sucked into this messy legal battle, it was easy and natural to start thinking legally and defensively. Yet I wanted to live up to a more noble challenge, letting Jesus show me how to be pure, honest, and undefiled.

In her soft-spoken way, Laura helped me remember I was Christ's workmanship, set apart for His own purposes, even in court.

The next day Laura's husband, Kevin, came for her. He had "roughed it" long enough without his dearly beloved and the mother of his six children. He was still smiling, but if you looked carefully, you could tell that sacrificing Laura to help me had taken its toll on him. They had seen precious little of each other since I had landed in jail. It was time for this dear family to be reunited and meet some of their own needs.

As if they had not done enough already, Kevin left me their minivan, so that I would have something to drive. It was a light gray-blue Dodge Caravan, and it would prove very helpful with all my meetings with lawyers or driving downtown to the civil defense building.

I had one more good talk with Laura, hugged her good-bye, and said a hearty "thank you" to Kevin. As they drove off together in a minivan that his parents were loaning them, I marveled that God had blessed me with such quality friends. *How can I ever repay friends like that?*

My heart was filled with thanksgiving. Throughout my journey, God had always placed just the right people in my path at just the right time. The debt of love I owe is ever increasing.

Oh, God, bless Kevin and Laura, I prayed. *Please reward them richly for all they have sacrificed for me. And for all the others who have shown me or my children kindness. Please bless them too, and lift them up in their hour of need.*

How wonderful it was to have Hannah come and live at Ann's with me! Earlier I had hoped she would be allowed to stay with her Evans grandparents to comfort and encourage her younger siblings during this stressful time. But since she was required to leave, I trusted that God knew I needed her more. And what a comfort and sweet companion she was!

One afternoon, she and I went to the jail to visit Evelyn. At the conclusion of our visit, Evelyn beamed at me and Hannah. "See!" she exclaimed. "God has already brought back one of your chiddren. It won't be long now befo' you'll have 'em all back!"

As I raced through Ann's door just before my 5:00 p.m. curfew, she greeted me with a smile. "The list of people who called for you today is on the telephone table," she said. "You'll find the notepad right on top. I think Alex Azzo called for you twice, so you should probably get back to him first thing. Oh, and an old friend of yours from Phoenix called . . . Lucy something. I wrote her name and number there on the paper."

Word had spread like wildfire about our situation, and that I had been bonded out of jail. Word had also spread about how I could be reached. Ann's phone rang frequently as caring friends called, wanting to know the latest.

Articles were appearing in the newspapers and snips of our court case were being broadcast over news channels. It was strange to be scrutinized by the media.

Ann had quickly proved to be a wonderful help. She enjoyed meeting my friends in person or over the phone. She seemed to relish this break from living alone. Some of these callers were old friends whom I had not talked to in years. Others were Mennonites whom we had met along our way while in hiding. I even heard from a few people I didn't know at all, who just wanted to offer their help. All of this encouragement was heartwarming indeed.

Nonetheless, I was tense about tying up Ann's phone line so

much. In spite of her good-natured response to this barrage of calls, I decided to get a second phone line for myself. This would give Ann some privacy in her otherwise disrupted world. If I didn't do something immediately, she might feel like my full-time secretary in her own home. I did not want that!

While I was in jail, Alex Azzo had explained that, as a defense attorney, his job was to defend me against my criminal charges. "Your criminal case is very closely tied with the family case, but they are two separate cases. The whole thing started out shortly after Ron died, when Dr. and Mrs. Evans sued for grandparental rights. Since you never showed up in court, they changed their suit, pleading for custody. You still didn't show up in court, so by default, they were granted full custody. You were then legally charged with interfering with child custody and that is when the case escalated to the criminal court level."

I had stared at him, shaking my head.

"The time has arrived, Kay," he had explained, "for you to retain a family-law attorney as well. You need two types of legal assistance—both criminal and family law. A family lawyer will go to family court, working to repeal the earlier rulings that gave your in-laws custody of your children. He would work specifically to help you get your children back. I am only helping defend you in criminal court against the charges of interference with child custody."

I began gathering names of family lawyers and praying about how to pursue the family-law issue. As I did this, I also gathered counsel from a few Christian men whose wisdom I had come to respect. I knew I needed godly counsel to be sure my approach to these legal decisions would not be in violation of God's laws. I wanted to maintain a clear conscience while getting untangled from this legal mess.

I fidgeted in my seat and sighed deeply as I looked at the wall clock again. It was two o'clock sharp on January 17. Any moment now I would begin my first interview with a woman custody specialist. I sat nervously, trying to look at ease but feeling quite the opposite. I had a lot to be grateful for.

I smiled at William and Violet Bear and Phil and Connie Bear sitting around the long conference table. Both couples had flown in from Maryland to be a support for me and to help me select a family lawyer. I was so grateful they had come. Just a few days earlier, Phil had called when I was especially distressed about some of the deadlines and pressures placed on me.

Alex Azzo kept gently prodding me to find a family lawyer. I had interviewed one already and decided it ranked among my least favorite things to do. Yet he urged, "You cannot keep putting this off, Kay. You simply must get a family lawyer right away—one that specializes in custody issues."

After I had shared with Phil Bear some of my prayer needs, he asked, "Would you like for me and Conn and maybe a few others to fly down and go with you to interview some of those lawyers, and maybe give you some counsel?"

Overwhelmed, I found myself consenting to this incredibly gracious offer. As it turned out, he and his wife Connie and his parents, William and Violet Bear, came. The following day Arthur Shirk from Pennsylvania and Jim and Mary Grizzard from Colorado all flew in, forming a support team to assist me. I was deeply moved by these generous acts of love and grateful for this multitude of counselors, as is mentioned in Proverbs 11:14.

I had scheduled three family-lawyer interviews during the time some of these people would be with Hannah and me. We must have looked like a mob going into lawyers' conference rooms. I suppose being interviewed this way could have put extra pressure on those lawyers, but I was overjoyed for the extra support.

Entering the room briskly, the female lawyer gave everyone a curt welcome and sat down next to Hannah and me. She was the picture of a successful career woman. After only a brief attempt at small talk, she put on her glasses and set to work leafing through the thick file in her hands.

Alex Azzo had supplied copies of documents about my case so that she would know what she was dealing with. But now, as she reviewed the papers, the silence was deafening.

What is she thinking? How did that thick file look in the eyes of a custody specialist lawyer? I wondered.

Only an occasional shake of her head and an irritated sigh let me know she was not impressed. Finally she broke the silence.

"Well. Your in-laws certainly dotted every *i* and crossed every *t*. You, on the other hand, certainly did not! From the looks of these files, I would say you don't even have a prayer!"

She looked at me disdainfully above her glasses, perched critically on her nose. What could I say for myself? I felt as if I had been slapped in the face.

"I always have a prayer," I managed to say weakly.

In my mind the interview was over. I had prayed that the Lord would make clear to me what to think of this woman. Her very first words helped me make that evaluation. If I retained her as my lawyer, she would base everything on facts and files. I needed a lawyer who could get past all of that—one who trusted in God.

My group of friends and counselors all felt the same way I did about this lawyer, which gave me an extra measure of peace. Nonetheless, what she had said certainly affected my mood. My spirit was downcast. Undeniably, I had made mistakes after Ron died. While Ron's parents had been busy dotting all their *i*'s and crossing all their *t*'s and making sure they were doing everything in a manner that would look good to an earthly judge, I was merely crying out to God, desperately trying to break loose from the control of my in-laws.

The path I had chosen did not look good on paper. Neither had it looked good in the courtroom. And there were a number of people in my life who felt it their duty to tell me they disagreed with my choices.

In Ann's home that night, my heart was heavy. I was sorely missing my younger children. *They would have loved being part of this evening and seeing these friends,* I thought. And besides missing my children, I was despondent because the lady lawyer had made me feel like a dunce. I felt I could cry any second.

As our little group talked about the day's events, I couldn't help expressing myself. "Sometimes when I listen to people like that lawyer today, it does sound like I really blew it years ago, like she said. In spite of my desire to just please God, I made so many mistakes."

Before I went further, Brother William Bear interrupted me. "Oh, Kay, don't you see that God has chosen this path for you? He is the One who has used all of these things to bring your family out from the environment you needed to part from."

It was the soothing counsel of a father. Somehow I felt it was the counsel of my heavenly Father as well. His tender words made me weep. It was so reassuring that this godly man, whom I had grown to respect so much, felt I had done the right thing. Somehow in this moment, it mattered little that others did not approve.

On Friday, January 21, I was once again sitting in an unfamiliar lawyer's office, this one in an elegant skyscraper in downtown Houston. My friend Linda Stevenson accompanied Hannah and me to this interview. I sat at a long table in a dimly-lit conference room facing a wall of windows.

The tall, lanky lawyer strode into the room looking as if he could play the part of Abraham Lincoln. He shook my hand with an almost lighthearted grin on his face as he glanced around the room at each of us. He casually folded himself into a chair beside me and talked a few minutes, as if to feel me out.

I waited to see what he would say. We sat frozen, watching him while he spent a few moments shuffling papers with his long fingers, scanning through the pages, stopping occasionally to pore over a document. Scratching his head, he turned to me quizzically and announced, "Well, frankly, my friend, heaven would have to move earth in order to get you out of *this* mess."

"Well, that's been done before," I replied quietly. The Lord had answered my prayer again with the first words out of the lawyer's mouth. He, too, had disqualified himself. As far as I was concerned, the interview was over.

One lawyer's name had come up several times in my homeschool circles—Tom Sanders. Although he practiced family law, his credentials did not include being a custody specialist. Linda knew him and spoke highly of him. I called his home to see if he might be available while my friends were here to assist me. He was willing to schedule a meeting.

We were all tired of the "stuffed shirt" interviews and meetings. Since Linda already knew Tom Sanders, she suggested I invite him to join all of us at her house over lunch for something more informal.

Tom turned out to be a tall, slender man with a big grin and bushy eyebrows. He came across as a very laid-back, friendly man who had a way of putting everyone at ease.

Pork chops sizzled on the backyard grill as the men stood around watching them, occasionally flipping one while they discussed our case.

Before long, we were all seated casually in Linda's dining room on folding chairs. We must have been an interesting crowd to this Houston lawyer. The lady guests all wore long dresses and coverings on their heads. The men wore dress shirts, but not one of them wore a tie. Here Tom was, not only surrounded by us but being interviewed by us as well.

Forks scraped on plates as everyone enjoyed each bite of the delicious pork chops sent from Maryland. When the Bears had flown down, they had brought with them an ice chest of meat donated by a butcher in their fellowship. Light conversation could be heard off and on, mostly about the food, with everyone trying to act natural.

Then it happened. Arthur Shirk's fork slipped. We saw him quickly drop his chin, looking down at his shirt. Yep. There sat an ugly glob of ketchup, splattered right onto the front of his nice shirt. Arthur chuckled as he reached for a paper napkin and tried to wipe away the evidence.

Tom, seated next to him, broke into one of his big grins and elbowed him. "See, if you had been wearing a tie, it would have protected your shirt!"

The room erupted with laughter to imagine this Mennonite man wearing a tie. The gentle jibe was a wonderful icebreaker and from then on the conversation was easy.

After lunch we all sat around the dining room table and at Tom's request, I shared part of my story. He listened thoughtfully, pausing from time to time to shake his head and say, "Praise God." It was so different, sharing details of my recent years with a lawyer who saw things from a Christian standpoint.

Eventually he shared a few things about himself, his wife and family, and about his perspective on life and law. He felt God had been directing him more into mediation and away from his former law practice. He had met my husband years ago at a homeschool gathering for dads, a fact which was very interesting to me. When he heard of our family's troubles following Ron's death, he felt a tremendous burden for us and had been praying for us ever since. If I decided to retain him, I wasn't to worry about payment. His desire to work on my case was driven by the burden of his heart, not the money.

When he left, he paused at the door and gave Hannah a fatherly hug. How could he have known how much that meant to her?

After our counselors flew back to their homes, Alex Azzo recommended another custody specialist to us. This man was very well-known and respected in legal circles but was also very expensive. Alex went with Hannah and me to interview him, but after the interview I still wasn't sure what I thought. The man had asked Hannah to step out of the conference room during the interview, so I couldn't even ask what her impressions were of him.

January 24 was the night of decision. I could not postpone it any longer. I still leaned strongly toward Tom Sanders because he was a God-fearing man, but I wanted to know for sure who the Lord's choice was.

After staring at the phone a few seconds, I took courage and dialed William Bear's home in Maryland and gave him my impressions about the new lawyer. Then I asked the big question: "Brother William, by tonight, I have to decide which lawyer will represent us. This is such a huge decision, and I don't want to make a mistake. Would you mind terribly much if I just lay this whole decision in your lap and let you see which man God lays on your heart?"

At first there was silence. Then he agreed to take this load off me and pray about it with his wife and Phil and Connie.

"Oh, what a relief! Thank you so much. Hannah and I will be praying for God to give you His counsel on this, and we won't stop until we hear back from you. Oh, and there is one Scripture that keeps coming to mind that I would like for you to consider. It's Psalm 20:7, *Some trust in chariots, and some in horses: but we will remember the name of the* LORD *our God.*

With that, I closed the conversation and hung up the phone. Hannah and I immediately fell to our knees. We prayed for the next few hours, waiting for the phone to ring.

Hannah clearly wanted Tom Sanders to be our family lawyer. "Mommy," she asked, "could it even be God's will if I want it this badly?"

When the phone rang at last, I picked it up instantly. Hannah sat very still, watching me intently.

"All right," I said. "I appreciate that. Okay. Well, I want to thank you for your input on this. Uh-huh. Well, tell your wife and your son Phil and his wife thank you. Y'all have a good night."

Hannah sat frozen on the bed, certain they had recommended the expensive lawyer, since I didn't seem excited.

I looked at her. "Well, who do you think it is?" I asked.

"Not Mr. Sanders," she said in a small voice.

I showed her a slip of paper on which I had scrawled the decision. It said simply, "Tom Sanders."

She squealed with delight, and we hugged each other. Oh, were we ever excited! "Our God does love to use humble vessels to do His work! Won't it be exciting to have a lawyer we can pray with? Oh, God is so good! Thank You, Father!"

CHAPTER 33

The Weight of Evidence

K ay:

The plates were carefully loaded into the dishwasher. I dumped in some soap and shut the door, pressing the "Normal Wash" button. Just as it started, the phone rang. Ann picked it up in the living room. A moment later she appeared in the doorway.

"Kay, Alex Azzo is on the phone for you."

I quickly finished wiping the counter and dropped the dishcloth into the sink. After drying my hands on a towel, I reached for the phone.

"Hello?" I said, striding into my bedroom where I could concentrate more fully. Sitting on my bed, I pulled out my notepad and pen, ready to take notes.

As Mr. Azzo finished updating me on what was going on, a thought struck me. He was my lawyer, and of all people, he should know what to hope for in court. I felt prompted to ask him a question.

"Mr. Azzo, how do you think I should be praying in regard to my criminal case? In other words, in your professional opinion, what is the very best I can hope for in court?"

Silence. Maybe he wasn't accustomed to a client asking such a question.

Finally he spoke. "The very best we could hope for," he said matter-of-factly, "is that the state would dismiss your case and acknowledge that the indictment was issued by mistake. If that happens, we could possibly forego a trial, and it would be much easier for you to get an expunction."

Jotting this in my daily time log, I wondered why I hadn't asked him this before. "Thank you so much!" I said. "This gives me some specific direction, and I really appreciate it."

Alex Azzo sat across the deep mahogany desk from me with his hands folded soberly. "I just heard through the opposing attorneys that Dr. and Mrs. Evans plan to bring further indictments against you."

I leaned back in my chair. *What now?* I groaned silently.

I had no idea what these new accusations would be. The thought was overwhelming. *Lord,* I prayed silently, *I cast it all upon You. I feel too weak to even worry about it.*

Alex continued, "I also want to prepare you for the strong possibility of going before the grand jury. This would mean that neither I nor Mr. Lindeman would be allowed to accompany you. You would enter the courtroom alone to testify before the jury."

The thought of testifying to a grand jury was petrifying. As I drove home, the scenario played over and over in my mind. I continuously brought my fears and concerns to the Lord. "Lord, what would I do? What would I say?"

There was no way I could adequately defend myself. I already knew what the courts thought of what I did years ago. As I continued begging God for direction and deliverance, I finally found genuine peace that, if that were to happen, I would just have to plead for mercy. I saw no other choice.

"Mommy, this stack is folded and ready to be put into envelopes. The envelopes are stamped and addressed and are in that bag."

I pulled up the blue Wal-Mart bag and peered inside. "How many of these letters are we sending out, anyway?" I asked, chuckling.

"A lot," Hannah assured me. She had worked very hard trying to personally answer each note we received, but it seemed impossible to keep up with the task.

It was Friday, February 4, 2000, and Hannah and I were

sitting in the van just outside Alex Azzo's office. I needed to take him some papers, but having arrived early, we used the time to stuff letters into envelopes.

We were determined to set aside most of the day for getting a form letter in the mail to all the dear people who were concerned about us. The letter would inform our prayer supporters of the latest developments and express our gratitude for their crucial role in our lives.

I glanced at my watch, and whistled. "Whew, where'd the time go? We are supposed to be up there in two minutes. Let's finish this later."

Pushing open the heavy wooden door, we stepped into Mr. Azzo's office. His secretary was on the phone, but when she noticed us, she gasped and excitedly motioned for us to wait.

Covering the receiver with her hand, she said, "Alex has been looking all over for you! He told me that if you come in, I am not supposed to let you leave!"

She brought her phone conversation to a close and called Mr. Azzo on his cell phone to tell him she had found us.

Hannah and I looked at each other with raised eyebrows.

"I wonder what's going on?" I whispered.

"She certainly acts like it's something urgent," Hannah responded.

But we would save our questions for Mr. Azzo himself. We slipped into the conference room and sat down.

At long last, the door burst open and Mr. Azzo and Mr. Lindeman strode in triumphantly, looking absolutely jubilant.

They look extremely thrilled about something, I thought.

Hannah and I stared blankly as they stepped wordlessly to the table and handed each of us an identical stack of papers. Eagerly I began examining the state-issued memorandum. "MOTION TO DISMISS," it declared boldly across the top. My name and prisoner ID number were scrawled on the appropriate lines, along with an abbreviation of my offense. Scanning down the page, I found a list of ten possible reasons why the case had been dismissed, with a box to check by each one. A bold check mark graced only one box. Beside it was the simple statement, "Insufficient Evidence." In addition, the words were circled, giving it double emphasis.

At the bottom of the page was a signature—Judge Belinda Hill. I had never before noticed how lovely her name looked until I saw it signed so elegantly on this form, completely dismissing my criminal charges.

Speechless, we looked up. My face was flushed with excitement.

"Is this real?" I gasped.

"Yep! This is definitely real!"

"It is incredible, but it is definitely real!" they assured us.

"God has answered our prayers! This is so exciting!" Hannah and I exclaimed as we leaped to our feet and embraced.

Ecstatic, we looked delightedly at one another and then at the lawyers.

"Tell us how this happened, please," we begged.

Eagerly, they began to fill us in on the details of their exciting day at the courthouse.

Then Mr. Azzo's excitement changed to concern. "I realize, Kay, that up until this time you have not been interested when the media has asked to interview you. And I can understand that. But this is just too good to pass up! It's not every day that a woman is jailed on a $3,000,000 bond, and then later her charges are totally and mysteriously dismissed by the district attorney's office. This is big news! I mean BIG news! Would you let me call and put the *Houston Chronicle* on the phone to speak with us?"

I must have consented, because in only moments we were having a speakerphone conversation with a reporter about this wonderful news of the day, a miraculous answer to prayer.

Climbing into the van I pushed the form letters out of my seat. "These letters are outdated now," I said, still beaming with excitement.

"I'm so glad," Hannah said, sighing happily. "Even if it does mean we have to write a new form letter. What splendid news we have!"

"Hannah, did Mr. Azzo really and truly say what I thought he just said up there in his office? That the district attorney's office mysteriously dropped my charges?"

"Yes, ma'am, that's exactly what you heard, that the district attorney's office decided there wasn't enough evidence, so they dropped your charges."

"It's almost too good to be true, isn't it?"

"Yes, ma'am. Mommy, God's ways really are mysterious, aren't they?"

"Yes, Hannah, indeed His ways are wonderfully mysterious." I started the van and pulled out onto the busy street. "Hey, I'm hungry. What about you?"

"Yeah, me too," Hannah agreed.

"Well, I don't have to rush home tonight because, for once, I'm not required to make it home by curfew. He said the monitor people will be coming over to Ann's later this evening to take my ankle monitor off once and for all. It'll be nice to have a relaxed drive back to Ann's and not go through the usual routine of sweating to make it through her door by curfew," I said.

Hannah nodded, and I went on, "I can hardly believe the criminal case is completely over! I feel like pinching myself to make sure this is really happening. All the criminal charges against me have been totally dropped. Imagine that! We saw it in print for ourselves. And best of all, with the restrictions now lifted, I can resume contact with Lissa, Isaiah, Beverly, Grace, and Emily. This is definitely a day to celebrate! Think about it, Hannah. God has done the impossible! I stand in tremendous awe of Him!"

"Me too, Mommy."

Now that the criminal case was over and the restrictions lifted, the next priority was to reestablish contact with my younger children. My in-laws still had full legal custody, so this had to be approached carefully. But I could hardly wait! It had been more than two months since I had seen my younger children, and I was so eager to hug each one.

I pulled up to the sidewalk and peered at my in-laws' nice brick home.

"I have a feeling that this visit is going to be highly scrutinized. I'm dreading that part, but I am very eager to see the children."

Yesterday Hannah and I had packed up the borrowed Dodge Caravan to make the long drive to Amarillo for this exciting event. Planning the visit was stressful, and we had fervently prayed about it. Mr. Sanders, our lawyer, had counseled me how to approach things, and then I called my in-laws and scheduled a time for us to see the children.

Hannah spoke from the backseat. "Grandfather is already here. See him in his truck over there?"

I nodded. "Sure enough, there is Dad. Bless his heart for coming out here and doing this for me. Thank you too, Sue Beth, for coming along. The way you and David have supported me means so much."

I pushed the door open and grabbed my purse. "Hannah, that gift bag we brought with stuff for the children is in my purse, right?"

She nodded and shut the side door. "Yes, I put it there just this morning."

As we started up the sidewalk, my dad joined us and reached out his arms to hug me.

"Hello, sugar," he said.

"Hi, Daddy. Thank you so much for coming!"

He looked down into my eyes and smiled kindly. "No problem, honey."

Lissa:

I heard Grandmom's shoes clicking on the tile as she hurried toward the door and peered through the valance over the window. She returned to the living room, her face tight with concern.

"Officer Jones, Kay is here with her dad and sister-in-law and her daughter." She looked at us and said firmly, "Children, quickly go back to the study. You may watch a video or something, but Granddad and I want you to stay there until we come get you. We need to talk to your mom privately before you visit with her. Go."

I got up from the couch and motioned for the children to join me, but how I wanted to stay and watch as Mommy and Hannah stepped through the front door. Nonetheless, we dutifully made our way down the hall, straining our ears for the sound of Mommy's voice. I flopped onto the couch and looked at Grace.

"Oh, how I want to be out there!" I said.

Beverly stamped her foot on the carpet. "Me too! It's not fair."

"But why did Grandmom have that policeman come over?" Isaiah asked.

I closed my eyes and tried to feel gracious toward my grandmother. "Isaiah, she doesn't trust Mommy, so she wants someone here to make sure the visit is under control. I know. It's irritating, isn't it?"

He nodded and pulled out a box of Legos and sat down, trying to busy his hands.

Kay:

Just as I reached for the doorbell, the door opened, and Walter greeted us in his usual friendly manner.

"Welcome. Come on in." His lips formed a smile, but he looked as tense as I felt. Nonetheless, he hugged Hannah and me formally and shook my dad's hand. I stepped past him into the hall as Jan appeared and gave Hannah and me token hugs.

"Hello, Kay," she said.

I smiled faintly and nodded. "Hello, Jan."

She looked at me awkwardly and turned toward the living room. "Y'all can come in and sit down."

I looked around the tastefully decorated living room. *It hasn't changed much since I was last here,* I thought.

Hannah and I stepped around the coffee table and sat down on the plush green couch in the middle of the room. Sue Beth and my dad seated themselves on the hearth facing us. Seeing their faces was reassuring in the strained atmosphere of the room.

Jan spoke to the policeman in hushed tones as they took their seats behind us against the wall.

"Well, I want to thank each of you for coming," Walter began as he eased himself into a folding chair across the coffee table from Hannah and me. "I wanted to speak with you privately a few minutes before the children come out to see you. First of all, I want to say that Jan and I are extremely disappointed in you, Kay. You have not chosen to promote peace now that you are pursuing us in court and filing for custody of the children. After the visit tonight, you will be permitted to visit the children only one more time before the upcoming court hearing."

I heard a door close down the hall. *That was one of my children!* I thought. *Oh, I wish he would just finish talking so that I can see my precious children!*

But his words rolled on and on. ". . . So Hannah, you will not be allowed to contact Lissa either at the college campus. You know she is studying her high school work in the library there."

Lissa:

"Emily," Grandmom said as she opened the door, "you may now come with me to see your mother and sister in the living room."

Beverly hopped up eagerly, "But Grandmom, can't I come too? I want to see them!"

Shaking her head, Grandmom raised her eyebrows. "Beverly, you may come when I get you. Granddad thinks it's a good idea to let you children into the room one at a time."

As the door closed behind them, Beverly groaned. "Oh, how much longer do we have to wait?"

When it was finally my turn, I rounded the corner to see Mommy and Hannah surrounded by Isaiah, Beverly, Grace, and Emily. Nearly everyone in my family was crying. We were all so happy to see each other. But because we knew we couldn't stay together, it was a bittersweet reunion.

Emily sobbed, hiding her face in Mommy's sweater. Tears streamed down Mommy's cheeks too, as she reached out and hugged me.

Kay:

It felt incredible to have my arms around my children again. I couldn't stop the tears that flooded my eyes.

"Isaiah," I said, touching his cheek, "it is just so good to see you again." Bending low, I whispered into Grace's ear, "How is school going?"

"No whispering!" Jan's voice broke in behind me. "Speak in normal tones."

Startled, I gritted my teeth at one more restriction being placed on our visit. It had been two whole months since I had seen some of my children, and my time with the others had been sparse as well. I continued chatting with my little daughter.

"Grace," I asked quietly, "do you like your teacher?"

She nodded. "Yes, she is really nice, Mommy."

Lissa:

Glancing at the coffee table in front of us, something caught my eye. A small, silver object was partially hidden by the carefully arranged magazines. Instantly, I knew what it was.

Oh, it's that small tape recorder Granddad bought last week, I thought.

I nudged Mommy. "We are being taped," I whispered. "There's a tape recorder on the coffee table, but I can't turn it off without being noticed."

Mommy's face grew concerned, and she peered discreetly at the silver object.

I glanced around, grabbed a magazine from the coffee table and casually laid it over the recorder. *Hopefully that will hinder it from picking up our conversation.*

"Mommy," I said, nearly whispering, "there is something I really want you to have, but it's in my room."

I stood up. "I'll be right back," I said as I left the couch. "I'm just going to my room."

Granddad nodded and then looked back at the police officer who was listening intently as Grandmom explained the severity of our case.

In my room I quietly opened the drawer by the computer and pulled out the small blue disk. I held it in my hands, and bit my lip.

How am I going to do this? I wondered. This was my journal on disk, and I wanted desperately to give a copy to Mommy to read. It would be a poor replacement for the long talks we were accustomed to, but it would give her an inside peek at life here, living under my grandparents' thumb.

On impulse, I stuffed the disk up my sleeve and glanced in the mirror to see if it showed. I stared at the sleeve of my maroon cape dress. *Good, but I shouldn't move my arm too much, just in case.*

Returning to the living room, I sat down on the couch, and snuggled up to Mommy, placing my hands in her lap. "Mom," I whispered, "I've been keeping a journal on disk that I'd like for you to take with you as you leave. I'm hiding it in my sleeve right now. Do you think we could transfer it to your sleeve?"

She nodded with an amused expression in her eyes.

Gingerly I took the disk from my sleeve and slipped it up hers while we chatted and tried to look casual. We were successful, and the transaction went unnoticed.

Smuggling was actually thrilling, with the elements of danger and excitement. *What would I have done if Grandmom had caught me?* I shuddered at the thought.

Kay:

As Isaiah told me about his class at school, Walter broke in. "Kay, why don't you and your children sing together before you go. I have heard the children sing, and they tell me you all sing as a family."

We sang three songs together, one of which was Spanish. I couldn't sing without choking up, but it was so beautiful to hear my children's voices again.

After this, Walter asked my dad to close the meeting in prayer. Dad prayed a very touching, heartfelt prayer.

When it was almost time to end the visit, I turned to Jan. "May I be excused to go to the restroom?"

She nodded coldly, and I scurried off, securely locking the door behind me. I set my large purse on the counter and pulled out a crinkled pink gift bag that I had stuffed into the bottom. Inside, Hannah and I had placed letters from us and other friends, postage stamps, lotion—just a few things to remind my children of our love.

But where shall I hide it? I wondered, looking around the flawlessly clean bathroom. I carefully pulled open a drawer and peered inside. *Well, I'll just wedge the bag in the back. Hopefully, Lissa will find it.*

I jammed the small gift bag behind the brushes and combs and slid the drawer shut. As I joined Hannah and the children in the front room, my dad and Sue Beth stood waiting by the door. Apparently, it was time for us to go. I turned and hugged my children tightly, wishing I didn't have to leave them.

Lissa:

I watched as the door closed and was locked securely behind them. It was so very depressing to turn around and face the reality of being here. I walked into the bathroom, fighting tears.

"Now, Mommy said she hid something in the drawer in here," I murmured, pulling several drawers open. Finally I spied the small package awaiting me. Clutching it tenderly, I stepped cautiously into the hall and dashed to my room, locking the door behind me.

Kay:

I waited in the van as Hannah ran into the post office to check our mail. We had begun to receive so many letters that we decided to rent a post office box. Hannah pushed the glass door open and hurried toward me with a smile and an armful of envelopes. I reached across to open her door.

"We got a lot of mail today!" she exclaimed joyfully.

She jumped into the van and set the stack on her lap. "Why don't you read some out loud to me as I drive?" I suggested.

Carefully I backed out of the parking space and exited the parking lot to join the heavy Houston traffic.

Hannah thumbed through the stack of mail to see who had written. "May God bless all these people who are writing to encourage us!" she said.

"Amen," I agreed.

"Oh!" Hannah cried excitedly. "Here's one from Lissa!"

"Really?" I exclaimed. "Save hers for last."

It was a highlight for us to find a letter that Lissa had sneaked off to us during her day on the university campus. Living in a big city like Houston meant we spent quite a bit of time just getting from one point to another. Lissa's letters were a treasured way to pass our time in traffic.

"Dear Mommy," Lissa wrote, "I wish I could talk to you right now rather than write. But I'm grateful I can at least write. This morning was very difficult."

For Lissa, writing was a form of release. As she poured out her heart to us, she wrote in vivid detail, mingling humor with exasperation. Sometimes we laughed until our sides ached. These letters were a glimpse into what my children were experiencing in the home of their grandparents. It also let us know how to pray for them.

———————

Hannah:

As Mr. Sanders began researching the history of our case, he grew increasingly concerned. He introduced us to a colleague of his, Tim Telge, a quiet, God-fearing man. Mr. Sanders asked Mommy's permission to bring Mr. Telge in on the case.

"Believe me," Mr. Sanders assured us with a smile, "two heads are better than one."

God had already shown Himself so powerful, so able to deliver, in the way the criminal case so suddenly and mysteriously ended. But now it was time to delve into the family-law case in an attempt to have custody returned to Mommy. Mr. Sanders sat on the couch in the office above his garage, leafing through the thick stack of court files and discussing the matter with Mr. Telge. Although he did not seem exactly discouraged, he looked at Mommy and me gravely.

"Kay, the family case against you, just like the criminal case, was thoroughly sealed. While you and the kids were in hiding, your in-laws went to court and tied you so completely in knots that, humanly speaking, there is just no way you can get out. I mean," he said with an uneasy laugh, "your in-laws made sure there were absolutely no loopholes." He raised his bushy eyebrows in exasperation. "I'm tellin' ya, they did their homework!"

We listened soberly. Now, we understood better what the first custody specialist had meant when she said my grandparents had dotted all their *i*'s and crossed all their *t*'s.

"But you know," Mr. Sanders went on hopefully, "this problem is not too big for God. He doesn't need loopholes to work through anyway. He can make a way when there seems to be no way! And let's all remember, He is the Father to the fatherless and the Defender of widows. Hey, let's stop and pray about it," he suggested.

How thrilling it was to be reminded that God Himself was fighting for us.

"Kay, you won't believe what I found on the Web site this morning!" Linda exclaimed as she hurried into her study and pulled out a chair. "Here, sit down, I want you to see this."

She connected to the Internet and entered "United in Christ Network." Hannah leaned over my shoulder, eagerly looking on.

"Ah, here it is." Linda pointed to the page as it popped onto the screen. "Welcome to the Kay Evans Information Site."

"Now I know you've seen this before," Linda assured me, "but there's a new page now."

She clicked on a blue tab labeled "Prayer." A page flashed onto the screen. I carefully read the paragraph at the top.

With less than two weeks remaining until Kay's next custody hearing, our friends at United in Christ Network have resumed their round-the-clock prayer vigil. The goal is to have people praying continuously for Kay between now and Wednesday, April 12, 2000. If you would be interested in participating, please sign up. This may well be the final hearing, so please pray that all parties involved will be blessed with a double portion of God's wisdom. Continue to lift up Judge Linda Motheral, Ms. Ellen Yarrell, and Kay's attorneys, in order that they might make the right decision regarding the future of the five younger children.

Below the paragraph was a chart covering each day hour by hour. Beside each hour was a block with a name.

"From 8 a.m. to 9 a.m. today R. Smith will be praying," I read.

Hannah pointed to the screen. "And look, J.M. is praying right now, whoever that is . . . "

I looked into Linda's and Hannah's faces. "Just think, someone is always praying for us!"

How precious when the body of Christ pulls together for one another.

CHAPTER 34

Baby-Sitter With a Gun!

Hannah:

Stepping onto the elevator, I glanced at the slip of paper stating the office number. I pressed the button marked "2", and the elevator doors slid shut. I tried to ignore the knot in my stomach. I was unaccustomed to visiting lawyers' offices alone.

Judge Motheral had appointed an *ad litem* for Lissa, Isaiah, Beverly, Grace, and Emily. Rather than defending either of the opposing sides fighting over the children, the *ad litem* takes the children's side, listening to them, speaking up for their concerns, and defending their rights.

The door quietly closed behind me, and I approached the receptionist at the desk. "My name is Hannah Evans. I am here to see Ms. Yarrell."

The receptionist's blue eyes sparkled. "She will be out in just a few minutes. You may take a seat right over there," she said, pointing to an elegant love seat.

I sat down and looked around the tastefully furnished office. Beautiful, framed pictures decorated the room accented by royal wallpaper. On the coffee table before me, I spied a large photo album. Lifting it onto my lap, I began turning pages.

Hmmm. I see Ms. Yarrell handles quite a few adoptions, I mused as snapshots of smiling children peered back at me.

I had seen her only once before, and that was in court. I recalled how she had appeared totally at ease in the courtroom, as if it were her stage. I liked her way of translating legal dialogue so that regular folks could understand what was going on. Ms. Yarrell spoke confidently and articulately and was clearly influential with the judge.

But I was concerned about one thing: she was reportedly a personal friend of one of my grandparents' attorneys. *Will that cause her to be more sympathetic toward their opinions?* I wondered. *I hope not.*

"Are you Hannah?"

I looked up into Ms. Yarrell's pleasant face. She was a tall, slender woman whose graying hair hung neatly down to her shoulders.

Standing quickly, I smiled. "Yes, ma'am."

"Well, why don't we go back to my office? I am eager to hear about you and your family."

She led me into her office, and I took a chair across the desk from her. She was very professional but also very nice. As she listened to me, I appreciated her open and understanding spirit. God calmed my fears, and I felt in my heart that the Lord had chosen this woman to play a special part in our case.

Kay:

"Oh, and one more thing, Kay," said Tom Sanders' voice over the phone, "I heard something from Dr. and Mrs. Evans' lawyers that you might want to take note of. They said one of Walter's reservations in relinquishing the children to you is that you don't have a house for them to live in."

I frowned but said nothing.

"So," his voice continued, "I think it would be helpful if you would have an address to give the judge on the 18th when we're in court. Try to get a house rented by then, okay?"

My forehead wrinkled. "What? That gives us exactly two days to find a house!" I appealed frantically. "I don't know how I can do that."

Mr. Sanders was unfazed by my weak response. "Aw," he said, laughing, "you've moved faster than that before!"

And so began the frantic house-hunt. We were already busy preparing for the court hearing only two days away. Friends and family were traveling into town, and on top of all that, we now needed a house.

We began searching the want ads. The first house we looked at was very fancy and didn't feel right for my family of seven. But was this the time to be picky?

The next morning the phone rang. "I'm sorry," the real estate agent said, "the owners have decided not to rent their house to you since you have so many children."

We breathed a huge sigh of relief. But now we had only one day to find a house!

Hannah and I stood at two pay phones, a newspaper with highlighted ads between us.

"If you get an answering machine, just hang up," I told Hannah. "We're in too much of a hurry to deal with leaving messages."

Hannah nodded and carefully dialed a number. "Uh, hello. You put a rental ad in the paper, right? Do you mind renting to a family with six children? Oh, that won't work? Well, thank you very much anyway." She hung up and looked at me. "This could be interesting . . ."

I crossed the ad off. "Well, just go to the next one," I said. "I'll call this one here," pointing to a small, unimpressive description of a three-bedroom house. After I dialed the number, I heard a recording, "You have reached . . . "

I sighed and looked at the paper for the next possibility. My hand was still resting on the phone when it rang unexpectedly. Hannah and I looked at each other curiously. This was strange!

"Are you supposed to answer a pay phone if it rings?" I asked no one in particular and gingerly answered. "Hello?"

"Hi. Did you just call me?" a lady's voice asked.

"I don't know. I am looking for rental houses."

"Well, I have one," the voice chirruped.

"Well, do you mind if we come look at it this afternoon?"

The voice paused and then said, "How about three o'clock?"

"Sounds great; we'll look forward to it. Can you give me directions?"

Hannah stared at me in surprise. I beamed and held my hand over the mouthpiece whispering, "We have an appointment!"

At three o'clock I parked the car by the sidewalk and peered at the small brick house.

"This definitely looks more our speed," Hannah said excitedly.

We walked up the sidewalk and knocked on the door. A short lady immediately opened it.

"Come on in!" she said, holding the door wide.

"Thank you so much for being willing to come out this afternoon," I said.

She shook my hand and closed the door after us. "Oh, it's my pleasure."

I looked around at the dining room. "Well, I want to tell you before we even look at the house that our family is in the middle of a very unusual situation," I said. "I thought you may want to read this before you decide if you want to rent to us." I handed her the most recent newspaper article concerning our case. "In fact, if we do rent this place, we need to begin renting today."

She took the paper and nodded, her eyes glued to the bold letters printed across the top. "All charges dropped in custody case."

Hannah and I took a quick look around. We both felt this place could definitely work. It had a nice, large living area, and even a big bedroom where all the girls could be together. We returned to the front hall just as the woman finished reading the article.

"What do you think of the house?" she inquired.

"Oh, it would be just right," I assured her. "But would you mind renting to us?"

She laughed. "Oh, everybody has a story!"

So we rented the house on the spot, and drove away rejoicing. God knew our deadline and had provided us with just the right house on the day before the hearing. Why had we worried?

———————————

Lissa:

"Emily," Grandmom called from the front seat, "come sit in my lap while Granddad gasses up the van."

I opened one eye and groggily watched Emily climb over sleeping Beverly and Isaiah. We were once again on our way to Houston so that Granddad and Grandmom could go to a hearing.

"Good girl," Grandmom crooned as Emily slid into her lap. Grandmom hugged her tightly and bent close to her ear, whispering.

I don't think Grandmom knows I'm awake, I thought, *but maybe if I listen closely, I can learn something.*

Quietly leaning forward, I caught the words, ". . . and your mommy wants to take you and go into hiding again."

I was infuriated. How could she dare try to brainwash Emily! I cleared my throat loudly.

Grandmom jumped. "Lissa, you are awake," she said, forcing a smile.

I was more than awake; I was mad! "Grandmom, I heard what you said, and that is not true. Mommy is not going to kidnap us!"

She pressed her lips together into a tight line, and looked away, not saying a word.

I heard the bathroom door click shut, followed by the sound of the shower. I rolled over on the firm hotel bed and squinted at the clock. It was 5:45, February 18, 2000. Grandmom stood by the mirror in her bathrobe, carefully curling her hair.

I sighed and pulled the covers over my head wishing I could go back to sleep. Today would be another court hearing. As my eyelids slowly closed, I suddenly remembered something and my eyes flew open. *The policeman!* I sat straight up, my heart thumping.

"Grandmom."

She whirled around, holding the curling iron close to her head. "Good morning, Lissa!"

"Yes, good morning. What time does the policeman come?"

She glanced at the numbers glowing on the clock and said, "Oh, in about an hour."

I swung my legs over the side of the bed and stretched. "I need to get a shower as soon as Granddad comes out."

I didn't want to be caught in my pajamas when the policeman arrived.

Grandmom nodded in agreement.

At each court hearing, my grandparents faced the dilemma of finding someone to supervise us while they were gone. Yesterday Grandmom had told me they had made arrangements for a policeman to baby-sit us. I had stared at her, speechless. I couldn't believe it! And what made it worse is that I wanted to be in the courtroom. It just wasn't fair that Granddad and Grandmom would get to see Mommy and Hannah, but we couldn't. Instead, my little brother and sisters and I would all be stuck in a hotel room with someone we had never met before—and a policeman at that!

Imagine, I thought, *we will have a baby-sitter with a gun!*

I had just finished Emily's French braid when a firm knock resounded on the door. My heart thumped.

Grandmom hurried importantly to the door. "Oh, good morning, officer! Thank you so much for doing this for us. We can never thank you enough."

The uniformed officer's badge glittered in the light as he stepped into the room. Around his waist was slung a belt with ammunition and his holstered pistol.

Here is our baby-sitter! I thought. *If ever there was a time I didn't want to irritate a baby-sitter, it is now!*

Minutes later Grandmom looked at her watch and announced, "Walter, it's time to go."

He nodded and finished tying his shoelace. "Children, be good, okay?"

Our eyes followed them as he and Grandmom hurried toward the door. We heard it click shut behind them.

We children sat meekly on the bed, staring in silence as the officer hesitated and then stepped to a chair by the window to sit down.

He looked at us and said, "So, how are you kids doing?"

I smiled weakly. "Fine," I managed.

"Good." He nodded and glanced out the window.

Dear me, I thought, *this is going to be a long morning.*

Awkwardly, I tried starting a conversation. "Um, have you ever had this kind of an assignment before?"

A smile spread easily across his face as he shook his head. "Nope," he admitted, "this is definitely a first. Why exactly did your grand-parents call the police station to hire a baby-sitter?"

Emily crawled off the bed and began playing with her doll by my feet.

"It's sort of a long story," I said with a sigh. "My mom and grand-parents are both fighting for custody of us."

His eyes focused intently on me as I spoke. He leaned back in his chair and locked his hands behind his head. "Since I was given so little information before coming, I thought this might be a setup by druggies," he confessed with a chuckle. "We were just told that someone wanted a policeman to do some baby-sitting for a few hours. That's all. But why are you with your grandparents?"

"Well, have you heard of Kay Evans?" I asked.

He shook his head. "The name doesn't sound familiar."

"Have you heard about the lady with the three-million-dollar bond?"

"Oh, yeah, I have definitely heard of her!" he exclaimed. He straightened up in his chair, looking at me curiously.

"Well . . . she's our mom."

His eyes grew wide in surprise.

"And we do NOT want to be with our grandparents; we want to be with her. She is innocent!"

He shook his head in amazement. "Among the police force, there has been a lot of talk about this lady in jail with the huge bond."

Our conversation was interesting, but eventually we ran out of things to say. He stared out the window, and we sat on the bed wondering what to do.

Hannah:

I followed Mommy into the courtroom and slid onto the bench beside her. "I can hardly believe how many people are here to support us!" I whispered excitedly into Mommy's ear.

The bailiff glared at me. I sat still, looking into my lap. *I guess I wasn't quiet enough,* I thought.

But it had been very uplifting to see the hall lined with supporters. I shook my head, still amazed that people we didn't even know would come to encourage us like this. The courtroom was filling quickly, and Mommy and I scooted farther down to make more room on the hard wooden bench.

Mr. Sanders hurried over. "Kay, you and Hannah and your dad can go sit in those jury chairs over there," he whispered. "We are simply running out of room in here."

I grabbed my purse and followed Grandfather and Mommy. I had a fluttering feeling in my stomach, typical of these court days. But today it was stronger than usual, because Mr. Sanders had said he might want me to testify.

Looking toward the door, I noticed another group of people entering the room. There wasn't space for them to sit down, so they stood just inside the door.

Whew! I thought. *This is a packed courtroom!*

The bailiff grimaced at the crowd unhappily. Marching to the benches, he announced gruffly, "Everyone under the age of sixteen needs to leave so that we can make room for the adults."

Disappointed youth and children stood and made their way out the door to wait in the hall. Judge Motheral entered the room, and everyone stood.

"You may sit down," she said, motioning casually with her hand.

Court was now in session.

Mr. Sanders got up. "Would all the witnesses I spoke with please come up front at this time?" he said.

I quickly stood and joined the small group of people gathering by Mr. Sanders. There were about ten of us. It was such a blessing to look into each face, knowing each one was there to help Mommy. There was dear Grandfather, who was more than willing to speak a good word on behalf of his only daughter. There was the CPS worker, as well as her boss, who had interviewed us after Daddy had died.

Aunt Elaine had come too. *She will probably pay the highest price of anyone testifying today,* I mused, as I looked into her determined eyes. *Aunt Elaine is here to testify on Mommy's behalf even though her own parents will be listening to her every word. That will be tough,* I thought, taking a deep breath.

Our nurse friend, Debbie, who had helped us so much during Daddy's sickness, had come also. She had written a convincing letter about how things went during my dad's illness. Her letter was being presented to the judge.

There was an old friend of ours, Kent Dowden. And next to him was Mr. Azzo. It warmed my heart to see him. He had really put his heart into our case, and now that the criminal side was over, he wanted to do anything he could to help out on the family case.

Our missionary friends, Vernon and Kim Martin, had flown in from Guatemala, and then there were Mommy and me.

"Come," Mr. Sanders said, motioning, "we need to go up to the judge's bench and be sworn in, or affirmed."

I could feel my heart thumping wildly. *What will I say if I am called to be a witness?*

After we had raised our right hands and affirmed that we would tell "the truth, the whole truth, and nothing but the truth," we were ushered to the door. The witnesses were not allowed to be in the courtroom while another witness was testifying, lest they alter their story to fit what someone else had said. Consequently, all of us witnesses filed out except Mommy.

Kay:

I felt almost calm as the potential witnesses were ushered out of the courtroom, because I had been told I would not likely testify today. I was ready to put all my efforts into praying for those who would be placed on the witness stand. But as I stepped toward my seat, I heard one of the opposing lawyers call my name. I was horrified.

"I'd like to hear from Kay Evans first."

It caught me totally off guard. *I am to testify now?* My mind reeled. Shakily, I turned and walked to the witness stand. Seating myself before the microphone and the audience, my mouth went totally dry. Only the sound of the microphone being adjusted to my height could be heard.

Lawyer Ward Cope stalked up to me like a cocky rooster determined to do battle. He wasted no time.

"Isn't it true, Kay, that you purposely evaded your obligation to show up in court while you were running with your children?"

"Well, I had not personally been handed a subpoena by a court-appointed official."

"Yes, but isn't it fair to assume you knew there was a court case against you when you were leaving the country?"

"Yes, that is true."

"Objection, Your Honor!" shouted Tim Telge, shooting up from his chair.

The judge waved her hand, motioning for Mr. Telge to sit down.

Mr. Cope grinned smugly and continued to hurl one accusation after another.

I was unprepared for the intense grilling.

"It is pretty obvious you were disobeying the law in order to take your children and run. What do you have to say for yourself?"

"Well, sir, as a Christian, I know it is my duty to obey the laws of the land as long as those laws do not conflict with my higher authority, Jesus Christ."

"Yes, uh hum . . . So just what is it about your in-laws that you object to so strongly that you cannot even allow your children to be alone with them?" he asked sarcastically.

"Well, I believe their influence on my children has been spiritually damaging and confusing. I feel it is my duty, as their mother, to protect them from that influence."

"Yes, I see," he sneered, as he wheeled around and gave a meaningful glance toward my in-laws.

Once he was finished with me, I felt completely deflated. It seemed as though I crawled back to my seat among the audience.

Next was the private investigator who had been employed by my in-laws. "Now you traced this case and followed this woman's tracks during the years she spent in hiding. Is that right?" the attorney asked.

"Yes, sir," he admitted.

"If you were to rank this woman, Kay Evans, on a scale of one to ten, judging by how difficult she was to locate, with ten being the most difficult, how would you rank her?"

The silver-haired man paused for a moment and then leaned toward the microphone. "I'd give her a nine," he spoke flatly with his Texas drawl.

"Thank you. That will be all," the attorney said, dismissing him. The investigator could not have known the secret of how my family eluded him those three and a half years. I had no special knowledge or "street smarts" that kept us out of his reach. God alone had kept us hidden, as if in the very palm of His hand, for the exact length of time that He meant for us to be tucked away.

Thou shalt hide them in the secret of thy presence from the pride of man: thou shalt keep them secretly in a pavilion from the strife of tongues.[1]

I sat attentively as Judy, the CPS caseworker; my dad; our

1. Psalm 31:20

nurse friend, Debbie; and my sister-in-law Elaine each climbed into the witness stand and, one by one, answered questions. I was humbled at their willingness to speak out so boldly in my defense.

"Thank You, Lord," I whispered.

Hannah:

I scooted forward on the hard wooden bench, and sighed. The halls were quiet. Only Kim was busy, her skillful fingers pulling and looping yarn through her crochet hook as she waited.

"I should have thought to bring something to do," I commented as she looked up, smiling. I shook my head at the thought. "No, I don't think I really could handle a needle and yarn while my stomach is in such knots."

Kim glanced at the door. "How long does this kind of hearing take?" she asked.

"It varies," I answered. "This could be a long one."

The door swung open, and we all looked up eagerly. Mr. Sanders poked his head out and called, "It is your turn, Elaine."

Aunt Elaine stood and followed him through the door.

I elbowed my cousin sitting next to me. "Lauren, what do you think Granddad and Grandmom will say to her after this?"

She looked down at her hands and twisted her watch around and around her wrist. "I don't know, but I doubt it will be pleasant."

The hall grew silent again, and the tension seemed to grow. Lunchtime came and went. I leaned back against the cold wall, and closed my eyes, praying and waiting.

Lissa:

With her nose pressed into the glass, Beverly peered out over the cars that snaked down the highway. Grace and Emily jumped up and down on the bed, giggling. I sat on the floor staring again at the journal page in front of me, but I couldn't seem to focus.

What is going on in the courtroom? I wondered again. I glanced at the clock on the nightstand and shook my head. *We have been here almost nine hours!* My eyes drifted back to the girls jumping on the bed. *I really should tell them to stop, but what else is there for them to do? Surely they'll tire soon.*

But they didn't, and soon Isaiah and Beverly joined them. Up, down, up, down.

My thoughts went again to the courtroom. *When will we be let out of this room?* Up, down, up, down, the children jumped on and on.

Hannah:

I started when the door burst open and people poured out.

"It's over for today," someone said.

What? What had happened? I rushed into the courtroom and saw Mommy's lawyers talking to her. I glanced around at the huddles of people talking in hushed tones. As I was wondering why the hearing had ended so abruptly, Mr. Sanders walked up to me.

"Well, do you have any questions?" he asked kindly.

"Yeah," I mumbled, "what happened?"

He looked at me apologetically. "Oh, Hannah, the judge has placed a 'gag' order on everyone that was in the courtroom until the next court date. Then the other testimonies can be heard, but I can't give you any details about the case now."

I stared at him in disbelief, trying to make sense of his words. I thought of all the people out in the hall and the witnesses that had gone to a tremendous amount of effort and expense just to get here today. Others had flown and traveled many miles to show their support. To have the hearing delayed was certainly discouraging.

"But," Mommy consoled me, "God did show Himself strong through the testimonies that were heard. Apparently we are just not through learning to be patient."

"Excuse me," a voice broke in behind us. I turned to see Ellen Yarrell holding her briefcase. "I would like for you and Hannah to come to my office right away. Can I plan on seeing you there in a little bit?"

"Oh, yes, certainly," Mommy assured her.

I pulled the van door shut and snapped my seat belt into place. Laura turned the key in the ignition and carefully backed the minivan out of the crowded parking lot.

"Kay, I'll drop you and Hannah off at Ellen Yarrell's office and then head over to my mom's. You can just call me when you need me to come pick you up, okay?"

"Laura, thank you so much. I really appreciate all you do for me."

"Oh, you're certainly welcome," she said, with a smile.

After a few minutes, I turned to Mommy. "Well, I am just bursting with questions about the hearing today," I said, breaking the silence. "But I know y'all can't tell me a thing."

"Hannah, it is going to be a real challenge not to say a word about it, but we've got to keep mum on this until the judge lifts the order."

I looked out the window at the tall buildings flashing by and sighed. "I know."

As we arrived in Ms. Yarrell's reception area, she greeted us and hurried us back to a more private office.

"Walter and Jan are bringing the children," she told us with a twinkle in her eye, "so I need to get you back to the conference room before they show up."

Mommy's eyes grew wide in amazement, and she flashed me an excited smile.

"Now you wait here," Ms. Yarrell said quietly. "I'll be near the door to greet them."

Lissa:

"I'll be done with the children in about an hour," Ellen Yarrell told Granddad and Grandmom. They nodded and thanked her before they stepped out the door, leaving us alone with her in the office.

"Now, children," she said, smiling pleasantly as she led us down a hallway, "I have some people back here I want you to see."

I eyed her curiously but didn't really care what she wanted. I was just relieved to be out of that dreadful hotel room. Pushing open a door, Ms. Yarrell motioned for us to go in. I peered inside.

"Mommy! And Hannah!" I squealed.

We dashed toward them and wrapped them in tight hugs. This was a delightful, unexpected reunion! Ms. Yarrell kindly stepped out of the office and left us alone to talk for a few minutes.

When she returned, she wanted to see me. "Now Lissa, I would love to leave you in here with your family, but I need to ask you some questions in my office."

I smiled at her, eager to be of assistance. *She has already proved she is sensitive to our desires to be with Mommy,* I thought gratefully.

"Lissa, I want to ask your permission to read this," Ms. Yarrell said, pulling out a folder and placing it on the desk in front of me. "Tom gave it to me, but I want to make sure it is all right with you."

I flipped open the front and immediately recognized the content. It was the computer journal I had kept on disk and then slipped to Mommy on that visit at my grandparents' place.

"I know this is personal to you," said Ms. Yarrell, "but it could be very helpful in the courtroom."

I thumbed through the pages and stared at the entries. Each one recounted events and emotions I had experienced over the recent months. Ms. Yarrell waited quietly as I held the journal, and then I cleared my throat. "Well, it will certainly be humbling to let you read this, but if it can somehow be used to put our family back together, I am all for it. Yes, you may use it."

Kay:

Ellen Yarrell had just finished speaking with several of my children, when Jan and Walter returned.

"Hey, could I try a meeting with you and your in-laws?" Ms. Yarrell asked. "I'd like to get an idea of the chemistry of your relationship."

"Sure," I said with a shrug.

She led me into a conference room, "Okay, just seat yourself at the table, and I'll be back," she instructed as she disappeared into the hallway.

Moments later, she returned leading Walter and Jan into the room, motioning toward the glass table. Ms. Yarrell took a seat beside me as Walter and Jan sat across from us.

I gulped. *This is going to be really uncomfortable,* I thought.

We all stared at one another awkwardly. I tried to smile, but felt no inclination to begin the conversation.

Jan broke the silence. "The hearing today was most unusual, Kay," she said indignantly. "We just could not believe the untruths that were told today in court. Why," she said, sighing heavily, "even our own daughter . . ." Her voice trailed away. "It was just most unusual."

Walter nodded. "Yes, it was rather disappointing."

A long pause followed, and Ms. Yarrell nudged me encouragingly. "Why don't you say something?"

I looked back into her eyes. "What's the point?" I whispered.

My relationship with my in-laws had been strained even in better times. But now that we were on opposing sides of a court case, I did not feel free to say anything to them.

Jan started again, "It is very disheartening when people are not willing to represent the truth . . ." she droned on and on.

Finally Ms. Yarrell sighed. "Okay, I don't think we're getting anywhere. Let's go back to the lobby where the children are waiting."

Lissa:

I could tell by the expression on Mommy's face that the dialogue with Granddad and Grandmom had not gone well.

Ms. Yarrell spoke up clearly. "Walter, Kay told me a friend of hers is having a bunch of the people over tonight who have traveled in for this case. I heard they will be having snacks there, is that correct, Kay?"

Mommy nodded and Ms. Yarrell continued, "Walter and Jan, I think you should take the children there to see their friends."

I watched with keen interest as she told Granddad exactly what she thought he should do. Her personality was commanding and instantly demanded respect.

"Yes, I think we can do that," Granddad agreed, "but I don't know how to get there."

Ms. Yarrell smiled triumphantly. "That should work out perfectly, since Kay and Hannah were dropped off here. Kay," she said turning to Mommy, "you don't have a ride over to your friend's house, do you?"

Mommy shook her head with a puzzled look on her face. "Walter, could you give Kay and Hannah a lift over there?" Ms. Yarrell asked. "They could give you the directions, and it would do you both a favor."

Grandmom looked at Granddad uncomfortably, but he meekly

nodded at Ms. Yarrell. "Yes, Kay and Hannah may certainly ride with us."

The room was silent for a moment, and Ms. Yarrell said, "Good."

Mommy stroked Emily's hair. "Before we leave," she said, "would it be all right if my children and I sing a song together?" Mommy's voice faltered and her eyes grew misty. "Singing has been one of our favorite things to do together, and it has been so long . . ."

"But of course," Ms. Yarrell assured her, stepping back to listen.

Hannah and I looked at each other. "What shall we sing?" I questioned. Hannah glanced up thoughtfully and then suggested, "What about 'Faithful Love'?"

We had sung that song a lot just before we were captured in Novillero.

"Sounds good," I said and hummed a starting note. But before we began singing, I told myself, *Lissa, you cannot cry, okay? Be strong!*

So, standing there in the office lobby, we sang as a family again, for the first time in a very long while, our arms wrapped around each other. As we started the second verse, I couldn't hold back the tears any longer. No matter how hard I blinked, the tears streamed down my cheeks. It was beautiful to be singing together again.

Kay:

We stepped up on the porch as my friend Linda smiled and held open the creaky door. "Welcome!" she cried. "Oh, and the kids came along too! And your in-laws . . . Come on in, everyone!"

I held Emily in my arms and stepped into the well-lit living room. The room was packed with eager faces, all looking our way. Some were old friends of mine, some were new, some were unknown to me altogether, but they wanted to show their support. We felt very grateful for everyone's desire to come and encourage us.

My children, whom I had scarcely seen over the past two and a half months, were the focus of everyone's attention. Some people wanted to meet them. Old friends were eager to see them again after our years of absence. It was a strange and emotional gathering.

"Kay, it is so wonderful to see you and the children together!"

a friend exclaimed as she passed, balancing a plate loaded with food.

I nodded but felt incapable of handling the pressures suffocating me within these walls.

How can I smile, introduce my in-laws around, and pretend everything is fine? I thought helplessly.

My five-year-old, Emily, held tightly to me, struggling to cope as well. Her eyes swam with tears at the overwhelming scene, not even sure who she was allowed to cling to. I glanced around and slipped through the crowd to a corner and sat in a recliner where Emily and I could be all by ourselves. I scooped her into my lap and held her close as we sobbed mournfully together.

Oh, God, please protect my little daughter in this cruel season of her life, I prayed as I buried my face in her blond hair. *Hold her tenderly for me when I cannot. She is so precious to me.*

All too soon I would be told the children must go, but for now I wanted to cherish this rare moment with my little girl.

CHAPTER 35

Decorations, Negotiations, and Celebrations

Kay:

The van clock glowed 11:42 p.m. just as I pulled up into the driveway of our rental home.

Hannah sighed. "Ah, home at last. That drive from Amarillo doesn't get any shorter, no matter how many times we drive it."

I nodded as I reached down and grabbed an armful of stuff to be taken in. "Yes, I'm eager to fall into bed. Let's see how fast we can get this van unloaded."

As I pushed the stubborn van door shut, my thoughts drifted back to the wonderful weekend we had enjoyed with the children. We had stayed at my dad's farmhouse, and Hannah and I had relished the time to catch up on the children's lives. We had also spent some time with David and Sue Beth and their children.

At the front door, I fumbled with the keys. Hannah stood patiently behind me, her arms loaded with bags and clothes.

"I'm sorry, I'm having a hard time getting the door to open. Oh, here, I think I've got it."

The door swung open, and I felt around on the inside wall until my fingers found the light switch. Flipping it on, Hannah and I sleepily blinked in surprise.

"Oh, Hannah!" I gasped.

"Oh, Mommy!" she returned.

We had left the house with only a few pieces of furniture, but now we found ourselves in a beautifully furnished and professionally decorated home. I couldn't believe my eyes! We had never lived in a home that looked this nice.

The table in the dining room was elegantly covered with a cloth that accented the new curtains draped in the window. The living room looked like something you would find on a magazine cover. The couch was artistically placed and invitingly draped with a rich red cover. There were curtains and lace hanging decoratively in the windows. There was even an artificial tree carefully placed in a corner of the room that would have otherwise looked dull and empty.

Hannah dropped her armload on the couch and stood with wide eyes and gaping mouth, surveying the transformed house.

I opened the pantry door and stood shaking my head. "Why, they even stocked the pantry with all kinds of groceries, Hannah!"

I heard her voice faintly from the girls' room, "And Mommy, you should see what they have done in here!"

We both walked around and around inside the house for about two hours, forgetting how tired we were.

"Can you believe this?" I said over and over again.

We marveled at how our needs had been provided for each room. People had anonymously donated furniture, curtains, and brand-new bath sets. They had also provided various forms of labor, repairing and improving things here and there.

"Oh, God, bless the servants of Yours who have ministered to us so lovingly. I am unworthy of the ways You lavish Your love upon us through so many kind people."

Before Hannah and I had left for Amarillo, word had spread among the homeschooling community as well as various churches about our situation and the unfurnished house I had rented. People I didn't even know had rallied to the cause right along with old friends. Someone donated a couch and two living room chairs. A washer and dryer suddenly appeared in our garage. A piano was delivered. Someone brought over a nice wooden dining table just the right size for a family of seven. A yard crew showed up and mowed and edged our lawn.

My sister-in-law Elaine and her husband Allen had generously parted with some of their own nice things to get us started too. One afternoon Allen brought over their second refrigerator, which they had found helpful with their growing family. When I thanked Allen and Elaine, she paraphrased Luke 3:11, altered to fit the occasion. "She who has two refrigerators, let her give to her who has none," she said with a twinkle in her eye.

Word must have gotten around too, that the *ad litem* was planning to come look our house over carefully. It would be her job to make sure this was a suitable place for my children to live. We had heard our house might be more easily approved if I could provide an individual bed for each child. The only problem was that we currently had only two beds.

Before I could consider what we would do about this need, a well-known mattress company, The Mattress Firm, called to offer new beds and mattresses; they only needed to know how many we needed. I was elated!

Our house had buzzed with activity while people came and went bringing their contributions. One lady mailed us beautifully printed Scriptures that we framed and put up on the walls. My dad and brother rented a U-Haul trailer and brought some of our old things that had been stored for years in my brother's barn. Little by little our house had become more livable, even if it was a hodgepodge of styles and colors.

When the time came for Hannah and me to leave for Amarillo to visit the children, Elaine had called. "Kay," she asked, "would you mind if a few people worked on some things inside your house while ya'll are away?"

I had told her that would be fine and had left a key for her under the doormat.

"But Hannah, I certainly wasn't expecting this!" I said as I sat down on the couch and surveyed the transformed room. "Oh, if this beautiful house will not pass the *ad litem's* inspection, nothing will!"

"God delights in doing abundantly above what we can even imagine," Hannah sighed contentedly.

———————————

Lissa:

Click, click, click . . . My shoes were the only sound in the quiet hallway as I passed the college classes in progress, with teachers' voices droning monotonously. Through open doorways, students looked up as I walked by. They always stared.

It seems the students on campus will never get used to seeing me. I smiled, shaking my head.

I had a backpack like everyone else, but that is where the similarities ended. I wore a dress and a white veil, and this seemed to be the strangest thing many of these people had ever seen. Oh, well . . . I wasn't a nun, they discovered, or a nurse. "Then what could she possibly be?" their questioning expressions seemed to ask.

Each morning after the children were sent off to school, Granddad and I headed to the university where he taught and where I studied by myself. Although I was enrolled in a high school correspondence course, being on the campus made me feel like a college student. This certainly was a new experience for me, as I had always been home-educated.

Several of my cousins also attended this university. One of them, Ben, I saw quite often, and he always took time to talk with me. He took me to see his latest art project and wasn't embarrassed to have me sit at his table, despite my unusual attire. It was always reassuring to see him.

Uncle Leo taught in the law department at the university. Despite his busy schedule, he encouraged me to drop by his office if I ever needed anything. My grandparents did not keep my siblings and me informed about the court case at all, and we rarely heard the latest developments. I guess they saw no reason to update us since we were not on "their side" anyway.

Even though Uncle Leo did not agree with how Mommy had handled things, he always told me what was going on with the case when I asked. He even encouraged me to ask if I had questions. It had been a long time since I had heard anything, and today I felt desperate for some straight answers, so I decided to take him up on his offer.

Reaching Uncle Leo's office, I knocked lightly at his door and waited. I heard a chair squeak and seconds later the door opened. "Hey, Lissa, come in and have a seat."

I slid my heavy backpack off my shoulder and onto the floor. Sitting back in a chair, I began, "I haven't heard anything about the case for several weeks. Can you please tell me what's going on?"

He ran his fingers through his brown hair, leaning back in his swivel chair. I always appreciated his explanations of how the court process worked, simplifying the big legal words I did not understand.

"Well, Lissa, your mother is hoping to regain full custody of y'all, but I think it's quite unlikely. Even if she does, it will take some time."

I stared at the large oil-on-canvas painting of a stern-looking judge centered on the far wall.

How dreary court life is! I found myself thinking.

Uncle Leo continued, "It would take a long time because she wants complete custody with no restrictions, whereas Granddad and Grandmom want to help make the decisions about your future."

I nodded. "It sure is taking a long time!"

He leaned forward. "What is happening right now is that your mother sends a proposal, but Granddad and Grandmom refuse it. Then they write her one, and she refuses to accept their terms. Get the idea?"

I nodded and sighed. "It just gets wearying sometimes." I glanced at my watch and stood up. "Well, thank you, Uncle Leo, for letting me ask these questions. It means a lot to know what is really going on."

He smiled and hugged me. "Hey, any time, Lissa."

Kay:

"Let's pray," Tim Telge said fervently. We all bowed our heads and closed our eyes. "Dear Lord," he pleaded, "Your Word says You defend the fatherless and widows. We are trusting You to prove Yourself faithful."

Each time, before any meeting or court proceeding, Tom Sanders and Tim Telge would pray with Hannah and me. It was so comforting to lay such a secure foundation for the day, asking God's direction before attempting these stressful legal proceedings. This time it was March 14, and we sat waiting in a mediation office.

"Mr. Sanders, I would be amazed if my in-laws and I come to any kind of agreement through this mediation today. You and Mr. Telge know I can't in any way compromise my convictions for how my children should be raised. And I really can't see my in-laws willing to budge either."

He nodded understandingly. "Kay, you are probably right. This attempt at mediation may not accomplish a thing. But let's just go through with it for the judge's sake. Okay?" I nodded.

Moments later the door opened, and Ellen Yarrell walked in, accompanied by another woman.

"Good morning," the other woman spoke. "I will be the official mediator for you and Dr. and Mrs. Evans today. They will be in another conference room like this one. I will go between the two parties and see if we can work something out. Do you have any questions?"

Hannah and I sat at a table facing Mr. Sanders and Mr. Telge, who explained the message the mediator had brought.

"Kay, your in-laws want to be involved in the decisions you make for the children's future. They want to be able to take your husband's place and have equal authority in the decisions made concerning the children. Would you be willing to agree to let them have fifty percent of the authority?"

I shook my head firmly. "No way! I can't be unequally yoked. No, I just want to have the full authority a parent rightfully has."

Proposals flew back and forth, but I stood firmly, insisting that I must be able to raise my children the way the Lord directed me. Ms. Yarrell came in and listened to my desires. I could tell by the expression on her face that she wished I would be a little more flexible.

"No, I need to be the sole guardian over my children. I know things would go easier for me now if I bend, but I cannot. There is just too much at stake."

The mediator sighed and leaned against the table. "Okay, we are not getting anywhere. Jan and Walter are not willing to compromise, nor is Kay. Who knows how many petitions have gone back and forth this morning, and none of them have been accepted. I think this will have to be resolved in court."

I nodded.

Tom Sanders looked down at his watch. "Well, we are scheduled to be in court in an hour anyway. I guess we should all head over in that direction now. Thank you," he said, standing up and shaking the mediator's hand.

"Oh, you're welcome. I just wish something could have been accomplished." She smiled graciously and opened the door to the waiting room.

Hannah:

The windshield wipers swept back and forth across the glass. I closed my eyes and leaned back against the seat. Mommy drove carefully on the wet downtown streets. The sound of the wheels splashing in the puddles was accented by the rain pounding on the roof.

"It is really coming down," Mommy commented as she peered at the sheets of rain falling from the dark clouds high above us.

I was lost in deep thought. The morning had been rather discouraging. Mediation seemed to have been a waste of time, and Granddad and Grandmom hadn't even brought the children with them to Houston, so we had no hopes of seeing them today.

"Well, Hannah," Mommy said, touching my shoulder, "it's one o'clock. I parked pretty close to the courthouse, so we don't have far to walk."

I grabbed my purse and quickly hopped out of the van. Holding my jacket close to me, I followed Mommy's quick steps. Dashing across the wet street and jumping over the swollen gutter, we climbed the steps to the courthouse. Mommy shook the rain from her sweater and tucked a strand of wet hair back into her limp veil.

I laughed. "We may look like drowned rats, but we are here!"

She rolled her eyes and smiled. "Okay, we had better hurry up to the courtroom."

As we sat down, several ladies on the bench in front of us turned around and smiled. There were quite a few women from the homeschool group.

"I had no idea so many of our friends would show up for this hearing!" I said.

I listened as Ward Cope spoke persuasively to the judge. "Your Honor, the children are adjusting very well to public school. Their grades are improving, and it seems obvious that they need to be kept in such a healthy educational environment."

He paused as he broached his next point. "In order for Dr. and Mrs. Evans to feel they can relinquish custody to their daughter-in-law, they must know that the children are going to be properly provided for academically."

Judge Motheral leaned forward in her seat and spoke. "I'd like to have a private counsel about this."

We all waited in the hall while the lawyers and judge discussed the issues of our case. As soon as they were done, a deputy called Mommy and me back to a simple jury room where both of our lawyers joined us. They wanted to explain what Granddad and Grandmom were asking of us.

"They really want to know if you are open to having the children continue their education in public school," Mr. Telge explained as he looked down at his small yellow notepad.

Mommy bristled and furrowed her eyebrows.

"I really think your in-laws' attorneys are getting desperate," Mr. Sanders whispered. "The judge knows what needs to be done, but I think she is just waiting to give your in-laws a chance to give over the children voluntarily. I don't think she wants to force them unless she has to."

The door opened and Ellen Yarrell strode in, joining our circle. "Kay," she said pointedly, "I would still like you and your in-laws to come to an agreement. I strongly suggest that you be willing to put the children into public or private school . . . even just to finish out the school year."

Mr. Sanders and Mr. Telge both nodded. "At least consider it, Kay," Mr. Sanders suggested.

We gathered back in the courtroom and the lawyers and Ellen Yarrell stood before the judge.

The judge spoke up, "I want everyone, Dr. and Mrs. Evans, and Kay Evans to have psychological testing within the next ninety days. And for now, I want the children to be brought from Amarillo to spend the rest of this week with their mother. They won't miss any school since this is spring break."

Mommy broke into a smile, and grasped my hand excitedly. "Now we are getting somewhere!" she whispered gratefully.

Encouragement flooded us like a welcome rain after a long drought. "Thank You, Lord!"

Kay:

"I thought of something, Kay, that I really think might prove helpful in the courtroom." Mr. Sanders' voice sounded confident over the phone.

"All right," I paused, "what is it?"

"Well," he said, "you know how much of the discussion in court yesterday was about the children's education. I really don't think that is an issue, but of course, Walter and Jan do. My thought is this, why don't you have Hannah tested to see where she places academically? Even though she is no longer a minor, if her scores turn out well, surely the court would realize that the children's educational future would be just as promising under your teaching. If Hannah's scores don't turn out well, then we can just trash the results and forget it."

We decided to pursue testing Hannah.

"Mrs. Juren lives in Pearland," I said, handing the directions to Hannah.

She took the paper and peered down at the map. "It looks like it could take at least an hour to get there," she concluded.

"Mr. Sanders told me Mrs. Juren has a master's degree in education but is now a home-educating mother," I related. "Apparently she can test you at her house and then send off the forms to Bob Jones University where they will be scored."

Hannah and I were both nervous about this test.

"Mommy, I hope my scores turn out well, but I'm a little scared," she said, looking at me apprehensively.

I gripped the wheel tightly. "Well I'm nervous too, but let's trust God. I am going to drop you off at her house and then go park somewhere and pray for you during the test."

"Oh, thank you," Hannah whispered.

Hannah:

Joann Juren greeted me warmly at the door. "Oh, come on in. You must be Hannah," she said, hugging me. Her bubbly manner instantly put me at ease. She led me into the dining room. "I have the test and a few sharpened pencils right here for you. Just fill in the answers on this chart here. Would you like a glass of water before you start?"

I shook my head. "No, thank you, I'd rather get started."

She nodded. "Very well. And don't worry about the test," she said comfortingly. "I am sure you will do just fine."

I carefully worked a math problem, checked it and then filled in the bubble on the answer chart. *I wonder how I am doing?* I thought. The problems didn't seem as hard as they could have been. At least I often knew what they were talking about. On and on I tested. My eyes grew tired, because I had forgotten my glasses. I held the paper at arm's length so I could make out the words. Once again, I bent over the paper and painstakingly filled in the answer.

"Hannah," Mrs. Juren's voice spoke from the kitchen, "do you need a break? Feel free to take one if you want."

Looking up, I replied, "Thank you, but I am almost done." At last I put my pencil down and sighed. "Finally, I'm finished!"

I glanced at the clock on the wall. "Oh! It's nearly 10 p.m!"

Kay:

Hannah and I stood by the door as Mrs. Juren spoke. "I will let Bob Jones University know it's urgent that this test be scored promptly, as it may be used for a pending court case. And I'll ask them to mail the results to you the fastest way possible."

I hugged her gratefully. "Thank you again for doing this for us," I said. "It is such a blessing!"

She shook her head. "Kay, I am just glad to be of assistance to you. Please call on me again sometime if there is anything else I can do to help."

Out in the van I asked Hannah, "How was the test?"

She buckled her seat belt and sighed. "Well, it wasn't as bad as I thought it might be. But I do wonder how I scored."

In just a few days, the results came in the mail. We hesitated nervously as we stared at the large envelope. "Do you want to open it, Hannah?" I asked.

She shook her head. "No, would you please?"

With a trembling heart, I tore open the packet. "What do all those numbers mean? Hmmm . . . it appears you did fine on everything."

Hannah looked relieved. Later that day, Mrs. Juren called me. "I also received a copy of Hannah's results, and I just want to assure you that she passed everything very well. In fact, she actually placed at college level. I think those results would be very beneficial in court."

I thanked her and weakly hung up the phone. God had been so good to us. I went out to the backyard to be alone and cried, "Sweet Lord, You have proved Your power to us yet again!"

"Mommy!" Hannah called from the dining room window, "Uncle Leo just got here with the children. Oh, they are actually here!"

I centered the picture frame on the wall and stepped back, examining my work. "Does that look okay?" I asked her.

"It looks great."

"Good," I said, quickly laying the hammer on the counter and hurrying down the hall. "Oh, I am so eager to see them!"

For the past week, Hannah and I had been putting our personal touches throughout the house. We had excitedly culled through old pictures, framing different ones and arranging them carefully on the walls. During our hiding years, we had only two tiny pictures from our past to carry with us, so I knew my children would be excited to see photos from long ago. I wanted each of the children to walk through the house and see their own pictures carefully placed here and there, so that they would feel that this was their own home.

Hannah and I had even decorated one wall to remind us of our years in Central America. We had hung a colorful Guatemalan blanket on the wall as the backdrop for photos displaying scenes of our happy years there. We had dreamed of living together again as a family like old times. This week would be an exciting reunion, a taste of things to come.

Isaiah flew into my arms. "Mommy!"

I hugged him tightly, and cried, "Oh, it is so good see you again!"

Emily pranced around me. "Mommy, we are finally here. The

drive took a long time."

Lissa looked up at the brick home and said, "So this is our house!"

I wrapped all the children in a tender embrace. "Oh, it is so good to be a family again!"

Leo slammed the minivan door and picked up two bags of the children's clothes.

"Thank you, Leo, for bringing the children all the way here. I really appreciate it."

He smiled. "Hey, I'm glad to do it. Where do you want me to put these bags?" he asked.

"Oh, you can just set them down inside the door."

Beverly pulled me by the hand. "C'mon, I want to see inside our house."

I followed my eager children through the front door as they excitedly began looking through the house.

"Would you like something to drink, Leo?" I offered.

"Sure," he responded, accepting a cup from my hand. He sipped slowly and looked around. "The place looks very nice, Kay. You have done a good job."

"Oh, we have done very little of the decorating in here. So many people have worked on this home to make it look the way it does. Hannah and I can hardly believe it ourselves."

CHAPTER 36

On the Wings of Prayer

Hannah:

"But Your Honor," Ward Cope complained, "Kay and her lawyers failed to inform us of that."

I looked quickly at Mommy and leaned toward her. "What is he talking about? What didn't we do?"

She looked concerned. "I don't know. Let's listen and see if we can figure it out."

There seemed to be some piece of information our side had failed to give them, but what was it? It must have been an oversight.

"Oh, no!" I worried, wringing my hands. "And it happens right now when the judge seems to be leaning in our favor."

Ellen Yarrell stepped forward confidently in her bright red business suit. "Yes, you're right," she spoke boldly to Ward Cope. "Kay's lawyers failed to get that information to you, but you also failed to notify them that you recently had the children psychologically tested again."

Her eyes flashed. I leaned forward in my seat to catch every word.

"But, Ellen," Mr. Cope said, weakly justifying his negligence, "I hadn't had a cha . . ."

"Ward," Ms. Yarrell broke in, "I thoroughly examined those tests myself right after I received them yesterday." Ms. Yarrell was clearly upset.

Mr. Cope was taken aback at her onslaught. Stammering, he attempted to recover his position, but to no avail.

Judge Motheral watched Ellen Yarrell intently as she continued.

"When the children first returned to the States, they were psychologically evaluated. Those first test results showed that the children were fine. But Dr. and Mrs. Evans had the children reevaluated last week, without informing me, or Kay, or her lawyers!"

Mr. Cope looked down at the gray carpet, but Ms. Yarrell went on. "Ward, the recent test results came back stating the children are now clinically depressed. The test administrator even jotted on the test papers, 'The children need to be returned to their mother.' "

Ms. Yarrell turned to the judge. "These test results are the most conclusive evidence we have seen yet," she declared. "It seems urgent to me that the children be returned to their mother!"

Why were these tests administered without our knowledge? I wondered. *If my grandparents had hoped to use the results to help their cause, it definitely backfired, and God is using it to bless us instead. This battle is the Lord's!*

The words of the Prophet Isaiah came to my mind. *No weapon that is formed against thee shall prosper.*[1]

After a private counsel between the judge and attorneys, our lawyers met Mommy and me in the hallway. We learned from them that my grandparents had submitted a proposal requesting visitation if they would relinquish custody. They wanted to have the children for two weeks every summer.

Without hesitation Mommy shook her head, turning it down. Mr. Sanders and Mr. Telge both nodded in agreement as they disappeared down the hallway.

Returning a few minutes later, we learned my grandparents had agreed to give the children back to Mommy one week from today when she would be granted temporary custody.

"Kay, your in-laws want you to notify them about medical and educational decisions," Mr. Sanders said.

Mommy was disturbed that my grandparents were still trying to maintain some level of control over our family.

"Now, Kay, don't worry about these minor details because this is only temporary custody we are talking about today. The stipulations they place on temporary custody may not have any effect at all on permanent custody."

"Really?" Mommy looked relieved.

"Oh, and Kay, there was no mention of you being required to send the children to public or private schools. So, you have complete liberty to

---

1. Isaiah 54:17

home-educate. That's good news, isn't it?" he asked, raising his eyebrows.

Mommy's face brightened.

"Kay, I think this second proposal is something you can live with, and I believe you should accept it."

"I wholeheartedly agree," Mr. Telge asserted.

Mommy looked from one lawyer to the other. "All right then," she said. "I will."

Both men sighed with relief, grateful for her agreement. Mr. Telge pulled out his pocket calendar and thumbed through its pages quickly. Finding the month of April, he paused and studied it.

Looking at Mommy thoughtfully, he said, "Let's see, you'll be getting your children back on April 19. Isn't that what the judge said?"

Mommy and I nodded.

"Kay, I don't think it is coincidental that your children will be delivered to you this close to Passover, which commemorates the Israelites' deliverance from the bondage of the Egyptians."

Mommy stood pondering this insightful comment before it was time to return to the courtroom and finalize the day's proceedings. Mommy turned to me as we walked excitedly toward the courtroom. "Hannah, isn't God good? To think, they are actually making definite plans to give me the children back in a week!"

"Mommy, I know. This is such an answer to prayer."

Kay:

I stared at the computer screen before my fingers finally began to move over the keys. God had worked in such an incredible way, and I was eager to inform our prayer warriors of the latest developments.

April 14, 2000
To My Brothers & Sisters in Christ:
  I want to say thank you for all the prayers that have been offered up on behalf of my family over the past four and a half months since we were captured in Guatemala. I am so grateful for the time you took out of your busy schedules to pray for my family, asking

the Lord to deliver us from our difficult circumstances and to reunite us as a family.

I also appreciate other ways you've gone out of your way to show us you care about us in the midst of our struggle. I owe a tremendous debt of love to you for helping carry our burden in the ways that you have. I don't know how to repay you except to ask the Lord to reward and bless you and your families for helping me through this time. And I believe He will do that, and in a way that will be a much greater benefit to you than anything I could do.

In case you haven't heard, the Lord has answered your prayers and has delivered me and my family from our recent fiery trials of being separated from one another. This was quite a test for me and my children, but God carried us through on the wings of your prayers.

On April 12th (this past Wednesday), Judge Motheral issued "temporary custody orders" to give the children back to me this coming April 19, 2000. Then, we expect to have another more private meeting with her on June 26, 2000, to reevaluate and determine how things should proceed from then on.

Perhaps this does not sound very permanent or settled, but I believe it is progress. I'll just need to trust and to continue petitioning God for the completion of the whole process. I hope I am learning that God's ways and His timing are always perfect.

Often I want everything worked out completely right now, but waiting may be just what I need for God to complete His refining process for me.

I thank you for your love and your prayers for us! God has proven Himself Mighty yet again and I know He will continue to. If you don't mind, I would still really appreciate your prayers as God completes what He has begun on behalf of my family. Thank you for sharing our burden, our prayers, our tears, and now our victory, because of the Lord who is enabling us to be a family again.

Much love and gratitude from a sister in Christ,

Kay Evans

CHAPTER 37

Light at the End of the Tunnel

Lissa:

Granddad, arms laden with suitcases, held the hotel room door open with his foot.

"And, Walter, don't forget to go to the lobby and check us out," Grandmom called after him.

"Yes, Jan," he answered dutifully.

I finished twisting a rubber band tightly around the end of Emily's braid and flopped onto the bed. I was bursting with questions. *Why was today's hearing so unusually short? Why is Grandmom so perturbed?*

I intently scrutinized Grandmom's face as she methodically folded her bathrobe and very carefully laid it inside the open suitcase before her.

Suddenly I could contain my curiosity no longer. "Grandmom," I pleaded, "can't you tell us anything about the court hearing? We've been waiting all this time to find out what's going on."

Grandmom zipped the black suitcase and then looked up, annoyed. Forcing a smile she announced, "Well, Lissa, it looks like you will be returned to your mother in exactly one week."

She walked over to the bathroom counter and snatched up the toothbrushes and slid each one into its plastic container. Dropping them into the cosmetic bag, she closed the lid, fastened it shut, and turned to face us.

"Children," she said deliberately, "I want all of you to know something. Your granddad and I have hoped for this all along. We simply wanted to help you out and take care of you until your mother could get her problems resolved."

My feet thumped lightly down the steps, and my heart was singing. The sky was slightly overcast, but the day seemed gorgeous to me. Clutching her bag, Beverly jogged beside me as we made our way toward the van. Her sparkling eyes and wide smile assured me she was every bit as delighted about this exciting news as I was.

"I can hardly believe we'll actually be going to live with Mommy and Hannah in one week!" she chattered. "I feel like jumping up and down, I'm so excited."

Nearing the van, I whispered back, "Me, too, but we need to be careful how we act around Granddad and Grandmom. I don't think they are one bit excited about it."

My little sister nodded, but I could tell her mind was far away. "You know," she said, "I am going to begin packing as soon as we get back to Grandmom and Granddad's house."

When we reached the van, she set her bag by the van door. "And I'm leaving every shirt and pair of pants right in the drawer!" she said firmly.

———————

The small chapel was full, and I squirmed in my seat. Acquaintances of the past four months filled the pews for a farewell service. Granddad stood in front and expressed his deep gratitude to the many supporters.

"The children will be leaving this week to live with their mother in the Houston area. Jan and I are very delighted for the children that they will be reunited with their mother. In fact, this is what we have wanted all along."

I stole a glance at Grandmom who nodded at him and smiled persuasively.

"And we want to thank each one of you who have donated money or clothing or brought food to our home. Well, it would take too long to list all of the kind things you dear people have done for us over the past months and years . . ."

I leaned back on the soft, padded bench and closed my eyes. *Mommy told me she and Hannah would be coming here tonight. Oh, I am so eager to see them!*

Opening my eyes, I absentmindedly stared at the stained-glass window high above Granddad's head. I crossed my legs and sighed, trying not to fidget too much. I was just so eager for this to be over.

Suddenly, Granddad paused and stared. Quickly regaining his composure, he smiled broadly. "Welcome, Kay and Hannah," he called out. "Just c'mon in and take a seat."

I craned my neck to look. Mommy and Hannah were standing in the doorway, obviously ill at ease! Heads turned to eye them as they walked to the front row and squeezed in next to us.

Hannah's face flushed with embarrassment, and Mommy whispered to me, "I thought you said this was at seven-thirty."

I nodded. "Yeah, that's what I heard, but somehow everyone else got here earlier. Sorry," I answered, feeling terrible for them.

Granddad wrapped up his speech. "I think what we will do is have Kay and the children line up down here and everyone can come by and speak a few words of farewell."

Mommy looked up, startled.

"Oh, no!" I groaned silently. "This is going to be very awkward," I whispered under my breath.

The next thing I knew, our family was standing in a line near the pulpit as an endless blur of smiles and words, handshakes and hugs, were given to us as face after face filed by, introducing themselves or bidding us farewell. Finally the line dwindled away as the last people shook our hands and left the chapel.

I looked over at Mommy and sighed. It was so good to be with her again.

With one final tug, I smoothed the thick comforter over the high double bed and carefully arranged the pillows at the head. Straightening up, I surveyed the room thoughtfully. Warm morning light streamed in, illuminating the green curtains. The closet door stood open, revealing the empty clothes rack. The dresser drawers were empty too, while on the floor my open suitcase bulged with my belongings.

My eyes drifted to the computer desk where a stack of books waited to be packed. I gathered them up and knelt on the floor, studying the pile.

"Hmmm. Where can I fit these in?" Slowly, I worked them in like pieces to a puzzle while the clock ticked steadily on the nightstand. Finally, I grabbed the clock too, staring into its expressionless face.

Mommy and Hannah should be here in half an hour! I held the clock for a moment before wedging it between my books.

My grandparents had seemed withdrawn all morning, but I had been so excited about leaving that I hardly noticed.

The house will be very quiet after we leave, I thought. I zipped up my suitcase and then sat back on my heels. *My grandparents' home has been a flurry of activity for the past four and a half months. I wonder if they're breathing a big sigh of relief now that their lives can return to normal . . . and silence.* I grinned.

"They're here!" Isaiah called excitedly from the front room.

I heard Trixy barking and then the girls' feet pounding down the hall toward the front door. I pushed my bedroom door open just in time to see Emily disappear into the living room. I dashed outside after her, the glass door slamming shut behind me. The soft, green grass of the lawn was cool under my feet as I joined the happy circle around Mommy and Hannah.

Grace wrapped her arms tightly around Mommy and sighed. "I can hardly believe you're actually here, and we can go home with you!"

Mommy bent down and kissed her. "Me, either!"

Hannah hugged me tightly and said, "I am so glad to see you!"

"Me, too!" I whispered in her ear.

After several minutes of enjoying this happy reunion, Mommy said, "Well, let's go inside and say thank you and good-bye to Grandmom and Granddad, and then it will be time to go home."

"Yea!" Grace squealed.

Granddad held the door open for us, and greeted Mommy and Hannah stiffly.

After a few minutes of awkward pleasantries, we were ready to leave. We loaded all our luggage into the van, and Mommy turned the key. Slowly we pulled away from Granddad and Grandmom, left standing alone in the yard. We waved until they were out of sight, and then settled back into our seats, delighted to be with Mommy and Hannah once again.

"Children," Mommy said happily, "I am so grateful God has

allowed us to be together again, even if it is just under temporary orders."

A chorus of "Me, too" was heard throughout the van. Yes, we were all grateful to be a family again.

Setting down the heavy suitcase, I looked around at the kitchen.

"Where are the cups?" I called as Hannah stepped through the front door, her arms loaded with bags and pillows.

"Oh, the cups are to the right of the sink. First shelf, yes, right there."

Pulling down a small glass, I paused. "Thanks. It seems really odd not to know where things belong in my own home," I confessed.

"You just need to do the dishes a few times, and you'll figure it out," Hannah teased, heading back out the door.

In the hall were several old family pictures; memories flooded over me as I looked at them.

Mommy's voice spoke up behind me, "How does it feel to see these old pictures?"

"Wonderful!" I said. "It is just so good to be home."

Kay:

The heavy wooden door clicked shut behind Lissa and me as we stepped into the lawyer's conference room. Long shelves lined the wall, well-stocked with thick, drab-looking volumes of law books. Alex Azzo and Jim Lindeman stood up from the dark, polished table, greeting us professionally with a handshake.

"Hello, Kay. Hi, Lissa. Would either of you like a Coke or something before we get started?" Mr. Azzo offered.

"Oh, no, thank you," I responded.

"No, nothing for me either."

"Please, won't you take a seat then?" Mr. Azzo invited as we pulled out plush chairs from the table and sat down. It was May 1, 2000.

I had found myself in this room many times since I had been set free from jail. In this room I had trembled when Mr. Azzo explained how grim my case was. But this room was also where God had shown His mighty hand. It was here that these lawyers handed Hannah and me the dismissal papers on that glorious afternoon of February 4.

"Well, Kay, today we want to discuss with you the matter of expunction. As I said over the phone, you're eligible to apply for an expunction because the district attorney's office dismissed your charges."

One of the side benefits of being sued is that going through all the court proceedings ends up increasing one's vocabulary. I had never heard the word *expunction* until my defense attorneys began throwing the term around impressively near the end of my court case. Finally, I learned it is just a legal term which means that one's criminal charges are all erased from the record. In fact, if someone is expunged, it is as if he had never been charged with a crime at all.

Imagine that! It reminds me of what God's forgiveness means to a Christian, for when God forgives us, He also chooses to forget our past sins, wiping them all away. To someone who had worn the tag of "criminal," the thought of expunction was music to my ears. Now that God had moved the district attorney's office to mysteriously dismiss my charges, Alex Azzo and Jim Lindeman wanted to present this proposition.

"Jim and I think it's only fair to inform you that expunctions are only rarely granted," Mr. Azzo said, scooting a stack of papers aside on the table and looking at me soberly. "Kay, if you decide to apply, we don't want you to become too hopeful. You see, if the district attorney signs the form granting you an expunction, it's almost as if he's admitting his office made a mistake in the first place."

Sitting forward in his seat and raising his eyebrows, Mr. Azzo continued. "And Kay, that is one office that really hates to admit making mistakes," he said with emphasis. "Do you understand? It could make them look bad."

"Yes, I certainly see what you mean," I replied.

"So, Kay, it is your decision whether you want to apply for an expunction or not. We would be happy to help if you indeed want to pursue it. The cost would be minimal and there is very little procedure involved on your part. Basically you just pay the fee, sign your name, and wait."

"Okay, that's good to know. It sounds pretty straightforward to me. Actually, I have already prayed about this, and I want to apply. And if God wants me to be granted an expunction, then He will make it happen."

I turned the pages of my Bible, finally coming to the cross-stitched marker. *Let's see; it's May 24, 2000, and I think I'm at Ezra 4 this morning,* I thought, pulling the desk lamp closer and bending over the pages in front of me.

> *Now when the adversaries of Judah and Benjamin heard that the children of the captivity builded the temple unto the LORD God of Israel; then they came to Zerubbabel, and to the chief of the fathers, and said unto them, Let us build with you: for we seek your God, as ye do; and we do sacrifice unto him since the days of Esarhaddon king of Assur, which brought us up hither. But Zerubbabel, and Jeshua, and the rest of the chief of the fathers of Israel, said unto them, Ye have nothing to do with us to build an house unto our God; but we ourselves together will build unto the LORD God of Israel, as king Cyrus the king of Persia hath commanded us. Then the people of the land weakened the hands of the people of Judah, and troubled them in building, and hired counsellors against them, to frustrate their purpose, all the days of Cyrus king of Persia, even until the reign of Darius king of Persia. And in the reign of Ahasuerus, in the beginning of his reign, wrote they unto him an accusation against the inhabitants of Judah and Jerusalem.*[1]

I put my finger at the end of the paragraph and looked thoughtfully out the window through which the early morning light streamed. *This Scripture sounds a lot like my situation. Ron and I wanted to build temples for God in our children.*

---

1. Ezra 4:1-6

The chair squeaked as I leaned back, deep in thought. Through the twenty years of our marriage, I could see that my in-laws had a different "blueprint" for life than did we. We declined their offer to share in the work of "building" our children. When following Ron's death I still wouldn't allow them to share in this work, my decision was considered "politically incorrect." And yet God blessed my heart's desire to assist Him in helping my children become set apart for His own purposes. My family had suffered through these experiences, but we had also learned many priceless lessons.

———————

It was June 5. I reread the e-mail again in awe. "Lord, this is incredible!"

In big, bold letters the title announced, "U.S. Supreme Court Rules in Favor of Parents."

It had been sobering to learn of several other custody cases similar to ours. My family and I had been following these stories with keen interest, particularly a grandparental case much like our own, which was before the U.S. Supreme Court.

"Children, come look at this e-mail from Mr. Telge. It is GREAT news! Do you remember what Judge Motheral said?"

My children gathered around me and the computer and looked at me curiously.

"Well, recently she told the attorneys she has been waiting for a Supreme Court ruling on a pending custody case involving grandparents. She said the ruling would definitely impact our case. Well, a decision was finally reached. And the court ruled six to three IN FAVOR of curbing grandparent access laws in custody cases!"

Isaiah peered intently over my shoulder at the computer screen. "Yes, but what does that mean, Mommy?"

I turned and faced my six children. "Well, that means that in custody cases where the parents and the grandparents both claim rights to the children, the parents have now been given more favor. Hallelujah! This is a very timely answer to prayer."

———————

Hannah:

"Mommy, I just hate going there," Beverly complained as Mommy backed out of the parking space. "Even though the lady is nice, she asks so many strange questions. She even asked some of the questions more than once. Often she just stared at me, and then wrote something in her notebook. It made me nervous. Do we ever have to go back there?"

"No, Beverly, that was the last psychological evaluation. So we have now fulfilled the judge's requirement."

"Good. I'm glad," Beverly stated with emphasis.

"Me, too," confessed Isaiah.

"What did the lady say to you, Emily?" Mommy asked, looking back at Emily in the rearview mirror.

"Oh, we mostly just played games."

"I see."

"Yeah, the lady played games with me too," Grace volunteered.

As Mommy pulled our van into the street, I asked, "Mommy, was it hard for you to see your children being psychologically evaluated? I mean, you never would have chosen for any of us to be examined by psychiatrists."

Mommy turned on her blinker and moved into the left lane. "Oh, no, I would have never wanted that. Never! I would have been afraid that psychiatrists or psychologists would put harmful ideas into the minds of my impressionable young children.

"When I was in jail and found out that y'all were being sent to psychiatrists, it really scared me. All I could do about it in jail was pray God's protection over each of you. I pleaded with God every day to guard each of your minds and hearts from any harmful influences, whether it was from Grandmom and Granddad, public school, movies, or yes, even psychological evaluations. And He has protected you.

"And you saw what God was able to do with the results of those earlier tests. He actually used them to help reunite us, didn't He? I could never have imagined that. So, I am sure He is just as able to use these tests for good too. I just need to trust Him and to remember His ways are not my ways. I am learning He knows what He is doing. And Hannah, His ways are always perfect."

"Yes, I want to remember that," I answered, nodding slowly.

"Hey, Mommy, how far is it to the jail from here?" Isaiah asked as we left the psychiatric appointment. "I want to see what it looks like."

Mommy slowed to a stop at the red light and looked at Isaiah thoughtfully.

"That's right. You have never been there, have you?"

"No, ma'am."

Mommy was quiet for a moment. "Let's see. I guess I would turn left here, if I need to get to Fannin. Hannah, does that sound right?"

"Um, yes, ma'am, I think so."

Soon the tall downtown buildings rose high around us. The sidewalks were littered with trash, and a soggy newspaper lay in the gutter.

Carefully parking the big van by the sidewalk, Mommy said, "Children, I want to see if I can take y'all up to the fourth floor of the jail."

Emily's small voice piped up. "Is that where you were?"

Mommy turned in her seat and smiled. "Yes, honey, that is where I stayed for thirty-seven days. Come on, let's get out and go in."

I shuddered as we stepped inside the dreary building. This place did not hold good memories for me. Mommy had been an inmate here, dressed in a horrid orange prison outfit and confined behind bars and glass.

And now, just standing in line to talk with the officer at the counter, I felt the same wave of heaviness wash over me. We inched our way up to the metal counter where Mommy explained what we wanted.

"I didn't actually come to visit anyone. I used to be an inmate in here. Would there be any way I could take my children to the fourth floor and just show them what it looks like?"

The officer shook his head emphatically. "No, ma'am. You can't go up there unless you're planning to visit a specific inmate."

Mommy's face fell, and we turned and made our way outside.

Grace shook her head sadly. "I wanted to see where you stayed, Mommy."

I breathed a sigh of relief. "Oh, it is so good to get out of there!"

Suddenly, Mommy had another idea. "Let's go into the building next door so y'all can see the criminal law courtroom my case was tried in!"

Isaiah nodded eagerly. "Oh, yeah, Mom, that would be great!"

Apparently everyone was excited about this too, except me. That building represented dark court days, long hours of dreary waiting, and grim prospects. Trying to ignore the knot in my stomach, I followed my family into the Harris County Criminal Justice Center.

Outside the familiar courtroom door, Mommy turned and whispered,

"Just wait here in the hallway while I check things out."

Just as she grasped the brass door handle, a lawyer pushed the door open, his eyes intent on a notebook in his hand.

He looked up and paused. "Oh, excuse me, ladies," and noticing Isaiah, he added, "and sir!"

Mommy smiled. "Pardon me," she said, "but is the court in session at this time?"

"No," he said, looking at her curiously.

"You see," Mommy explained motioning into the courtroom, "I just wanted to introduce my family to the judge I had during a recent case."

The lawyer nodded and smiled, sliding his notebook into his briefcase. "I can escort you inside. Follow me."

The courtroom was hushed. A few secretaries typed on computers, and the judge sat examining papers at her desk.

Our lawyer escort cleared his throat. "Your Honor, may I approach the bench?"

Judge Hill nodded, and the lawyer motioned for us to follow him.

When we stood before the stately woman in her black robe, Mommy spoke respectfully. "I'm not sure if you remember me, but I just wanted to personally thank you for your part in my criminal case. I also wanted to introduce you to my family." Mommy put her hand on Emily's shoulder.

With an air of gracious dignity, the judge smiled faintly. "Yes, I do remember you," she said, studying our little group thoughtfully. "You all look very happy to be back with your mother."

We smiled and nodded, assuring her that we were indeed happy. Then we told her good-bye, excused ourselves, and filed quietly out of the courtroom.

As we stepped back into the empty hall, I thought, *I'm actually glad we did that, now that it's over. It's just that seeing the same courtroom and facing the same judge again brings back a flood of unwanted emotions.*

Carefully closing the door behind him, the lawyer said, "Ma'am, you all must be a homeschooling family. If you would like to observe a court in session, feel free to enter any one of these courtrooms and just sit in the audience. You are most welcome."

"Well, thank you. We just might do that," Mommy responded gratefully.

And we did. Quietly we opened the door into another courtroom and slid onto a bench near the back. It was fascinating to listen to someone else's case and to see the lawyers and the judges working together to mete out justice. We found the judicial process so interesting that when the hearing ended, we walked down the hall and slipped into another courtroom. What an educational day!

Part of my memorization had been 1 John 2:1, 2. *My little children, these things write I unto you, that ye sin not. And if any man sin, we have an advocate with the Father, Jesus Christ the righteous: And he is the propitiation for our sins: and not for ours only, but also for the sins of the whole world.*

I thought about how it applied to the courtroom scenes we had just visited. In one of the cases we observed, a man had been charged with assault. His lawyer asked the judge, "If this man is convicted, what will follow?"

"He would be taken into custody on the spot," the judge had answered promptly.

Justice! And no recourse for mercy or forgiveness! I thought again about my memory passage. What a wonderful realization! Jesus is not only our "lawyer," but because of Him, there is mercy and forgiveness too! God made those verses come alive for me during our courtroom visit.

Kay:

It was July 3, my birthday, and we were running errands as a family.

"Children, just one more stop, and then we can get lunch at Taco Bell. After that we'll head home."

It was wonderful being together again, even if it was only under temporary orders. My in-laws and I still needed to come to a final agreement for the permanent custody. Petitions had flown back and forth many times since the children had arrived in Houston, but my in-laws and I had very different opinions as to what should be in the terms of agreement the judge would sign.

In the last petition I had received, they had again asked for joint authority over the children's schooling, medical care, and even where we would live. Apparently they wanted to replace Ron and be active in the parenting process. Even thinking about it was stressful. I couldn't agree to being unequally yoked.

"I must turn down these propositions," I had told my lawyers. "I should have the freedom to raise my children the way God directs me."

My lawyers and I stuck resolutely to our original proposal, stating that I must have all the authority, and that Walter and Jan have none. Of course they didn't like that, so they wrote another petition, conceding me just a little more than their previous petition. But it still wasn't complete authority, and so we had turned it down as well, sending our petition again.

Both sides were unyielding. Would either side wear down and just sign, agreeing to the other side's terms and putting an end to this game? We began to wonder, but we were determined it would NOT be us.

A court date was scheduled, and if there was no agreement before then, we would have to hash it out in court. The date came closer and closer, and still no agreement. Time was running out.

I steered the van into a parking lot and scanned for a parking space. As I parked, my cell phone rang. Quickly digging it out of my purse, I punched the "talk" button and held the phone up to my ear.

"Hello?"

It was Mr. Telge, and he was very excited about something. The children sat silently in their seats, not wanting to miss anything.

"Yes, Mr. Telge, what was that you said? Are you serious? You say Jan and Walter actually signed our proposal today just like it is? And they aren't sending back another counter proposal?"

I looked around excitedly at my children, hardly able to contain myself. "Oh, praise the Lord! What a blessing. Oh, yes, sir, God is definitely awesome! He surely is! Well, thank you so much for letting us know. All right, I'll talk to you later. Okay, goodbye."

I sat stunned, the phone still in my hands.

The children exploded with a chorus of questions. "Mommy, what happened? What did he say?"

Still hardly comprehending the wonderful news myself, I blurted out, "They signed our order! Praise the Lord! He said Grandmom and Granddad at long last signed our order! Isn't God good?"

We all sat there trying to take it in. Yes, they had actually signed OUR order. Walter and Jan had agreed to do things the way we wanted. After it had looked as if we might never reach an agreement, they had finally, and with no explanation, given in.

Most women want their husbands to remember their birthday in some special way. And here was God, my eternal Husband, showing me His tender affection in this way. That was so touching to me. God had delivered us from one problem after another throughout this whole ordeal, working miracle after miracle. Now, it seemed He was "icing the cake" by having my in-laws sign the proposed order, granting me back full and permanent custody in just the way I had requested. And He had caused them to sign their names, making it official, right on my birthday!

A meager "thank you" sounds so weak when God does something that big. God was so good! This definitely called for a praise service right there in our van. And that is exactly what we had!

He doth execute the judgment of the fatherless and widow. He is thy praise, and he is thy God, that hath done for thee these great and terrible things, which thine eyes have seen.[1]

We were in a mood to celebrate. Here it was, the fourth of July. With flags displayed in front of so many homes on this national holiday, it almost appeared that the whole country, or at least our neighborhood, was sharing our joy.

Excitement was in the air at our house. Hannah burst through the front door, her hands full of grocery bags and a song on her lips.

---

1. Deuteronomy 10:18, 21

"Jesus, name above all names!
Blessed Redeemer, Glorious Lord!
Emmanuel! God is with us!
Beautiful Savior! Living Word!
His name is Jesus, Jesus!
Sad hearts weep no more.
He has healed the brokenhearted,
Opened wide the prison doors.
He is able to deliver evermore![1]

"Mommy," she exclaimed joyfully, "as I was driving to the grocery store, the Lord reminded me of this song. Isn't it absolutely perfect?"

I nodded, "Yes, it surely is."

After all, it was only yesterday that we had gotten the marvelous news. My family lawyers and their wives and children, as well as Allen and Elaine and their children, were all coming over to our house for a celebration brunch. We went all out, serving pancakes piled high with real whipped cream, fresh strawberries, and blueberries.

I jabbed the last bite of pancake on my plate and glanced around the circle in our living room. Everyone was in a festive mood. Both of my lawyers teased the children. The stress of the case was finally over.

When the meal was over, and the dishes cleared away, Tom Sanders led us in a worship time. It was most appropriate, since it was God who had brought us to this celebration. I was indeed grateful for both Tim Telge's and Tom Sanders' help with the family custody issues. Their wives had even pitched in and helped out on the case, through prayer or typing or whatever else was needed. Allen and Elaine had also helped us countless times and were a continual encouragement.

But all of these dear Christian people understood that they were tools in the hands of the Almighty God in what had just taken place. The real applause was reserved for Him alone.

---

1. JESUS NAME ABOVE ALL NAMES by NADIA HEARN.
©1974 Scripture In Song (c/o Integrity Music)/ASCAP
c/o Integrity Media, Inc., 1000 Cody Road, Mobile, AL 36697

CHAPTER 38

A Song for Your Honor

– 8:30 a.m. July 5, 2000 –

Kay:

The tall, downtown buildings towered above us, as we hurried toward the courthouse. Cars and buses roared past on the busy streets, while the sidewalks were a thoroughfare of men and women in business suits.

A man stood at the corner holding a tarnished trumpet to his lips. As the wind ripped at his thin, brown suit, his fingers danced over the keys. Notes bounced off the concrete walls and disappeared in the roar of the heavy traffic. An occasional passerby tossed a coin at his feet.

As we walked by, his eyes rested briefly on us, and the music paused. With a twinkle in his eye, he took a deep breath and began playing the notes to "Amazing Grace." I smiled at his kind gesture.

We were heading to the Family Law Building for our last court hearing. I could hardly believe this was really the last time I would have to enter this building.

As I stepped out of the elevator, the familiar, depressing atmosphere washed over me. Strangers sat on benches, looking gloomy and hopeless. Bulletin boards lining the hallway walls displayed articles about divorce and other unpleasant things family court had to deal with.

Hannah turned to me. "You know, Mommy," she commented, "I've spent so much time in these halls during court sessions that I've read all these pathetic articles. This hallway has been where

I've waited and wondered what was happening in that courtroom."

She shook her head and sighed. "I get butterflies just being here again. But, Mommy, God has done such miracles in this place for us! We've prayed in this hallway, waited nervously here, and rejoiced as well. And now, here we are, one last time. I praise God to think we don't ever have to return here."

I smiled at each of my children. Today I considered myself to be the happiest mom on earth!

The courtroom still wasn't open, so we waited out in the hall with Elaine, who had come to witness the final signing. Other friends also began showing up. When people had asked me if they should come for this hearing, I simply repeated what my lawyers had said—it was merely a formality.

We already had an agreement; we just needed to appear before the judge and sign the papers. But friends who had stood with us when things looked grim also wanted to be with us in the final, joyful moment.

A photographer for the *Houston Chronicle* appeared, looking very out of place in his cargo shorts and T-shirt with a big camera hanging off his shoulder. "I need to get several shots of your family," he said, "for tomorrow's paper."

He escorted us back down the elevator to a big window overlooking the busy street where the lighting was better. After lining us up against the wall, he shot several pictures.

Then we trooped back up to our floor, and the children sat on the benches lining the hallway while a reporter interviewed me.

Finally the great courtroom doors were opened, and we quietly filed in and took seats. The benches quickly filled, jam-packed with mostly unfamiliar faces of lawyers and their clients. It looked as if there would be many divorces here today and many children fought over. Looking from face to face, I saw the misery of homes at war.

"Family court is an awful place—a sea of broken hearts," Mr. Sanders had told us sadly.

I was comforted that at least one good thing would happen in this place today.

Mr. Sanders sat down next to Hannah. "You know," he whispered to her, "I don't really feel worthy to get to watch this today."

Finally, a door on the far side of the courtroom opened, and the bailiff ordered everybody to rise to their feet as the judge of the 257th District Family Court entered.

Judge Motheral stretched her hand toward the crowd and smiled. "You may be seated," she said quietly.

She wore the usual black robe, but a white collar peeked out from beneath. She seemed serious as she took her seat. Her eyes scanned the audience, assessing how full her day would be.

Names were read from a list to see if each case on her docket was represented. "Here, Your Honor," was heard in different parts of the room.

It could be all day before she ever gets to us, I thought after more than a dozen names were called.

Then Judge Motheral asked, "Is anyone here for the Evans case?"

All five lawyers stood. "We're all here, Your Honor," one said.

After the last name on her docket was called, Judge Motheral paused thoughtfully. "I think we will bring the Evans case to the head of the class today," she announced. "Will those here for that case please come forward?"

As the five lawyers started for the bench, Mr. Telge turned and motioned for us to follow. "C'mon, Kay. Bring your family up."

Hearts thumping and mouths dry, we stood and filed up after them. We were quite a crowd: five attorneys and a family of seven, walking to the front of the room. Only my in-laws were absent from the scene.

As we gathered before the judge, one of the lawyers handed her the order, and she looked our family over thoughtfully. Then she said, "Kay, please step forward and swear that you will speak the truth, the whole truth, and nothing but the truth."

"Your Honor, may I affirm?" I asked.

"Oh, of course," she assured me.

Then she slid a paper toward me and pointed where I was to sign. I was too short to reach the counter comfortably, so I stood on tiptoes. Taking my pen in hand, I studied the paper before me.

It was amazing. I was officially being given back total liberty to raise my children however God would lead me. The only condition placed on me was also placed on my in-laws—that we would inform each other of any address changes. My in-laws could visit my children only after obtaining my consent. Every right of parenthood had been restored to me. In fact, with the court's approval, I could protect my children better now than before.

God had turned everything completely around. I was grateful to Judge Motheral, but in my heart, I knew a far greater Judge had brought about the results of this day. I stood silently in awe of Him.

As I signed the form, my children faced the judge. Standing in front of a judge isn't so terrifying if she is smiling.

"Hi, kids. How are y'all doing?" the judge asked in a friendly, Texan manner.

They smiled nervously. "Good," they said. Seeing fresh, happy, young faces in the courtroom was probably a rare thing! Upon her request, they introduced themselves.

And then, just like that, it was all over. We were done. Our legal case was finished! After all those years of hiding and then being found, after all those court dates, it was really and truly and finally over.

With our permanent custody order signed, our business here was complete, and it was time to leave. The judge obviously had plenty of other cases to attend to today.

"Thank you, Your Honor," I said.

The judge watched us wistfully as we turned and started for the door.

"Well, now I've met the children," she said to Mr. Telge, "but I didn't get to hear them sing."

"Well, Your Honor, we can fix that!" Mr. Telge assured her. "Come back and sing a song for the judge," he directed.

We could hardly believe our ears. "What should we sing?" Hannah whispered as we returned to the bench. We took our places, nervously facing the judge.

Ellen Yarrell leaned forward. "Judge, shall we have them sing the song I once told you about? You know, children, the one you sang in my office? I think it was called 'Faithful Love.'"

So, there in that oppressive courtroom, filled with so much hate and bitterness and suffering, we sang. From the mature voices, all the way down to Emily's childish tones, every word and note floated to the very ceiling of the room. Except for our voices, the courtroom was perfectly silent. When the song died away, we once more thanked the judge and turned to leave.

People in the benches were dabbing their eyes. Then spontaneous applause erupted all over the courtroom.

There were so many miracles tied into our story, so many special touches that only the Lord could have come up with. It was thrilling! This story was planned entirely by God. Singing in the courtroom was like the grand finale. It was an unbelievable moment, before man, praising God for His goodness.

As we left the courtroom, we left so much behind us—the separation, the stresses of the court case. Yes, it had been an agonizing experience, but God had never once left us comfortless. He had been with us every moment. When life had been so dark and hopeless, we simply had to lift our faces to Him, and He wiped our tears away.

God was faithful, even when we failed and made mistakes. He never failed us, nor did He forsake us. We did not know what the future held, but we could walk securely forward, knowing God would be with us every step of the way.

"FAITHFUL LOVE"

Faithful love, flowing down from the thorn-covered crown,
Makes me whole, saves my soul, washes whiter than snow.
Faithful love calms each fear, reaches down, dries each tear;
Holds my hand when I can't stand on my own.

Faithful love is a friend just when hope seems to end,
Welcome face, sweet embrace, tender touch filled with grace.
Faithful love, endless pow'r, living flame, Spirit's fire;
Burning bright in the night, guiding my way.

Chorus:
Faithful love from above came to earth to show the Father's
love.
And I'll never be the same,
For I've seen faithful love face to face, and Jesus is His name.

---

1. *"Faithful Love"* by Ken Young. Used by permission of Hallal Music.

CHAPTER 39

Forgiveness and Hope

Hannah:

After the dust settled from our court case, life slowly returned to normal. But I learned that something remained unfinished.

Once, while traveling, our family was listening to a sermon on tape about honoring parents. "We need to honor our parents, even if they are not godly," the speaker said.

I was convicted. Had I always honored my grandparents during the time I lived in their home? I fidgeted in my seat knowing that, at least in my heart, I had not.

The speaker told of a man who asked his dad's forgiveness for not honoring him.

My heart thumped. *Oh, Lord, do You want me to do that too?* I prayed quietly.

A couple weeks later in morning devotions Mommy read from the Bible about loving those who are unkind to us. When she finished, she closed the Bible and looked up at us. "Does anyone have any thoughts about what I just read?" she asked.

"Yes," I said. "What can we do to show Grandmom and Granddad love?" God was still working on my heart.

"Well, let's see," Mommy replied. "We are planning to head to Amarillo next week to visit them. Your grandmom likes coconut cake, if I remember correctly."

"Really?" I responded eagerly. "Then, let's bake her one and take it to her."

It would be a very small deed, but I hoped it would convey the love of Christ nonetheless. We often prayed that God would help us forgive them, but I found it hard.

On our trip to Amarillo, we listened to a book on audiocassette called *God's Smuggler* by Brother Andrew. Mile after mile, we inserted one tape after another. These were fascinating stories about a man who deeply loved God. Smuggling Bibles into communist countries, he experienced difficult trials, but God brought him through each one. Inspired by how God's love overcame evil in the impossible situations he faced, we thought surely God could do the same for us in relating to our grandparents.

As we got closer to Amarillo, a strange thing began to happen. We all began to *feel* love for Granddad and Grandmom. God was preparing us to see them. We greeted them, walked inside their house, and presented them with the cake.

My uncle was there also. *God probably doesn't want me to apologize to my grandparents while my uncle is here,* I rationalized.

At one point he left the room, but he wasn't gone long enough for me to gather courage and say anything important to my grandparents. Soon it was time to go, and I still had not apologized.

"Oh, well, too bad," I said to myself, trying not to dwell on my failure. But my dear heavenly Father did not give up on me that easily.

After we left and headed for my other grandparents' home for the night, Mommy had an idea. "Let's surprise Grandmom and Granddad and show up at their church Sunday morning," she suggested.

My heart beat faster. I knew apologizing was the right thing to do, but it sure was challenging to put into words. *How will I do it?* I worried.

Sunday morning came and my family and I filed awkwardly into the large, well-filled auditorium and seated ourselves beside my grandparents. They realized we had chosen to come to their church for the Sunday morning service to see them, so they decided to skip the Bible class that followed in order to visit.

I knew God was placing the opportunity right into my lap. But I did not want to talk to them amidst a crowd. Finally I approached my granddad nervously and asked, "May I talk with you and Grandmom privately?"

"Certainly!" he assured me, reaching for Grandmom's arm.

I walked to the side of the auditorium and sat down, dreading the next few minutes. *I really can't get out of it now,* I thought soberly as they approached.

"Um," I began awkwardly, "I just feel like I need to apologize to both of you because I did not honor you while I was living in your home."

They looked at me, surprised.

"Will you please forgive me?" I continued.

Tears formed in my granddad's eyes as he nodded slightly. I wish I could have known what he was thinking, but no words came.

One day, an enormous box was delivered to our door bearing a familiar address.

"What could it be?" we asked one another as we gathered around curiously.

We cut the tape and pulled open the box. There were all kinds of art supplies inside: paints and paint brushes, paper of varying kinds, blank cards meant for water color. We were delighted.

But what meant the most to me was not the assortment of gifts for the children, but a veggie-chopper underneath all the art supplies. We realized this must be meant for Mommy. Grandmom knew how much Mommy loved to cook.

Oh, that blessed me so much! Could it be that after all we had been through with my grandparents that something was beginning to happen in their hearts? Even with little tangible improvement in our relationship, we pray God continues working in their hearts *and in ours* toward a full reconciliation.

Epilogue

With the court case behind us, we prayed that the Lord would lead us to a fellowship of believers we could become part of. I needed godly authority to help guide us as I raise my family for Christ. North Carolina became our home some months later, and it is here that we have written the bulk of our story.

Writing this book has been a long, grueling task and has been more time-consuming than we ever dreamed. But at the same time, it has been a blessed reminder of God's goodness to us as we reviewed each step of our journey.

As each year passes since that memorable last day in the courtroom, I continue to stand in awe as I ponder what mighty miracles the Lord has done for us. Within a year of our family being reunited, Alex Azzo contacted me with the wonderful news that I had been granted expunction. Clearly, God delights in showing us that His ways are abundantly above all that we can ask or even imagine. All glory to God, the Defender of widows, and the great and powerful Deliverer!

I am very thankful for the Lord's faithfulness in using the very things which could have harmed us, for our good, as He did in the life of Joseph of the Old Testament. God has also helped me realize that our true enemies are not people, but rather Satan and our selfishness, as is true for every follower of Jesus Christ. God has replaced the bitterness toward the grandparents with love, as only He can do, for He is the God of love.

We find ourselves in need of prayer as we relate to the grandparents. It is our desire that they see and experience the love of Jesus Christ in the way we treat them. They are very important people in our lives, and if the Lord prompts you to pray for them and for us and for our relationship, we would be very grateful.

We do not wish to "settle in" and mistakenly assume that what we experienced in this story was our one difficult assignment from God. Rather, we desire to be sharpened by this and earnestly hope that God will consider us available, willing, and ready to suffer for His worthy name in the future.

I believe as the endtimes approach and the persecution of Christians becomes more prevalent, stories like ours will become more commonplace. Even now, God is sifting His people throughout the world, making manifest who the true Christians are.

Please note: I am in no way advocating that others should follow our example of fleeing when faced with persecution. I have no special information or techniques that helped my family or would help anyone else's to successfully go into hiding. It was simply God who kept us out of sight for as long as He did.

May our story inspire you and help you realize that no matter what God may require of you, He has a rich supply of grace available to carry you along even the roughest way. It is exciting that God uses mortal flesh to bring honor to His worthy name upon the earth. Whether or not your own struggles end on a happy note, as in this story, there will be a sure and lasting reward for all those who remain faithful to Jesus Christ.

October, 2004

Christian Light Publications, Inc., is a nonprofit, conservative Mennonite publishing company providing Christ-centered, Biblical literature including books, Gospel tracts, Sunday school materials, summer Bible school materials, and a full curriculum for Christian day schools and homeschools. Though primarily produced in English, some books, tracts, and school materials are also available in Spanish.

For more information about the ministry of CLP or its publications, or for spiritual help, please contact us at:

Christian Light Publications, Inc.
P. O. Box 1212
Harrisonburg, VA 22803-1212

Telephone—540-434-0768
Fax—540-433-8896
E-mail—info@clp.org
www.clp.org